W9-CTA-211

MUSEO DELLE TERME, ROME; ALINARI

THE HORIZON BOOK OF
ANCIENT GREECE

NATIONAL MUSEUM, ATHENS

AMERICAN HERITAGE PUBLISHING CO., INC./
BONANZA BOOKS
NEW YORK

THE HORIZON BOOK OF

ANCIENT GREECE

BY THE EDITORS OF

HORIZON MAGAZINE

WILLIAM HARLAN HALE

AUTHOR AND EDITOR IN CHARGE

AMERICAN HERITAGE
PUBLISHING CO., INC.

Staff for this Book

EDITOR

William Harlan Hale

MANAGING EDITOR

Norman Kotker

ART DIRECTOR

Emma Landau

PICTURE EDITOR

Phyllis Iselin

ASSISTANT EDITOR

Jane Hoover Polley

COPY EDITORS

Ruth H. Wolfe

Kaari I. Ward, *Assistant*

EDITORIAL ASSISTANT

Regina Wirth Kane

EUROPEAN BUREAU

Gertrudis Feliu, *Chief*

Copyright © MCMLXV
by American Heritage Publishing Co., Inc.
All rights reserved.

This 1984 edition is published by Bonanza Books,
distributed by Crown Publishers, Inc. by arrangement with
the American Heritage Publishing Co., Inc.

Manufactured in Hong Kong

Library of Congress Cataloging in Publication Data
Hale, William Harlan, 1910-
    The Horizon book of ancient Greece.

    Originally published: New York : American Heritage
Pub. Co., 1965.
    Includes index.
    1. Greece—Civilization—To 146 B.C.   2. Greece—
Antiquities.   I. Horizon (New York, N.Y.)   II. Title.
III. Title: Ancient Greece.
DF77.H32   1984   938   83-25884
ISBN: 0-517-435454
h g f e d c b a

NATIONAL MUSEUM,
ATHENS; HARISSIADIS

*The bronze mirror above, supported by the figure of a woman, was
made in Corinth in the fifth century, when Greek culture was at its
height. Of the same period is the bas-relief on the half title page,
which shows a seated woman burning incense. On the title page is
a small bronze of the goddess Athena, perhaps modeled after one
of the colossal cult images of the Athenian Acropolis. On page 6
the Erechtheum, one of the Acropolis temples, is seen in the sunset.*

CONTENTS

MARIO DI BIASI, PICTORIAL PARADE

THE HAUNTING PRESENCE

On an April day in 1811—a year in which Europe was briefly at peace—two vessels, each on an unusual mission and each with interesting passengers aboard, fell in with each other while outward bound from the Piraeus, the port of Athens. One was a chartered open boat bearing two young English architects, Charles Robert Cockerell and John Foster by name, along with a German, Baron Haller von Hallerstein, who was also an architect and, moreover, a protégé of the art patron, Crown Prince Ludwig of Bavaria. The Cockerell group had set out for the island of Aegina, some twenty miles to the south of Athens, with the object of exploring, measuring, and digging out the ruins of a classical temple on that once famed island—a temple thought to have been dedicated to Zeus, and possibly rich with fallen sculpture.

The other vessel was a British naval transport, and aboard it was no less a person than Lord Byron, fresh from making love to Mrs. Spencer Smith and other ladies in the Mediterranean area, swimming the Hellespont, and writing the first cantos of *Childe Harold's Pilgrimage*. In its

hold lay a cargo of twenty cases containing marble figures hauled down off the Acropolis as a private acquisition of His Majesty's late envoy at Constantinople, Lord Elgin.

Cockerell's boat gained on the laden British craft, and when the young men came astern of it they sang out a song to announce their presence. The poet looked overside, recognized them as acquaintances, and had them invited aboard for a glass of port. After the wine, the vessels resumed their separate courses: Cockerell's sailed to Aegina, where his party soon uncovered a great trove of sculpture which Ludwig of Bavaria promptly bought for his collection in Munich; the other steered homeward with its rare freight, which ended up in the British Museum.

Though the encounter of these young visitors came by chance, it was a symbolic and prophetic one. Here were several bright spirits from the West converging upon the classical land, no longer content to learn about it at second or third hand, as their fathers had, but bent on rediscovering and experiencing it themselves, all seeking to draw some inspiration or sustenance from it. And though highly individual spirits, they were at the same time exemplars of a whole new European generation that had suddenly fallen head over heels in love with ancient Greece. The era of modern man's return to Hellas had begun—an era marked also by the hauling away of its monuments.

The return was both spiritual and physical. It was spiritual in that the romantic, restless, often revolutionary generation of 1800 had turned to far-off Athens in the belief that it would find there an embodiment of its own ideals of freedom, respect for man's individual worth, and indeed of his ability to attain something like earthly perfection. The return was physical in that first a few men, then dozens, then hundreds, and finally thousands from many lands, armed with calipers and maps, picks and shovels, and using Pausanias' ancient descriptions of long-lost sites as a Baedeker, were to undertake the most massive exhumation of a culture in all history. Classical Greece came back to life for the modern age, first through the passion of the romantics, and then by long and weary work with the spade.

It is difficult for us today to conceive, now that Greece has become a popular mecca and museum, how very little there was to see of its ancient presence a century and a half ago, when the country was still a grubby and backward fief of the Turks, neglected and depopulated by more than three centuries of Janizaries' misrule. Resurrection of the monuments of classical Rome had been going on ever since the Renaissance, and many of its greater structures had survived the preceding centuries almost intact; but most of the physical vestiges of the earlier Greece had lain submerged until the age of the master diggers, from Heinrich Schliemann in the 1870's, to Sir Arthur Evans, to those of our own day. (The variety of names in the field—Curtius and Holleaux, Dörpfeld and Blegen, Thompson and Papadimitriou—tells of the international range of the effort.)

To be sure, the Acropolis still loomed over Athens, but as a kind of rubbish heap of history, overrun in turn by Goth, Slav, Norman, Venetian, and Turk, its Parthenon converted first into a Christian church and then into a Turkish mosque (with minaret attached), its walls partly topped by Frankish towers, its Erechtheum turned into a harem, its Propylaea into a crenelated palace, and the Panathenaic Way into a parade ground for Moslems. The great sanctuary of Athena finally became an ammunition storehouse that was blown up when the Venetians bombarded it in 1687, scattering Parthenon marble all over the mount. But though there were enough stones left standing atop the Acropolis to enchant a Byron or a Chateaubriand, or to arouse the interest of Lord Elgin, the ancient city of Athens below it had almost completely disappeared. A maze of Byzantine alleys and hovels—with churches, other buildings, yards, and gardens intermixed—thickly covered the area where the spacious Agora, or market place, of Periclean times had stood. Not until the mid nineteenth century were the first excavations made on that site and not until 1931 was its systematic exhumation begun—a crowning project of the American School of Classical Studies at Athens.

Where was Olympia, the early sanctuary of Zeus that had grown into a whole city of monuments, palaestrae, treasuries, and the temple of Zeus that housed Phidias' immense gold and ivory statue of the god, which was once accounted one of the Seven Wonders of the World? What had not been destroyed by edict of the emperor Theodosius II in A.D. 426, had been shattered by earthquakes and so smothered by landslides and floods that silt and meadows now overlay it. True, a Frenchman had spotted the site in 1725, but it was not until a century and a half later that intensive digging commenced there, carried out by thorough Germans.

Apollo's shrines at mountainous Delphi and on the sacred island of Delos showed but a few traces above the surface. Centuries of avalanches followed by resettlement had helped obliterate much of Delphi, while pillage, massacre, and total abandonment had helped do the same to Delos, until the French in the late nineteenth century began their long labor of unearthing both. Once-proud Corinth lay buried under later habitations, and the great healing center of ancient Greece, the shrine of Asclepius at Epidaurus, with its marvelously designed theatre, was all but lost to sight until spades went to work in 1881.

And what of Homer's Troy, his Mycenae "rich in gold," and the ninety cities he had spoken of as thriving on the island of Crete? Since almost no traces of these had been found, students all over the world had come to the conclusion that the rich palaces and kingdoms described in Homer's poems were probably only mythical, and the Trojan War itself just a legend. Until the day in 1871, that is, when Schliemann made his first inspired strike at Troy, to be followed shortly thereafter by his uncovering of the ancient citadel of Mycenae. Within a few decades, all man's perspectives on Greece were altered and vastly lengthened. To learn that much we had thought to be fable was indeed fact—to discover, with Schliemann, that the Troy of Priam and Hector had been a real place, that there had been a Mycenae whose House of Atreus was indeed rich, meant to realize that the Greeks were not simply poetizing when they wrote of ages, golden or other, that had existed in their land long before the rise of Athens. Then a whole earlier culture that had flourished in the Aegean, centuries before Mycenae, came to light when Sir Arthur Evans and others began unearthing Minoan remains in Crete in the 1890's. The ancient Greeks had only guessed at their past; now, as spades dig deeper, we know far more about it than they ever did.

Still, for all this mighty endeavor, how much remains about Greece that we do not know! In 1952 Michael Ventris deciphered the hitherto baffling Linear B script—found first at Knossos, in Crete, and then at sites in mainland Greece—which scholars had thought to represent a pre-Greek tongue; he revealed that Linear B was actually an early form of Greek, and thus that Greek had been written many centuries earlier than anyone had supposed. But as to the spoken language of Greece, we do not know exactly how it was pronounced; we do not know what a line of Sappho or Aristophanes sounded like. The Greeks were intent on music, and in Pythagoras they produced the first scholar of sound; but though we have a few inscriptions that suggest a musical score, and have mathematical knowledge of what Greek intervals were, we are unable to reconstruct an actual piece of their music. We know that the tragedians Aeschylus, Sophocles, and Euripides among them wrote some three hundred plays; but so far, only thirty-three of these have been retrieved. We also know that well over a hundred other men in classical Greece wrote tragedy; but of their work not one play survives. The Greeks wrote of "glorious Apelles," their leading painter; but none of his art is extant—nor have we any classical Greek paintings save those on pottery.

From these vases, as well as from steles and other reliefs, we know a great deal about Greek dress, household furnishing, entertainment; we have a good idea of what a Greek dwelling as a whole looked like, although no house from the classical period has survived upward of its foundation. Though sculpture is our most glorious trove from Greece, we cannot but think of all that has been lost: the great figure of the Olympian Zeus, for instance, carted off to Constantinople by Theodosius for its gold and ivory and lost in a fire there; or Phidias' two statues of Athena that once topped the Acropolis, lost without a trace; or the friezes and pediments of innumerable temples ruined by man and nature. And whatever sculpture was made of bronze was, for the most part, melted down at some later time for gain or weaponry—save that which by merciful accident was lost during sea voyages. The surrounding sea—the "blue museum," as one writer has called it—which served Greek traders so well, has served history too by preserving some of Greece's greatest treasures safe from the hands of marauders, yielding up some of them in our day to divers and the nets of fishermen.

We know much, but wish we knew more. We are fairly certain now that there was a war at Troy, and that Troy was destroyed by men; but so many questions still persist as to just who the attackers were, or just when and why they came, that a leading classicist, M. I. Finley, recently suggested that until we learn more, "the narrative we have of the Trojan War had best be removed from the realm of history and put back into the realm of myth and poetry."

Geologically, Greece is a promontory of a land largely submerged. Archaeologically, much of it is also lost to view. Mile after mile, hour after hour, as one tours Attica or the Peloponnesus today, one is struck not so much by what one sees standing of antiquity as by what is not there to see, other than in the mind's eye. But what survives in its rarity is incomparable.

Perhaps this awareness brings us closer to the singular spell that Greece has cast—for spell it has been all along, and would be, whether Olympia or Troy had been dug out or not. Whenever before or since have a people who left so few physical survivals of their greatness exerted so mighty an influence over the ages? Everyone knows that Greece immensely stirred the imagination of the Romans, who passed the Greek legacy on to the West. What some overlook is that much of the impact was conveyed to conquering Rome at a time when Greece was already in decline, whole cities having been sacked by the invaders. Thus Alpheus of Mytilene, a Greek poet of about the time of Caesar Augustus, laments:

> Lost now are the homes of the heroes. Scarce here and
>   there a city
> From the dust lifts its head a little, where the sons of
>   the gods were born.
> And such wert thou, Mycenae, as I passed, a thing of
>   pity—
> Even the goats of the mountain have pastures less for-
>   lorn.
> The goatherds pointed toward thee. And I heard an
>   old man say,
> "The Giant-builded City, the Golden, here it lay."

The Romans in Greece, seeking to attach themselves to a tradition more cultivated than their own, dutifully copied the art they saw there, though they had more difficulty following Greek ideas. The theologians of the Middle Ages, on the other hand, to whom physical Greece was remote and paganism anathema, were fascinated by many of its ideas and looked on ancient Aristotle as "*the* philosopher." Each successive age has found something it especially sought in classical Greece, and surely the mightiest force of Greece has been that of its image impressing itself upon each age—often becoming much transfigured in the process. One could say that Hellas, the Western world's greatest creator of myths, has over all the centuries gone on creating myths about itself in the eyes of its beholders.

For each generation has had a way of constructing its own vision of Greece, according to its own predilections. Some have turned to Greece as the embodiment of the world's lost youth; others, as that of perfected form and wisdom. Medieval versifiers imagined a knightly Troy and composed pale romances dimly based on Homer; earthy Chaucer and Boccaccio wrote somewhat more lusty versions of his tales. The Renaissance was so busy reviving

Rome that it viewed Greece chiefly through Roman eyes. Another idealizing style was set when Nicolas Poussin, moved by visions of an Arcadia he had never seen, painted his idyllic canvases of Greek goddesses and heroes decorously disporting themselves in sylvan groves. (Had he actually visited Arcadia and observed how harsh and forbidding much of that fastness in the Peloponnesus is, he might have made his portrayal of it less serene.) The same sense of exquisite harmony courses through C. W. Gluck's eighteenth-century operas, which were inspired by Greek myths; while to Richard Strauss, writing his own operas in the twentieth about Iphigenia, Orestes, and Electra, ancient Greece is all angry discord and violence. Even in the same generation the impulses that drive men back to Greece may differ widely. The tender Wordsworth, secluded in his Lake Country, felt chiefly nostalgia:

> So might I, standing on this pleasant lea . . .
> Have sight of Proteus rising from the sea;
> Or hear old Triton blow his wreathèd horn.

The archrebel Shelley, on the other hand, felt Greek ideals to be a rallying cry for freedom and revolution, and with this in mind wrote his *Prometheus Unbound*.

It would be false to say that Greece has been all things to all men. Yet if it has been so many things to so many different men, it must be in great part because Greece was so many different things to itself. For it was a culture both uniform and diverse. We speak of Greek order; yet we are always conscious of Greek contrast. On one hand we see those drives toward clarity, balance, reason, restraint, that are reflected in Hellenic architecture and philosophy; on the other, those urges of instinct, passion, boundless ambition, and excess, that are reflected in Hellenic myth, drama, religious cult, and so often in politics. The Apollonian mean constantly confronts the Dionysian extreme; and Apollo's temple at Delphi would not have had engraved on it the cautionary words "Nothing to Excess" unless the Greeks had been so given to just that.

What makes the Greeks so endlessly absorbing to us today is that in their tensions and diverse urges we can sense so many of our own. We speak of the Greeks' democracy, and with right we regard as the first ancestor of our own republic their stirring invention of a state ruled by citizen suffrage rather than by an absolute monarch. Yet at the same time we recall that many of the best minds of Athens—none more than Plato—were disillusioned with popular government and called for a return to absolute leadership by an elite. There is nothing that has been said or felt in our own last three agonizing decades of struggle between democracy and authoritarian government that was not prefigured by what was said in the Athenian Agora 2,500 years ago.

The Greeks also experienced their own collisions between science and religion, between physical evidence and traditional belief—as what people since has not? Some of the scientists and advanced thinkers made fun of their gods (many of whom were, to be sure, pretty shabby in their behavior), and the devout in turn denounced the impious. Nonconformists, people with notions of their own, which they could not resist spreading, were sometimes silenced: thus the end of Socrates.

In a few ways, to be sure, the classical Greeks remain distant from the modern West, despite all transmissions and migrations of their spirit. Though they held that man could and should enlarge his capacities, they did not believe in progress as our centuries have taught us to do. To most Greeks the general world they lived in was just the afterglow of some better, earlier, "golden age," when gods and godlike heroes had walked on earth, and which was never to be equaled or recovered. Nor did they seriously believe in immortality and fulfillment in afterlife, in the sense that most Christians do, or profess they do. They felt that glory won or honor done on earth would be sufficient fulfillment, and that such immortality as there was consisted in memory of their praiseworthy deeds among men who came after them.

Yet despite these differences, Greece remains constantly in us and around us, though we may not always be conscious of it. We are in the presence of Greece, though at some remove, when we look at innumerable court houses, banks, and porticoed mansions built in America in the Greek Revival style. Some men hold that when Roman Catholics revere the Virgin Mary, they are unconsciously the inheritors of Greek and pre-Greek worship of a mother goddess, or that when they light candles to their patron saints they are distantly linked to ancient Greeks, who made oblations to their local deities. Plato has sometimes been called a precursor of Christ.

However all this may be, the central truth remains that there is hardly an area of aspiration known to us on which the Greek mind before us had not also exercised itself. The concept of natural law—that the physical world is not simply the plaything of dark powers, but is intelligible and can be studied in search of first principles and order—this is Greek in origin, and on it all the law and the prophets of more than two millennia of science and natural philosophy have stood. The idea of gods (or, shall we say, God) as increasingly responsible to men and solicitous of them, and of man at his best, able to walk in godliness: that too—so different from the Babylonian's submission to animal spirits and the Egyptian's to his god-kings—is Greek as well as Hebrew in origin, and has profoundly affected all our religious thinking since. And the ideal of the uttermost development of all the faculties of man, as if in praise for his creation, leading to grace of body, freedom of spirit, high discipline of mind, and the love of truth: this is the very light of Greece and, though often dimmed, it has never gone out.   W. H. H.

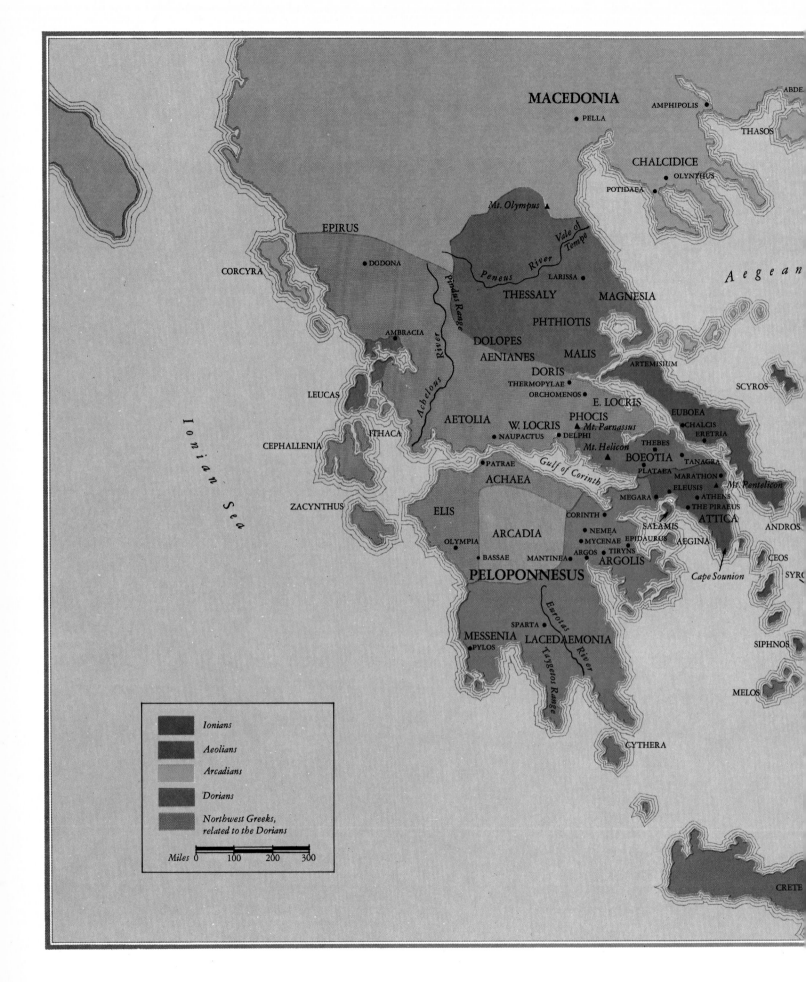

THE GREEK HOMELAND

The lands where Hellenic civilization arose were settled by various branches of the Greek race. The brilliant and creative Ionians inhabited the Asia Minor coast, the central islands, and the region around Athens. The Dorians, a sterner breed, controlled most of the Peloponnesus, the southern islands, and the southwestern coast of Asia Minor. In the north were the Aeolians, who, like the other two groups, stood in the vanguard of Greek culture. The other Greeks were less advanced, and there were relatively few city-states in their territories.

	PEOPLE AND POLITICS	ART AND ARCHITECTURE
BRONZE AGE c.3000–c.1100	c.2700–c.2000 Early Helladic culture on mainland Early Cycladic culture in the islands c.2000–c.1700 Mycenaeans enter Greece c.1700–c.1500 Height of Minoan culture on Crete c.1400 Beginning of Mycenaean sea supremacy c.1200 Trojan War Fall of Mycenaean states c.1150 Dorian migrations begin c.1150–c.1100 Aeolian migrations to Asia Minor	c.2700–c.2000 Cycladic and Helladic primitive figurines c.1700–c.1400 Great Minoan palaces; frescoes; pottery c.1400–c.1200 Mycenaean palaces; "beehive tombs"; goldwork
DARK AGE c.1100–c.800	c.1100 Final destruction of Mycenae Early city-states ruled by kings c.1100–c.1000 Ionian migrations to Asia Minor c.900 Dorian migrations to Aegean islands and Asia Minor	c.1000–c.700 Geometric pottery
ARCHAIC PERIOD c.800–c.500	c.800–c.700 Kingships replaced by aristocracies 776 Traditional date of first Olympic games c.750–c.550 Age of colonization by city-states 621 Draco's code of law in Athens c.600 Coinage introduced 594–593 Solon, Athenian lawgiver, makes constitutional and economic reforms 566 Panathenaic festival established 560–527 Pisistratus is leading Athenian politician 546 Persian conquest of Greek Asia Minor 507 Cleisthenes' democratic constitution	c.720–c.550 Archaic and orientalizing style of pottery; Attica and Corinth are leading manufacturers c.660–c.580 First life-sized statues; frontal, stylized *kouros* and *kore* figures c.620–c.530 Attic black-figured pottery c.600 Early Doric stone temples at Olympia, Corfu, Delphi, Aegina, Cyrene Architectural reliefs c.580–c.535 Increasingly naturalistic sculpture c.530 Temple of Apollo at Delphi c.530–c.400 Attic red-figured pottery
CLASSICAL PERIOD c.500–c.400	490 First Persian invasion of Greece Battle of Marathon 480 Second Persian invasion of Greece Persians defeat Spartans at Thermopylae Athens occupied by Persians Greeks defeat Persians at Salamis 479 Persians defeated at Plataea 454 Treasury of the Delian League transferred to Athens 448 Peace with Persia 443–429 Pericles leads Athens during Golden Age 435 Corcyra incident 432 Revolt of Potidaea 431–404 Peloponnesian War 431 *Pericles' funeral oration* 430 *Plague in Athens* 415 *Mutilation of Herms in Athens* *Athenian expedition to Sicily* 411 *Year of revolts in Athens* 404 *Athens surrenders to Sparta*	c.490–c.417 Phidas 438 *Athena Parthenos* c.480 Transition to early classical style *Ephebe* by Critios fl.c.480–c.445 Myron; sculptor c.450 *Discobolus* c.480 *Running Maiden* of Eleusis fl.c.475–447 Polygnotus; painter c.470 *Charioteer* of Delphi c.470–450 Bronze sculpture of Poseidon or Zeus c.450–406 Periclean building program in Athens 447–438 *Parthenon* c.450 *Temple of Hephaestus* 437–432 *Propylaea* 427–423 *Temple of Athena Nike* 421–406 *Erechtheum* fl.c.450–405 Polycleitus; sculptor and theorist c.450–425 Earliest Corinthian capital, at Bassae c.440 Temple of Poseidon at Sounion
LATE CLASSICAL PERIOD c.400–c.330	c.395–c.340 Warfare among rival Greek leagues 384–322 Demosthenes; Athenian orator, statesman 351 *First Philippic* 371 Thebes defeats Sparta at Leuctra 338 Battle of Chaeronea Philip of Macedonia leads Greek states 336–323 Reign of Alexander the Great	fl.c.394–351 Scopas of Paros; sculptor fl.c.370–330 Praxiteles; sculptor c.350 *Hermes with Infant Dionysus* c.350 Theatre at Epidaurus c.350–c.320 *Apollo Belvedere* fl.c.342–300 Lysippus; sculptor of statues of Alexander fl.c.332 Apelles; painter
HELLENISTIC AGE c.330–c.30	c.323–148 Macedonia ruled by Antigonids Greek city-states enjoy varying degrees of independence Frequent warfare among rival leagues 200–196 First Roman victories in Greece 148 Macedonia becomes a Roman province 146 Corinth destroyed by Romans 86 Athens sacked by Sulla	c.200 *Nike* of Samothrace *Venus de Milo* c.160–c.130 Laocoön group c.197–c.156 Altar of Zeus at Pergamum

LITERATURE	SCIENCE AND PHILOSOPHY	EVENTS ABROAD
*c.*1750 Linear A script *after* 1500 Linear B script		3100–2160 Old Kingdom, Egypt *2575 Cheops' Pyramid built* 3000–2000 Sumerian civilization 2133–1625 Middle Kingdom, Egypt 1792–1750 Hammurabi rules Babylon 1567–1085 New Kingdom, Egypt 1460–1200 Hittite empire in Asia Minor *c.*1200 Hebrews invade Canaan Sea peoples invade Egypt
*c.*1100–*c.*900 Art of writing is lost		*c.*1000 King David rules in Jerusalem Rise of Phoenician sea power 875–630 Height of Assyrian empire 875–520 Age of Hebrew prophets 814(?) Carthage founded
*c.*800–*c.*700 Homer composes the *Iliad* and *Odyssey* *c.*700 Hesiod writes the *Theogony* *fl.c.*600 Sappho; lyric poetess Aesop; originator of fables 534 First playwriting competitions in Athens	*c.*636–*c.*546 Thales of Miletus; founder of Ionian school of natural philosophy *c.*611–*c.*547 Anaximander of Miletus *c.*582–*c.*507 Pythagoras; mathematician and philosopher *c.530 Establishes mystical and political brotherhood at Croton* *fl.c.546* Anaximenes of Miletus *c.*535–*c.*475 Heraclitus of Ephesus; last of the Ionian philosophers *c.*500–*c.*428 Anaxagoras of Clazomenae; natural philosopher	800–500 Height of Etruscan power 753(?) Rome founded *c.*715 Midas; king of Phrygia 612–538 Babylon rules the Near East *c.*560–546 Croesus reigns in Lydia 538 Cyrus I of Persia conquers Babylon
525–456 Aeschylus; playwright *467 Seven Against Thebes* *458 Oresteia* 518–438 Pindar; lyric poet *c.*496–406 Sophocles; playwright *441 Antigone* *c.429 Oedipus the King* *413 Electra* *c.*485–406 Euripides; playwright *438 Alcestis* *431 Medea* *415 Trojan Women* *c.*484–*c.*425 Herodotus; father of history *c.*460–403 Critias; poet and critic *c.*460–*c.*400 Thucydides; historian *c.*450–*c.*385 Aristophanes; playwright of Old Comedy *423 The Clouds* *411 Lysistrata* *406 The Frogs*	*c.*495–*c.*435 Empedocles of Acragas; philosopher and scientist *c.*490–*c.*430 Zeno of Elea; mathematician *c.*485–*c.*411 Protagoras of Abdera; Sophist 469 Birth of Socrates *c.*460–*c.*370 Hippocrates of Cos; physician *c.*460–*c.*370 Democritus of Abdera; originator of atom theory 436–338 Isocrates; Sophist *c.*428 Birth of Plato *c.407 Plato becomes disciple of Socrates*	538–333 Persia rules the Near East 486 Egypt revolts against Persia 485 Xerxes I becomes ruler of Persia after death of Darius I 483 Persia quells Egyptian revolt 464 Artaxerxes I becomes king of Persia after Xerxes I's murder
*c.*430–*c.*354 Xenophon of Athens; historian and essayist *c.*400–*c.*320 Middle Comedy; only fragments remain	*c.*400–*c.*315 Diogenes; Cynic philosopher 399 Trial and death of Socrates *c.*387 Plato founds Academy in Athens 384–322 Aristotle *367 Joins Plato's Academy* *343 Tutor to Alexander of Macedonia* *c.335 Founds Lyceum in Athens*	396–300 Romans conquer the Etruscans; rise of Roman power Height of Carthaginian power 331 Battle of Gaugemela; Alexander the Great conquers Persian empire
*c.*342–291 Menander; playwright of New Comedy *c.317 Dyskolos* *c.*310–250 Theocritus of Syracuse; bucolic poet *c.*300 Alexandrian library founded *fl.c.*200 Apollonius of Rhodes; head of Alexandrian library, poet *c.*203–*c.*120 Polybius; Greek historian of Rome	*c.*342–*c.*271 Epicurus; philosopher *c.*310–230 Aristarchus of Samos; mathematician and astronomer *fl.c.*300 Euclid; mathematician and physicist, author of the *Elements* *c.*300 Stoic school founded in Athens *c.*287–212 Archimedes of Syracuse; mathematician, physicist, and inventor *c.*275–194 Eratosthenes; scientist, historian, literary critic, head of Alexandrian library	323–30 Ptolemies rule Egypt 312–64 Seleucids rule the Near East 282–133 Attalids rule Pergamum 264–241 First Punic War 241 Rome conquers former Greek colonies in Sicily 218–201 Second Punic War 149–146 Third Punic War *146 Rome destroys Carthage* 69–30 Cleopatra; last of Ptolemies 31 Battle of Actium

A RUGGED
SETTING

Climate and landscape play an important role in the for-
mation of every civilization. In many places societies seem
to have arisen because natural advantages made the area
ideal for permanent settlement; in Egypt, for example,
crops sprang abundantly from the fertile soil deposited
by the Nile's annual floods. In Greece the factors were
very different, and helped produce another kind of civilization. The face of Greece, like the islands that seem to
be extensions of the mainland, is dominated by mountains and little valleys, though a few plains exist. The
meagerness of arable soil caused the growth of small communities rather than large ones in Greece, and the difficulty of land communications kept them from uniting.
Each region was fiercely independent, just as its individual
citizens were, for the land provided little opportunity for
the collective irrigation and farming that had helped mold
earlier, more unified cultures. Greece could not support an
enlarging population; its inhabitants were forced to the
sea (opposite, a view of the Bay of Salamis), which cut
into the peninsula at every side, to seek new sites for
colonies and sources of food; in the process they became
expert navigators. Their land, though harsh and inhospi-
table, was bathed by sunlight that exposed the finest detail of the terrain. From its hard outlines the Greeks derived
aesthetic ideals which were to be fulfilled in works of art.

15

BOISSONNAS

ROLOFF BENY

It was natural for the ancient Greeks to believe that the great gods had conquered the mighty, rugged mountains which defied man. The ancients felt that the clouds hovering about the top of Mount Olympus (the snow-capped mountain in Thessaly in northern Greece that soars almost 10,000 feet above a rocky plateau) hid away the glorious home of those gods, where, in a climate of perpetual springtime, they lived and cavorted and held council. Two views of the mountains are shown here: the craggy peak (opposite) and a view from the north of the Olympus range (above).

OVERLEAF: Sunlight flickers through the branches of the silvery trees in the largest olive grove on the Greek peninsula. Located far below the towering cliffs of Mount Parnassus at Delphi, in a seaside valley that cuts into the mountains of central Greece, the grove stretches for ten miles. The olive was indigenous to Hellas and grew wild in all parts of the country; it was one of the land's few natural advantages. The ancient Greeks not only ate olive oil on bread and used it profusely in cooking but they also anointed themselves with it and burned it in their lamps.

DESCHARNES

Although there were plains in ancient Greece, not all of them were arable, and they comprised less than one fifth of the total area of the country. Barren, arid landscapes—like that shown below in a photograph of an area in the Peloponnesus about fifty miles from Athens—were a far more common sight. Because there were no large rivers in Greece farmers had to depend on small streams like the one opposite, and on springs, which were plentiful, to supply them with water.

HASSIA

MANOS, MAGNUM

OVERLEAF: *At the tip of Attica the steep headland of Cape Sounion—topped by the remains of a temple to Poseidon—juts out into the waters of the Aegean. Past its rugged cliffs, Athenian mariners sailed homeward with their cargoes.*

HANS HANNAU, RAPHO-GUILLUMETTE

A row of stately cypresses towers high above a stand of olive trees in a rich meadow in the Peloponnesus. Throughout Greece, even in ancient times, such pleasing rural landscapes became increasingly less common as the land was denuded by the indiscriminate cutting of trees and shrubs, and by the ravages of warfare.

HASSIA

1

THE LEANEST LAND

When on the East the sheer bright star arose
That tells of coming Dawn, the ship made landfall
And came up islandward in the dim of night.
—Homer, the Odyssey

Ancient Athenian sailors, threading their course homeward with a cargo of timber from Thrace or grain from beyond the Bosporus, were careful to hug the headlands and islands along the way, since they traveled without compasses or charts and were well aware of the dread storms the sea god Poseidon might send down on them if they ventured too far offshore. Yet some of the harshest waters they had to cross lay close in—none closer or more treacherous than those just off Cape Sounion at the tip of Attica itself, where winds funneled down through the narrow strait between the bony island of Euboea and Andros, another island outcrop. There the blasts often met with others whistling down from the strait of Chalcis, to the northwest, to churn up a narrow cauldron of conflicting seas. To get under the lee of Sounion—"holy Sounion," Homer called it—was every captain's need: not until he rounded it, looking up as he did so at the great temple the Athenians had built at its peak to the sea god, could he be sure that now only a short day's coasting would bring him to safe haven in the Piraeus.

As he beat his way around the bleak promontory, he passed over a singularly dark patch of water. It is still dark today, reflecting perhaps the sudden depth below. It marks the spot below the cliff on which, according to one legend, Aegeus, a mythical king of Athens, had stood watching the ship of his son Theseus returning from Crete. Because of an oversight, it approached under black sails rather than white (the prearranged signal); he believed mistakenly that Theseus had perished in his struggle with the Cretan Minotaur, and so hurled himself headlong into the sea—the sea that thereupon became known as the Aegean.

All ancient Greece begins with myths—and, one could say, with storms as well. The expedition against Troy—the war that forms the subject of the *Iliad*—began with a contrary high wind, the norther that bottled up more than a thousand Greek ships at their assembly port of Aulis and prevented Agamemnon and his fellow chieftains from making sail for Troy. It was only when King Agamemnon, at a soothsayer's behest, sacrificed his own daughter Iphigenia on the altar to angry Artemis that the blow abated. The high wind was an ill wind too; for the deed the king performed to allay it brought about the fulfillment of an ancestral curse upon his house: because he sacrificed their daughter, his wife Clytemnestra murdered him on his return, and their son Orestes in turn murdered her.

The *Odyssey*, in dealing with the return voyage of some of the warriors who had fought at Troy, abounds in tempests unleashed at the caprice of contentious gods. Thus, after the marooned Odysseus was helped by the nymph Calypso to escape her island

26

on a raft, Poseidon was so bent on tormenting the hero that,

> *Brewing high thunderheads, he churned the deep*
> *With both hands on his trident—called up wind*
> *From every quarter, and sent a wall of rain*
> *To blot out land and sea in torrential night.*
> *Hurricane winds now struck from the South and East*
> *Shifting North West in a great spume of seas,*
> *On which Odysseus' knees grew slack, his*
> *Heart sickened, and he said within himself:*
> *"Rag of man that I am, is this the end of me?"*

Homer could hardly have composed such a passage unless the perils and excitements of the sea lay deep within his consciousness; indeed they were a part of the everyday experience of the Greeks, one of the world's first great sailor folk.

All Greece begins with its surrounding sea, the "wine-dark," turbulent waters swirling around three sides of a peninsula thrust out like a bony hand from the European main. Rarely more than thirty miles removed from the sea even when in the mountainous interior, Greece's early settlers were drawn to it despite all dangers. They called it *pontos*, which also means "passage" or "road." And road it became for them, beckoning them toward a far horizon and making the Greeks very different kind of men from the haughty lords and the serfs that peopled the river valleys of sunbaked Egypt and the Middle East. As early as the dim Mycenaean age in the second millennium before Christ—an age that Homer's sagas are now thought to reflect in part—venturers from the Peloponnesus set up trading posts as far away as Italy and Syria. At the beginning of the first millennium Greeks were settling in Asia Minor. In the eighth and seventh centuries B.C. they were establishing settlements around the shores of the western Mediterranean and sailing northeastward against the currents of the Bosporus and all the way to the Crimea. All Greece, one could say, begins with the pursuit of adventure, despite the interfering gods, and with the reward and knowledge gained thereby.

Today the image of a storm-tossed, god-tormented Greece may seem somewhat remote. A current handbook *Tourism in Greece* advertises "balmy climate . . . enchanting islands amid sparkling waters." Byron wrote rhapsodically of Greece's "eternal summer." Painter and poet, scholar and tourist alike, have helped compound a genteel Western notion of a Hellas of balm and amplitude.

The ancient Greeks, however, saw a different kind of country: a land lean rather than rich, divided by mountains often impassable, meager of soil and water, without navigable rivers, its "sylvan groves" few and far between, discomforts great, and surrounded

NATIONAL MUSEUM, ATHENS; HARISSIADIS

A detail of a gold Mycenaean cup, which shows a herdsman roping a cow, tells of the early pursuit of animal husbandry in a land where men eked out their sustenance with difficulty.

Poseidon is shown running with his trident in his hand in a detail from a vase painting made early in the fifth century. In Greece, where no region was more than a few dozen miles from sight of the sea, his worship was widespread.

WILLIAMS COLLEGE MUSEUM OF ART; ANDRE EMMERICH GALLERY

by seas often more malignant than benign. In such an environment life was bound to be hard-working and difficult. Homer would hardly have recognized his homeland in the courtly paintings of it done in the seventeenth century by Poussin (who had never been there); in them all waters are ample and still, goddesses are graceful presences among the copses, and no leaf stirs. Homer himself spoke of Greece as a violent land: seas are always heaving, winds and torrents are always rushing, tall trees are trembling, and gods and heroes are constantly colliding, burning with passion and intent on doing in their enemies.

Eternal summer? In the early seventh century B.C. the poet Hesiod warned:

> *Beware the month of Lenaeon—foul days, all of them, of sharp air that would flay an ox; beware the cruel hoar-frosts that Boreas brings when he blows upon the face of the earth.*

> *Over Thrace the land of horses he blows, and breathes upon the wide sea and lifts it up. Earth also and her forests bellow aloud.*

Ample, generous valleys? There were some, of course; but Plato, speaking in his *Critias* of the Attic landscape, says that it looks like "the skeleton of a body wasted by disease." Ease of life? Herodotus, the first and perhaps the greatest Greek historian, writes in one stark sentence of the land that he had traveled well: "Hellas has always had poverty as her companion."

Even today, despite much work to reclaim and terrace its eroded uplands, hardly one fifth of Greece is arable. The rest is mostly tortuous ridge and pitching declivity, from the Pindus range down through the limestone spines of Attica and the Peloponnesus that reach out toward stony islands. There are watered plains beside the Ionian Sea in the west, and some in Thessaly, Attica, Boeotia, and around Corinth too; but in many parts of the east and south the strata tend to rise abruptly from the Aegean; and before the Greek is fairly out of sight of the sea he is likely to find himself on a lonely height where no grain grows, where only lean sheep graze, and where, higher up, the only inhabitant, feeding on stunted growth, is the ubiquitous goat, the symbol of his country's ageless poverty.

Between the heights lie isolated valleys, often fertile, without a river system worthy of the name to connect them. In such terrain, communities tended to remain detached from those beyond the next ridge; often communication between them by sea around the capes was more feasible than overland. Zeus's shrine at Olympia in the west, pleasantly sited in a vale at the confluence of two streams, with cypress and oleander all about, was hardly sixty miles from Sparta, as the crow flies; but to the Spartan athlete journeying there for the Panhellenic games it involved a trek of a week or more, winding by trail across the Peloponnesus. A journey to Apollo's oracle at Delphi, high on the flanks of Mount Parnassus, is today just three hours by car from Athens, but in ancient times it was a major undertaking, involving long days' marches along dry river beds, or across torrents in winter, followed by a slow ascent from the gorges—and, if you hailed from the southern part of Greece, it involved a trip by boat across the Gulf of Corinth as well. Yet so great was the importance attached to the Delphic oracle that there was a stream of traffic to it of individual seekers and messengers of state from all over the Greek world and sometimes from foreign kingdoms as well.

Though well-favored Olympia had its streams, most inland waters are hardly what we should consider rivers at all. They resemble nothing so much as the arroyos of the arid American Southwest—torrential with flash-floods when the rains come, but waste beds of rubble and lizards in the dry season. No wonder far-traveled Herodotus was impressed by the Nile and Euphrates when he saw them—broad rivers that actually kept flowing all the year around.

Lacking constant water coursing across his land, the Greek relied primarily on local springs, of which there was a happy abundance. Along with them was a store of myths about sacred wells and the gods who had beneficently caused them to arise. The earliest Athenians, when they chose the sheer limestone Acropolis as site for a town and citadel, could hardly have made it livable or defensible unless there had been fresh water there. And water there was, its origin according to one legend being this: In very early times Zeus's elder brother Poseidon, the sea god and earth-shaker, vied with Zeus's daughter Athena for the role of protector and patron of the city. To show his power, Poseidon struck the stones of the Acropolis with his trident, and up sprang a gushing well. Athena, for her part, cast her spell upon the stones and produced a thriving olive tree. The citizens of Athens, asked to choose between the deities, chose Athena by a majority of one vote—the winning ballot being a woman's (which was the last time that women in Athens were allowed to vote). Vengeful Poseidon, a version of the legend tells us, then sent a flood upon Athens; but his well remained. It is known that in Mycenaean times a fountain existed deep in a seam of the rocks and supplied water for the Acropolis' dwellers. And today there are still travel-

The Greeks supplemented a diet that was short of meat with food from the peninsula's many surrounding waters. Above, a painted dish depicts the harvest of the sea, which included fish, shellfish, and the ubiquitous squid.
LOUVRE; GIRAUDON

29

LOUVRE; GIRAUDON

ers who, bending low over the fissures, insist that they hear the murmur of Poseidon's ancient waters far beneath.

And if a traveler now, as in ancient times, makes a pilgrimage to Delphi, the first welcome sight, as the dusty, hairpin road from Athens attains the heights, is that of a fountain of coldest water bursting forth from a cleft in the vertical red seams of Parnassus overhead, no matter how dry the season. This is the unfailing sacred spring, as inviting to the tourist or shepherd today, as he scoops his hands to drink of it, as it was to the petitioner even in the age of Homer.

Four millennia and more of settlement, plus the tramplings of innumerable conquests and a history of poor husbandry, have taken their toll of Greek land and resource. Denuded by woodsmen, chewed over by voracious goats, in turn fought over and abandoned when the local populations were decimated or enslaved and carried away, the upland has been eroded. Today it probably sustains far fewer cattle than it did in Homeric times. Yet the process of impoverishment began early—so early that Plato, looking back over the past of Attica, speaks of its soil in his time as only "a remnant" of what it had been, much that had once supported fine herds before the coming of great "deluges" and "ravages" having since been washed away into the sea. In Homer's tales, heroes are constantly feasting on meat; in early times a whole province of Greece was named Boeotia—"land of the cow" —for the herds that grazed on it. But such herds appear to have declined almost to the vanishing point by Periclean times. Meat was eaten only on festival days, when animals were sacrificed to the gods; otherwise, two meals a day of barley and other grain dishes were the rule—a diet so austere that the Persian invaders complained of it. Even today, the rural Greek subsists on two meals a day, and a dinner of meat is a festive occasion.

The bees of Mount Hymettus provided honey (there was no sugar). The olive provided cooking oil (there was no butter) and, on its subsequent pressings, oil for personal cleansing (there was no soap) and for lamps as well, after which its lees were used for fuel. The goat provided cheese, a little grudging milk, and an occasional muscular haunch for the pot (if one was ready to destroy the goat for the sake of eating the meat). Lean sheep provided the wool that Greek wives and their maidservants spun and wove into the plain oblong lengths that provided the basic year-round garment of man and woman alike. There was some flax, and it was made into linen, another popular material for clothing. Cotton was yet hardly known, and silk was not cultivated in Greece until long after the time of Christ. There were a few fruits

30

—chiefly the fig, pomegranate, apple, and pear—but the citrus stands that now grace the western Peloponnesus did not exist then.

Grapes there were in plenty, best grown in Chalcidice and Thrace, on the islands of Thasos, Chios, and Samos, and in Attica; and the Greeks were a wine-drinking people. They were, according to legend, taught the art of the vine by Dionysus, the strange, wild god who had come down from the north and for long was not quite accepted by the Olympians. But though Dionysus was the patron of great revels, wine was by no means identified with them only: it was drunk daily and somewhat abstemiously, usually diluted with one or two parts of water, as the only enlivening accompaniment to a generally monotonous diet. And the Greek palate for the grape was hardly a discerning one. A story has it that the Athenians, anxious to save their stocks of wine during the Persian invasions by making them unpalatable to the thirsty eastern intruders, doctored their storage jars with resin from their pine trees. This stratagem had a paradoxical result: though the Persians found the mixture not potable, when the Greeks themselves reopened the rejected amphorae, they discovered that, indeed, it was, and have been drinking *retsina*, with its strong taste of turpentine ever since. A more likely explanation is that resin was used to seal the porous clay wine jars, affecting the wine's flavor, and that the Greeks grew to like the odd taste.

Finally there were fish, with so many seas about, but the notion of ample Aegean fisheries is another literary illusion. Good fishing grounds demand strong marine vegetation; the Aegean's translucent, opalescent, stone-bottomed depths have been as bare of clouding sea-growth as Attica, throughout historic times, has been of grasslands. The result was that the fisherman was often lucky if he could haul in a handful of paltry sardines or spear an octopus for his long day's work.

One thing his country did possess: a steady climate, rather than weather that changed daily, and upon this much depended. Jutting into the sea, between cloud-hung Europe and the hard stare of Africa's sun, Greece lived under seasons that alternated but that promised half a year of almost constant warmth and light. In fall came fertilizing rains for next year's crops, in winter, torrential ones; then, as if by clockwork, in April or early May the atmosphere lifted to bring azure days that might go on uninterrupted by any cloud or rainfall for six months, until in late fall, skies thickened again, and traders and fishermen beached their boats, shepherds brought their flocks down off the heights, and ephors and councilors of state suspended wars and other expeditions until the following spring. During the long, bright summer season storms

METROPOLITAN
MUSEUM OF ART,
ROGERS FUND

The agricultural people who lived in Greece before the coming of the Hellenes developed a simple but sophisticated art. Above, a small Cycladic statue dating from around 2500 B.C. shows a seated harpist. Opposite is a female idol, probably representing the mother goddess.

31

did indeed assault the coast; but such are the peculiarities of Greek atmosphere that an undimmed sun and pleasant breezes could be bathing the Acropolis while high crests of sea were driving boats into cover at the Piraeus, four miles away. And even in midwinter—Hesiod's "month of Lenaeon"—with all the winds unloosed, there might remain over Attica that extraordinary, penetrating Hellenic light.

Such a climate, so clear, firm, and hospitable throughout much of the year, left its profound impress upon the mind and ways of Greek man. He saw no fogs, as northerners do, no misty mornings of low-hanging sun mingling with gray haze and overcast. He looked up into the hills and saw instead, day after day, dry, hard, sculptural forms of nature cast into bold relief as the sun began its climb in Helios' chariot (though very few Greeks actually believed in the chariot); and then, as the orb rolled westward, he saw these forms changing in all their facets—highlights were very high, shadows were very dark, and there was little softness in between.

This sense of great clarity of form and of sharp, even violent, contrast we shall see running through all Greek consciousness and art. One first encounters it, inevitably, in the temples or remnants of temples that survive—those structures upon which the Greeks lavished their greatest care and cost, and which in the eyes of so many bespeak the very landscape itself, being so hard, spare, and lean of line, resembling Mount Pentelicon's own marble rocks in the way in which they catch the strong, contrasting, ever-changing play of sun and shade.

They were temples, moreover, open to all weathers. Though each had its walled-in, central sacerdotal chamber, windowless and dark, its greatest beauty lay in its surrounding treelike colonnade, windswept and sun-crossed like all Greece itself. Indeed, almost all the surviving Greek architecture one can see or detect today (apart from the deep tombs of Mycenae, the walled-in treasuries of Delphi, or the council chamber at Athens) was outdoor architecture—the colonnaded temple, the portico, the hillside theatre, the roofless stadium. This in turn tells of an outdoor people, living in close communion with sun and landscape. The Athenian's place of business was the Agora, originally a broad cleared field below the Acropolis; his exercise and recreation place was the gymnasium courtyard; his walking and talking place, particularly under high summer sun or when winds and the rains came, the covered portico, or *stoa*; his parliament, the slope called the Pnyx. It was only in the harshest months that he spent much time in his uncomfortable dwellings, poorly warmed by braziers, hibernating

A Hellenic coin depicts a stalk of wheat, a crop that was never abundant on the Greek mainland. Large Greek cities imported grain from colonial regions on the Black Sea coast, Sicily, or Italy, where this coin was made.
BIBLIOTHEQUE NATIONALE; GIRAUDON

awhile in structures so modest that they have yielded little but rubble to the archaeologist's spade.

In any season the Greek had time to reflect upon his unique homeland, so exposed to the surrounding seas and thereby in danger of conquest, so divided by inland heights and cut in two by the Gulf of Corinth, so inchoate, and yet so strategic, athwart the water routes from east to west, north to south. It was a land, first of all, that called for a tough, hardy people, able to make do with little and to supplement by their own resources what they lacked from nature's gods. It was a land turned outward, in need of commanding every sea around it if it was to survive and grow, and yet one of small population. Asia had empires at a time when Greece yet had only sparse settlements, with local kings ruling over hamlets. Even martial Sparta at its strongest was able to place only five thousand citizens in the field against the Persians at Plataea in the year 479 B.C.; and though great Athens and its allies mobilized against the Persian invaders a force numbered in tens of thousands, this was still a small one to throw against one rumored to consist of hundreds of thousands.

The Greek's greatest strength and irreducible asset, as the world was to know, lay in intangibles—in his conception of himself and of his relation to his gods and fellow men. Did his physical environment play some deep part in forming these, calling forth some special genius of race? And what was it that caused men to come to the land of Greece in the first place, to become there the Hellenes of history?

There was no single race that came; there was an amalgam of several. From both east and north, early men and influences came to the land. Neolithic mounds and implements have been found at many sites from northern Thessaly down through the Peloponnesus to Knossos on Crete, and they tell of tribes with a knowledge of farming, which spread into the Aegean world from the grasslands of the ancient Near and Middle East, where, so far as we know, the art of agriculture first sprang up. By the early third millennium, Bronze Age cultures in Mesopotamia and Egypt—characterized by commerce, kingship, the skills of writing and of working in bronze—were spreading their influences to coastal Asia Minor, the Aegean islands, and primitive mainland Greece.

An exuberant and luxurious culture arose on Crete, which was peopled by a dark-haired Eastern stock. This civilization, known as Minoan after the legendary monarch Minos, was influenced by Egypt and Asia Minor, but showed a marked departure from ponderous Eastern styles in the grace and delicacy of its arts. Far inferior to the brilliant Minoan culture flourishing on Crete in

Although in early times the Greek land was lush enough to support herds of cattle, by classical times only goats and sheep could survive on the rocky, eroded hillsides. This Bronze Age figure depicts a shepherd with a ram.
ARCHAEOLOGICAL MUSEUM, HERAKLEION; DESCHARNES

this period were the Helladic culture in parts of still rudimentary agricultural mainland Greece and another, in the nearby islands, called the Cycladic. These societies are dim to our knowledge when compared to what succeeded them in the second millennium at Mycenae, Tiryns, Pylos, Orchemenos, and other sites on the mainland, where a ruling people called the Mycenaeans, who were strongly influenced by Minoan culture, established a strong and highly organized society, building proud bastions on high hills. They have left behind numerous remains—among them ornate golden cups from which they drank, their women's marvelously wrought jewelry, and even more marvelous, the traditions and tales that were later woven into the *Iliad* of Homer.

These Mycenaeans gave Greece its first age of power and brilliance. Until recently, some scholars believed them to be offshoots of the Minoan race, but in 1952 Michael Ventris deciphered the script known as Linear B and found it to be a primordial form of Greek. Now it is believed that the Mycenaeans, who used this script, were in fact the earliest Greek-speaking peoples of the mainland. It is supposed that at the beginning of the second millennium they arrived in Greece as barbaric tribesmen, sweeping down and conquering the original inhabitants. Their incursion unsettled the whole Aegean area: vocabularies and races intermixed in the land and turbulence governed the times.

Much about their origins remains a riddle. We do know, however, that they came in close and beneficial contact with the highly civilized Minoans of Crete, and that sometime around 1400 B.C. they may have conquered that island; under their rule the palaces and culture of Crete flourished for centuries more, like the Mycenaean kingdoms on the mainland. Mycenaean traders and rovers sailed as far as Italy, Egypt, and the Syrian coast, and the Hittites in Asia Minor became aware of a Mycenaean tribe or people they called the "Ahhiyawa"—a name very like Homer's name for the inhabitants of Greece, the Achaeans. But then, amid all this stir and bustle, toward the end of the millennium a second descent from the north took place, led apparently by another and less civilized Greek-speaking tribe which had hovered long at the outskirts of the Mycenaean world, and which history was to call the Dorians. Precisely how and when these people assaulted the Mycenaeans, we do not know either; we do know that in the twelfth and eleventh centuries the lights of Mycenaean culture went out, and that in the seizures and brutalities of the age the invaders toppled the Mycenaean kingdoms, took their women and subjected their peasants, but assimilated little of their high culture. After about 1100 B.C., mainland Greece reverted to a stage far

BOTH: ARCHAEOLOGICAL MUSEUM, HERAKLEION; HIRMER

A fresco (above) from the palace at Knossos shows the bull games that were practiced by the Minoans of Crete; in them, young acrobats leaped upon the backs of bulls and jumped to safety. The classical Greeks had but dim memories of the Minoans, who had flourished centuries before their time; most of Minoan civilization was lost, and even now most Minoan scripts have not yet been deciphered. One puzzling Minoan form of picture writing is shown on the terra-cotta "Phaistos disk" at left; it is more primitive than the syllabic scripts known as Linear A and Linear B, also found on Crete.

more primitive than that of the preceding eras. We call the four centuries that followed 1100 the Greek dark ages; at least, they are dark to us.

They were dark, or at least mysterious, to the Greeks of classical times too. Men of the classical age in the fifth century were fascinated by their origins, though they had only vague and mythic knowledge of their ancestors. Yet they were aware that into their making there had gone not one but several sources of blood. They were conscious of some distinction between a primordial folk who had lived in their land from time immemorial and a spate of later arrivals from elsewhere who had come to mingle with them. The proud Athenians in particular liked to insist that they themselves were descendants of aboriginal or indigenous Pelasgians. And though modern scholarship knows nothing about any Pelasgians as actual pre-Hellenic ancestors, the Athenian claim is not all sheer mythmaking. For the very name of Athens, like that of its patron goddess Athena, is paradoxically non-Greek and may hark back to some earlier native language.

Herodotus, the first Greek student of the past, remarks on the survival of what he calls this "barbarian language" down to his own day, and argues that one should distinguish between the Dorians and the Ionians (those who settled in Asia Minor) as two main branches of the Greek people, the latter being of Pelasgian roots. This again displays the Greeks' awareness of diversity in their midst. This diversity was to become quite visible as Ionians raised settlements on the pleasant Asia Minor coast, while the Dorians concentrated more and more on the rugged Peloponnesus. The former produced the first Greek literature and philosophy, together with spirited and lively forms in art, whereas the latter stressed that strength and austerity which one associates with early Sparta and the shape of the emerging Doric temple.

This development took centuries. It was to take centuries, also, for these differences across land and sea, between tribes and tongues, to result in what can be called the Greek fusion. In the fifth century Herodotus (himself a Dorian) could write of certain general or joint qualities that had marked the Hellenes as a whole during their struggle against the oncoming Persians. These were, he said, "our common language, the altars and the sacrifices of which we all partake, the common character which we bear." And of these the last, the "common character," was to be the greatest. On a meager land, thinly peopled, divided by geography, racial origin, political differences, and often conflicting impulses a common culture was in process of creation. This was the central Greek achievement; from it, what is best in Greece springs.

ROLOFF BENY

DAWN IN THE AEGEAN

According to Greek tradition, in most ancient times Minos, the king of Crete, ruled the seas, put down piracy, and brought order to the Aegean world. In the *Iliad* Homer speaks of ninety rich cities established on the island of Crete, but by classical times the power of Crete had vanished and the island had become relatively unimportant. Only myth and poetry recalled the memory of Europe's first civilization, which had flourished there during the second millennium. In those centuries the culture that we call Minoan reached a peak of artistic splendor comparable to that of the contemporary civilizations of Egypt and Mesopotamia. From the Cretan towns, with their vast palace complexes, traders sailed throughout the eastern Mediterranean. Palace storerooms were filled with great jars of wine, grain, olive oil, and figs. Atop these palaces stood horns of consecration, such as the pair shown at left at Knossos; they resembled the horns of a bull, a beast that played an important role in Minoan religion, being a symbol of fertility like Crete's major deity, the mother goddess. In many aspects of its culture, Minoan Crete strongly influenced the early Greeks of the mainland and through them the classical culture that was to arise there. Late in the second millennium the mainland cities Argos, Pylos, Tiryns, Orchomenos, and most notably Mycenae, the city rich in gold, mingled Cretan and Hellenic elements to give the peninsula its first great age of splendor.

ARCHAEOLOGICAL MUSEUM, HERAKLEION; JOSEPHINE POWELL

ARCHAEOLOGICAL MUSEUM,
HERAKLEION; JOSEPHINE POWELL

*A faïence figure of the bare-breasted mother god-
dess of Crete shows her carrying serpents, and with
a bird on her head; both animals were often associated with her. At right a bronze statuette depicts an acrobat landing on the back of a bull.*

COLLECTION OF
E. G. SPENCER CHURCHILL,
GLOUCESTER

THE CULT OF THE GODDESS

The cult of the mother goddess dominated Crete. Her images and emblems were everywhere. She was worshiped primarily as a goddess of earth and of fertility, and her power over nature was symbolized by many representations of her taming wild beasts. Often, too, she appeared as a bird or with a bird; in later times the Greeks, whose goddesses retained many of her attributes, associated Athena with the owl and Aphrodite with the dove. It seems likely that the Cretans sacrificed bulls to their goddess; indeed the Minoan bull games may have originated in a ritual celebrated in her honor. These games were played by nimble athletes—youths and maidens—who performed the difficult feat of somersaulting over the back of a fierce bull. To do this they seized one of the bull's horns and, when he tossed his head in anger, sprang head over heels, to land on the animal's back; then they jumped to safety. After the bull had been ritually conquered in this manner, its sacrifice to the goddess probably took place.

THE PALACE OF MINOS

The palace at Knossos was the richest and most extensive in Crete. The vast complex, constructed around 1700 B.C., contained storerooms and artisans' workshops, ceremonial halls and private chambers. Its walls were adorned with frescoes that depicted the varied life of the island—youths marching in procession, bull-leaping games and the crowds that watched them, wide-eyed Cretan maidens with hair in ringlets and breasts exposed. And everywhere there was the double axe, or labrys, the most common cult object of the Minoan religion, which gave its name to the labyrinth that Minos supposedly built. The Greeks' first encounter with this enormous palace probably inspired the tale of the mysterious labyrinth through whose endless corridors no man could find a way.

ROBERT E. GINNA

Griffins painted on either side of the alabaster throne in the throne room of the Knossos palace symbolized the divine protection of the Minoan ruler. From the hallway shown on the opposite page rises the grand staircase of the palace. Beside the stairway stand tapering columns, thicker at top than at the bottom. They surround a lightwell, one of several that opened to the sky to illuminate the interior of the palace.

HIRMER

HARISSIADIS

MYCENAE, RICH IN GOLD

When the great king Agamemnon marched his men off to Troy through the Lion Gate of Mycenae, he left behind a rich kingdom that prospered through its extensive commerce. From Greece, Mycenaean ships carried abroad textiles, terra-cotta vases, beads, trinkets, and oil, and in return imported metals and grain. In this, Mycenae was similar to the Hellenic city-states of a later age. Its government, however, was quite different. The Mycenaean king was venerated almost as a god, and the place of his burial was revered. His subjects were tightly ordered into ranks; and each one, from noble to peasant, was dedicated to his service. Under military dynasties Mycenae and the other early Greek kingdoms flourished until the thirteenth and twelfth centuries, when less civilized Greek tribesmen from the north invaded, as the Mycenaeans themselves had done long before.

Above the gateway (right) that leads into the citadel of Mycenae stand two lionesses of stone that were placed there to guard the rulers and inhabitants of the ancient city. Within the massive walls of the city, which overlooks the fertile Argive plain, was a circular enclosure where Mycenaean rulers were buried in deep shaft graves. (The stone-walled grave circle can be seen in the view of the citadel above.) When the kings of Mycenae were interred, golden masks, such as the one shown opposite, were placed over their faces. Although this mask is generally known as the Mask of Agamemnon, it was made several centuries before 1200 B.C., the approximate date of the Trojan War, when King Agamemnon supposedly reigned.

ALISON FRANTZ

NATIONAL MUSEUM, ATHENS; HARISSIADIS

ALL FIVE: NATIONAL MUSEUM, ATHENS; HIRMER

A WORLD THAT VANISHED

Sometime around the year 1400, Mycenaean warriors from the mainland swept down into Crete and overthrew the Minoan power that had flourished so long on the island. There they set up another Mycenaean kingdom, with Greek as its language; but they continued to patronize the traditions and art of their native subjects. Minoan culture was not alien to them; in their homeland they had long been influenced by it. The bare-breasted lady shown in the fresco opposite comes from Tiryns, a stronghold near Mycenae, but she is dressed in Minoan costume. The religion of the Mycenaeans incorporated elements that also appeared in Minoan worship, particularly the cult of the mother goddess. But despite its assimilation of Cretan ideas, Mycenaean culture remained distinctive. It was far more martial than that of Crete had been. Mycenaean warriors raided over wide areas; indeed the tale of the Trojan War may be a memory of one such raid. From these expeditions, Mycenaean warlords brought back slaves who labored to produce textiles or grain, or served as palace attendants. This rich and turbulent world was to disappear, but echoes of it lingered for centuries in the epics, myths, and religious traditions handed down to classical Greece.

The fresco of a woman opposite comes from Tiryns, as does the seal ring at bottom right, which shows four demons before a goddess. Three other rings, from Mycenae, depict sacred trees, long-skirted worshipers, and (second from top) a goddess seated beside a double axe.

OVERLEAF: *In a detail of a vase made around 1200 B.C., Mycenaean warriors march off to battle. The soldiers, wearing crested helmets, carry shields and have sacks of food attached to their spear shafts.*

NATIONAL MUSEUM, ATHENS

2

GODS AND ANCESTORS

Earth, the beautiful, rose up,
Broad-bosomed, she that is the steadfast base
Of all things. And fair Earth first bore
The starry Heaven, equal to herself . . .

—*Hesiod*, Theogony

The gods were there early in Greece, though not at the outset of things. "In the beginning God created the heavens and the earth," says Genesis; but the Greek preferred to see the process the other way around, believing that a dawning universe was first, rising out of primeval Chaos to bring forth its gods. Then Genesis tells us that on the sixth and culminating day "God created man in his own image"; but the Greek had different ideas about this too. Uncertain in his own mind as to what the images of his gods actually were before the origin of man, he inclined to the belief that the creation of man was probably not the act of any supreme godhead at all; rather it was an assignment given by Zeus and his peers to a demigod, Prometheus, who fashioned humans from clay and water and then went off the celestial reservation, so to speak, and brought down heavenly fire, without authorization, to assist his protégé.

The ancient Egyptians had bowed to a whole armory of animal-like gods embodying the dread spirits of nature; the Babylonians were obsessed by the terrifying presence of demons everywhere. It has been said that it was the Greek's great departure, as his centuries advanced and he built shrines to a beautiful Apollo, a wise Athena, a lovely and chaste Artemis, and a humane and ever-helpful Hermes, to be the first to erect gods in man's own image. This is not only false but it also ignores the beginnings of Greek religion and oversimplifies and distorts both the Greek's mind and his history. In classical times he did assemble a gallery of stately and more or less responsible and urbane Olympian deities; but he also retained the memory of dark, inscrutable powers that had ruled him in earlier times, and from whose spell he was never to be quite free.

A sense of the awesome, the mysterious, the numinous, remained with him even during the peak of the Periclean enlightenment: grottoes and caves were peopled by strange spirits, dread Hecate of the underworld did deeds of darkness at ghostly crossroads when the moon was down, the sea monster Triton was to be feared as Poseidon's son, and sacred snakes were to be respected. Long after the sixth-century Ionian philosopher Thales had laid the groundwork for Greek scientific thought, and even during the fifth century when Pericles was preaching democracy and Aeschylus was writing his noblest dramas in Athens, the snake—totem of many primitive peoples—was still being worshiped on the Acropolis. It is possible that even in the century of Plato human sacrifice was still practiced in the back country. In a fourth-century document called the *Minos* (a dialogue sometimes attributed to Plato) there is a reference to rumors of human sacrifices still taking place in secret places in the Arcadian hills in the Peloponnesus.

Far from being humanized deities, the early gods of Greece were all either inhuman or subhuman, in contrast with the Hebraic (and also Christian) concept of the godhead; indeed, so acute is this contrast that one stops to ask how these two traditions could ever have met and mingled. Yet mingle they did, early Christian thought owing almost as much to Greek religion and philosophy in their later, refined stages as to Hebraic theology. At the outset, though, we have on one side the single vision of an all-knowing god-father, creator of all things visible and invisible, and maker of man, "the masterwork of all yet done," as John Milton was to write. On the other side we have a tortuous and prolix collection of Greek creation myths, beginning with some primordial Chaos out of which a semblance of order gradually sprang.

Among the early recorders of myths, the poet Hesiod stands out. He became so fascinated with the stories of his people that he put them together in a kind of genealogy of some 1,000 bardic lines. (Scholars disagree on Hesiod's dates; but, unlike Homer, he is a definitely established historical personage and lived probably sometime around the beginning of the seventh century.) If you go by his particular organization of mythology in his *Theogony*, what happened was that "first Chaos came into being, next wide-bosomed Gaea (Earth), Tartarus, and Eros (Love). From Chaos came forth Erebus and black Night." Another version has it that Night and Erebus between them strangely produced Love, which in turn brought forth Light and Day, after which, in a manner unexplained, Earth came into being. Then Earth (personified by the aboriginal goddess Gaea) united with Heaven (in the form of Uranus) to bring forth a race of creatures ranging from the immense Titans to the one-eyed Cyclopes to a trio of monsters, each possessing fifty heads and one hundred hands. According to one fable, Uranus became incensed at the behavior of his monster offspring and imprisoned them. This in turn aroused Gaea, who appealed for help. The Titan Kronos answered and rose against his father and castrated him; from Uranus' blood there sprang up another race of monsters, the Giants, who in their turn were accompanied by the fearful Erinyes, or Furies, pursuers of evildoers.

As legend has it, Kronos and his sister-goddess Rhea ruled the universe for aeons, while a host of lesser divinities of land, sea, and cave sprouted up beside them. Then, as the sixth of their progeny, they brought forth Zeus, whom Kronos wished to devour (he had already swallowed his first five children), having learned from a prophecy that one of his sons would unseat him. But the boy Zeus was secreted by his mother in a mountain cave

SPIROS G. PONTY COLLECTION; ANDRE EMMERICH GALLERY

In classical times the worship of the "humanized" Olympians was most important, but vestiges of old religious practices lingered. Above, a fifth-century worshiper pours a libation, just as the Mycenaeans had done, to propitiate darker gods.

The detail of an early fifth-century vase painting above depicts Zeus, the supreme ruler of the gods. The worship of Zeus probably entered Greece during the Indo-European invasions that started early in the second millennium.
LOUVRE

on the island of Crete and thereby escaped Kronos' murderous intent; on growing to maturity, he in turn raised revolt against his sire and most of the other Titans and Giants too. Upon winning this celestial civil war, Zeus drew lots for rule of the universe between himself and his brothers Poseidon, who became lord of the sea, and Hades, who became king of the underworld, realm of the dead, while he himself became ruler of the sky. With the ancestral monsters now disposed of, all might have proceeded smoothly with the invention called man, had not Prometheus, "the forethinker," exceeded instructions and made himself man's champion. Prometheus, it appears, having first disobeyed Zeus by stealing heavenly fire in order to make man strong on earth, next proceeded to deceive the reigning god in a most humiliating fashion. Carving up a great ox that was to be sacrificed by men to the gods, he separated the good flesh from the bones, concealing the first heap under ugly entrails and hide, and the second under a handsome wrapping of fat. Then he asked Zeus to select the heap he preferred. The god chose the handsomer-looking one, only to find, when he came upon bones underneath, that he had been tricked. From then on, the old story says, men held back the best meat of the animal for themselves, and offered to the gods chiefly that part of the beast that was inedible.

In his wrath Zeus determined upon two punishments—one to be imposed upon Prometheus, and another upon man himself. For his double effrontery, the rebel demigod was chained to a rock in the Caucasus, to be visited each day by an eagle that would tear out his liver, after it had grown in again each night. (Another reason for Zeus' vengeance against Prometheus appears in Aeschylus' *Prometheus Bound*: Zeus, like his father Kronos before him, had an inkling that a son of his own would dethrone him, and only Prometheus knew who this would be. This secret the ruler of the gods tried to extract from Prometheus by torture, without success.)

As for man, he was to undergo another form of torment. As Hesiod puts it, Zeus exclaimed, "I shall give man an evil as the price of fire: they will clasp destruction with laughter of desire." So he brought about the creation of young Pandora, beautifully garlanded and bejeweled, seductive and irresistible to men—the Eve, so to speak, of Prometheus' Adam, and the author of many of his woes. (A different version of the Pandora myth tells of her as the bringer of trouble to man not through her innate evil, but simply through her lightheadedness. Incurably inquisitive, she could not resist opening a jar that the gods had given her but had forbidden her to touch, with the result that mischief and evil flew out to spread among men everywhere.) Later, still angry at man's ways, Zeus, according to a further account, drowned the whole earth under great torrents with the aid of his brother Poseidon. Only the peak of Mount Parnassus was left showing—upon which, paradoxically, the only two humans to find refuge and so survive the deluge were Pyrrha, daughter of trouble-bringing Pandora, and Deucalion, son of rebellious Prometheus.

All told, it is hardly an elevating creation story. Neither, of course, is that of the Hebrews, with its tale of man's first disobedience, Cain's murder of his brother, and Yahweh's brutal extermination of all wicked mankind save Noah and his kin. Zeus, to be sure, as the incoming father god of the Greeks, is a very different presence from Yahweh, notably in his rutting activity, for he was intent upon impregnating every female whom he could lay hands upon, goddess or near goddess, from Io and Europa and Themis and Mnemosyne to Dione, Maia, Leto, Aegina, Semele, Niobe, and his sister-wives Demeter and Hera. The resulting offspring included Apollo, Artemis, Persephone, Hebe, Ares, Aphrodite, Hephaestus, and the Graces, Muses, and Hours—along with Athena, who sprang from his own brow. (A genealogical chart of the chief Greek gods and near gods and their offspring appears on pages 60–61.) Yet while Yahweh in his austere and omnipotent majesty seems to stand poles apart from lusty Zeus, the thunderer who was so slow-witted at times that Prometheus could readily trick him, some correspondences between the Greek and Hebraic stories stand forth—the equivocal role of woman and the sending down of some great primeval, punitive flood—a dim memory shared, in various forms, in much of the Near East.

The early Hebrews were fortunate in their own eyes, and have perhaps remained so in ours, because they received from Moses the God-given tablets of law. Upon that rock they erected their system and belief, with a priesthood to support it, and no doubt banished in the process many tribal customs and superstitions that had existed before. With the Greeks all was different: there was never to be among them dogma or an agreed theology; there was never in fact to be a professional priesthood or caste or Mother Church or universal Olympian ritual. There remained, instead, over the centuries a mixture of gods high and low, divinities old and new, deities above the earth and below it, spirits local and distant, and an accumulation of ancestral beliefs to which each Greek man either subscribed or did not, according to his lights. The result, as against the stern single-minded Hebraic belief in Yahweh, was disorder—polytheistic and often frivolous. Yet out of this an impulse was to arise in Greece that in its way paralleled

Above, Persephone pours out a libation to her mother, Demeter, the gentle and kind goddess who had control of the earth's fertility. The crowned earth deity holds one of her attributes, a stalk of wheat; grain was one of her gifts to man.
NATIONAL MUSEUM, ATHENS; ANDRE HELD

the Judaic one: to build an ethical religion in which man would be God's responsible agent, not his slave, and in which God (or the gods) would be responsive to man. For all their differences, this was to set both Greek and Jew many ages apart from the subservient folk of other lands around them. The savage Zeus of legend became in Aeschylus a high moral power comparable to the God of Moses whose laws presaged the teachings of Christ.

Dense population—if not overpopulation—is the mark of the Greek spirit world, with its nymphs, centaurs, daemons, harpies, gorgons, sirens, dryads, satyrs; its Furies, Fates, and Graces (three of each); its Muses (Calliope of epic poetry, Clio of history, Erato of lyric poetry, Euterpe of flute music, Melpomene of tragedy, Thalia of comedy, Terpsichore of the dance, Polyhymnia of mimic art, and Urania of astronomy); its Hours (goddesses of the seasons varying in name and number from place to place); its ruling clan of a dozen Olympian gods and goddesses, supported by a flock of lesser ones (from Eros to Pan and Persephone) and by a few mortals become gods (the hero Heracles and the healer Asclepius), all in addition to earlier, remoter deities (Gaea and Uranus, Kronos and Rhea). This multiplicity tells of many Greek characteristics, but above all of an immense imagination, peopling with wondrous beings almost every nook and cranny of the known earth, together with the air above and the deep below. It tells also of numerous traditions ranging far over time and space and of a Greek impulse, when conquering or absorbing some town or countryside, to absorb its old gods also, rather than abolish them, as later conquerors and civilizers often did. Zeus' many "marriages" are a mythical way of expressing the union of the religion of the incoming Greeks with ancient mother goddesses or cults long present. The Argonaut Jason, on reaching the faraway harbor of Colchis in quest of the Golden Fleece, made libation to the local deities "in accordance with ancient custom," says a Greek commentator; Alexander the Great in his recorded conquests was to do the same much later.

Some of the traditions hark back to prehistoric fertility rites, magic incantations, propitiatory worship of certain beasts and of the dead; others came into Greece variously from Crete, from the Near East, from the Thracian north, with the result that intermarriages occurred between gods and spirits that in their way mirrored the intermixture of tribes that was taking place in Greece. The worship of bull-like Zeus may have been preceded by worship of an actual bull (though most scholars now dispute this); he is generally believed to have arrived in Greece as an Indo-European thunder god; then, in Homer, he emerges as the "Father of

A detail from a sixth-century amphora (above) illustrates one of the most famous Greek myths. Athena, goddess of organized warfare, is born, already dressed for battle, from the head of her father Zeus; he conceived her without female help.
MUSEUM OF FINE ARTS, BOSTON

Gods and Men" not, to be sure, endowed with a high sense of morality, but still the dispenser of rough justice. "Cow-eyed" Hera, his consort, may have been at first quite literally a sacred cow; then she became a kind of local earth mother in the wake of the earlier Gaea; and in Homer she becomes the enthroned first lady of Olympus, and an extremely difficult one too—haughty in her role as protectress of marriage, and implacably angry at Zeus' irrepressible rounds of amours.

Athena, the wise one, was supposedly born from the brow of Zeus as the embodiment of heavenly wisdom. Her chief symbol in Athens, the owl, suggests her evolution from a pre-Hellenic deity worshiped in association with birds. She seems to have been connected with the palace goddess held in high esteem among the Mycenaeans for her martial virtues and her protection of the home, her attributes having been a snake, a shield, a tree, and a bird. Much later, Homer on occasion has her take the form of a bird: "Even as she spoke, Athena left them—seeming a seahawk, in a clap of wings. . . ." (The very epithet Homer constantly uses to describe Athena, "flashing-eyed" or "bright-eyed," can also be translated as "owl-faced," again conveying a memory of an earlier incarnation.) Scholars have long asked whether the Greeks, coming down from the north, may not have brought with them a martial, Valkyrie-like figure whom they identified with the ancient native goddess, resulting in the virgin of classical times who denied herself ordinary love and marriage. In any case, Athena finally developed from a flying spirit and tutelary house goddess into the patroness of Greek culture at its greatest—later, moreover, to be identified in part with the image of *Hagia Sophia*, or Holy Wisdom, of the Eastern Christian Church. (To complete the transformation process, Western Christians were to mistranslate or misunderstand what was meant by *Hagia Sophia*—an idea, not a person—and conclude that there was a Saint Sophia.)

And who at the start was Artemis, supposed sibling of Apollo as a result of Zeus' union with the Titan daughter Leto? She was not at the outset the "queen and huntress, chaste and fair" of whom Ben Jonson speaks. In her first being, so far as we know, she was rather "the many-breasted Great Mother of Asia"—a primeval fertility queen encountered by the Greeks when they colonized Ephesus in about the year 1000 B.C., and represented in images that show her bosom erupting in multitudinous mammae, or eggs, with figures of rams, lions, hinds, griffins, and sphinxes decorating her barbaric bodice. Yet this alien deity too was taken into the Olympian pantheon and there transformed into the classical one of youthful grace and chastity—though the Greeks also

The nymphs were lovely female spirits, not as important as the goddesses, but still divine. They were the guardians of things in nature like mountains and streams and trees; three are shown above in a detail of an archaic relief.
ACROPOLIS MUSEUM; HASSIA

entertained thoughts that she had some linkage with Hecate, underworld spirit of the evil eye.

Other deities were later arrivals in the Greek godly circle—none with greater effect than the love goddess Aphrodite, whose origins were also eastern, and the wine god Dionysus, who came down from Thrace in the north. Though Aphrodite traveled far, finally becoming the Venus of the Romans, her nature, unlike Artemis', did not change greatly in the process: her cult often promoted frank sexuality, and the Greeks of classical times used the very word *aphrodite* to denote the sex act itself. Hesiod and later poets described her rising at birth from sea foam off Cythera; and her cult flourished particularly on nearby Cyprus, an island where Greeks and Semites mingled. She seems to have been derived from the sex and fertility goddess worshiped far and wide in the Near East as Ishtar, Astarte, or Ashtoreth; Herodotus tells of such a goddess, named Mylitta, whose cult involved sacred prostitution, as did Ishtar's, and relates Aphrodite to her: "The Babylonians have one most shameful custom. Every woman born in the country must once in her life go and sit down in the precinct of Aphrodite, and there have intercourse with a stranger. . . . A woman who has once taken her seat [in the enclosure] is not allowed to return home till one of the strangers throws a silver coin into her lap, and takes her with him beyond the holy ground. When he throws the coin he says these words, 'I summon you in the name of goddess Mylitta.' (Aphrodite is called Mylitta by the Assyrians.) . . . A custom very much like this is found also in certain parts of the island of Cyprus." A comparable cult also established itself at Corinth, headquarters of Aphrodite's new-found precinct in Greece, though travelers passing through that strategic port at the junction of the Greek mainland and the Peloponnesus were usually accommodated by temple professionals.

Homer, however, while calling Aphrodite "the Cyprian," also says that she was the daughter of Zeus by Dione, one of his sub-wives or celestial mistresses, which places Aphrodite high in the hierarchy, despite the nature of her cult. We are also told variously that she was the spouse of the crippled and foolish Hephaestus, smith god and armorer of the Olympians, and, in a later account, that by union with Anchises of Troy she became the mother of Aeneas, who was presumed (chiefly by Vergil) to be the founder of Rome. Her partisanship for Troy against the attacking Achaeans, or Greeks, was ardent and continuous according to the *Iliad* (and this may testify further to her Asia Minor background); yet for all Aphrodite's devious and complicated history, the ancient Greeks evidently relished greatly her presence and ministrations.

MUSEO NAZIONALE ARCHEOLOGICO, TARANTO; LEONARD VON MATT

The terra-cotta plaque, above, depicts Hermes, the messenger god, in his winged apparel, climbing aboard Aphrodite's chariot. It is drawn by a female spirit and Eros, the goddess' son. Aphrodite herself was the Olympian goddess of love; Hermes was only one of the many gods and mortals attracted by her sensual beauty.

The strange, daemonic, orgiastic Dionysus, so foreign in his make-up to the Olympian family when it had grown lofty and dignified, was thought by Herodotus to be of eastern, possibly Egyptian, origin. Yet it seems established now that his cult entered Greece by way of the northern mountains from Thrace, perhaps brought in by invaders, and that it mingled with local "mysteries" and fertility rites. These rites, about whose origin there has been much speculation, may trace back to a pre-Greek religion that survived in the form of secret societies. They involved initiation, rituals of purification, fasting, perhaps worship of sexual symbols, and beliefs in the magic powers of those who had risen to the highest level among the *mystai*. Though Homer knows of a Dionysian religion that may have become mixed with these ancient practices, his references to it are only incidental, and it appears to have played little part in the society he describes. Its force, with its emphasis on seeking utter freedom and escape from human limitations by momentary, total communion with the god in an ecstasy brought on by wine, music, and torchlit dancing by night, may have been felt only in later times. Still the question remains as to just when it did take strong hold in Greece—for its effects were to be immense. What we do know is that when the Dionysian cult spread southward, it was first met with considerable distaste in the more cultivated cities, whose citizens perhaps felt in it a throwback to primitive forms of worship; thus in the fifth century Euripides, in the *Bacchae*, his drama about the cult, has King Pentheus of Thebes worry about its intrusion into his realm:

> *I happened to be away, out of the city,*
> *But reports reached me of some strange mischief here,*
> *Stories of our women leaving home to frisk*
> *In mock ecstasies among the thickets on the mountain,*
> *Dancing in honor of the latest divinity,*
> *A certain Dionysus, whoever he may be!*

Whoever he was, he became a very potent god indeed—despite the disdain of what might be called the Old Society of gods and men alike—and Greek mythmakers, always anxious to provide a place for every interesting deity, claimed he was the son of Zeus and Semele. Dionysus was the deity not only of revels and abandon—attended by his company of female maenads, or "mad ones," god-possessed in their frenzy—but of festivals and spectacles in general, of poetic inspiration, and, through his ceremonies, the begetter of Greek tragedy in particular. Though few temples were ever erected to him, Aeschylus, Euripides, and Sophocles built the greatest of shrines to him when they wrote their dramas for performance at his festivals, in which celebration of human joy and fulfillment was mixed with recognition of the tragic condition of man.

For Dionysus, the reveler, the beneficent bringer of the vine, was at the same time a tragic god. In fact, he was the only truly tragic deity in the pantheon save Demeter, the corn goddess, who also knew sorrow and suffering in a way the other Olympians, disporting themselves on high, did not. The seat of the gods above the mists, which hung between their mountain top and the world of men below, was an ineffable, well-lighted place. Thus Homer describes it in the *Odyssey*: "Athena went away to Olympus where evermore they say the seat of the gods stays sure: for the winds shake it not, nor is it wetted by rain, nor approached by any snow. All around stretches the cloudless firmament, and a white glory of sunlight is diffused about its walls. There the blessed gods are happy all their days. . . ." Crop-bringing Demeter, however, was not one of these ever-happy beings. Supposedly a sister of Zeus, as well as another of his mates, she gave birth to the lovely Persephone, embodiment of the spirit of the spring. But Persephone was torn from her by Hades and carried off to the underworld, with the result that the grieving mother left Olympus and wandered about the earth, trying to recover her. During this time all crops withered and desolation lay across the land. Finally, in order to win Persephone back, Demeter had to make a truce with Hades, under which her daughter could return to earth for certain months but had to remain below for the others—the origin, in myth, of the alternation between fruitful seasons and the death brought by the drought of the Greek summer.

While the Olympians enjoyed their endless pleasures, Demeter, in her agonized pilgrimage, seemed to draw near to man and his perennial searches and sufferings. The "Eleusinian mysteries" that sprang up as a popular cult about her—recalling her visit to Eleusis in her quest—were akin to some of the rites that figured in the worship of Dionysus, who was a god of seasons and the life and death cycle too. For Dionysus, despite all his exuberance, was the vine that must be pruned back to bare stock every autumn, once the grapes were in; and thus he embodied the coming and going of all things, and particularly of man himself. As the renowned American student of mythology Edith Hamilton writes of Dionysus: "His death was terrible: he was torn to pieces, in some stories by Titans, in others by Hera's orders. He was always brought back to life; he died and rose again. It was his joyful resurrection they [the Greeks] celebrated in his theatre." The "Eleusinian mysteries," in turn, were to remain a special adjunct or cult of Greek religion throughout its lifetime, the subject of

Just as many a cured patient today leaves an offering at a shrine, those who were miraculously healed in ancient Greece gave gifts affirming their gratitude and faith. Above, a detail of such an offering, a votive plaque, depicts Asclepius, god of medicine, healing the suppliant.
NATIONAL MUSEUM, ATHENS; GERMAN ARCHAEOLOGICAL INSTITUTE, ATHENS

curiosity and wonder in the minds of some men, of disdain in those of others, and of veneration in very many.

No deity would seem at first glance more distant from this troubling outsider among the gods than the most noble of Olympians, shining Apollo, god of light, truth, grace, law, and order. Yet a remarkable thing occurred—and nothing could better illustrate the leaps of imagination, the talent for accommodation, and, if you will, the paradoxes of Greek religion. For three winter months every year, Apollo relinquished his high shrine at Delphi, from which oracular word went forth to all Greek society, to none other than Dionysus. In those months of the revel god's occupancy, his unloosed maenads performed their mystical fertility dances on the heights above the sacred precincts. Thus Sophocles, after describing such a scene, has a chorus in the *Antigone* invoke the presence of Dionysus himself:

> Leader in dance of the fire-pulsing stars,
> Overseer of the voices of night,
> Child of Zeus, be manifest,
> With due companionship of maenad maids
> Whose cry is but your name.

So sky god and earth god meet, and cults of lofty reason and the magic spell and oracle mingle, in the Greek effort to reconcile all forms of worship of the unseen but immanent. Such an impulse inevitably involves not only compromise and paradox but leads to a certain ambiguity as well—and in the outcome most Greek deities were to be quite ambiguous in their own persons. Almost without exception there were no wholly "good" Greek gods and no wholly "bad" spirits either; there were spirits from above and below who in their own persons mixed the good with the not-so-good and the downright hostile and selfish and vindictive, even as men themselves often do. And this is probably what made the Greek gods seem so much like men, and the Greek himself seem so much like his gods.

Beautiful Aphrodite, so enchanting to men, is also malicious and dangerous, out to enslave them. Dionysus, for all the beneficence and inspiration that came from him, embodies the brutalizing powers of excess. The wise Athena is at the same time a war-making goddess. Apollo, well-beloved as the exemplar of supreme grace and the champion of lucidity and measure in all things, is on occasion heartless and mean. In their unpredictability and caprice the Greek gods were often menaces to mankind as well as to one another. Moreover, because these deities were images or personalities which had been compounded from many sources, they were often seemingly at loggerheads with themselves.

MUSEO JATTA, RUVO; ALINARI

METROPOLITAN
MUSEUM OF ART,
ROGERS FUND

The Greek spirit world was made up of a rich variety of creatures. The most important divinities, and many lesser ones, had human form like Hebe (above). Daughter of Zeus and Hera, she personified joyful youth. At center is a silver image of Pan, from a bracelet; half-man, half-goat, he was god of flocks and sometimes caused unreasoning fear—panic—in men and beasts. Below, winged Eros, eternally a boy, catches a rabbit to give to a pair of lovers.

SANFORD C. FRUMKER COLLECTION, CLEVELAND; ANDRE EMMERICH GALLERY

None was more so than Apollo, who has been prized down to our own day as "the most Greek of all the gods" or "the very embodiment of the Hellenic spirit." Centuries of sculptors and painters have represented him affectionately, even adoringly, as this glorified ideal, and perhaps no more noble Grecian marble has come down to us than the heroic, mid fifth-century B.C. figure of him at Olympia (illustrated on page 71). When you confront it in that bare hall of the Olympia Museum you find yourself gazing at a supreme classical image—a godly male at the peak of bodily perfection, marvelously balanced between tension and repose, bow-arm outstretched over a writhing struggle between the savage centaurs and civilized Lapiths about him, yet so calm and sure that right and reason under his governance will prevail that he sees no need to shoot an avenging arrow or enter the fray, but instead looks out above the battleground with serene and restrained majesty.

This is Apollo at his highest—Greece at its highest, if you will. Yet there were other sides to Apollo, darker ones, suggesting that the god of light and reason also had a daemonic aspect harking far back. The Pythian priestess who speaks for him from her oracular crypt under his shrine at Delphi is no reasoning woman: she is a sybil in a trance, pronouncing often incomprehensible words of mysterious import, herself possessed by Apollo. How Apollo got to Delphi—how he got to Greece, in fact—remains a fascinating mystery. He was definitely a non-Hellenic god. Some scholars have argued that he came with other gods from the north, possibly from the lands of the obscure Hyperboreans; others, that he was of eastern, perhaps Anatolian descent, since on the Asia Minor coast the Greeks may have encountered an Apollo-like god of Hittite origin named Apulunas (the fact that this greatest of Greek gods sided with the Trojans of Asia Minor against the oncoming Achaeans of the West also testifies to an Eastern background); still others, like Gilbert Murray, believe that he may have been a compound of both.

Greek mythology tells us little about Apollo's origins; it simply holds that he, like Artemis, was born of Zeus and Leto. But the fact that he was particularly worshiped both on the island of Delos, his supposed birthplace in the mid-Aegean, and on the heights of Delphi along the passes from the north, suggests a multiple origin. Perhaps he himself was the amalgam of several gods and layers of being and feeling, able in the end at Delphi to make marriage, so to speak, with the contrasting Dionysus just because he too encompassed so much. Aeschylus suggests as much when he refers to Apollo—Apollo, not Dionysus—as "the ivied, the Bacchic, the prophet," and Euripides speaks of "Paean Apollo of the tuneful lyre."

Long before the time when Aeschylus and Euripides wrote, however, a very slow yet mighty process had been going on, in which Greek man civilized and humanized his gods, and in which one could say that the gods helped humanize the Greeks in turn. Like other men, the early Greek had begun life in lonely fear, anxious to propitiate the unknown; then he had populated all nature with spirits, thereby making the surrounding world less threatening, since he could now meet and mingle with them as familiars; finally he imagined these spirits to be more and more like himself, his gods being akin to men in their motives and passions and differing from them only in their superior powers and in their one special attribute—immortality. Some gods even came down to earth to sire mortals, while on the other hand a few mortals rose to join the Olympians. Yet both the gods and men alike were subject to the inscrutable providence of *moira*, or ultimate fate. So there was a constant interplay—one might even say an intimacy—between Greek men and their gods, the deities being fallible, and man at his noblest being almost godlike.

Almost, but not quite: the heart of much of the highest of Greek writing tells of the dark fate that may overtake a man who presumes too much, even when he thinks he has obtained some promise from the gods or some compact with them, as Agamemnon had. A "holy fear" should still pervade all mortals. As Pindar writes: "There is one race of men, one race of gods; both have breath of life from a single mother. But sundered power holds us divided." Icarus must not attempt, as he did, to soar too high: to come too near to the heat of heaven invites disaster.

Greek godmaking and mythmaking received their early culmination in Homer, who was to be the great organizer and expositor through his poetry of the splendid presences on Mount Olympus, both lifting them out of the Titanic hierarchy of terror that had gone before and bringing at least some of them close to man. Hesiod, in his *Theogony*, was to go further, by enlivening and humanizing them. The vision remained a glorious fantasy, to be sure, but how did it come about? One of the great students of the emergence of Greek thought and feeling, the German philosopher Friedrich Nietzsche, remarked that the Greeks—whom he saw as not "classically" composed at all, but as emotionally extremely intense—must have been so painfully alive to the terrors and horrors of existence that in order to make life possible at all, they set up this gleaming Olympian dream. However that may be, having set it up, they proceeded to emulate it.

This relief from a sanctuary of Artemis, goddess of the hunt and patroness of beasts, shows her seated before worshipers and a deer, which was her favorite animal. She was the twin sister of Apollo; but while he was rarely vengeful, Artemis often was. She demanded that honor be paid her and severely punished those who neglected her. Nevertheless, she assisted mothers through childbirth and protected the young.
NATIONAL MUSEUM, ATHENS

THE DIVINE FAMILY

Unlike conventional genealogical charts, that at right, of the ancestral line of Greek gods and their children, requires a suspension of belief in both fact and time. Of course it is all legend; and it exists outside of time in that generations mingle without sequence as we know it.

URANUS, personification of the heavens, and GAEA, the earth mother, existed outside of or before time, producing Titans, Cyclopes, and Giants who ruled the universe for untold aeons. Chief of the Titans was KRONOS, who overthrew Uranus, and who begat many of the twelve Olympians. That generation, led by Zeus, rebelled against its monstrous parents to become the new and more human rulers of the universe.

ZEUS (the Roman Jupiter) overthrew his father and became the chief of the Olympian gods. He was ruler of the heavens, but he also had a hand in almost all of man's undertakings. He was variously thought of as god of the home, hearth, hospitality, liberty, law, order, property, and fertility, all of which functions he shared with at least one of the other deities.

POSEIDON (Neptune) was the violent and powerful god who ruled over the sea; he was also god of horses and earthquakes.

DEMETER (Ceres) was the goddess of corn and therefore of fertility and agriculture.

HERA (Juno), both wife and sister of Zeus, was patroness of women and of marriage.

ARES (Mars) was the hated god of war.

HEPHAESTUS (Vulcan), the smith god of fire and crafts, promoted cities and civilization.

HERMES (Mercury) performed myriad functions. Among other things, he was messenger and herald to the gods; the patron god of luck and wealth, thieves, merchants, and travelers; and the bringer of dreams.

APHRODITE (Venus) was daughter of Zeus and DIONE in one myth, although according to another she sprang from sea foam. At first the goddess of lustful love, she came to be protectress of a higher, purer love.

ATHENA (Minerva) was conceived by Zeus himself; she sprang from his head "fullblown," armed and armored, to be patroness of orderly battalions, as well as learning.

ARTEMIS (Diana) was the virgin goddess of the hunt, of wildlife, childbirth, and youth.

APOLLO, Artemis' twin, was the god of light, order, music, archery, prophecy, and youth.

DIONYSUS (Bacchus) was the son of Zeus and *Semele*, a mortal. A latecomer to the Olympic pantheon, he was the dying god of autumn, resurrected each spring, and the god of wine who inspired music and poetry.

HESTIA (Vesta) was one of the original Olympians. She was replaced by Dionysus when he rose, but she remained very important to every Greek as goddess of the hearth and the personification of all that was good in the home and family.

ASCLEPIUS, originally a hero, eventually became god of medicine.

HEBE was the handmaiden of the gods.

PROMETHEUS was the god who made mankind of clay, and then stole fire for him.

ATLAS was condemned to support the sky.

MNEMOSYNE was the goddess of memory.

THEMIS was the personification of justice.

THE MUSES, nine in number, were inspirational goddesses of the arts.

THE HOURS were goddesses of nature.

THE FATES controlled man's destiny. Clotho spun the thread of each man's life, Lachesis determined its length, and Atropos cut it off.

THE GRACES personified loveliness and waited on more important goddesses.

HERACLES was the son of Zeus and *Alcmene*, a mortal. He was the greatest of Greek heroes, noted for courage, strength, and good humor, if not for brains. After his death he was made a god.

Europa was carried off by Zeus in the guise of a bull; subsequently she gave birth to *Minos, Rhadamanthys*, and *Sarpedon*, the greatest warrior among the allies of Troy. Minos and Rhadamanthys, although mortals, were made gods of the underworld. Among mortals sired by gods, *Lacedaemon* was the founder of Sparta. *Leda* was raped by Zeus and bore twin brothers, the Dioscuri, and Helen and Clytemnestra. Legends vary as to which were Zeus' children and which her husband's.

Helen was carried off to Troy, which the Greeks besieged for ten years to get her back. *Castor* and *Pollux*, the Dioscuri, were the mortal twins who came to be worshiped as courageous fighters and protectors of sailors. *Perseus* was the forebear of the Persians. *Electra*, daughter of Atlas, gave birth to *Dardanus*, forebear of the kings of Troy. *Antiope* with Zeus had twin sons, *Zethus* and *Amphion*, who built the Theban walls. *Aegina* mated with Zeus and gave birth to *Aecus*, a forebear of *Achilles* and *Ajax*.

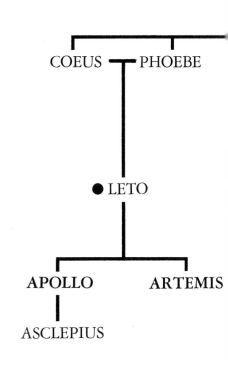

COEUS — PHOEBE

● LETO

APOLLO — ARTEMIS

ASCLEPIUS

CLOTHO
LACHESIS
ATROPOS

POLYHYMNIA
URANIA
EUTERPE
CLIO
THALIA
ORPHEUS ← CALLIOPE
MELPOMENE
TERPSICHORE
ERATO

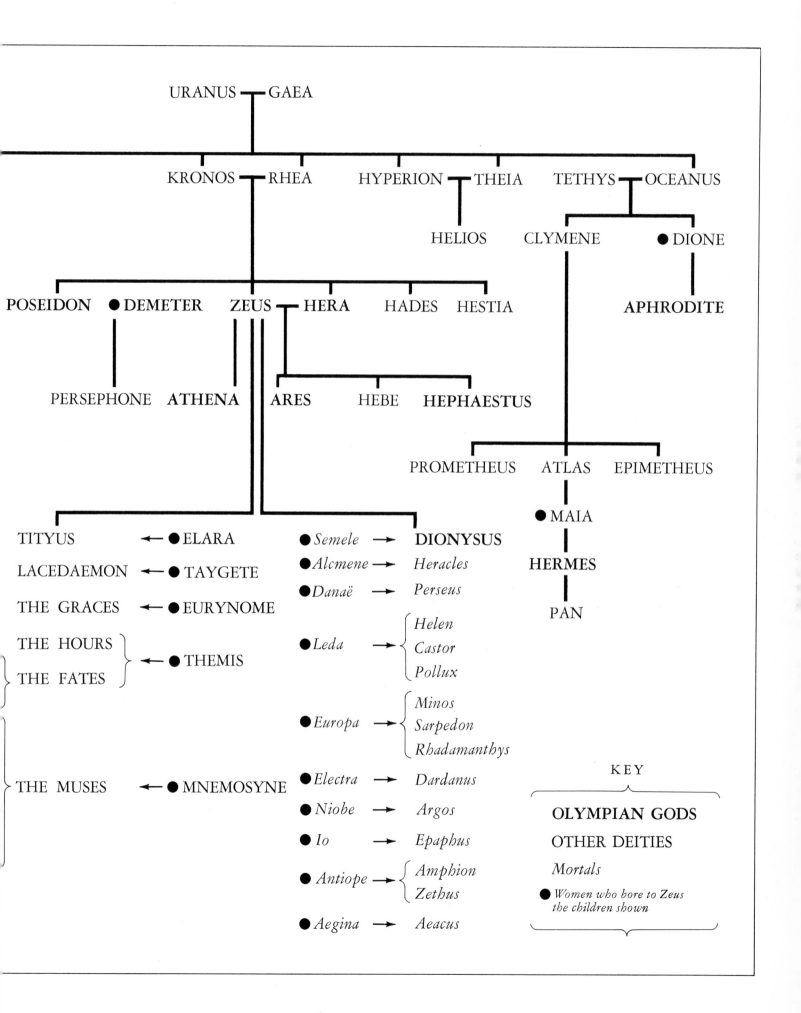

URANUS —— GAEA

KRONOS —— RHEA   HYPERION —— THEIA   TETHYS —— OCEANUS

HELIOS   CLYMENE   ● DIONE

POSEIDON   ● **DEMETER**   **ZEUS** —— **HERA**   **HADES**   **HESTIA**   **APHRODITE**

PERSEPHONE   **ATHENA**   **ARES**   HEBE   **HEPHAESTUS**

PROMETHEUS   ATLAS   EPIMETHEUS

● MAIA

HERMES

PAN

TITYUS   ←—● ELARA   ● *Semele* —→ **DIONYSUS**

LACEDAEMON   ←—● TAYGETE   ● *Alcmene* —→ *Heracles*

THE GRACES   ←—● EURYNOME   ● *Danaë* —→ *Perseus*

THE HOURS ⎫   ● *Leda* —→ ⎰ *Helen*
           ⎬ ←—● THEMIS   ⎱ *Castor*
THE FATES ⎭   *Pollux*

● *Europa* —→ ⎧ *Minos*
              ⎨ *Sarpedon*
              ⎩ *Rhadamanthys*

KEY

THE MUSES   ←—● MNEMOSYNE   ● *Electra* —→ *Dardanus*

● *Niobe* —→ *Argos*   **OLYMPIAN GODS**

● *Io* —→ *Epaphus*   OTHER DEITIES

● *Antiope* —→ ⎰ *Amphion*   *Mortals*
                ⎱ *Zethus*
                              ● *Women who bore to Zeus
                                the children shown*

● *Aegina* —→ *Aeacus*

NATIONAL MUSEUM, ATHENS

THE TWELVE OLYMPIANS

When the Indo-European invaders moved into Greece early in the second millennium, they found a society whose religion was dominated by earth goddesses, bestowers of fertility who were equally capable of withdrawing it. This world was inhabited by hosts of demons and animal spirits whose dark malevolence could only be appeased by human sacrifice and primitive rites. The religious beliefs of the invaders were far more civilized; their sky gods dwelt high on Mount Olympus and ranged over heaven and earth. The very majesty of these beings, who looked like man and often acted like him, elevated mankind. As the invaders began to intermarry with the conquered peoples, so did their masculine Olympian gods begin to marry the indigenous mother goddesses. The Olympians took on some of the characteristics of local heroes or male deities—even of some animal spirits—but in turn, their consorts became more "humanized." As the two groups slowly merged, the Olympians prevailed and their worship spread throughout Greece. The reverence paid each god varied from place to place; so sometimes did his legend. Though they were at times immoral, selfish, and foolish, in one or another of the Olympians the grace, intelligence, wit, beauty, and strength that humans strove for reached perfection. The recently found fifth-century bronze opposite depicts either Zeus or Poseidon and represents the Greek ideal of divine majesty.

MUSEUM, OLYMPIA; HIRMER

HERA AND ZEUS

The most important deity to arrive in Hellas with the invaders was Zeus, who became the supreme ruler of the gods, according to one myth, by drawing a lot which awarded him the sky as his domain. Deferred to by immortals and mortals alike, the majestic king ruled with great power, enforcing his decrees with thunderbolts. His wife —stately Hera—had probably been one of the indigenous mother goddesses, although classical myth said she was Zeus' sister. None of the Greek gods was perfect in himself, and for all their authority Zeus and Hera often became involved in undignified situations. Hera took her duties as guardian of marriage very seriously and became a jealous, nagging wife, not without reason perhaps, for Zeus sought to ease his cares in the arms of one lovely lady—human or divine—after another. The results were not only dozens of children but also dozens of plots by Hera against Zeus' paramours. Yet despite the many times that Zeus seemed more human than divine and Hera seemed as conniving as a mortal wife, they presided over a universe that was far more orderly than that of the dark gods who had preceded them.

The head of Hera, left, is part of a cult image carved c. 600 B.C. At right, in a fifth-century terra-cotta figurine, Zeus is shown abducting Ganymedes, the most beautiful boy in the world. Like many of the men who worshiped him, Zeus was not attracted to women alone.

OVERLEAF: *A fifth-century relief shows Aphrodite, goddess of love, being born out of sea foam, aided by two maidens. The seductive goddess was wed to lame Hephaestus, the gods' armorer, whom she often cuckolded.*

MUSEO DELLE TERME, ROME; ALINARI

MUSEUM, OLYMPIA; HIRMER

65

NATIONAL MUSEUM, ATHENS; HANNIBAL

METROPOLITAN
MUSEUM OF ART,
CESNOLA COLLECTION

OVERLEAF: *Among the most widely worshiped deities in
the Olympian pantheon were Athena and Apollo. A
detail of a recently discovered bronze of Athena, goddess of truth and justice, is shown at left; at right is a
detail of the classical marble of Apollo from Olympia.*

LEFT: NATIONAL MUSEUM, ATHENS; ROLOFF BENY. RIGHT:
MUSEUM, OLYMPIA; HOYNINGEN-HUENE, RAPHO-GUILLUMETTE

BRITISH MUSEUM; HIRMER

DEMETER AND PERSEPHONE

Demeter, shown at right in a fourth-century marble, was the giver of fertility to the earth. She had
a beloved daughter Persephone, who was so
beautiful that Hades carried her off to his dark
domain. (An impression of a carved gem, above,
depicts the act.) After months of frantic search
for her child, Demeter entered Eleusis, where she
taught the inhabitants, who had treated her
kindly, secret rites which came to be performed
there annually. In her wrath and grief over the
loss of her daughter, she shriveled all things that
grew in the earth, threatening the very existence
of mankind. In consequence Zeus finally arranged to help her get her daughter back. Three
fourths of each year Persephone was to spend
with Demeter, but during one quarter she had
to be in the underworld. (Thus the Greeks symbolized the death of the land during the summer
drought and its rebirth in the fall.) Over-
joyed, Demeter brought forth plants again and
sent Triptolemus, an Eleusinian youth, around
the world to give man grain and teach him
cultivation. Opposite, Triptolemus receives his
commission as Persephone (right) looks on.

LOUVRE; GRAUDON

NATIONAL MUSEUM, ATHENS

ARTEMIS AND APOLLO

Both Artemis and Apollo, twin children of Zeus and Leto, were born on Delos—the small mid-Aegean island that was to become a chief center of worship of Apollo, the other being his mountainous shrine at mainland Delphi. As goddess of the hunt and patroness of wild creatures, Artemis was an expert archer; Apollo, as well as being god of light, truth, and law, was also the archer god, shooting deadly arrows against powers of evil. Above, in a fifth-century vase painting, brother and sister appear together with their weaponry. Both are complex figures in the Olympian circle: Apollo, the beneficent healer, the intermediary between gods and men at his oracle at Delphi, the inspirer of poetry, art, and music, was sometimes remorseless and cruel; Artemis, the chaste lover of the wilderness and goddess of childbirth, was also vengeful, associated with cold moonlight. Opposite, she is shown in a bronze discovered in 1959.

HEPHAESTUS, ARES, AND HERMES

Three others of Zeus' children were also sufficiently important to be included in the Olympic pantheon. Ares was Zeus' son by Hera; he was hated by his parents and by the other gods, for as god of warlike frenzy he was bloodthirsty and savage. Despite his strength and fury the men he championed could always be beaten if Athena took the other side, because she was the goddess of orderly war. Unlike his half brother Ares, Hermes was well loved by the Greeks and the gods; he was the god's messenger and patron of inventors and merchants. Hephaestus was a smith; he forged Zeus' thunderbolts and watched over craftsmen.

DUMBARTON OAKS,
WASHINGTON, D.C.

74

Hephaestus is shown opposite in a mid fifth-century bronze; the position of his hands indicates that they probably once held a blacksmith's hammer. Below, in a detail of a frieze from Delphi depicting the primeval battle of the gods and Giants, Ares (the armed figure at left) is shown charging the host the Olympians eventually vanquished. The bronze of Hermes at right was made in the sixth century. Like Hephaestus, he was a patron god of craftsmen, so he is shown wearing the short, tight chiton of a worker; he carries a ram, for he was also a god who watched over shepherds and flocks.

MUSEUM, DELPHI; ALISON FRANTZ

MUSEUM OF FINE ARTS, BOSTON

OVERLEAF: *A detail from a vase painting shows Dionysus (left center), the god of wine, being offered a libation by a maenad, one of his possessed followers; satyrs also bring offerings. Though not originally an Olympian, by classical times Dionysus had become such an important subject of worship that a place had to be made for him on Olympus. He was also a fertility god who died and was resurrected periodically; his cult stressed ecstatic freedom, and at his festivals dramas were performed.*

LOUVRE

3

THE AGE OF HEROES

Sing, MOUNTAIN GODDESS, *sing through me*
That anger which most ruinously
Inflamed Achilles, Peleus' son,
And which, before the tale was done,
Had glutted Hell with champions—bold,
Stern spirits by the thousandfold;
Ravens and dogs their corpses ate.
—Homer, "Invocation of the Muse," the Iliad
        (translated by Robert Graves)

One night, according to an ancient tale, the ever-amorous Zeus visited Alcmene, bride of the Theban general Amphitryon who was then away fighting, and, having disguised himself as her husband, bedded with her and spawned a child who grew up to be Heracles (in later, Roman usage of his name, Hercules), the mightiest of mortals. This man, or rather this superman, whose strength was enormous though his mental powers were somewhat limited, accomplished a series of stupendous feats or labors, most of them in order to expiate a monstrous crime he had committed in a fit of madness. Raised in Thebes and having helped the Thebans against their enemies, he was given in marriage their princess Megara, who bore him three sons. But Zeus' wife Hera, always resentful of the god's extramarital exploits, caused Heracles to become insane and kill Megara and their children. Recovering his mind, he sought out the Delphic oracle and was told that by Zeus' order he must perform any twelve punitive labors that his cousin King Eurystheus might dictate.

Placing himself at the oracle's bidding into the service of Eurystheus, who was king of Argos (of Mycenae, according to some versions of the tale), he slew the marauding Nemean lion and the feared nine-headed Hydra; he cleansed the vast stables of King Augeas at Elis in a single day by diverting two rivers to flush them; he brought back from a far western island the cattle of the horrible three-bodied Geryon, erecting, as he did so, two mountainous rocks at the Mediterranean's end—the Pillars of Heracles; he also brought back from the ends of the earth the golden apples of the Hesperides, and on that same venture, moreover, freed long-suffering Prometheus from the shackles that bound him to a high mountain of the Caucasus.

This was not all. He spent a year tracking down the stag with golden horns, sacred to Artemis, and brought it back to Argos. He trapped a great boar lowering on Mount Erymanthus. He drove off the swarm of monstrous birds that had plagued the people of Stymphalus. He sailed to Crete to seize for his master the great snorting bull that Poseidon had given to King Minos. He vanquished the man-eating mares of King Diomedes of Thrace. He brought home to Greece the girdle of Hippolyta, queen of the Amazons. He descended into the lower world to seize barehanded its three-headed watchdog Cerberus, and while he was there rescued his fellow hero Theseus from the oblivion below.

These twelve labors were not the only adventures of Heracles. As formidable indoors as outdoors, he was also capable of possessing in one night some fifty women—the daughters of King

Thespius. Perhaps most remarkable of all, he vanquished in a wrestling encounter the death spirit Thanatos (some versions say it was Hades himself) on another quest to the world of the shades, this time to bring back his friend Admetus' recently lost wife Alcestis. These and other deeds made Heracles believe himself the equal of the gods, which in many respects he manifestly was: his arrows had greatly helped the Olympians put down the primeval Giants. But in other respects he was not their equal. "Cow-eyed" Hera, Zeus' official consort, had always been filled with hatred of her mate's children by others, and had several times tried to destroy Heracles, on occasion by vipers, on occasion by sending fits of madness down upon him. Indeed, as we have seen, Heracles was under such a spell when he murdered his wife and children. Not knowing his own immense strength and, furthermore, easily angered, he was likely to kill when he did not really mean to do so. Thus, when provoked, he killed the centaur Nessus who was ferrying him and his new bride Deianira across a river. Nessus, dying, gave her some of his own blood, telling her it would serve as a charm to keep the hero from loving other women. Later, when Deianira found Heracles straying, she smeared some of the blood on a shirt which he thereupon donned only to fall into horrible torment. After learning what she had unwittingly done, Deianira killed herself; and Heracles, unable to bear the torture, immolated himself on a tall pyre.

So even the greatest of heroes must die. Achilles, the greatest of the heroes who came after him, remarks in the *Iliad*:

> *For not even the strength of Heracles fled away from destruction,*
> *Although he was dearest of all to lord Zeus, son of Kronos,*
> *But his fate beat him under, and the wearisome anger of Hera.*

Yet Heracles, unlike other heroes, was raised from death and made a god. Some stories say he was wafted upward in a cloud from his funeral pyre; others that he was borne aloft in Athena's four-horse chariot and guided by swift-footed Hermes to the portals of Olympus. The hero Odysseus, who on his long voyage home visited the shades to seek advice from the spirit of the blind prophet Tiresias, saw there the wraithlike figures of many departed kings and warriors and the *eidolon*, or phantom, of Heracles as well; but Heracles himself, Odysseus adds, is

> *Feasting amid the gods, reclining soft*
> *With Hebe of the ravishing pale ankles,*
> *Daughter of Zeus and Hera, shod in gold.*

This gargantuan, ancestral tale, compounded of many elements

The mightiest of Homeric heroes was Achilles, who is shown here in a fifth-century vase painting. Achilles' powers were so great that the Greeks were unable to conquer Troy without his aid.

VATICAN; ALINARI

Many of the monstrous beasts of Greek mythology, such as the centaur Nessus, who is seen here fighting a losing battle against Heracles, were originally fierce nature spirits. To the Greeks, the centaurs, creatures who were half horse and half man, came to represent the forces of barbarism that continually challenged Hellenic civilization.

NATIONAL MUSEUM, ATHENS; SKIRA

and accretions over early centuries, seems far removed from the light and reason of classical Greece. Yet despite all its crudities, it remains one of the greatest of tales, conveying on one hand the richness of Greek mythmaking imagination and on the other the scope of Greek feeling about the capabilities as well as the faults of man. It tells, in particular, of the Greeks' absorption with the heroic ideal and their veneration of it, even while aware of the inscrutable fate that overtakes the all-too-human hero.

The Greeks did venerate Heracles over many centuries, erecting altars to him and making a cult of the man who for his deserts had become a deity. The frieze of Zeus' temple at Olympia was given over entirely to sculptures celebrating Heracles' labors. The idea came to prevail that the work of this primeval giant—roistering, foolhardy, and often barbarous—exemplified man's power to overcome inhuman obstacles and his desires to ride abroad redressing wrongs. Nevertheless, in the sophisticated fifth century, many Greeks were to look with disdain on some of their old legends. Herodotus, who was not only the Greeks' first historian but their first student of comparative mythology as well, wrote at one point: "The Greeks tell many tales without due investigation," and scoffed at what he called a "silly fable" about Heracles among the Egyptians. What he was trying to show was that there had been two Heracles—one the Greek hero and the other an Egyptian god—and that the Greeks had mixed up the stories. The dramatist Euripides, who was also critical of much that was handed down in Greek legendry, made Heracles a blunderer, almost a buffoon, in his *Alcestis*; yet he was so taken with his presence that he also made him into a great tragic hero in his *Heracles*. And Sophocles, similarly engaged, devoted *The Women of Trachis* to the final episode in Heracles' life—the story of the robe poisoned with Nessus' blood and of the destiny that comes upon those who think they are all-powerful.

Every society, from the savage ones on up, creates its myths; the anthropologist Bronislaw Malinowski has argued that these are not mere storytellers' yarns retold for their entertaining interest, but arise out of some act of belief and live as statements of some "primeval, greater, and more relevant reality." The far-reaching analyst Carl Jung has looked upon myths as expressions of the "collective unconscious"—fantasies arising in the primitive psyche as it awakens with its desires and passions, but which are often repressed below the conscious level until they finally emerge as wish-fulfilling tales. Thus there are the recurrent fables of some great quest into the unknown; of the winning of great treasures, talismans, or magic weapons; of descent into the underworld to wrestle with the monster and perhaps bring back the beloved. However one may choose to interpret their origins, there are fascinating correspondences between such tales as they emerge in cultures far apart in time and place.

The Sumerians of Mesopotamia, for instance, told of a legendary king, Gilgamesh of the city of Uruk, which flourished in the fourth millennium B.C. Gilgamesh fought with giants, lions, and a monstrous bull, and made a descent into the underworld to contend with Death itself. In Greek mythology, not only Heracles but also Dionysus, Theseus, Orpheus, Odysseus, and Aeneas of Troy were to visit the realm of the dead. Furthermore, Mesopotamian cuneiform tablets, recording a very ancient tradition, tell of the imprisonment of a fertility goddess in the underworld—a story strikingly similar to the Greek legend of the detention of Persephone in Hades. The story of the foundling and of the divine or semidivine king also appears in Eastern as well as Greek lore. What is perhaps most significant in the mythmaking process is the cult of the hero and its relationship to the cult of the dead— nowhere more pronounced and prevalent than in Greece, where there was an ancestral belief among its people that doers of great deeds exerted some extraordinary power from the grave.

In the Greek mind, hero worship (often actual worship of a mortal hero in his tomb) was combined with worship of the gods, and this, in turn, reflected a sense of some earlier, heroic age when men had been greater, loftier, and closer to the gods than they were in times present. No doubt this accounts in part for the wondrous proliferation and persistence of Greek myths about humans, which were in effect a part of religion. The great Greek problem was to try to resolve the coexistence of gods and men and to explain, or at least to indicate, the presence of the divine in man. What better solution, then, than to relate man to his gods by actual blood ties, and to dream back to a splendid race that we might call Founding Fathers—and mothers, too—all descended from the loins of great Zeus himself.

Many kings, dynasties, noble families, and emerging cities encouraged this process, anxious to claim for themselves a lineage of godly origin, and many imaginative bards were on hand to aid it. Thus King Minos of primeval Crete was made out to be the son of Zeus, who had appeared in the form of a bull to Europa, daughter of the king of Sidon. From Minos' union with Pasiphaë came Catreus, the father of Aërope; she slept with King Atreus of Mycenae (also supposedly a descendant of Zeus) to become the

The mythological founder of Thebes was the Phoenician prince Cadmus, who was obliged to perform the difficult task of killing a dragon; the feat is depicted above. Many Theban aristocrats traced their ancestry back to some of the armed men who sprang from the ground when Cadmus sowed the dragon's teeth as the goddess Athena had advised him to do.
LOUVRE; GUILEY-LAGACHE

The hunter Actaeon (above) accidentally encountered the virgin goddess Artemis bathing in a spring. He was punished for breaking an ancient taboo against approaching a god unbidden by being turned into a stag and then devoured by his own hunting hounds. In some parts of Greece, Actaeon was thought of as an evil ghost who destroyed crops.

MUSEUM OF FINE ARTS, BOSTON

ancestor of that tragic house. Perseus, who became king of Tiryns, near Mycenae, after fetching the head of the Gorgon Medusa, was described as the offspring of Zeus and another princess, Danaë. Helen of Sparta, Menelaus' spouse and the cause of so much mischief and bloodshed at Troy, was said to be the result of Zeus' mating with the mortal Leda, whom he had visited in the guise of a swan. Athens prided itself on having had as its first great hero the brave king Theseus, vanquisher of the Minotaur and the son of the city's founder Aegeus—though some claimed he was the son of Poseidon, Zeus' brother. And in Thebes genealogists and bards worked out a scheme by which the royal Theban line went back to Cadmus, born of Zeus and Io (whom Zeus had conveniently turned into a heifer in order to deceive ever-prying Hera)—a lineage that produced a veritable *Almanach de Gotha* of heroes and other royal figures, among them Creon, Jocasta, Oedipus, and Antigone. Even the great god Dionysus was included, for (according to the Thebans) he was born of the never-flagging Zeus and Cadmus' daughter Semele, and as such was the grandson of their own King Cadmus.

All this fabric of imagination about gods and men interbreeding helped to establish in Greece a particular form of ancestor worship. The kings of Mycenae were laid to rest in spacious tombs and surrounded (not unlike the Pharaohs of Egypt) by their treasure and instruments of daily living, with the thought evidently in mind that they would continue to use them. True, Homer speaks of the departed spirits among the shades as "strengthless." Yet though among the mythical heroes only Heracles rose to Olympus, glorious Achilles (son of Thetis, a sea nymph, and great-grandson of Zeus) was said to enjoy immortality on earth, off on an island in the Euxine, or the Black Sea, and there he became the subject of particular worship. Local cults sprang up: at Athens, of Theseus; at Colonus, of Oedipus of the Theban line; at Sparta, of beautiful and ill-starred Helen; on the island of Lesbos, of Orpheus, the fabulous musician (appropriately, son of a Muse)—his cult eventually produced an agglomeration of poetry and ritual that came to be part of a cult of Dionysus that was known as Orphic religion.

What the Greeks believed about their past heroes varied not only from place to place but from generation to generation. Many heroes, like many lesser gods, were revered as ancestral spirits simply in one locality, the next having its own. As one family rose and another fell, the genealogies of heroes changed too. Through early centuries the multiplication and alteration of tales was probably immense and chaotic, and it was not until the emergence of Homer—presumably at some time between the years 800 and 700—that a bard came forth who was both a great recorder of myths and one who could impose some order on them. With him, both the heroes and the Olympians become organized in relationships, and a rough *ethos*, or scheme, of values is cast over them all and their actions. Thereafter, the vast body of saga about great ancestral deeds, compounded of folklore, travelers' yarns, and tales devised to glorify this or that dynasty or town, begins to coalesce into a national legacy of heroic poetry and moral teaching. Much later, in the fifth century, Pindar is found trying to distinguish between myths that are based on historical evidence and those that are based on imagination; and Euripides, who was often called "the destroyer of illusions," reexamines the great tales too, rejecting some but making use of others as subjects for his dramas to illustrate the tragic issues confronting man.

After the four or more "dark" centuries following the extinction of Mycenaean civilization, during which the knowledge of writing was apparently lost, the written word reappears; but the telling of old tales remains for a long time an art of reciting them, not of writing them down—and each recitation, since there was no text, contained its own possibilities of invention. There are parallels between eighth-century Greece, emerging slowly from the dark, and early medieval Europe, emerging from long submersion more than two millennia later. In both, the civilization that survives is centered in isolated, crudely built strongholds, with few comforts, separated by lonely and dangerous valleys; their lords, for the most part, are unlettered, and communications difficult and rare. But there is the welcome arrival of some traveling bard or minstrel, bringing to those within their rubble walls some information or remembrance of the outside world as he sings for his supper. The *jongleurs*, harp in hand, intoned the song of brave Roland, and the *Minnesänger* of the dragon-killing Siegfried of the Nibelungen. Bravery and monsters were the stock in trade of the storyteller of ancient Greece too, and he could ring wondrous changes on such subjects.

He told, for instance, in one of the oldest sagas handed down, of the fabulous voyage of the Argonauts—notable because many Greeks seem to have thought of it as one of their first major overseas expeditions, preceding that to Troy by a generation or more, and also because it included in it so many illustrious figures. A precise list of those who accompanied Jason on the good ship

Charon, who appears above in a detail from a vase painting, ferried the dead across the Styx, one of the nine rivers that divided the world from Hades. To pay his fee, the Greeks placed a coin in the mouth of each corpse before they buried or cremated it. Another of the rivers crossed was Lethe, the river of forgetfulness, whose waters were drunk by the dead.

NATIONAL MUSEUM, ATHENS; ALISON FRANTZ

Argo to the Black Sea was never established, innumerable Greek families claiming, as they climbed to high estate in later centuries, to have had some ancestor aboard, as if it were a kind of *Mayflower*. But Pindar and later poets, culling the legends, agreed that Jason's vessel had undoubtedly carried such figures as Peleus, the father of Achilles; the inseparable twin sons of Zeus and Leda, Castor and Pollux; the archmusician Orpheus; and for a while the mighty hero Heracles himself was aboard, along with a band of the noblest youths of Greece.

It seems that once upon a time a prince of Thebes named Phrixus was about to be sacrificed on the altar for the sake of procuring crops. (The legend of the ruler who was put to ceremonial death to ensure a good harvest is of great antiquity and appears in many cultures, recalling a time when such sacrifices actually took place.) However, a miraculous ram with a fleece of gold appeared and wafted Phrixus away to the remote lands of the wild Colchians beyond the Hellespont, where the precious fleece came into the possession of the Colchian king. Later young Jason, heir to a kingdom in northern Thessaly that had been usurped by a blood relative was told that he could have his patrimony if he brought back the Golden Fleece. The bravest of Achaeans joined Jason in this adventurous quest and on the way they met with immense perils. Though they dallied pleasantly enough for a while with the women of Lemnos, after which Heracles parted company with them, they were set upon by the mighty-clawed, flying Harpies, "the hounds of almighty Zeus"—this in spite of the fact that Zeus' mate Hera, and Athena too, were warm partisans of Jason. Escaping these monsters, the Argonauts had to pass through a narrow strait (the Bosporus) that was guarded by the Clashing Rocks, or Symplegades—vast boulders that rolled together and smashed every vessel that tried to pass between them. Barely getting clear, they eventually came to the land of the warrior Amazons and escaped them too. Finally, after passing close by the Caucasus and seeing Prometheus in agony bound on a peak, they reached Colchis, only to be faced with further danger. For the Colchian king Aeetes, angry at this intrusion into his realm, told Jason that he could have the fleece only if first he himself harnessed two fierce fire-breathing bulls to a yoke, plowed a great field, and sowed it with the magic teeth of a dragon. From each dragon's tooth a fully armed warrior would spring up, who must be immediately cut down.

Jason knew he could not possibly perform such a feat, and that the unloosed dragon-seed warriors could well overcome his com-

The prince Phrixus was saved from being sacrificed by a golden ram which carried him away to safety; at right the two are shown fleeing.
METROPOLITAN MUSEUM OF ART, ROGERS FUND

The figures below may represent the Argonauts, the heroes who sailed from Greece in search of the fleece of Phrixus' golden ram. Led by Jason, the Argonauts sailed past many perils to the eastern coast of the Black Sea, where the Golden Fleece was kept. Jason succeeded in seizing the prize and bringing it back to Greece.
LOUVRE; GIRAUDON

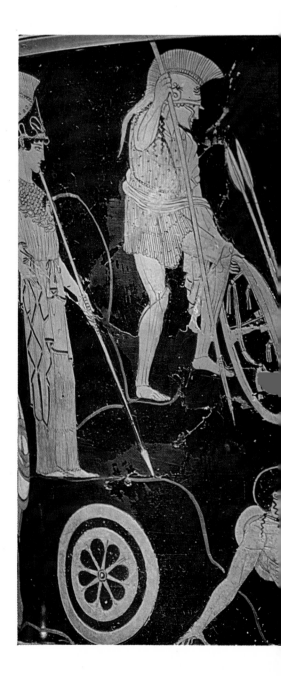

pany. But on Olympus, Hera and Athena connived and persuaded Aphrodite to have her son Eros shoot one of his love-bringing arrows at the heart of the king's daughter Medea, causing her to conceive a passion for Jason and therefore seek to help him out of his predicament. This Eros did, and with good result, for Medea, as it happened, was a princess possessed of great powers of magic and spells, which she now applied in Jason's behalf.

To make a long story short (which, however, was never the aim of a Greek bard, his listeners evidently liking a good tale to go on and on), Medea gave Jason both ointments and stratagems by which to overcome the suicidal task imposed on him by her father. These he used successfully, yoking the bulls and downing the seed-warriors, only to find that the astonished King Aeetes would not keep his side of the bargain. Medea then charmed to sleep the serpent guarding the fleece, after which the lovers made what we could call a classic getaway—fleece safely aboard, broad sails straining toward Greece, Jason promising to wed Medea, and King Aeetes, impotent in wrath, left standing on the shore.

Yet this was not quite the end of the tale. It was said that Medea, in her passion to escape with great Jason, either slew her pursuing and avenging brother or caused him to be slain. What happened to her and Jason when they returned to Greece with their treasure remained obscure to many story tellers. But as the legend grew over the centuries, some additions suggested that the bewitching Medea had herself been a human monster, and Jason, for his part, a good deal less than honorable. Just when these accretions arose, no one can tell; but when Euripides came to write his *Medea*, the returning Jason had become both a cowardly avenger and a faithless lover: cowardly in that he turned to ever-helpful Medea to rid him of the treacherous usurper Pelias; and faithless in that after siring two children by her, he jilted her and planned to wed the king of Corinth's daughter instead. Medea, for her part, became not only the murderess of Pelias but of Jason's bride and, in her frenzy, of the two sons she had borne to Jason as well.

Though Jason emerges from this story a very tarnished hero, and everyone in it from the gods on down behaves amorally and deceitfully, there is yet present in it, as in the tale of Heracles, that fascination with past fame, daring deed, and far place—particularly the daring deed in a far place—that marks all Greek epic poetry making. For poetry it was, created by certain powerful imaginations to inspire others. The theme of wonderment, of the quest of the faraway, of fabulous and glorious adventure once

Reverence for the winds was common in Greece. Above, a Boreiad, a creature of the North Wind, pursues two Harpies, wind spirits that supposedly carried off people. Below them is a sphinx, another monster reputed to kidnap youths.

MUSEO NAZIONALE DI VILLA GIULIA, ROME; GERMAN ARCHAEOLOGICAL INSTITUTE, ROME

A small sixth-century vase from Corinth is made in the form of a satyr, one of the mischievous and lewd creatures that represented the wild life abounding in the woods and hills. Often satyrs were shown as half man and half goat.

LOUVRE; GIRAUDON

lived, runs through and inspirits all of it. And not all the tales told of ancestors were brutal, either; some were most poignant. Heroes descended into the underworld on brave missions to rescue the dead: Heracles, to find Alcestis; Theseus of Athens, to try to bring back Persephone; and Orpheus, armed only with his lyre, to bring back his beloved bride Eurydice. Orpheus, the archsinger and musician, schooled by Apollo, so moved Hades with his melodies that the king of the underworld gave up Eurydice on condition that Orpheus would not look back on her, as she followed him from the world of the shades, until they had both reached the light of day. But Orpheus, always the lover, could not forbear, as they ascended, to cast his eyes on Eurydice, and so she was forever lost to him.

Then, too, there were early morality fables of bold men who, apparently forgetting the fate that had overtaken the archrebel Prometheus, behaved toward the gods in ways arrogant or importunate, and who as a result received interminable punishment. Though not all these men were heroes in the Promethean sense of helping man, the theme of revolt against the gods evidently fascinated the Greek mind, and the early Greek imagination devised exquisite forms of torture for those mortals who had overstepped the line. This was so, particularly in the cases of Tantalus and Sisyphus, two legendary kings who ran afoul of Olympus.

Tantalus, reputedly a son of Zeus, and ruler of Sipylos in Lydia, was and remains a baffling figure. Favored by the Olympians to the point where they came to dine at his palace, he was so seized by some obscure motivation that he served them a ghastly banquet of which the main dish was the flesh of his own son Pelops, whom he had caused to be killed for the occasion. One explanation, to which Robert Graves as a leading modern student of Greek mythology subscribes, is that Tantalus found that he did not have enough food for the gods' dinner, and so, either to test Zeus' omniscience or just to show his goodwill, he sliced up and offered his son. Another has it that Tantalus' fell purpose was to make the gods unwittingly become cannibals. In any case, for this monstrous deceit he was condemned to stand forever in Hades in water up to his neck, athirst and deprived of nourishment: whenever he stooped to drink, the water disappeared; whenever he reached upward to grasp the branches, laden with fruit, which hung overhead, a wind tantalizingly wafted the grapes and figs out of his reach.

The character of Sisyphus, a king of Corinth and son of the wind god Aeolus, is more understandable—though his fate was no less agonizing. His crime was simply that he gave away an amorous secret of ever-lusting Zeus to a friend, the river god Asopus. When Asopus came to Sisyphus, lamenting that his lovely daughter Aegina had disappeared, Sisyphus replied that he had seen her borne off by an immense eagle (that is, Zeus in the shape of one) to an offshore island, and gave him directions for pursuit. In return for this information, Asopus supplied Corinth with an ever-running spring. But for thus revealing Zeus' love nest, Sisyphus paid a heavy penalty: he was doomed to remain in Hades and endlessly roll a rock up to the top of a hill from which, each time he had placed it there, it rolled down again.

Remote and strange as these two tales seem, their sequels lead us into the midst of a familiar company—the heroes of Homer. For the gods resurrected Tantalus' butchered son Pelops, who, in turn, sired Atreus, founder of the tragic dynasty (the House of Atreus) that produced Agamemnon and Menelaus. Fair Aegina, for her part, whom Sisyphus had observed at the wrong moment, in due course had a son by Zeus, and it was that son's son, Peleus, who mated with the nymph Thetis to bring forth the hero Achilles.

With Homer we emerge from shadowy realms into a sudden, brilliant, immediate presence. Homer has been called variously the first articulate European, the author of the bible of the Greeks, and, by Dante, "the sovereign poet"—all of which he was. Perhaps what most of all strikes a reader on first looking into Homer is his immense vividness and concreteness. He is not spinning a tale of highly improbable persons in an abstract landscape, outside of time and known space; he is narrating one particular episode in one particular war at Troy in which many heroes participated (all listed in Book II of the *Iliad* together with their cities of origin, the strength of their cohorts, and the number of their respective ships). He follows this tale with another detailed account of the adventures and struggles of one of the victors on his voyage to regain his home and kingdom in Ithaca. To be sure, Homer does not say just when all this took place or what happened before and after; yet he speaks with such detail and absorption about the customs and accoutrements of his heroes—their methods of rule, their dress, their food, their weaponry, their siegecraft, their manual skills, their codes of conduct toward both men and women—that he evidently regards it integral to his story to recall and evoke some past society and environment in which his heroes lived. This he does with unending delight—from descriptions of Achilles' tent and shining armor to menus of banquets and sum-

Probably some time during the sixth century the epics bearing the name of the blind Ionian bard Homer, who is portrayed above, reached their final form, providing the richest single source of Greek mythology for future ages.
MUSEUM OF FINE ARTS, BOSTON

According to tradition, Aesop was a slave and storyteller of Samos, to whom a great body of folk tales was attributed. Above, a fifth-century Attic cup depicts him and the fox who played so prominent a role in several of his fables.
VATICAN MUSEUM; ANDERSON

When the Trojan slave girl Briseis, a part of Achilles' war spoils, was taken away from him by Agamemnon, Achilles refused to continue fighting against Troy. Instead he remained sulking in his tent while the inconclusive siege dragged on. The hero is shown above, his face veiled in grief for the girl's loss.

BRITISH MUSEUM

maries of speeches made at councils of war. And this he accompanies with searching characterizations of all that was most human in his heroes: the sulking egotism of great Achilles; the indecisiveness of not-so-great Agamemnon, a poor leader of men; the saving guile of Odysseus; the bluff bravery of Hector; the garrulousness of Nestor, a kind of Homeric Polonius; the fatuousness of Helen's lover, Paris; the irresponsibility of Helen herself; the tired yet manly dignity of aged Priam, the Trojan patriarch; the artfulness of Penelope, spinning her endless web and (at least supposedly) standing off her army of suitors during her twenty years' wait for her husband's return; the boyishness of her son Telemachus, so keen to play the man; the matronly sturdiness of Eurycleia, guarding Odysseus' treasure room; the still but imperturbable faithfulness of Eumaeus, his devoted swineherd.

But what was that past society of heroes of which Homer tells? Did it ever exist as he describes it? First of all one must confront that question, Did Homer himself ever exist as a person? Herodotus thought that he had, and placed his life and work some four centuries before his own—which would put Homer somewhere in the ninth century before Christ. Though Greek sculpture represents him as a venerable, bearded bard ("deep-browed," John Keats was to describe him in his splendid sonnet written on first looking into the Elizabethan George Chapman's translation of Homer), nothing actually is known of the identity of the man, save that the language or dialect of the *Iliad* and *Odyssey* suggested that he was of Ionian origin. Mythical biographies were made up about him—he was variously said to have been a son of the Muse Calliope, or a son of the stream Meles that passed through the city of Smyrna, or a descendant of Orpheus—but the very word "Homer" was not a personal name at all but a term widely used to designate a fellowship or group.

Later scholars, however, were less and less convinced of Herodotus' identification; instead, they began to think more and more of Homer not as a person but as a tradition, and of the epics called Homer's as the sheer accumulation of stories recited by several centuries of fraternities of minstrels. And a particular Homer had of course left nothing in writing to prove individuality of authorship: the earliest texts of the *Iliad* and *Odyssey* appear to have been assembled in Athens in the sixth century, possibly by order of the Athenian ruler Pisistratus in order to establish an agreed version to govern reciters at public festivals. By that time innumerable variants and interpolations must have entered into what had come down by word of mouth. What is important is not the changes—since no one knows what may have gone before—but the fact that the Homeric tales persisted in the Greek mind, while other tales gradually evaporated or at least were never brought together as a kind of canon. Homer's poems, recited endlessly by minstrels in a society that remained unlettered for centuries, became, in effect, Greek religion. Herodotus remarks that it was Homer who first fixed for the Greeks the genealogy of their gods and assigned them their titles and functions. Homer was also telling tales with some remote foundation in fact, as against pure fantasy. In humanizing or, up to a point, civilizing the gods, he was also providing a body of precept and example for generation after generation. The singsong of his repeated epithets and images —the "wine-dark sea," the "rosy-fingered dawn," the "flashing-eyed Athena," the "Odysseus of many wiles," the "silver-footed Thetis"—are the almost ritual lines used by bards as a refrain when going on with their story, night after night; but the heave and bulk of a great chronicle was always there, both brutal and humane. No doubt many further changes entered into the texts in subsequent centuries, by the hands of copyists and editors; for the oldest manuscripts that we presently possess are medieval ones, supplemented by a few ancient papyrus fragments.

Our own era has seen an impulse to return to the concept that there actually was a poet named Homer. In view of the marked differences in style, imagery, and construction between the epics, there may even have been two poets: one the compiler-author of the *Iliad*; the other of the *Odyssey*. The *Iliad* is all action, tense, swift, bold, built about one central theme—the wrath of Achilles before Troy (brought on by the fact that he was deprived of his prize, the captive girl Briseis); the *Odyssey* moves from episode to episode, as its hero does from place to place, in what often seems like a marvelous, spacious dream of adventure and revenge. The ancients felt this distinction as we do, Aristotle remarking that the *Iliad* was simple and disastrous, the *Odyssey* complicated and moral, while the Roman commentator Pliny thought that there was far more "magic" in the *Odyssey*. It does have the quality of a fairy tale, as against the brusque and bloody *Iliad*. Hellenistic scholars who had lingered over the notion of a single Homer regarded the *Iliad* as a work of the poet's maturity but the *Odyssey* as one of his garrulous old age.

Modern belief in the historical existence of a Homer (or, if need be, two Homers) rests chiefly on the sheer literary values of the poems. They are so superior to other early Greek tales that have survived, in terms of unity, coherence, imagery, plausibility of

Achilles was enamored not only of Briseis but of the hero Patroclus as well. Above he is shown tending his wounded companion, winding a bandage about his arm. It was only after Patroclus had been killed by the Trojans that Achilles would return to the battle in order to revenge his death.
STAATLICHE MUSEEN, BERLIN

89

One of the climaxes of the Iliad comes when Achilles slays the Trojan champion Hector. Here the aged Trojan king Priam is shown coming to beg Achilles for the return of his son Hector's body, which is seen lying beneath the Greek hero's couch.

KUNSTHISTORISCHES MUSEUM, VIENNA

characters, and ethics (roughhewn as these were), as to suggest the controlling presence of an individual of very great creative powers who gave them the shape we know. And one Homer or two, in view of all the contrasts between *Iliad* and *Odyssey?* This problem may remain insoluble—if indeed it is a problem. If we did not know from records that there had been a playwright named Shakespeare, it would be difficult to conceive that works so utterly contrasting as *King Lear* and *A Midsummer Night's Dream* could have been written by one and the same hand.

Yet now we come to the other question. Homer tells vividly of a long-remembered past: But what does he really know about that past as an actuality, and to what extent is he in effect describing instead the age in which he himself moved, poetizing and projecting his images far back in time? Some knowledge had evidently come down to him in the eighth century, of an earlier civilization of which Mycenae was a center, but the knowledge was dim. Mycenae's splendor by his time had been effaced from all but legend, and was to remain so until the brilliant archaeologist Schliemann brought it back to light in the late nineteenth century, discovering the Bronze Age culture that had flourished there and revealing many remarkable correspondences between Homeric descriptions and Mycenaean artifacts. Yet despite these correspondences, in many ways Homer and history meet only to part again. The weapons he describes resemble the bronze ones of the Mycenaeans, but his anachronisms are legion: he speaks of temples, whereas the ancestors of the Greeks appear to have built none; he tells of Achaeans cremating their dead, whereas in the heroic age, of which he purports to speak, they buried them.

He tells of one great ten-year war against Troy, but for all Schliemann's and later scholars' studies, we still have no historical proof of it. There may well have been not one but several wars or raids against Troy in the Mycenaean age, but the notion of a ten-year siege, in an era of small kingdoms that were often hardly more than country households, is probably sheer fantasy. Herodotus, though he accepted the traditional story that the Achaeans, "for the sake of a single Lacedaemonian girl, collected a vast armament, invaded Asia, and destroyed the kingdom of Priam," thought that the idea of their fighting for ten years for the sake of a woman was foolish. But this problem of duration never troubled Homer; on the contrary, he assumes it as the dramatic background for his superb opening, plunging at once into what proves to be the climax of the war—the wrath of Achilles amid chieftains Greek and Trojan. made savage by nine years of frustration and slaughter.

These chieftains, as we get to know them, are tribal leaders in a world not yet made up of states, but of clans. Their kingdoms consist of a palace or citadel and a few villages surrounding it. Their wealth lies in stock-breeding and in their land, owned by the family or clan, which they cultivate themselves: thus King Odysseus boasts that he can drive a furrow as straight as any man. They drop their plowshares to lead their fiefmen or serfs in war (little is said in Homer of the supporting hosts, large as they are made out to be; all drama concentrates on individual combat between heroes). They have slaves—particularly female ones, procured on this raid or that—and of these, like Agamemnon's Chriseis and Achilles' Briseis, they make concubines, their wives having nothing to say in the matter. Their wives, in turn, are not only mistresses of the household but are probably also accomplished in various crafts—witness Penelope, who by devising a shroud became the most famous weaver of antiquity. Their so-called palaces are mostly of rough brick set upon stone foundations. Their arts consist chiefly in the hammering of metals for armor and ornament; both Achaean men and women, as Homer describes them, wore jewelry. Their morals, finally, find their strength in codes of manly friendship, in a religious respect for the duties of hospitality, and above all, in a dedication to the idea of heroic excellence, or *arete*.

To what extent Homer in all this is describing a remote, heroic age of which he had only intimations, as against that which he had himself seen and known, remains a matter of some debate. But when he moves from supposed remembrance of things past to portrayal of mind and manner and belief, we stand with him on timeless ground—indeed, on the fundamental ground of Greece. For he is speaking, in every book of the *Iliad* and *Odyssey*, of the necessity of valor, even though it is very likely to lead to one's own destruction. He is saying that a man should fill his life with brave deeds; that the only weakness is cowardice, or the failure to seek heroic goals; and that a hero's main duty is toward himself, for by finding honor he will attain near-godly glory.

The Homeric hero is often selfish, blind, and brutal—none more so than Achilles, whether sulking in his tent or monstrously maltreating the body of his slain foe Hector—but he is also chivalric, loyal to his oath, his blood tie, and his friend (in Achilles' case, Patroclus). To be sure, he is a good deal more chivalric than the gods, who in the way the Homeric imagination organizes them, become in effect the senior partners of one or the other contending sides before Troy, and very prone to chicanery, deceit, and un-

Another of Achilles' victims was Memnon, the mythical king of Ethiopia, who fought on the Trojan side. Above, his mother Eos, goddess of dawn, is seen carrying him away; each morning, supposedly, she weeps tears of dew in her sorrow for him.
LOUVRE; GIRAUDON

sportsmanlike intervention in behalf of their favorites. Thus the whole abduction of Helen by Paris, we are told, was contrived by the ever-mischievous Aphrodite—who also lifts her weakling favorite out of battle at the moment when he is about to be properly speared by avenging Menelaus. Apollo, Artemis, Ares (with whom Aphrodite was discovered in bed in one episode of the *Odyssey*, thus giving rise to much Homeric laughter) are on the side of the Trojans; Hera, Athena, Poseidon, and Aphrodite's awkward husband Hephaestus are on the side of the Achaeans; and though Zeus tries to adjudicate and bring about some order on Olympus, in a memorable scene in Book XIV of the *Iliad* his consort Hera wantonly seduces him in order to keep him from supporting the Trojan cause.

The gods live on—even though obscure Fate rules them, too, as Zeus learns in the *Iliad* when he finds his son Sarpedon is doomed—but the heroes must die; and the greater the heroism, probably the earlier the death. Achilles knows this, and when the gods offer him long life and mediocrity on one hand, or glory and an early death on the other, he makes the inevitable choice. His proudest foe, Priam's son Hector, knows it too, sensing that his days are numbered as are those of Troy itself. And in one of the most poignant scenes in the *Iliad*, when his tender wife Andromache comes to him, accompanied by a nursemaid with their infant son in arms, to remind him that Achilles has already killed her father and all her seven brothers and to plead with him that for her sake and the child's he abstain from further combat after all his past victories, his reply, again, is the only possible one: "I have learned to be valiant and to fight always among the foremost ranks of the Trojans, winning for my own self great glory, and for my father." Not to be in the forefront would be unthinkable, though Troy must fall.

In a touch that shows a poet at his peak, Homer then has Hector reach out to take in his arms the little boy—who, however, screams in terror at the sight of his father's helmet with its fierce horsehair plume. At this unsettling outburst, the parents smile; then Hector removes his helmet, places it on the ground, kisses his son, and prays to Zeus and the other gods to grant that this boy may be superior to himself. (A panel of contrasting translations of this noble passage, from Chapman's in the early seventeenth century to Alexander Pope's in the eighteenth to those of major translators in our own time, appears on pages 136–137. Homer's compelling power over the men who have translated his works into many languages, and the different readings that have

The Trojan horse, with which the Greeks treacherously gained entry into their enemies' town, was built at the suggestion of Athena and under her direction. Above, a sixth-century vase painting shows the goddess inspecting the horse.
MUSEO ARCHEOLOGICO, FLORENCE

been given him in many eras are subjects of great fascination.)

Soon thereafter Hector is slain by Achilles, who, however, knows that his own death is near, having been told by his mother Thetis (who may have had it from Zeus): "For you will not be with me long, but already death and powerful destiny stand closely above you." So the Trojan Hector, who is as superior to most of the gods in valor as his wife Andromache is superior to the goddesses in character, succumbs to a rival who is at once the most brilliant, the most brutal, and in the end the most knightly of men. Achilles, however, gloriously caparisoned with Hephaestus' armor, fights on, knowing that Apollo and Paris both have the secret of his vulnerable heel.

The gods themselves pale beside such presences as these, as Homer models his heroes with his images of flashing helmet or swift foot or well-greaved shanks or wily wisdom stalking for prey or the grace of honor. Indeed, though far more powerful than men, the gods seem less good than men. They are not moral by human standards: they show little pity, little magnanimity, and often little wisdom. They plan the ruin of a great city. They contrive against men and each other. They induce madness in a hero. They indulge in foul play or poor sportsmanship, as when rescuing the wife-stealing Paris by wafting him away from the Achaeans' avenging shafts. The heroes of Homer are men; the villains, always ready for mischief or a bargain, are gods. Perhaps this is what makes Homer the most heroic and humane of poets, and the preceptor of Greek man's own dignity.

An early end overtakes most of his heroes—as, indeed, an early end was to overtake the brief splendor of Greece. But Hector remarks eloquently—as a new translation by the American poet Richmond Lattimore renders it, seeking to recapture Homer's stately, dactylic rhythms:

> And some day one of the men to come will say, as he sees it,
> One who in his benched ship sails on the wine-blue water:
> "This is the mound of a man who died long ago in battle,
> Who was one of the bravest, and glorious Hector killed him."
> So will he speak some day, and my glory will not be forgotten.

Or, in the older version used by generations of readers of the Loeb Classical Library, "And some one shall some day say even of men that are yet to be, as he saileth in his many-benched ship over the wine-dark sea: 'This is a barrow of a man that died in olden days, whom on a time in the midst of his prowess glorious Hector slew.' So shall some man say, and my glory shall never die."

And so it was to be.

After Achilles' death, his armor was awarded to the bravest of the Greeks left alive. Odysseus was judged worthy of the award. Instead of keeping the armor, he presented it to Neoptolemus, the young son of Achilles (above).
KUNSTHISTORISCHES MUSEUM, VIENNA

GLYPTOTHEK, MUNICH; LEONARD VON MATT

THE WORLD
OF MYTH

The myths of the Greeks, those curious tales of god and mortal, of love and warfare, of trials of strength and intelligence, are unsurpassed as literature. Often brutal, often poignant, they have engaged the minds not only of the Greeks but also of the ages that followed them. Yet the myths are far more than literature. To historians they are of considerable value in corroborating archaeological findings, for they embody many memories of Minoan and Mycenaean civilization; indeed the important sites in the mythological tales—Argos and Thebes, Mycenae and Athens—were also major centers of Mycenaean culture. The myths, too, provided expression for the major concepts of Greek religion. With their fierce monsters and gentle spirits of wind and water, they enshrined many primitive beliefs about the world in which the Greeks dwelt. An important religious role was played by the cult of the heroes, those men, often of divine ancestry, whose astonishing feats dominate Greek mythology. The foremost among them, Heracles, who is shown opposite clothed in the skin of the Nemean lion that he had slain, was worshiped throughout Greece. Thousands of other heroes, probably spirits of the dead originally, were revered too, often only in specific regions near the place of their burial. Their worship, with its emphasis on relics and on the hero's intercession to aid the faithful, was similar in many ways to the medieval veneration of the saints.

LOUVRE; HIRMER

96

THE GREATEST OF HEROES

Hundreds of feats were attributed to Heracles, the most heroic of the heroes of the Greeks. Among these, the most famous and most difficult were the labors that his kinsman Eurystheus commanded him to perform—killing the Nemean lion whose hide was invulnerable to weapons, cleaning the Augean stables which were piled so high with dung that their stench polluted the entire Peloponnesus, and slaying the monstrous Hydra, which sprouted two more heads whenever any one of its nine was cut off. Heracles lifted the world on his shoulders, descended to the land of the dead, and ripped open a passage between the Mediterranean and the Atlantic, where he set the pillars that bore his name. Upon his death he was brought to Olympus to sit with the gods, the only mortal to do so.

MUSEO CIVICO, BRESCIA; HIRMER

Above, a detail from a late sixth-century amphora shows Heracles wrestling with the Nemean lion; Athena stands protectively beside him, her shield adorned with her symbol, an owl. Another of Heracles' labors is shown opposite. The hero has captured Cerberus, the three-headed beast who guards the entrance to the underworld, and brought him to Mycenae. Its king, Eurystheus, who ordered the feat, is terrified and hides in a vat.

97

MUSEO NAZIONALE, NAPLES

VATICAN MUSEUM; ALINARI

THE WRATH OF ACHILLES

The tale of the siege of Troy was one of the central themes of Greek mythology. From the story of the abduction of Helen by the Trojan prince Paris and the embarkation of a Greek army to recapture her and gain revenge, both the *Iliad* and the *Odyssey* and almost half the remaining body of Greek tragedies were drawn. The *Iliad* contains but a small portion of this material; it is primarily the story of the wrath of Achilles, the strongest of the Greek warriors, and of his re-fusal to join the battle against the Trojans. Only when his dear friend Patroclus is slain does he begin to fight, to revenge himself on the Trojan champion Hector. "The heart within him loaded with savage fury," Achilles killed Hector, turning the tide of victory to-ward the Greeks, and dragged his body three times around the city.

The funeral pyre of Patroclus, with the slain hero's armor upon it, is seen at the center of the vase painting at right. Achilles stands beside the pyre, pouring a libation, and a captive Trojan maiden kneels, about to be sacrificed in Patroclus' honor. Achilles' chariot appears beneath, dragging Hector's body. Above, another painting shows Helen, the cause of it all.

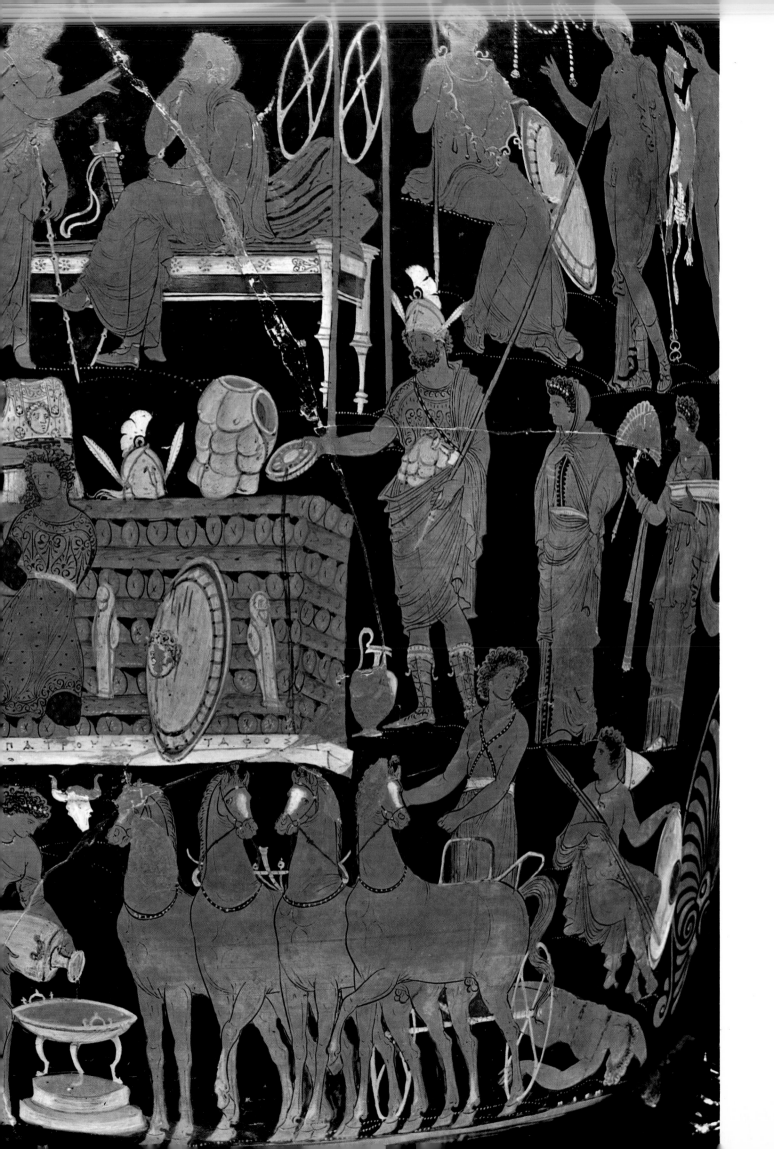

ΠΑΤΡΟΚΛ   ΤΑΦΟΣ

MUSEUM, MYKONOS, GERMAN ARCHAEOLOGICAL INSTITUTE, ATHENS

VATICAN MUSEUM; ALINARI

THE WARRIORS AT TROY

MUSEO ARCHEOLOGICO, FLORENCE; HIRMER

The Trojan War was fought not only by mortal heroes who sallied forth from the city walls or the Greek camp to engage in battle, but by the gods as well. They had their favorites among the warring heroes, and they too disputed the fate of the city. Above both gods and heroes stood Destiny, controlling the final outcome. Her judgment was inexorable, and warriors had to fight on, even when they knew death was imminent. "Now evil death is close to me . . . and there is no way out," Hector says during his battle with Achilles in the *Iliad*; "Let me at least not die without a struggle, inglorious, but do some big thing first, that men to come shall know of it." It was glory in arms that both Trojan and Greek warriors primarily sought. Yet it was not through force of arms that the Greeks finally won their war. It was through guile. They built a great wooden horse, concealed soldiers within, and left it for the Trojans as a token of peace. After it was taken into the city, the Greeks emerged in the dead of night and opened the gates to their companions. Taken by surprise, Troy was captured, its men slaughtered, its treasure plundered, and its women and children doomed to a life of slavery.

During the long and tedious siege, warriors, like Achilles and Ajax (above), must have distracted themselves with games. At left, Trojans march out of the city gate. Opposite is the Trojan horse, with Greek soldiers peering out of windows that are cut in its side.

MUSEUM, ELEUSIS; SKIRA

THE WANDERINGS OF ODYSSEUS

Condemned by the god Poseidon to roam the seas for a decade before returning home from Troy, Odysseus wandered past fearful hazards. Only his own guile and strength, and Athena's favor, preserved him from death along the way. But they were not enough to save his companions, who perished one by one. Some were devoured by the one-eyed giant Polyphemus, others by the Laestrygones, a cannibal race. Some were turned into swine by the enchantress Circe. Before he could reach home, Odysseus had to venture into the kingdom of the dead and pass by the island of the Sirens, whose singing turned men mad with desire. He had to sail past the sea monsters Scylla and Charybdis: one shattered the bones of sailors, and the other whirled them down to the depths of the sea. Some of the obstacles that diverted him on his homeward trip were less baleful. Chief of these was the beautiful nymph Calypso, who promised Odysseus eternal life and youth in exchange for his love. Although "he was constantly cared for like a god" all the time he spent on her island, Odysseus preferred his own homeland.

The winged Sirens, "weaving a haunting song over the sea" to entice Odysseus to his destruction, are shown in the vase painting below. As they rowed past the Sirens' island, Odysseus was lashed to the mast, and his men had their ears filled with wax to keep from being tempted by them. Odysseus is shown again, in another vase painting opposite, with Polyphemus, a Cyclops who had imprisoned the hero and his men in a cave, eaten some of them, and was planning to dine on the rest. In order to escape from the cave, Odysseus had to gouge out the monster's eye.

BRITISH MUSEUM

ODYSSEUS' HOMECOMING

When the long-suffering Odysseus finally regained his home, Athena disguised him as an old beggar in order to protect him from the powerful nobles who, considering him dead, were competing for his kingdom and for the hand of his wife in marriage. He made his way to his house, pretending to have news of its absent master, and was received by Penelope, his wife. He talked to her of Odysseus; "as Penelope listened, her tears ran down," Homer relates. "She mourned and wept for the man who at that very moment was sitting beside her." The time had come for her to accept a new husband from among the suitors. To choose one, she offered herself to the man strong enough to bend a mighty bow that Odysseus had left behind. None of the suitors was able to do it, but the old beggar, Odysseus himself, could. Armed with the bow, and aided by his son Telemachus to whom he revealed himself, he regained his wife and kingdom.

In a small terra-cotta relief made in the fifth century, Odysseus is shown, on his return to Ithaca, standing unrecognized (at right) before his wife Penelope, Telemachus his son, and his retainers.

METROPOLITAN MUSEUM OF ART, FLETCHER FUND

VATICAN MUSEUM; HIRMER

According to one version of his legend Jason was swallowed and then disgorged by the dragon who guarded the Golden Fleece. A painting above depicts the climax of the scene, with the goddess Athena watching; in the background the Golden Fleece hangs on a tree. During the Trojan War the Amazons joined in the battle against the Greeks. A fifth-century painting below shows the Amazon queen Penthesilea, collapsing under the sword of Achilles.

MUSEUM ANTIKER KLEINKUNST,
MUNICH; HIRMER

METROPOLITAN MUSEUM OF ART, HUNTLEY BEQUEST

THE TRIALS OF THE HEROES

The quests of the Greek heroes took them to mysterious lands, to overcome strange obstacles and battle with fierce monsters. Bellerophon fought the Chimaera, a fire-breathing beast with serpent's tail, lion's body, and two heads. For aid he enlisted another more amiable monster, the winged horse Pegasus. Mounted on Pegasus, he dispatched the Chimaera, and followed that triumph with another over the Amazons. His successes made him lose all caution, however, and he resolved to fly to Olympus. Zeus, angered, sent a gadfly to sting Pegasus, who reared and sent Bellerophon tumbling down to earth again. Another perilous journey was that undertaken by Jason and a great assemblage of heroes in search of the Golden Fleece. Before he gained the prize, Jason had to battle the terrifying Harpies and to kill hundreds of armed men who sprang up where a dragon's teeth had been sown. One of those who accompanied Jason was Orpheus, the founder of poetry and music, who played so beautifully that the stones and trees listened to him. Later he ventured alone into the underworld to bring back Eurydice, his beloved. But his journey was in vain; despite Pluto's command he turned to gaze at her before they left Hades and had to leave her behind.

At left an engraved bronze plaque from the seventh century shows Bellerophon, mounted on the winged horse Pegasus, attacking the Chimaera. A detail from a vase painting below depicts Orpheus playing on his lyre.

STAATLICHE MUSEEN, BERLIN

THE DOOMED HOUSE OF ATREUS

When he came home from leading the Greek armies against Troy, Agamemnon, the king of Mycenae, was killed by his wife and by the lover she had taken during his absence. His son Orestes, determined to avenge him, killed his faithless mother in turn. Inexorably, his action was revenged. For this unnatural crime Orestes was pursued through the world by the monstrous Furies, and driven mad by them. Agamemnon's death was not entirely undeserved; he had sacrificed one of his daughters to Artemis, in order to get a fair wind for the Greek expedition to Troy. His blood-stained family, the House of Atreus, overlords of the Peloponnesus, was cursed from its beginning; for Atreus, its founder, had committed the unforgivable crime of slaughtering his nephews, cooking them, and serving them up for dinner to his rival, their father Thyestes.

While his mother tries to restrain him, Orestes turns to slay her after having dispatched her lover. Behind her, her daughter Electra rejoices at their slaughter.
NY CARLSBERG GLYPTOTHEK, COPENHAGEN

MUSEUM OF FINE ARTS, BOSTON

*Vase paintings depict two of Theseus'
adventures that combined, as was often
the case, both his amorous and his martial talents. Above he is seen killing the
Minotaur; beside him stands Ariadne,
who loved him enough to betray her
father and teach Theseus how to find
his way out of the Minotaur's labyrinth.
Opposite, he is shown carrying off a
queen of the Amazons, Antiope, who
was to become so enamored of Theseus
that she later fought alongside him in
a battle against her former subjects.*

LOUVRE

THE SLAYER OF THE MINOTAUR

In the number of his brave deeds Theseus, king of Athens, emulated Heracles. His most notable feat was slaying the Cretan Minotaur, that monster, half man, half bull, to whom the Athenians were required to sacrifice seven youths and seven maidens each year. With the aid of a magic spool of thread, Theseus found his precarious way into the labyrinth where the Minotaur was kept, dispatched him, and then wound his way out again. His other enemies were less formidable; among them were the Amazons and Procrustes, who captured travelers to stretch or amputate their limbs. Theseus brought unity to Athens, and, according to one tradition, he established democracy there.

4

THE
GREEK
ERUPTION

We are as leaves in jeweled springtime growing
That open to the sunlight's quickening rays;
So joy we in our span of youth, unknowing
If God shall bring us good or evil days.
                    —Mimnermus of Colophon

If a great Trojan War actually occurred somewhat as Homer described it, one way of thinking of it is to regard it as Greece's first disastrous civil war. For before the walls of Troy Greek-speaking warriors from the peninsula battled warriors of the Asia Minor coast who worshiped the same gods and many of whom also spoke Greek. In the outcome Troy was totally destroyed and the decimated victors returned to their homes (if indeed they did return) to find their thrones or wives pre-empted, their kingdoms in disarray, and dark times ahead. When Odysseus visits Hades on his long voyage home, he encounters, among the shades of many heroes of either side, that of his commander-in-chief, Agamemnon of Mycenae, slain on his return by Aegisthus, lover of Agamemnon's wife Clytemnestra, along with the king's remaining men. Odysseus himself regains his own palace at Ithaca alone (all his followers perished along the way), reaching it after ten years of travel and travail only to find it overrun and despoiled by his wife Penelope's suitors.

Was there actually any such voyage as the fabulous one described in the *Odyssey?* To this day we have no clue. We know that the Mycenaeans had fallen heir to the Mediterranean trade routes of the great Cretan sea empire after its sudden destruction around 1400 B.C. But sometime in the twelfth century the Mycenaean kingdoms in turn fell prey to Dorian invaders, who came from the north. These warriors were content to settle the land and left the sea lanes to others, notably the Phoenicians, who set sail for far places perhaps as early as the tenth century. But as to tales of early travels, we remain in the realm of sheer myth and wild surmise. In legend the Argonauts explored the Black Sea, but we know little concrete of such a venture. In Homer's tale Odysseus ranges over a vast area of seas, islands, straits, and currents in his efforts to get home; various listeners or readers of the epic at various times have thought that his wanderings represented a voyage eastward beyond the Bosporus or westward as far as the Strait of Gibraltar. But we know nothing provable about this either. What we do know is that there is so much fascinating detail in Homer's telling that for fully two and a half millennia students of it have been bent on identifying with actual sites the strange places he mentions in bardic terms as visited by his hero. This just may have been history's most perennial guessing game, and if so, it is sovereign testimony to Homer's lasting spell; yet so many tantalizing geographical and navigational correspondences are embedded in the poem that some surmises about Odysseus' route may well be true.

The ancient Greeks believed wholeheartedly in the existence

of Odysseus—the great schemer who after Troy's fall became Hellas' greatest sailor—and in the actuality of his voyages. Thus Hesiod, perhaps less than a century after Homer, places some of Odysseus' adventures specifically in or around Italy. Herodotus identified the land where the Lotus Eaters gave Odysseus' crew their opiate of honey-sweet flowers with western Libya, on the North African coast. Thucydides and most ancient writers thought that the menacing sea monsters Scylla and Charybdis, between which Odysseus had to pass, referred to the Strait of Messina, with its dangerous rocks and currents. Tradition, in the wake of the old historians, has identified the seat of King Aeolus (the keeper of the winds who gave Odysseus' departing men a sack containing the worst of them, instructing them not to open it—which of course they did) with the Lipari Islands north of Sicily. Later the Roman Vergil in his *Aeneid* placed the cave of the one-eyed Cyclops Polyphemus in Sicily; and centuries later Dante in the *Inferno* describes his meeting Odysseus in Hell and has the hero recall the enchantress Circe with the words, "She who twelve months near Gaeta detained me"—Gaeta being a town north of Naples and close to the high promontory called Monte Circeo.

Over the centuries many travelers and scholars, noting Homer's comments on winds, currents, number of days traveled, and land seen, became convinced that Odysseus' farthest voyage of all—that which Circe advised him to make to the banks of the "Ocean stream," there to enter Hades and learn from the prophet Tiresias how to get safely home—referred to an actual expedition to the Strait of Gibraltar, the western limit of the Mediterranean world. Still, there were some who felt that possibly he had erred into the Black Sea between *its* straits, in the wake of Jason; others thought the Pillars of Heracles were simply a figment of the imagination.

What is relevant is that there lay in the Greek consciousness, as expressed by Homer, a tradition of belief in very early Mediterranean travel and exploration. The stories told of the Pillars of Heracles may have been transmitted by Phoenician seamen who had ventured out westward in advance of the Greeks and thus had contributed to the legend and folklore of Heracles. Homer, when he speaks of the "stream" (possibly a current?) of "Ocean" (the Atlantic?) is telling, many observers have thought, of something he might have learned from the Phoenicians—for a constant current flows in from the ocean through the Gibraltar straits to replenish the waters of the otherwise landlocked Mediterranean, evaporating under each summer's sun. We do know that if there was a historical Odysseus, he had obviously to sail west from Troy to get home. On this long voyage Odysseus encounters no other

MUSEO NAZIONALE, PALERMO; ANDERSON

The rapid expansion of the Greek city-states carried Hellenic culture overseas. This carving of Zeus disguised as a bull and abducting Europa was made in a Greek settlement in Sicily.

sail of any sort. Like a Columbus, he moves into regions previously unvisited and comes back freighted with lore.

Down to this day there are travelers, often in small boats, with the text of Homer beside them in the stern sheets along with sailing charts and pilot guides, who set out to retrace Odysseus' route, as Samuel Eliot Morison of Harvard did that of Columbus. One spirited British scholar-sailor, Ernle Bradford, has done just this. In his book *Ulysses Found* he identifies the home of the nymph Calypso, where Odysseus dallied for seven years, with Malta; the cave of Polyphemus, with a particular one just north of Trapani on the Sicilian west coast; the harbor of the gigantic, cannibal Laestrygones, who destroyed all Odysseus' ships but one, with Bonifacio on Corsica; and the rocks from which the Sirens sang, with the Galli Islands in the Gulf of Salerno of World War II fame. (Indeed Bradford, standing watch one night on a destroyer covering the Allied landings there, almost thought he heard the Sirens sing to him as he passed the Galli. At least he heard—or thought he heard—some low and almost human music coming from there. His shipmates smiled, thinking him gone dotty, but the captain steered in close just to see if anyone was on the rocks: no one. "There are plenty of rocky caverns and fissures just above sea level in the Galli Islands," writes Bradford, musing, "and such places are great originators of moaning sounds, whispers, and far-off wailing voices. But there was no wind on that night, and the sea unruffled." Imagination can play strange tricks on classicists as on others.)

Unlike Columbus' expedition, Odysseus' was involuntary. For he was, of course, simply seeking to get home to his kingdom of Ithaca, generally identified today with the island of that name off the western coast of Greece. For this purpose he had to round the southern Peloponnesian capes, but a strong offshore wind blew him out to sea and into the westerly unknown; and therewith his ten-year wanderings began. That westbound wind, the propellant of Odysseus, bears a striking resemblance to the one that many centuries later drove Saint Paul helplessly from Crete to shipwreck on the island of Malta; and anyone even in our own time who has skirted the southern Greek headlands under sail is familiar with the "Greco," or "Greek wind," particularly troublesome as it drives a boat westward off Cape Matapan.

At length, after his final and longest adventure—his thralldom to Calypso—Odysseus leaves her island and sails for seventeen days on a raft and (Poseidon having wrecked it in vengeance for Odysseus' blinding of the god's son Polyphemus) then for two days on a log, to be cast up on the land of the Phaeacians, which

MIGRATION AND COLONIZATION
c. 1150—c. 600 B.C.
→ DORIAN INVASION

→ IONIAN MIGRATION

→ AEOLIAN MIGRATION

▨ AREAS OF GREEK COLONIZATION

In the twelfth century, Dorian tribesmen migrated into Greece, forcing many of its original inhabitants to cross the Aegean and seek refuge on the Asia Minor coast. Beginning in the eighth century, Asia Minor and Greece saw another wave of migration, this time one made up of colonists setting out for new settlements along the coasts of the Mediterranean and Black seas. The map above shows the extent of their colonization. Another map, at right, shows one of the many guesses that have been made—this, by the contemporary English traveler Ernle Bradford —about the mythical route Odysseus followed through waters that were later to become familiar to the Greeks.

To Pillars of Heracle[s]

— Journey from Tr[...]
— Journey home
— Blown by winds to within sight of home and ba[...]
— To and from Pillars of Heracles

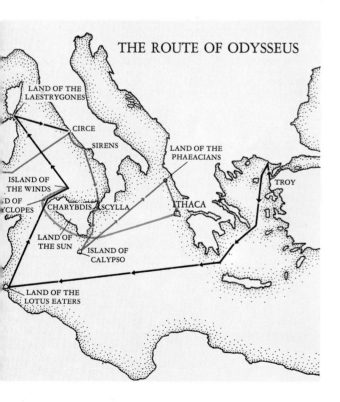

THE ROUTE OF ODYSSEUS

may have been Corfu, an island about sixty miles north of Ithaca. King Alcinous, hearing the tale of Odysseus' woes, aids him to make a swift descent onto his own kingdom—and to the greatest recognition scenes in all literature. These are the moments when Odysseus reveals himself to the faithful swineherd Eumaeus; when Telemachus throws his arms about the shaggy stranger, realizing from his bearing that this is indeed his noble father; when the old watchdog Argus wags his tail in greeting; when the servant Eurycleia, washing a stranger's feet, sees a scar she remembers from years ago; when Penelope, still wishing a final test of identity, orders Eurycleia to move outside the bridal chamber the bed that her own Odysseus had built, only to have him exclaim that this couldn't be, for didn't she remember that one of the legs of the bed had been a living tree growing in their chamber? (this was just what she wanted to hear); and when his aged father Laertes, plowing in the fields, hears him enumerate the vines and fruit trees the father had once given the son to tend. All these episodes are so immediate and compelling in their humanity that one can readily understand why the Greeks always felt so close to Odysseus, no matter how far he had sailed away on strange adventures. So do we still. For to read about him is to be on his side, so to speak, against all the forces arrayed against him (which is not necessarily so when one reads about Achilles or Hector, where one's loyalties may be equivocal or divided), and to feel in him the presence not only of an antique hero but of a very palpable man, sorely beset.

The poet, to be sure, is out to evoke just such a reaction from his audience; this he does through a long preparation, setting forth the loom of Odysseus' eventual return, and through his masterful use of the device of poetic irony. We know all along that the unlikely stranger who lands on Ithaca to seek restitution is in fact its rightful king, but the doubters and the suitors with whom he is to deal do not. Our foreknowledge of the outcome is at least equal to that of the gods (who have behaved all along in their usual contentious and meddlesome fashion); but all depends on the sureness of Odysseus' avenging bow-arm at the climactic moment.

As we close the pages of Homer, we come up inevitably to the actualities of Greek history. Was there in fact one great Trojan War, or were there sporadic raids extending over many years, or even generations, which some sovereign poetic imagination fused into one concerted drama of strife? And what happened to the rich civilization of the Homeric warriors? The discoveries of present-day archaeologists indicate that the Mycenaean kingdoms entered a time of troubles shortly before 1200 B.C. and were completely destroyed later, in the twelfth century. This is about the time the

Dorians invaded Greece, and we may conclude that these Greek-speaking but illiterate tribes from the north found an easy prey in the decadent and possibly war-weakened kingdoms. The lights of Mycenaean Greece went out, and many a goodly state disappeared in that long night which was followed, four centuries later, by a new dawn in which Greece reawakened, bursting with energy. Then, in a matter of a few decades, the Greeks moved into the light of history—not only that, but into the forefront of history.

Traditionally Greek history begins in the year 776, for it was from then that the Hellenes began to count time: they believed that the quadrennial Olympic games in honor of Zeus were founded in that year, and from then on great deeds and events were to be located in memory by a word or an inscription denoting in what particular Olympiad they had occurred. And Olympia provided more than a calendar. It marked the start of the Panhellenic impulse—an urge to bring Greek-speaking and Greek-thinking men from their scattered towns and hamlets together on a common ground. Some had already begun to converge on the high mount at Delphi to hear Apollo's oracle—as mentioned by Homer—but in the eighth century Delphi was probably only one of many local shrines, not becoming a Panhellenic one until the seventh.

The early seventh. century brings another significant scrap of information, too. In 683 the leading families of Athens had taken to electing one of their members to serve as archon, or chief of state, for a one-year term. This was the culmination of a long process in which the old monarchy coming down from Theseus' time was transformed into an aristocratic republic.

By this time a remarkable process of Greek state-making, expansion, and colonization had begun. But this had been preceded by several centuries of very gradual migration of Greek tribes into the eastern Aegean, a movement of which we have only the dimmest outlines. People who were later to call themselves Aeolians had begun wandering to the Asia Minor coast before the year 1000, possibly seeking new lands as refuge from the encroaching Dorians. They settled, for instance, on the island of Lesbos (where there are evidences of an earlier culture as well). Perhaps not long after, the Ionians had commenced moving to the far mainland as well, to be followed by the Dorians who began penetrating the Aegean islands and southern Asia Minor sometime after the year 900. Scholars today are inclined to doubt the supposed ethnic differences between "Aeolians" and "Ionians" and to hold that these terms were invented only when the process of systematic writing of Greek chronicles and histories began, centuries later. The "Ionians," for instance, hailing presumably from the northern Pelo-

Odysseus mourning his lost comrades, who failed to survive the terrible journey through unknown seas, is shown at right in an impression made on clay in ancient times from an ornamental belt buckle. Below, a redrawing of a scene from an early vase painting shows one of the many-oared galleys in which Greek mariners sailed throughout the Mediterranean. This galley has two banks of oars; others had three. According to the Odyssey, *when the wind died down the sailors "furled the sail, and stowed it away. . . . Then they sat down at their oars of polished fir and churned the water white."*

ponnesus and Attica, may have been a mixed folk who developed the culture we call "Ionian" only after they had crossed the sea.

By the eighth century this process of dispersion, previously cloaked in mystery, begins to take on some recognizable form. So-called Ionians, in their probings along the Asia Minor coast, had seized a settlement that was to become known as Miletus—a place possibly of Minoan origin, and then inhabited by what Homer calls the "barbarous-tongued" Carians, who had fought on the side of Troy. Now beginning in the seventh century, Miletus (its citizens supposedly descendants of Ionian men and the Carian women they had taken to wife after having slaughtered their husbands) sprouted dozens of offshoots of its own, some as far away as southern Russia.

AMERICAN SCHOOL OF
CLASSICAL STUDIES, ATHENS

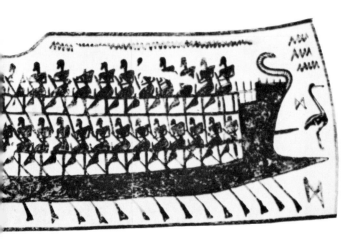

Other Ionian refugees had traveled to what was to become proud Ephesus, mingling there with an Asiatic tribe who worshiped a primeval mother goddess whom the newcomers blended with their own Artemis. ("Great is Diana of the Ephesians," was the protesting cry that went up many centuries later among its people when Saint Paul arrived seeking to convert them to the faith of Christ.) Aeolians, meanwhile, had set up five cities on fair, volcanic Lesbos, rich with vines and orchards, and produced there by the end of the seventh century a distinctive culture of much grace and charm—and the most famous of the Lesbians, the poetess Sappho. Aggressive Dorians, still energetic after subduing most of peninsular Greece, had organized Rhodes, the southernmost of the Asia Minor offshore islands, and established three independent cities there. Rhodes, to be sure, was not to shine in the immediate generations ahead with a light comparable to that of Lesbos or Ephesus or rich and many-talented Miletus, but its time was to come: in the era of Alexander the Great and after, it would emerge as one of the great Mediterranean trading centers.

And this was only the beginning. By mid eighth century, colonists from Euboea, the long island strip just to the north of Attica, were setting off to found settlements in Thrace—to the north—and in Italy, where Cumae and the offshore island of Ischia were probably the first sites (Cumae in turn established Neapolis, present-day Naples). Soon after, Naxos on Sicily was founded (named, some say, for the Aegean island of Naxos), and also Syracuse, a Corinthian colony that was to have an illustrious future. At about the same time Greeks began moving toward the Hellespont and in the following centuries they entered the Black Sea and founded numerous colonies on its shores. By the end of the sixth century the entire Mediterranean was encircled by Greek offshoots—ranging from Thrace and Asia Minor to Syria, Egypt,

MUSEE DE CHATILLON-SUR-SEINE

The bronze horses above are from a relief on a vase over five feet high, recently found in France. It was discovered along an ancient trade route that extended from Italy to Britain, where the Greeks obtained the tin necessary for making bronze. The vase was probably made in a Spartan colony and offered by a diplomatic merchant to the prince of the trading town.

Libya, Spain, southern France, and Italy. In areas like Syria and Egypt, where they encountered old, established local cultures, the Greeks had trading posts; elsewhere they founded replicas of their own city-states.

In some of these far-shore settlements culture and wealth grew fast—much faster even than on the parent peninsula itself. The geographer-historian Strabo, writing at the beginning of the Christian era, described one episode of this astonishing spread to southern Italy and Sicily: "Archias, sailing from Corinth, founded Syracuse about the same time that Naxos and Megara were established. They say that when Myscellus and Archias went to Delphi to consult the oracle, the god asked whether they preferred wealth or health. Archias chose wealth and Myscellus health, and the oracle then assigned Syracuse to the former and Croton to the latter." Thus Strabo conveys something of the gist of an original Greek process, which might roughly be summed up as this:

A given Greek city, having attained a certain degree of stability, is still subject to some degree of restlessness, perhaps because of expanding population or inadequacy of resource, or both. Some of its younger spirits conceive the idea of setting up beyond the seas a new town with more space or resource that will be related to the old, yet not beholden to it. They then choose a distinguished citizen as their *oikistes*, or city-founder, and consult the oracle as to whether this undertaking will be beneficial to all concerned. Finally, having been encouraged by Delphi, they proceed, carrying with them sacred fire from their old city shrine to ignite a new one; from then on they regard themselves as bound to the parent city by no ties other than those of filial friendship.

The motives of the Greek settlers were quite unlike those of the triumphant Caesars, seeking to acquire tributaries to be subject to Rome, or of the conquistadors, out for glory and gold for Spain. It was, instead of a true colonization, more in the nature of emigration; *apoikia* was a word Greeks used to define it, meaning an "away-home"—a thought no doubt comparable to that which stirred many settlers of North America. Impulses toward commercial exploitation played a strong part, but so did urges for new land; and the city fathers at home were wise enough to see that their emigrant sons had best be left to pursue their own fortunes— with some parental guidance.

Such a vast extension in relatively so short a time by so small a people (some scholars believe there were no more than 200,000 Dorian, Ionian, Aeolian, and other Greeks living in 700) leaves one still asking, How did they do it? One answer is that they embodied a new force at large in a surrounding vacuum. That vacuum was one of power and culture both. At the time when Greece came back to life seeking fresh horizons the ancient kingdoms of the East had either crumbled or were falling into decay. The Hittite empire in Asia Minor had long disappeared. The Phrygian kingdom that in part succeeded it was destroyed in about 700. The Lydian kingdom that in turn succeeded *that* was only just taking form under Gyges, and had not yet produced the Croesus who would threaten Ionian settlements along the coast. Egypt's glory had faded, and its dynasties lived in torpor, to be conquered in the early seventh century by the Assyrians. The Phoenicians had their share of Mediterranean trade; but not until they founded Carthage did they seriously menace the Greeks. Farther off to the east, the Persian realm had hardly begun to assert itself from its mountains. The Macedonians were still backward, northern hillmen. In Italy, the Etruscans had indeed made themselves known to the Greeks, and were carrying on a lively trade with them. But the Romans—a people still under Etruscan influence—were all but unknown.

In a sense, then, the Mediterranean world of the eighth and seventh centuries was singularly open. As the classicist H. D. F. Kitto writes, "The ironies of history are many and bitter, but at least this must be put to the credit of the gods, that they arranged for the Greeks to have the eastern Mediterranean almost to themselves long enough to work out what was almost a laboratory experiment to test how far, and in what conditions, human nature is capable of creating and sustaining a civilization."

The ideas the Greeks carried with them were those of self-determination and individuality; and their "peculiar institution," the *polis*, or city-state, both embodied and furthered these notions, encouraging men as they set off to a far shore to be as self-reliant and independent abroad as their fathers were at home. Vigorous competition between daughter cities, diversity in their mores and make-up, vitality in their sense of freedom, and the pursuit of excellence—all this was of the essence of the Greeks' uniqueness and success wherever they went in those centuries, for all the troubles it was to cause them in later ones.

The Greeks, the more they met and traded with the *barbaroi*, tended to look down on them. (The time was still far off when the Greeks, in the irony of history, were to be absorbed in the vastest of ancient empires, that of the "barbarian" Romans, to whom they had taught so much.) Only the Greeks, they knew, had brought forth the polis, and by this they meant a sovereign city or independent small state, but also something more: the word "polis" denotes not only a place but its people—a community acting together to govern itself under the idea that public affairs are the

ACROPOLIS MUSEUM; HASSIA

Ionian civilization developed along the Asia Minor coast, reaching a peak of prosperity and artistic influence in the sixth century. At that time a sculptor, probably from the island of Chios, carved this statue of a girl, which was placed as a votive offering on the Athenian Acropolis.

A small ivory statue portrays a priestess of the great goddess of the Ephesians. The Ionians, who colonized Ephesus and developed it into an important commercial port, identified the indigenous fertility goddess with their own Artemis.

ISTANBUL ARKEOLOJI MUZELERI

affairs of all its citizens. To be sure, this idea did not spring forth full-born, Athena-like, from the Greek brow. In the eighth and seventh centuries Greek city-states were ruled by aristocrats who ran them with little concern for the general interest. But the polis concept, once implanted, was rapidly to grow, creating a way of life that was diametrically opposite to that of the hierarchic Eastern and Mycenaean kingdoms, with their absolute despots. The Pharaohs were actually worshiped as gods and had abject subjects; the Greeks (though they had slaves too) were out to breed citizens. Later Aristotle was to remark, looking back over the origin and nature of the polis, that "while it grows for the sake of mere life, it exists for the sake of the good life."

A local form of government had come into being as a practical necessity in the chaotic times after the decline and fall of the Mycenaean kingdoms and during the tenuous growth of Greek settlements beyond the seas. What was remarkable was what the Greeks made of it, and how obstinately they were to stick to it. With survival uncertain, men in their isolated valleys had huddled for protection around some hilltop stronghold or citadel maintained by a vigorous local clan. These clans, each claiming descent from some ancestral hero or ruler, had gradually taken over the functions of decayed kingships by appointing some man or men from their own number to rule in their behalf. Sometimes they still styled these magistrates "kings" (Sparta, throughout its history as an independent city-state, had two such "kings" ruling concurrently); but actual, hereditary kingship in Greece had all but disappeared by the close of the eighth century, and all power lay in the hands of the local aristocracy and its representatives.

These feudal squires, or "first families,"—so we gather from the seventh-century poetry that tells of them—were a stout breed of men, greatly savoring the good life of war, love, and wine. They were also a jealous breed, intent on retaining sovereignty over their small specks of land. And how small some of these were: Boeotia alone, hardly the size of the smallest American state, brought forth all of twelve separate, independent city-states; the island of Ceos, only fifteen miles long and eight across, three; and all told, the number of self-governing Greek city-states was to reach a peak of perhaps fifteen hundred.

One might have thought that in time, as civil order revived in Greece along with a new sense of the community of all the Hellenes, this fragmented scheme of things would have been superseded by a drive toward over-all organization. Not at all. And here we come closest to what was both the genius and the eventual tragedy of the Greeks. They had found in the individual commune, in the self-determining locality, what seemed to them the most natural, workable, and responsive form of political life or polity—particularly as they developed the schemes of a council and of a public meeting of all citizens to hear and debate what their leaders had proposed. And though in the eighth century Sparta conquered and annexed the whole neighboring region of Messenia, and Athens expanded through Attica and later extended its influence and hegemony far beyond, the Greeks never became reconciled to any scheme stronger than that of a loose federation —certainly not to the idea of union. This was to serve them ill during the wars against Persia, when many reluctant or isolationist city-states either stood aside or gave in to the invader, not because they liked Xerxes and Darius more, but because their sense of common cause with Athens was less; and it was to prove suicidal in the end when Athens and Sparta, each proud, each vigorous, each aided by allies, but unable altogether to conceive of any general overriding Greek interest, went to war against each other in the late fifth century, to the second ruin of their land.

Yet even after that catastrophe of disunion, in the fourth century the two leading political philosophers of Greece were to go on arguing the case of the small, autonomous state, Plato in the *Republic* placing the ideal number of its citizens at 5,040 and Aristotle in his *Politics* arguing that a polis should be small enough so that all of its citizens could know each other by sight. What underlay all this thinking was a belief that every citizen should play some direct part in governance, which in turn implied a belief in the rule of law. As Pericles of Athens said, "Laws are all the rules approved and enacted by the majority in assembly, whereby they declare what ought and what ought not to be done." And the Greek mind, heady with this unprecedented idea, had doubts as to how the voice of the majority could effectively be delegated. Must not every individual citizen be permitted to stand up in the assembly and speak for himself? Even at the time of Greece's fifth-century strength there were probably no more than three city-states (Athens, Syracuse, and Acragas) with more than 20,000 citizens— the term "citizen" in the Greek context referring to those adult males who by reason of property, local birth, and other standing were eligible to vote and hold office. The citizens were only a fraction of the total population: thus while Sparta in its prime may have had 300,000 souls in its five communes and countryside, there were never more than 4,000 who could be called citizens.

The Greek respect for law, and particularly for law as enacted by will of the polis, was not of sudden birth. Centuries were needed to resolve such questions as, Whose law? For whom? One

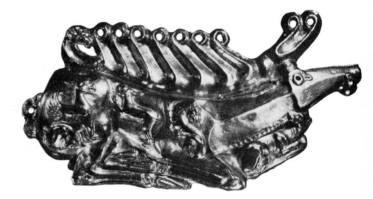

A gold ornament in the shape of a stag (above) was made by a Greek craftsman who was copying the Scythian art of southern Russia, where Greek merchants established trading settlements.
STATE HERMITAGE MUSEUM, LENINGRAD

A small bronze of a running girl comes from the Peloponnesus, the center of Dorian settlement; from here, as from elsewhere in Greece, colonists set forth to found new towns abroad.
BRITISH MUSEUM

The limestone head above is part of a representation of a mythological three-headed monster. It is from the pediment of a temple which was built on the Athenian Acropolis in the sixth century and dismantled during the Persian wars.

ACROPOLIS MUSEUM; HASSIA

law for rich and another for poor? and How to go about changing the law, once it had been set forth? The Greeks generally held that in the beginning, justice came from the gods, who punished transgressors against divine will (a paradox in later eyes, to be sure, since the gods themselves were thought to be so lawless). The early warrior-kings, ruling by fiat and caprice very much as the gods did, had naturally found it to their advantage to claim divine sanction for their acts. As man-made laws emerged, derived from ancient custom and religious observance, the Greeks felt that these laws stood under some divine protection and that their early lawgivers—such as Lycurgus of Sparta and Solon of Athens—had been directly inspired by the gods. As Demosthenes was to say to the Athenians in a celebrated address in the sophisticated fourth century: "The whole life of men, O Athenians, whether they inhabit a great city or a small one, is governed by nature and by laws. Of these, nature is a thing irregular, unequal, and peculiar to the individual possessor; laws are regular, common, and the same for all. Nature, if it be depraved, has often vicious desires; therefore you will find people of that sort falling into error. Laws desire what is just and honorable and useful; they seek for this, and, when it is found, it is set forth as a general ordinance, the same and alike for all; and that is law, which all men ought to obey for many reasons, and especially because every law is an invention and gift of the gods."

Yet it was by no means true, in the period when the aristocrats took over from the kings, that laws were "the same for all." The poet Hesiod, writing sometime around the beginning of the seventh century, spoke of "bribe-devouring judges" and complained that the ruling families tended to hand down judgments in their own favor. With the rebirth of literacy, a process began of codifying the laws that hitherto had come down orally, and of carving them on tablets (the oldest of these to survive being a city ordinance set up at Dreros on Crete perhaps in the mid seventh century); but for decades what was written down was feudal landlord's law, and it was administered by magistrates of that class. The code of the Athenian Draco, set forth in about the year 621, was particularly harsh in that it reaffirmed the right of a creditor to personally enslave a debtor for nonpayment, and even made petty pilfering punishable by death. A later biographer, Plutarch, wrote, "Those that were convicted of idleness were to die, and those that stole a cabbage or an apple to suffer even as villains that committed sacrilege or murder. . . . Draco's laws were written not with ink but blood."

Meanwhile, though, a new force was rising in the land, fired

122

by the oppressiveness of the hilltop lords, the leanness of life below, and the glimpse of better possibilities in the law. In Attica a massive protest arose among impoverished farmers, tenants, and small proprietors against the great, against the size of their holdings, and against their power to seize any person who, in a time of such scarce money, had not been able to meet his mortgage or his sharecrop payments on time. It was all very well to speak of the virtues of a community life and of self-dedication to the service of a polis. But so long as so many men remained with little land, or without land, or with their very persons pledged to some ancestral baron, wasn't this a sham?

Very many Greeks thought it was, and the late seventh century and the sixth were to see a class struggle that reached the dimensions of a social revolution. Aristotle recalled of this period that "the poor, with their wives and children, were enslaved to the rich," and had no political rights; and it was emancipation that they now demanded, turning in their turbulence to quite another type of man who might further them—the popular leader, seizing power from the nobles without any authority save his own. These men—a Pheidon of Argos, a Periander of Corinth, a Polycrates of Samos, a Gelon of Syracuse—were those whom the Greeks called *tyrannoi*, meaning self-appointed despots ruling supposedly in the people's interest; indeed, many of them did so, but enough ruled in their own interests to give the word "tyrant" the unpleasant meaning attached to it today.

Athens was to have its tyrant too in the person of Pisistratus, a most likable, benevolent, intelligent patrician who had placed himself at the head of the popular party, even as a "traitor to his class," and who shrewdly advanced the peasantry, chastened the landlord nobles, calmed civil strife, strengthened the power of Athens, and launched public works—above all, the building of the first great temples on the Acropolis. That he was able to do so much was, ironically, in part the result of the work of a man who had been put into office before him by apprehensive nobles to write reforms that would head off just such a tyrant as he.

That man, Solon, elected archon by his peers in 594 with extraordinary powers to revise their code, is one of the most appealing figures in all Greek history—as well as the first of the great Athenians. Of high birth, well-earned substance, wide travel, literary temperament, and profound humanity, he used the mandate given him to propose reforms that, while they did not satisfy all the radicals, astonished what we would call the old guard with their sweep and range. While he did not go along with the demands of the extremists that land should be redistributed, he

In the first half of the sixth century the marble sphinx above was mounted on a column more than thirty feet high and dedicated to Apollo at Delphi by the citizens of the island of Naxos.

MUSEUM, DELPHI; HARISSIADIS

CROESUS AND SOLON:

AN IMAGINARY INTERVIEW

*The historian Herodotus relates that when the fab-
ulously wealthy Croesus was ruling Lydia, he received at his court at Sardis the wise Solon of
Athens, then traveling in Asia Minor, and had
him shown over his splendid treasuries, after which
they had a conversation. The story is a fiction,
since actually Solon died about the time Croesus
came to the throne (560 B.C.), but Herodotus
makes a good one of it:*

*"Croesus addressed this question to him, 'Stranger
of Athens, we have heard much of your wisdom
and of your travels through many lands. . . . I am
curious therefore to inquire of you, whom, of all
men that you have seen, you consider the most
happy?' This he asked because he thought himself
the happiest of mortals: but Solon answered him
without flattery, according to his true sentiments,
'Tellus of Athens, sire.' Full of astonishment at
what he heard, Croesus demanded sharply, 'And
wherefore do you deem Tellus happiest?' To which
the other replied, 'First, because his country was
flourishing in his days, and he himself had sons
both beautiful and good, and he lived to see children
born to each of them, and these children all grew
up; and further because, after a life spent in what
our people look upon as comfort, his end was sur-
passingly glorious. In a battle between the Athenians
and their neighbors near Eleusis, he came to the
assistance of his countrymen, routed the foe, and
died upon the field most gallantly.' . . . Croesus
broke in angrily, 'What, stranger of Athens, is my
happiness, then, valued so little by you, that you do
not even put me on a level with private men?'
'Croesus,' replied the other, 'you asked a question
concerning the condition of man, of one who knows
that the power above us is full of jealousy, and
fond of troubling our lot. . . . I see that you are
wonderfully rich, and the lord of many nations; but
with respect to your question, I have no answer to give,
until I hear that you have closed your life happily.'"*

*Croesus ended by being vanquished and dethroned
by the Persians, with the loss of all his treasure.*

did abolish slavery for debt and furthermore abolished all existing debts involving land and rent payments, and he decreed that those Athenians who had been enslaved because of such debts should go free. The result was an immediate reduction in landlord power. Moreover, he wrote provisions designed to protect the poor against rule by the rich by setting up the right of appeal in court and that of a third party to seek justice in behalf of some accused person who might be unable to defend himself. No wonder that these reforms were celebrated by a public feast in the Agora when Solon pronounced them, for the foundations of Greek democracy and Athenian greatness were laid on that very day early in the sixth century—even though Greeks had not yet coined the term *demokratia* and though Solon's reforms were in the first instance to be administered by Pisistratus, a dictator related to him by blood.

Though later Greeks were to think that he had been inspired by the gods, Solon himself, ever urbane, felt he had been ruled by earthly good sense; he wrote in verse:

> *Such power I gave the people as might do,*
> *Abridged not what they had, now lavished new,*
> *Those that were great in wealth and high in place*
> *My counsel likewise kept from all disgrace.*
> *Before them both I held my shield of might,*
> *And let not either touch the other's right.*

Having accomplished this, he thereupon left Athens for a decade so that the polis would have time to try out his proposals without being embarrassed by his presence.

If Solon needed to enlarge his inspiration, he had the opportunity when visiting the cities of Ionia beyond the Aegean, then flourishing with commerce and arts far in advance of Athens' own, and whose literature and taste he knew well. For in prosperous Miletus, and in many other Greek settlements along the Asia Minor coast, mixtures of new blood with old, and contact with the Near East and Egypt had produced not only physical but intellectual enrichment and a life marked by lively curiosity, free self-expression, and a degree of oriental sensuousness. The art of personal, lyrical, or elegiac poetry arose, with the distinctive "measures" or rhythms in which to write it—never greater than when ever-amorous Sappho, a contemporary of Solon across the sea, wrote what is perhaps her most famous single line,

> Ἠράμαν μὲν ἔγω σέθεν, Ἄτθι, πάλαι ποτά
> *(I loved thee once, Atthis, long ago.)*

She would also compose so savage a stanza on some woman who had perhaps rejected her as this one:

Death shall be death forever unto thee,
Lady, with no remembrance of thy name
Then or thereafter; for thou gatherest not
The roses of Pieria, loving gold
Above the Muses. Even in Hades' House
Wander thou shalt unmarked, flitting forlorn
Among the shadowy, averted dead.

The worldly Ionians, by turns sunny and skeptical in disposition, and less concerned with the ancient menacing gods than with the intelligent enjoyment of a fleeting life, could well savor such a stanza as that by Mimnermus of Colophon which in translation heads this chapter. Or, relaxing in a way that their generic foes in Greece proper, the austere Dorians of the Peloponnesus, never could, they no doubt relished such a drinking song as this, by another accomplished poet of Lesbos, Alcaeus:

Zeus rains; a storm comes in its might
From heav'n, and freezes rivers tight. . .

Put down the storm! Pile up the fire,
Mix the sweet wine to your desire,
And round your forehead set
A dainty coronet.

To woe the heart must not give in.
In grief's no help. One medicine,
My friend, alone is fit—
Wine—, and get drunk on it.

Meanwhile there were more serious spirits in Ionia, who having some acquaintance with Babylonian astronomy and ancient Egyptian priestly wisdom, had then struck out to try to explain the nature of things without recourse to myth and the supernatural. Were they original in their efforts to pierce the riddle of the universe? The idea that the Ionian Greeks owed much of their dawning interest in science and philosophy to Babylonian and Egyptian sources, has until recently been widely accepted; but now some scholars discount this, believing that the unique scientific spirit of the Ionians was self-generated. A very new kind of thought sprang up in Ionia in the sixth century, particularly in the city of Miletus —the first Athens of Greece—where Western studies of the nature of things began.

Many stories have been told over many centuries about Thales of that city, the pioneer figure who always appears early in the first chapter of textbooks on the history of philosophy, and most of these tales are probably apocryphal. He is said variously to have been a shrewd Milesian trader who made a killing out of cornering the olive presses that served the market; to have been a stargazer

GLYPTOTHEK, MUNICH

Sappho, the poetess of Lesbos, was renowned for her many amorous attachments to men as well as to girls; following her death, her passionate lyrics became famous throughout Greece, and she came to be called the "tenth muse." In the vase painting above, Sappho is depicted with one of her friends, another poet of Lesbos, Alcaeus, who is shown strumming a lyre.

METROPOLITAN MUSEUM OF ART, GIFT OF J. PIERPONT MORGAN

In the eighth century, artists produced numerous small bronze animal figures like the stylized horse below and the centaur and man shown above. They were dedicated at shrines by worshipers, who customarily offered to the gods figures of the animals that were sacred to them.

METROPOLITAN MUSEUM OF ART, ROGERS FUND

who accurately predicted an eclipse of the sun that took place in the year 585; to have been an engineer who served as adviser to Croesus and who diverted the river Halys from its course. Renowned as one of the Seven Wise Men of Greece, Thales was as adventurous in thinking about the physical world as Solon was in thinking about the welfare of man.

The old creation stories of the world's rising out of Night or Chaos, with primeval gods and goddesses then mating to shape it, were simply not adequate answers to Thales' inquiring spirit. What *was* the origin and nature of the physical world—leaving the gods aside? Amid its manifold appearances, its riot of diversity, was there not some central physical scheme or substance from which everything had sprung? Thales pondered, and came forth with the surprising thought that the "world-stuff" was water, from which he thought all things had arisen and to which they would in the end return. This was a leap of the imagination that many later thinkers were to regard as challenging but naïve, but which today we do not regard as quite so naïve, with its first intimations of evolution and of the central role of hydrogen, a basic element from which other substances can be compounded. Gods were immanent in all things, Thales seems to have felt, but there was still some fundamental law or unity of nature greater than the gods; and his follower Anaximander, though disagreeing with Thales' water theory, went on—in another imaginative leap—to argue that "originally man was born from animals of another species," and that he was "like a fish, in the beginning."

Here, as Greece entered into the sixth century, was revolutionary thought—to remain revolutionary, indeed, until the priests and presbyters of the West finally yielded to Charles Darwin two and a half millennia later. But there was even more to this Greek eruption than the pursuit of natural science, poetry, and social polity. There was also a revolution in art, in this case influenced distinctly by the Orient. Egyptian heroic statuary, as known for instance to the early school of Hellenic marble carvers whose work has been found on Delos, inspired the first characteristic Greek free-standing sculpture—the tall, idealized figure of an athletic male, foursquare, left foot forward, arms firmly at his side like his Egyptian prototype. From the East also came new techniques of working in decorative metals and ivory, and the inspiration for a fanciful style of pottery painting which employed many oriental motifs. In architecture the Greeks turned from mere crude building and began to develop the distinctive styles that the world has treasured ever since.

The Mycenaeans had built no temples, only crude fortress-palaces and well-engineered subterranean tombs; what followed for centuries consisted of rude wood beams with clay or wattle sidings raised over stone footings. At some point the idea arose of extending the porch or colonnade (in the beginning fashioned of tree trunks or hewn timber) to surround a sanctuary and support its roof; and, once the idea had arisen, as in the early temple of Hera at Olympia, it led to gradual replacement of timber by stone, first in the form of monoliths, then in that of fluted drums once the original supports decayed. (Pausanias, visiting Olympia in the second century after Christ, saw one of the original oak supports of Hera's temple still standing.) In discovering the potential grace and magnificence of their own marble and limestone, the Greeks in one sense discovered themselves.

Their architecture arose from bold experiment in building and the use of native materials; their sculpture from searching thought as to grace and balance; their philosophy from inquiry independent of the gods; their style—from themselves. Conqueror had mixed with conquered; slavery was the fate of some, the idea of freedom the hope of others; the Orient helped inspire not only a Thales but a Pythagoras, the combination mathematician, musician, and mystic, who moved from Samos to southern Italy to set up his philosophic school there. This springtime of Hellas can perhaps be felt most closely in the mysterious so-called archaic smile that dominates its sculpture, as if these youthful beings and their mates had knowledge of some great though possibly short-lived fate to come. Their physical surroundings were long to remain lean and harsh, but not their intellectual ones: thus the men who designed the new temple at Corinth in the mid sixth century applied to it a most sophisticated refinement—the use of a slight correction, entasis, to swell their columns in mid-height to offset what otherwise might have been an optical impression from the ground of concavity or weakness of shape. And though the philosopher Pythagoras set up a cult surrounded by many a primitive taboo and mystic rite, and was called by his devotees a son of Apollo if not an embodiment of Apollo himself, he was the Greek who proposed the theorem that schoolboys have been asked to learn ever since, namely that the square on the hypotenuse of a right-angled triangle equals the sum of the squares on the other two sides. What is so important about that? two millennia's schoolboys have no doubt asked themselves when told to resolve it. What is important is that formulating this theorem demanded a stirring development of the human intellect. The emergence of Greece came about in large part because so many of its men were ready to make such demands on themselves.

A centaur in full gallop with his club raised and ready to strike is the subject of the sixth-century bronze above. The statue, which stands a little more than a foot high, shows the fine decorative work characteristic of the period.
METROPOLITAN MUSEUM OF ART, GIFT OF J. PIERPONT MORGAN

BRITISH MUSEUM

ΚΑΛΟΝΕ

POETS AND

TELLERS

OF TALES

*From the Muses and lord Apollo who shoots from afar
come the singers and harpers of earth; but from Zeus,
the kings.*
*Happy is he that the Muses love. When he sings,
sweetly speech from his lips forever flows.*
*Aye, though fresh troubles have crazed a man till he
knows*
*nothing but dread and despair, should a singer praise,
as the Muses' servant, the glory of ancient days,
the heroes and blessed gods of Olympus-crest,
the man will forget that he ever was darkly distressed,
such powers of healing to gifts of the Muses belong.*

Hesiod, Theogony
(*translated by Jack Lindsay*)

The Greeks particularly loved the spoken word, and the quality of their literature stems from it. Their language, with its high proportion of vowel to consonant sounds, lent itself admirably to fluid speech and rich verbal music. Swift movement combined with somber grandeur are the chief characteristics of their arch-poet, Homer. His way with words and images remained the model for subsequent centuries, and his flowing hexameter line was used for subject matter as diverse as Hesiod's homely poems of rural life and the fervent hymns sung at religious festivals as preludes to recitals of passages from the Homeric epics.

While Homer's influence was supreme, there was still place for the growth of other forms of Greek poetry. One was the choral ode, recited or sung by groups of performers and accompanied by a dance. Each stanza was designed to echo dance movements, and the meters were as complex as the dance rhythms themselves. These odes were originally dedicated to a god or hero; later, ordinary mortals were honored by them. Tragic drama itself arose from festival chants and declamation. Another type of poem was the simple solo song, originating in folksong, which reached sophistication in such hands as Sappho's. Like all Greek poetry, it was sung or recited, not just read, and usually was accompanied by music of the lyre or flute. From these songs derived the love lyric and also the elegies and epigrams written in honor of the dead, and often inscribed on tombs.

On the following pages a pair of famous episodes from the *Iliad* and the *Odyssey* are presented in recent translations, along with a selection of retellings of other Greek myths and readings of Greek lyric poetry. A panel of contrasting versions in English over the centuries of just one Homeric passage also appears as testimony to the fascination this poet has exerted over the ages.

A vase painting, opposite, depicts a bard reciting Homer at a religious festival.

ACHILLES FACES HECTOR

from the *Iliad*

(*translated by Richmond Lattimore*)

The climactic scene of the Iliad *comes in Book XXII when Achilles encounters the Trojan champion. Hector's parents, who had already lost most of their sons to Achilles, plead with Hector to avoid battle, but he refuses. He decides that either his or Achilles' death is inevitable and that he had best fight—though his courage briefly deserts him—and leave the outcome to the gods. (Here as elsewhere in the anthology pages, the spellings of proper names are those preferred by the individual translators.)*

"Better to bring on the fight with him as soon as it may be.
We shall see to which one the Olympian grants the glory."
So he pondered, waiting, but Achilleus was closing upon
him
in the likeness of the lord of battles, the helm-shining warrior,
and shaking from above his shoulder the dangerous Pelian
ash spear, while the bronze that closed about him was shining
like the flare of blazing fire or the sun in its rising.
And the shivers took hold of Hektor when he saw him, and he
could no longer
stand his ground there, but left the gates behind, and fled,
frightened,
and Peleus' son went after him in the confidence of his quick
feet.
As when a hawk in the mountains who moves lightest of things
flying
makes his effortless swoop for a trembling dove, but she slips
away
from beneath and flies and he shrill screaming close after her
plunges for her again and again, heart furious to take her;
so Achilleus went straight for him in fury, but Hektor
fled away under the Trojan wall and moved his knees rapidly.
They raced along by the watching point and the windy fig tree
always away from under the wall and along the wagon-way
and came to the two sweet-running well springs. There there
are double
springs of water that jet up, the springs of whirling
Skamandros.
One of these runs hot water and the steam on all sides

of it rises as if from a fire that was burning inside it.
But the other in the summer-time runs water that is like hail
or chill snow or ice that forms from water. Beside these
in this place, and close to them, are the washing-hollows
of stone, and magnificent, where the wives of the Trojans and
their lovely
daughters washed the clothes to shining, in the old days
when there was peace, before the coming of the sons of the
Achaians.
They ran beside these, one escaping, the other after him.
It was a great man who fled, but far better he who pursued him
rapidly, since here was no festal beast, no ox-hide
they strove for, for these are prizes that are given men for their
running.
No, they ran for the life of Hektor, breaker of horses.
As when about the turnposts racing single-foot horses
run at full speed, when a great prize is laid up for their
winning,
a tripod or a woman, in games for a man's funeral,
so these two swept whirling about the city of Priam
in the speed of their feet, while all the gods were looking upon
them.
First to speak among them was the father of gods and mortals:
"Ah me, this is a man beloved whom now my eyes watch
being chased around the wall; my heart is mourning for Hektor
who has burned in my honour many thigh pieces of oxen
on the peaks of Ida with all her folds, or again on the uttermost
part of the citadel, but now the brilliant Achilleus
drives him in speed of his feet around the city of Priam.
Come then, you immortals, take thought and take counsel,
whether
to rescue this man or whether to make him, for all his valour,
go down under the hands of Achilleus, the son of Peleus."
Then in answer the goddess grey-eyed Athene spoke to him:
"Father of the shining bolt, dark misted, what is this you said?
Do you wish to bring back a man who is mortal, one long since
doomed by his destiny, from ill-sounding death and release
him?
Do it, then; but not all the rest of us gods shall approve you."
Then Zeus the gatherer of the clouds spoke to her in answer:
"Tritogeneia, dear daughter, do not lose heart; for I say this
not in outright anger, and my meaning toward you is kindly.
Act as your purpose would have you do, and hold back no
longer."
So he spoke, and stirred on Athene, who was eager before
this,
and she went in a flash of speed down the pinnacles of
Olympos.
But swift Achilleus kept unremittingly after Hektor,
chasing him, as a dog in the mountains who has flushed from

a deer's fawn follows him through the folding ways and the
valleys,
and though the fawn crouched down under a bush and be
hidden
he keeps running and noses him out until he comes on him;
so Hektor could not lose himself from swift-footed Peleion.
If ever he made a dash right on for the gates of Dardanos
to get quickly under the strong-built bastions, endeavouring
that they from above with missiles thrown might somehow
defend him,
each time Achilleus would get in front and force him to turn
back
into the plain, and himself kept his flying course next the city.
As in a dream a man is not able to follow one who runs
from him, nor can the runner escape, nor the other pursue him,
so he could not run him down in his speed, nor the other get
clear.
How then could Hektor have escaped the death spirits, had not
Apollo, for this last and uttermost time, stood by him
close, and driven strength into him, and made his knees light?
But brilliant Achilleus kept shaking his head at his own people
and would not let them throw their bitter projectiles at Hektor
for fear the thrower might win the glory, and himself come
second.
But when for the fourth time they had come around to the well
springs
then the Father balanced his golden scales, and in them
he set two fateful portions of death, which lays men prostrate,
one for Achilleus, and one for Hektor, breaker of horses,
and balanced it by the middle; and Hektor's death-day was
heavier
and dragged downward toward death, and Phoibos Apollo
forsook him.
But the goddess grey-eyed Athene came now to Peleion
and stood close beside him and addressed him in winged words:
"Beloved
of Zeus, shining Achilleus, I am hopeful now that you and I
will take back great glory to the ships of the Achaians, after
we have killed Hektor, for all his slakeless fury for battle.
Now there is no way for him to get clear away from us,
not though Apollo who strikes from afar should be willing to
undergo
much, and wallow before our father Zeus of the aegis.
Stand you here then and get your wind again, while I go
to this man and persuade him to stand up to you in combat."
    So spoke Athene, and he was glad at heart, and obeyed her,
and stopped, and stood leaning on his bronze-barbed ash spear.
Meanwhile
Athene left him there, and caught up with brilliant Hektor,

and likened herself in form and weariless voice to Deïphobos.
She came now and stood close to him and addressed him in
winged words:
"Dear brother, indeed swift-footed Achilleus is using you
roughly
and chasing you on swift feet around the city of Priam.
Come on, then; let us stand fast against him and beat him back
from us."
    Then tall Hektor of the shining helm answered her:
"Deïphobos,
before now you were dearest to me by far of my brothers,
of all those who were sons of Priam and Hekabe, and now
I am minded all the more within my heart to honour you,
you who dared for my sake, when your eyes saw me, to come
forth
from the fortifications, while the others stand fast inside them."

Then in turn the goddess gray-eyed Athene answered him:
"My brother, it is true our father and the lady our mother,
taking
my knees in turn, and my companions about me, entreated
that I stay within, such was the terror upon all of them.
But the heart within me was worn away by hard sorrow for
you.
But now let us go straight on and fight hard, let there be no
sparing
of our spears, so that we can find out whether Achilleus
will kill us both and carry our bloody war spoils back
to the hollow ships, or will himself go down under your spear."
    So Athene spoke and led him on by beguilement.
Now as the two in their advance were come close together,
first of the two to speak was tall helm-glittering Hektor:
"Son of Peleus, I will no longer run from you, as before this
I fled three times around the great city of Priam and dared not
stand to your onfall. But now my spirit in turn has driven me
to stand and face you. I must take you now, or I must be taken.
Come then, shall we swear before the gods? For these are the
highest
who shall be witnesses and watch over our agreements.
Brutal as you are I will not defile you, if Zeus grants
to me that I can wear you out, and take the life from you.
But after I have stripped your glorious armour, Achilleus,
I will give your corpse back to the Achaians. Do you do
likewise."

Then looking darkly at him swift-footed Achilleus
answered:
"Hektor, argue me no agreements. I cannot forgive you.
As there are no trustworthy oaths between men and lions,
nor wolves and lambs have spirit that can be brought to
agreement
but forever these hold feelings of hate for each other,
so there can be no love between you and me, nor shall there be
oaths between us, but one or the other must fall before then
to glut with his blood Ares the god who fights under the
shield's guard.
Remember every valour of yours, for now the need comes
hardest upon you to be a spearman and a bold warrior.
There shall be no more escape for you, but Pallas Athene
will kill you soon by my spear. You will pay in a lump for all
those
sorrows of my companions you killed in your spear's fury."
    So he spoke, and balanced the spear far shadowed, and
threw it;
but glorious Hektor kept his eyes on him, and avoided it,
for he dropped, watchful, to his knee, and the bronze spear flew
over his shoulder
and stuck in the ground, but Pallas Athene snatched it, and
gave it
back to Achilleus, unseen by Hektor shepherd of the people.
But now Hektor spoke out to the blameless son of Peleus:
"You missed; and it was not, o Achilleus like the immortals,
from Zeus that you knew my destiny; but you thought so; or
rather
you are someone clever in speech and spoke to swindle me,
to make me afraid of you and forget my valour and war
strength.
You will not stick your spear in my back as I run away from
you
but drive it into my chest as I storm straight in against you;
if the god gives you that; and now look out for my brazen
spear. I wish it might be taken full length in your body.
And indeed the war would be a lighter thing for the Trojans
if you were dead, seeing that you are their greatest affliction."

So he spoke, and balanced the spear far shadowed, and
threw it,
and struck the middle of Peleïdes' shield, nor missed it,
but the spear was driven far back from the shield, and Hektor

was angered
because his swift weapon had been loosed from his hand in a
vain cast.
He stood discouraged, and had no other ash spears; but lifting
his voice he called aloud on Deïphobos of the pale shield,
and asked him for a long spear, but Deïphobos was not near
him.
And Hektor knew the truth inside his heart, and spoke aloud:
"No use. Here at last the gods have summoned me deathward.
I thought Deïphobos the hero was here close beside me,
but he is behind the wall and it was Athene cheating me,
and now evil death is close to me, and no longer far away,
and there is no way out. So it must long since have been
pleasing
to Zeus, and Zeus' son who strikes from afar, this way; though
before this
they defended me gladly. But now my death is upon me.
Let me at least not die without a struggle, inglorious,
but do some big thing first, that men to come shall know of it."
    So he spoke, and pulling out the sharp sword that was slung
at the hollow of his side, huge and heavy, and gathering
himself together, he made his swoop, like a high-flown eagle
who launches himself out of the murk of the clouds on the flat
land
to catch away a tender lamb or a shivering hare; so
Hektor made his swoop, swinging his sharp sword, and
Achilleus
charged, the heart within him loaded with savage fury.
In front of his chest the beautiful elaborate great shield
covered him, and with the glittering helm with four horns
he nodded; the lovely golden fringes were shaken about it
which Hephaistos had driven close along the horn of the
helmet.
And as a star moves among stars in the night's darkening,
Hesper, who is the fairest star who stands in the sky, such
was the shining from the pointed spear Achilleus was shaking
in his right hand with evil intention toward brilliant Hektor.
He was eyeing Hektor's splendid body, to see where it might
best
give way, but all the rest of the skin was held in the armour,
brazen and splendid, he stripped when he cut down the
strength of Patroklos;
yet showed where the collar-bones hold the neck from the
shoulders,
the throat, where death of the soul comes most swiftly; in this
place
brilliant Achilleus drove the spear as he came on in fury,
and clean through the soft part of the neck the spearpoint was
driven.
Yet the ash spear heavy with bronze did not sever the windpipe,

so that Hektor could still make exchange of words spoken.
But he dropped in the dust, and brilliant Achilleus vaunted
                                        above him:
"Hektor, surely you thought as you killed Patroklos you would
                                        be
safe, and since I was far away you thought nothing of me,
o fool, for an avenger was left, far greater than he was,
behind him and away by the hollow ships. And it was I;
and I have broken your strength; on you the dogs and the
                                        vultures
shall feed and foully rip you; the Achaians will bury Patroklos."
    In his weakness Hektor of the shining helm spoke to him:
"I entreat you, by your life, by your knees, by your parents,
do not let the dogs feed on me by the ships of the Achaians,
but take yourself the bronze and gold that are there in
                                        abundance,
those gifts that my father and the lady my mother will give
                                        you,
and give my body to be taken home again, so that the Trojans
and the wives of the Trojans may give me in death my rite of
                                        burning."
    But looking darkly at him swift-footed Achilleus answered:
"No more entreating of me, you dog, by knees of parents.
I wish only that my spirit and fury would drive me
to hack your meat away and eat it raw for the things that
you have done to me. So there is no one who can hold the dogs
                                        off
from your head, not if they bring here and set before me ten
                                        times
and twenty times the ransom, and promise more in addition,
not if Priam son of Dardanos should offer to weigh out
your bulk in gold; not even so shall the lady your mother
who herself bore you lay you on the death-bed and mourn you:
no, but the dogs and the birds will have you all for their
                                        feasting."
    Then, dying, Hektor of the shining helmet spoke to him:
"I know you well as I look upon you, I know that I could not
persuade you, since indeed in your breast is a heart of iron.
Be careful now; for I might be made into the gods' curse
upon you, on that day when Paris and Phoibos Apollo
destroy you in the Skaian gates, for all your valour."
    He spoke, and as he spoke the end of death closed in upon
                                        him,
and the soul fluttering free of the limbs went down into
                                        Death's house
mourning her destiny, leaving youth and manhood behind her.
Now though he was a dead man brilliant Achilleus spoke to
                                        him:
"Die: and I will take my own death at whatever time
Zeus and the rest of the immortals choose to accomplish it."

THE DEADLY BOWMAN
from the *Odyssey*
(*translated by Robert Fitzgerald*)

*When Odysseus returned home to
Ithaca, disguised as a poor wanderer, he
revealed himself to his son Telemachus
and to a few retainers. His long-wait-
ing wife Penelope, beset by suitors,
had declared that she would wed the
one who could string and shoot a great
bow Odysseus had left behind. None
was able to do it, and when the vagabond Odysseus tried to, they were out-
raged at his insolence. To their astonishment, he succeeded in stringing and
shooting the bow. He and his son were
now ready to battle and vanquish them.*

Eurýmakhos had now picked up the bow.
He turned it round, and turned it round
before the licking flame to warm it up,
but could not, even so, put stress upon it
to jam the loop over the tip
                        though his heart groaned to bursting.
Then he said grimly:
                                        "Curse this day.
What gloom I feel, not for myself alone,
and not only because we lose that bride.
Women are not lacking in Akhaia,
in other towns, or on Ithaka. No, the worst
is humiliation—to be shown up for children
measured against Odysseus—we who cannot
even hitch the string over his bow.
What shame to be repeated of us, after us!"
Antínoös said:
                                        "Come to yourself. You know
that is not the way this business ends.
Today the islanders held holiday, a holy day,
no day to sweat over a bowstring.
                                        Keep your head.
Postpone the bow. I say we leave the axes
planted where they are. No one will take them.
No one comes to Odysseus' hall tonight.
Break out good wine and brim our cups again,
we'll keep the crooked bow safe overnight,
order the fattest goats Melánthios has
brought down tomorrow noon, and offer thighbones burning
to Apollo, god of archers,

while we try out the bow and make the shot."
As this appealed to everyone, heralds came
pouring fresh water for their hands, and boys
filled up the winebowls. Joints of meat went round,
fresh cuts for all, while each man made his offering,
tilting the red wine to the gods, and drank his fill.
Then spoke Odysseus, all craft and gall:
"My lords, contenders for the queen, permit me:
a passion in me moves me to speak out.
I put it to Eurýmakhos above all
and to that brilliant prince, Antínoös. Just now
how wise his counsel was, to leave the trial
and turn your thoughts to the immortal gods! Apollo
will give power tomorrow to whom he will.
But let me try my hand at the smooth bow!
Let me test my fingers and my pull
to see if any of the oldtime kick is there,
or if thin fare and roving took it out of me."
Now irritation beyond reason swept them all,
since they were nagged by fear that he could string it.
Antínoös answered, coldly and at length:
"You bleary vagabond, no rag of sense is left you.
Are you not coddled here enough, at table
taking meat with gentlemen, your betters,
denied nothing, and listening to our talk?
When have we let a tramp hear all our talk?
The sweet goad of wine has made you rave!
Here is the evil wine can do
to those who swig it down. Even the centaur
Eurýtion, in Peiríthoös' hall
among the Lapíthai, came to a bloody end
because of wine; wine ruined him: it crazed him,
drove him wild for rape in that great house.
The princes cornered him in fury, leaping on him
to drag him out and crop his ears and nose.
Drink had destroyed his mind, and so he ended
in that mutilation—fool that he was.
Centaurs and men made war for this,
but the drunkard first brought hurt upon himself.
The tale applies to you: I promise you
great trouble if you touch that bow. You'll come by
no indulgence in our house; kicked down
into a ship's bilge, out to sea you go,
and nothing saves you. Drink, but hold your tongue.
Make no contention here with younger men."
At this the watchful queen Penélopê
interposed:

                    "Antínoös, discourtesy
to a guest of Telémakhos—whatever guest—
that is not handsome. What are you afraid of?

Suppose this exile put his back into it
and drew the great bow of Odysseus—
could he then take me home to be his bride?
You know he does not imagine that! No one
need let that prospect weigh upon his dinner!
How very, very improbable it seems."
It was Eurýmakhos who answered her:
"Penélopê, O daughter of Ikários,
most subtle queen, we are not given to fantasy.
No, but our ears burn at what men might say
and women, too. We hear some jackal whispering:
'How far inferior to the great husband
her suitors are! Can't even budge his bow!
Think of it; and a beggar, out of nowhere,
strung it quick and made the needle shot!'
That kind of disrepute we would not care for."
Penélopê replied, steadfast and wary:
"Eurýmakhos, you have no good repute
in this realm, nor the faintest hope of it—
men who abused a prince's house for years,
consumed his wine and cattle. Shame enough.
Why hang your heads over a trifle now?
The stranger is a big man, well-compacted,
and claims to be of noble blood.
Ai!
Give him the bow, and let us have it out!
What I can promise him I will:
if by the kindness of Apollo he prevails
he shall be clothed well and equipped.
A fine shirt and a cloak I promise him;
a lance for keeping dogs at bay, or men;
a broadsword; sandals to protect his feet;
escort, and freedom to go where he will."
Telémakhos now faced her and said sharply:
"Mother, as to the bow and who may handle it
or not handle it, no man here
has more authority than I do—not one lord
of our own stony Ithaka nor the islands lying
east toward Elis: no one stops me if I choose
to give these weapons outright to my guest.
Return to your own hall. Tend your spindle.
Tend your loom. Direct your maids at work.
This question of the bow will be for men to settle,
most of all for me. I am master here."
She gazed in wonder, turned, and so withdrew,
her son's clearheaded bravery in her heart.
But when she had mounted to her rooms again
with all her women, then she fell to weeping
for Odysseus, her husband. Grey-eyed Athena
presently cast a sweet sleep on her eyes.

The swineherd had the horned bow in his hands
moving toward Odysseus, when the crowd
in the banquet hall broke into an ugly din,
shouts rising from the flushed young men:

           "Ho! Where
do you think you are taking that, you smutty slave?"
"What is this dithering?"

              "We'll toss you back alone
among the pigs, for your own dogs to eat,
if bright Apollo nods and the gods are kind!"
He faltered, all at once put down the bow, and stood
in panic, buffeted by waves of cries,
hearing Telémakhos from another quarter
shout:
"Go on, take him the bow!

          Do you obey this pack?
You will be stoned back to your hills! Young as I am
my power is over you! I wish to God
I had as much the upper hand of these!
There would be suitors pitched like dead rats
through our gate, for the evil plotted here!"
Telémakhos' frenzy struck someone as funny,
and soon the whole room roared with laughter at him,
so that all tension passed. Eumaios picked up
bow and quiver, making for the door,
and there he placed them in Odysseus' hands.
Calling Eurýkleia to his side he said:

"T elémakhos
trusts you to take care of the women's doorway.
Lock it tight. If anyone inside
should hear the shock of arms or groans of men
in hall or court, not one must show her face,
but go on with her weaving."

          The old woman
nodded and kept still. She disappeared
into the women's hall, bolting the door behind her.
Philoítios left the house now at one bound,
catlike, running to bolt the courtyard gate.
A coil of deck-rope of papyrus fiber
lay in the gateway; this he used for lashing,
and ran back to the same stool as before,
fastening his eyes upon Odysseus.

         And Odysseus took his time,
turning the bow, tapping it, every inch,
for borings that termites might have made
while the master of the weapon was abroad.

The suitors were now watching him, and some
jested among themselves:

                "A bow lover!"
"Dealer in old bows!"

             "Maybe he has one like it
at home!"

         "Or has an itch to make one for himself."
"See how he handles it, the sly old buzzard!"
And one disdainful suitor added this:
"May his fortune grow an inch for every inch he bends it!"
But the man skilled in all ways of contending,
satisfied by the great bow's look and heft,
like a musician, like a harper, when
with quiet hand upon his instrument
he draws between his thumb and forefinger
a sweet new string upon a peg: so effortlessly
Odysseus in one motion strung the bow.
Then slid his right hand down the cord and plucked it,
so the taut gut vibrating hummed and sang
a swallow's note.

         In the hushed hall it smote the suitors
and all their faces changed. Then Zeus thundered
overhead, one loud crack for a sign.
And Odysseus laughed within him that the son
of crooked-minded Kronos had flung that omen down.
He picked one ready arrow from his table
where it lay bare: the rest were waiting still
in the quiver for the young men's turn to come.
He nocked it, let it rest across the handgrip,
and drew the string and grooved butt of the arrow,
aiming from where he sat upon the stool.

            Now flashed
arrow from twanging bow clean as a whistle
through every socket ring, and grazed not one,
to thud with heavy brazen head beyond.

           Then quietly
Odysseus said:

         "Telémakhos, the stranger
you welcomed in your hall has not disgraced you.
I did not miss, neither did I take all day
stringing the bow. My hand and eye are sound,
not so contemptible as the young men say.
The hour has come to cook their lordships' mutton—
supper by daylight. Other amusements later,
with song and harping that adorn a feast."
He dropped his eyes and nodded, and the prince
Telémakhos, true son of King Odysseus,
belted his sword on, clapped hand to his spear,
and with a clink and glitter of keen bronze
stood by his chair, in the forefront near his father.

SIX WAYS OF READING HOMER

Of all the modern European tongues, only Italian can approximate the rapid flow of classical Greek. Yet poets in many languages and centuries have sought to recapture the swift beat and imagery of Homer in particular, compelled by his bardic power. Here six English and American poets, translators of the Iliad *in several eras record one of the epic's most poignant scenes, found in Book VI, when Hector's little son is*

George Chapman, 1612

This said, he reach'd to take his son; who, of his arms afraid,
And then the horse-hair plume, with which he was so overlaid,
Nodded so horribly, he cling'd back to his nurse, and cried.
Laughter affected his great sire, who doff'd, and laid aside
His fearful helm, that on the earth cast round about it light;
Then took and kiss'd his loving son, and (balancing his weight
In dancing him) these loving vows to living Jove he us'd,
And all the other bench of Gods: "O you that have infus'd
Soul to this infant, now set down this blessing on his star;—
Let his renown be clear as mine; equal his strength in war;
And make his reign so strong in Troy, that years to come may
yield
His facts this fame, when, rich in spoils, he leaves the conquer'd
field
Sown with his slaughters: 'These high deeds exceed his father's
worth.'
And let this echo'd praise supply the comforts to come forth
Of his kind mother with my life."

Alexander Pope, 1715

Thus having spoke, the illustrious chief of Troy
Stretch'd his fond arms to clasp the lovely boy.
The babe clung crying to his nurse's breast,
Scared at the dazzling helm, and nodding crest.
With secret pleasure each fond parent smiled,
And Hector hasted to relieve his child,
The glittering terrors from his brows unbound,
And placed the beaming helmet on the ground;
Then kiss'd the child, and, lifting high in air,
Thus to the gods preferr'd a father's prayer:

"O thou! whose glory fills the ethereal throne,
And all ye deathless powers! protect my son!

Grant him, like me, to purchase just renown,
To guard the Trojans, to defend the crown,
Against his country's foes the war to wage,
And rise the Hector of the future age!
So when triumphant from successful toils
Of heroes slain he bears the reeking spoils,
Whole hosts may hail him with deserved acclaim,
And say, 'This chief transcends his father's fame':
While pleased amidst the general shouts of Troy,
His mother's conscious heart o'erflows with joy."

William Cowper, 1791

So saying, illustrious Hector stretch'd his arms
Forth to his son, but with a scream, the child
Fell back into the bosom of his nurse,
His father's aspect dreading, whose bright arms
He had attentive mark'd and shaggy crest
Playing tremendous o'er his helmet's height.
His father and his gentle mother laugh'd,
And noble Hector lifting from his head
His dazzling helmet, placed it on the ground,
Then kiss'd his boy and dandled him, and thus
In earnest prayer the heavenly powers implored.

Hear all ye Gods! as ye have given to me,
So also on my son excelling might
Bestow, with chief authority in Troy.
And be his record this, in time to come,
When he returns from battle. Lo! how far
The son excels the sire! May every foe
Fall under him, and he come laden home
With spoils blood-stain'd to his dear mother's joy.

frightened by his father's appearance in battle dress. Each poet, while reaching for Homer's spirit, reflects the style of his own times. Chapman (the first translator of Homer into English) writes with Elizabethan amplitude; Pope, with his era's artifice and elegance; Cowper, with echoes of Milton as recalled in late Georgian times; the American Bryant, with the floridness of the romantic period; and the contemporary Lattimore and Graves, with the earthy speech of our own times coupled with an imaginative use of pungent rhythm. Lattimore harks back to Homer's own pulse, without recourse to the device of rhyme, and Graves boldly invents his own rhythms. Thus Homer sings variously down through the ages, finding new voices in each.

William Cullen Bryant, 1870

So speaking mighty Hector stretched his arms
To take the boy; the boy shrank crying back
To his fair nurse's bosom, scared to see
His father helmeted in glittering brass,
And eying with affright the horse-hair plume
That grimly nodded from the lofty crest.
At this both parents in their fondness laughed;
And hastily the mighty Hector took
The helmet from his brow and laid it down
Gleaming upon the ground, and, having kissed
His darling son and tossed him up in play,
Prayed thus to Jove and all the gods of heaven:—
    "O Jupiter and all ye deities,
Vouchsafe that this my son may yet become
Among the Trojans eminent like me,
And nobly rule in Ilium. May they say,
'This man is greater than his father was!'
When they behold him from the battle-field
Bring back the bloody spoil of the slain foe,—
That so his mother may be glad at heart."

Richmond Lattimore, 1951

So speaking glorious Hektor held out his arms to his baby,
who shrank back to his fair-girdled nurse's bosom
screaming, and frightened at the aspect of his own father,
terrified as he saw the bronze and the crest with its horse-hair,
nodding dreadfully, as he thought, from the peak of the helmet.
Then his beloved father laughed out, and his honoured mother,
and at once glorious Hektor lifted from his head the helmet
and laid it in all its shining upon the ground. Then taking
up his dear son he tossed him about in his arms, and kissed him,

and lifted his voice in prayer to Zeus and the other immortals:
"Zeus, and you other immortals, grant that this boy, who is my
                                                        son,
may be as I am, pre-eminent among the Trojans,
great in strength, as am I, and rule strongly over Ilion;
and some day let them say of him: 'He is better by far than his
                                                        father,'
as he comes in from the fighting; and let him kill his enemy
and bring home the blooded spoils, and delight the heart of his
                                                        mother."

Robert Graves, 1959

He stretched out a hand towards little Scamandrius, who shrank away, hugging his pretty nurse-maid; the bronze armour terrified him, and so did the tall horsehair plume that nodded fiercely from his father's helmet-top. Andromache smiled; Hector smiled too. He removed the helmet, laid it shining on the ground, took Scamandrius in his arms, kissing and dandling him, and then prayed:

      "O ZEUS, Sole Ruler of the Sky,
      And all you other gods on high,
      Grant that my infant son may live
      To gather fame superlative.
      Reserve, I beg you, for this boy
      A bold, strong heart to govern Troy
      And shine as once his father shone.
      May the whole city muse upon
      His feats, as often as the car
      Brings him spoil-laden home from war
      (Spoil reddened with the owner's gore)
      To cheer his mother's heart once more;
      Then let all say, if say they can:
      'His father was the lesser man!'"

ENDURING MYTHS

Ancestral tales provided a great trove of subject matter for Greek poetry as well as for Greek drama. They were incorporated into individual odes or lyrics and into the Homeric hymns—festival chants written in the Homeric style. One of the most eloquent recounters of myths was Hesiod, whose long poems tell of the creation of the universe, the birth of the gods, and the five ages of mankind.

The Ages of Man
Hesiod
(*translated by Jack Lindsay*)

Then Zeus the Father again made humankind,
a breed of Bronze, far differently designed,
a breed from the Ash-tree sprung, huge-limbed and dread,
lovers of battle and horror, no eaters of bread.
Their hearts were hard, their adamant hearts: none stood
to meet their power of limb and their hardihood
and the swing of the terrible arms their shoulders bore.
Bronze were their homes, bronze the armour they wore,
and their tools; for no dark iron supplied their needs.
And they murdered one another with violent deeds
and down to the house of dank chill Hades they went
and left no name. In black Death's grasp they spent
their turbulence, and lost the land of day,
and in time the earth received and hid them away.

Again on the bountiful earth by heaven was sent
a worthier race; on righteous deeds they were bent,
divine, heroic—as demigods they are known,
and the boundless earth had their race before our own.
Some of them met grim war and its battle-fates:
in the land of Kadmos at Thebes with seven gates
they fought for Oedipus' flocks disastrously,
or were drawn to cross the gulf of mighty sea
for sake of Helen tossing her beautiful hair,
and death was the sudden shroud that wrapped them there.
But for some by grace of Zeus a fertile ground
apart from men, at the ends of the earth was found;
and there they dwell with never a care distressed,
by deep-swirled Ocean, safe in isles of the blest:
delighted heroes for whom in the fields of corn
honey-fruit thrice in the year is lusciously born.

Fifth is the race that I call my own and abhor.
O to die, or be later born, or born before!
This is the Race of Iron. Dark is their plight.
Toil and sorrow by day are theirs, and by night

the anguish of death; and the gods afflict them and kill,
though there's yet a trifle of good amid manifold ill.
And Zeus will smash them in turn on his chosen day,
when children at birth show heads already grown grey.

Father and child will quarrel and bring the end,
guest with host will quarrel, and friend with friend.
No brother will claim from brother the love once claimed,
and parents will quickly age, dishonoured and shamed,
and men will scorn them and bitter words they'll say,
hard-hearted, no longer god-fearing. They'll not repay
the cost of their nurture, but might their right they'll call,
and ravaging men will break through a city-wall.
No favour will then be found for the true or the just
or the good, but men will praise the creature of lust
and violence. Might will rule while decency dies.
Giving false witness and swearing to any lies,
the wicked will trick the worthy and strike them down.
Envy, that's foul of the mouth and dark with a frown,
will dog all mortals, for evil is his delight.
Down the broad paths of the earth for Olympus-height,
forsaking the human race for the gods, in flight
with beautiful bodies veiled in their robes of white,
Forbearance and Righteous Wrath will depart, and leave
evil too great to resist, and mortals who grieve.

The Birth of Apollo
A Homeric Hymn
(*translated by F. L. Lucas*)

But soon as Eileithyia touched Dēlos, suddenly
The birth-pangs fell on Lēto, and the longing to be free.
On the soft grasses kneeling, tightly her arms she cast
About the palm of Dēlos. And all at once there passed
A smile across the face of earth—and forth he sprang
To the light of day, Apollo! Loud through the island rang
The cry of the Immortals; and then, O Archer-lord,
Over thy limbs the water, stainless-clear, they poured,
And wrapped a robe of the fine-spun wool, snow-white,
                                          around,
And about thee for a girdle a band of gold they bound.
But the golden-sworded Apollo knew not his mother's
                                          breast;
Ambrosia sweet, and nectar, unto his lips were pressed
By the deathless hands of Thĕmis. And Lēto's heart grew
                                          glad
To think what a mighty archer, and stalwart son, she had.
But, at the taste of that food divine, no girdling gold,
No swaddling bands, O Phoebus, thy quivering limbs could
                                          hold.
And as thy limbs were loosened, in the Immortals' ear

The voice of Phoebus Apollo on a sudden rang out clear;
"Let me love the cry of the lyre, let me love the bended bow,
And the will of Zeus, that fails not, through *me* mankind
shall know."
Then up he leapt, far-striding o'er earth's immensity,
The Archer-god Apollo, with his tresses tossing free . . .

Pelops the Lover

Pindar (translated by H. T. Wade-Gery and C. M. Bowra)

When he came to the sweet flower of his growth
And down covered his darkening chin,
He lifted his thoughts to a bridal awaiting him,
To have far-famed Hippodameia
From her Pîsan father.
He went down beside the grey sea
In the darkness alone,
And cried to the loud-bellowing Lord of the
Trident.

And the God was with him
Close beside his feet: and Pelops said:
"If the dear love you had of me, Poseidon,
Can turn, I pray, to good,
Keep fast now the brazen spear of Oinomáos,
And on the swiftest chariots carry me
To Elis, and bring me to victory;
For he has slain thirteen men that wooed her,
And puts back the bridal day
Of his daughter. The danger is great,
And calls not the coward: but of us who must die,
Why should a man sit in darkness
And cherish to no end
An old age without a name,
Letting go all lovely things?
For me this ordeal waits: and you
Give me the issue I desire."
So he spoke, and the prayer he made was not
unanswered.
The God glorified him, and gave him a chariot of
gold,
And wing'd horses that never tired.
So he brought down the strength of Oinomáos,
And the maiden to share his bed.
She bore him princes,
Six sons eager in nobleness.
And now, by the ford of Alpheios,
He is drenched with the glorious blood-offerings,
With a busy tomb beside that altar
Where strangers come past number.

Anchises and Aphrodite
A Homeric Hymn
(translated by F. L. Lucas)

Therefore in Aphrodite Zeus awakened then
Sweet longing for Anchises, fair as the Heaven's kings,
As he kept his kine on Ida, mount of the many springs.
The laughter-loving Cypris, she saw him, and her heart
Maddened with measureless longing. Swiftly she fled apart
To her fragrant shrine in Paphos, far on the Cypriot shores,
Tree-girt, asmoke with incense, and shut its shining doors.
Round her the Graces gathered, and bathed her beauty there
With water, and oil ambrosial, that makes more fair
Even the Gods undying. New-clad and golden-bright,
Once more the Laughter-lover soared through the cloudy
height—
From the sweet airs of Cyprus to Troy and Ida's head,
Mount of the many waters, mother of beasts, she sped.
Over the hill, to the neatherds' byre, she passed; and as she
came,
The grey wolves followed, fawning, and lions with eyes on
flame,
And bears, and lightfoot leopards, devourers of the deer.
The Goddess smiled to see them; and on all, both far and near,
She cast her lure of longing—back to their forest-dens,
Pair by pair, they vanished, down the darkness of the glens.
But herself to the herdsmen's huts she came, built well and
fair,
And alone she found Anchises, left by his comrades there
In his god-given beauty. For all the rest were gone
With their herds to the mountain-meadows; and he was left
alone,
Striding forth and backward, while the cry of his harp rang
clear.
Then Zeus-born Aphrodite stepped forward and drew near,
Changed to the form and stature of a young unwedded maid,
Lest his eyes discern her godhead and the hero grow afraid.
Then Anchises saw and wondered—so beautiful she seemed,
So tall she towered before him, so gay her garments gleamed.
For the robe that rippled round her, shone like a fire ablaze,
Richly her twisted armlets, her earrings flashed their rays,
Round her soft throat fair chains of gold glanced fitfully,
Light from her soft breasts shimmered, like moonlight, strange
to see.
Then passion gripped Anchises. Swift was his greeting given—
"Hail to Thee, Queen, who'er Thou art among the Blessed in
Heaven!
Whether the bright-eyed Pallas, or Thĕmis high of heart,
Or Lēto, or Aphrodite, or Artemis Thou art,
Or one of the deathless Graces come earthward, it may be,
Who walk, men say, in Heaven in the high Gods' company;
Or one of the Nymphs that harbour in springs whence rivers
rill,
Or deep in the lovely woodland, or up the grassy hill.
Now on some far-seen summit that looks across the lands
For Thee will I build an altar, and bring Thee with my hands
Fair gifts through the circling seasons. . . ."

THE VOICE OF THE MUSE

. . . on love

Mimnermus (*translated by F. L. Lucas*)

Ah, what is life?—what is joy?—but Aphrodite the
                                        golden?
Let me die, when I am gladdened no more by things like
                                        these—
Her gifts honey-sweet, and the bed of love, by none beholden,
    And all the flowers of youth, that are so sweet to seize,
For the hands of man and woman. But he who is once o'ertaken
    By grim old age, that makes him ugly at once and base,
With misery and anguish his heart without cease is shaken,
    No more to the sun rejoicing, thenceforth, he turns his face.
Hateful he grows to boyhood, a scorn to women's gaze—
Such is the bitter burden God made life's latter days.

Moschus (*translated by P. B. Shelley*)

Pan loved his neighbour Echo—but that child
    Of Earth and Air pined for the Satyr leaping;
The Satyr loved with wasting madness wild
    The bright nymph Lŷda,—and so three went
                                        weeping
As Pan loved Echo, Echo loved the Satyr,
    The Satyr, Lŷda; and so love consumed them.—
And thus to each—which was a woful matter—
    To bear what they inflicted Justice doomed them;
For, inasmuch as each might hate the lover,
    Each loving, so was hated.—Ye that love not
Be warned—in thought turn this example over,
    That when ye love, the like return ye prove not.

. . . on death

Anonymous (*translated by Richmond Lattimore*)

When Leárete died her father set up a monument
which has beauty. But we shall nevermore see her alive.

Simonides (*translated by Richmond Lattimore*)

This is the grave of that Megístias, whom once the Persians
    and Medes killed when they crossed Spercheíos River; a
                                        seer
who saw clearly the spirits of death advancing upon him,
    yet could not bring himself to desert the Spartiate kings.

Anonymous (*translated by Richmond Lattimore*)

Whether you are a citizen or a stranger coming from
                                        elsewhere,
take pity on Téttichos as you pass by: a brave man
killed in battle, who there lost the pride of his fresh youth.
Mourn for him a while, and go on. May your fortune be good.

*Most of the lyrics that were written in Greece and Ionia during the heyday of the
short poem in the seventh and sixth centuries have been lost. Of the great majority
of poets who wrote at that time, most notably Sappho, we have but a few individual
poems, or fragments that survived only because they were quoted in the works of
later authors. The following pages present a selection, by various translators, of Greek
lyrics, some of which were written as late as the Hellenistic period. They show the
wide variety of form and subject matter that Greek poets were accustomed to use.*

Sappho (translated by F. L. Lucas)

Him I hold as happy as God in Heaven,
Who can sit and gaze on your face before him,
Who can sit and hear from your lips that sweetest
    Music they utter—

Hear your lovely laughter, that sets a-tremble
All my heart with flutterings wild as terror.
For, when I behold you an instant, straightway
    All my words fail me;

Helpless halts my tongue; a devouring fever
Runs in flame through every vein within me;
Darkness veils my vision; my ears are deafened,
    Beating like hammers;

Cold the sweat runs down me; a sudden trembling
Sets my limbs a-quiver; my face grows paler
Than the grass in summer; I see before me
    Death stand, and madness.

Sappho (translated by Richmond Lattimore)

Come to me from Crete to this holy temple,
Aphrodite. Here is a grove of apple
trees for your delight, and the smoking altars
        fragrant with incense.

Here cold water rustles down through the apple
branches; all the lawn is beset and darkened
under roses, and, from the leaves that tremble, sleep
        of enchantment

comes descending. Here is a meadow pasture
where the horses graze and with flowers of
        springtime
now in blossom, here where the light winds passing
        blow in their freshness.

Here in this place, lady of Cyprus, lightly
lifting, lightly pour in the golden goblets
as for those who keep a festival, nectar: wine for our
        drinking.

Sappho (translated by Richmond Lattimore)

This is the dust of Timas, who died before she was
        married
and whom Persephone's dark chamber accepted instead.
After her death the maidens who were her friends, with
        sharp iron
cutting their lovely hair, laid it upon her tomb.

Pindar (translated by Richmond Lattimore)

War is sweet to those who have not tried it. The
experienced man is frightened at the heart to see it
        advancing.

Theocritus (translated by Sir William Marris)

"O Pan, O Pan, where'er thou rangest now . . ."
"Master, approach: take to thee this fair pipe
  Bedded in wax that breathes of honey still,
  Bound at the lip with twine. For Love has come
  To hale me off unto the house of Death."
    Muses, forgo, forgo the pastoral song.

"Now let the briar and the thistle flower
  With violets; and the fair narcissus bloom
  On junipers: let all things go awry,
  And pines grow pears, since Daphnis is for death.
  Let stags pursue the hounds, and from the hills
  The screeching owls outsing the nightingales."
    Muses, forgo, forgo the pastoral song.

So said he then—no more. And Aphrodîtê
  Was fain to raise him; but the Destinies
  Had spun his thread right out. So Daphnis went
  Down-stream: the whirlpool closed above his head,
  The head of him whom all the Muses loved,
  Of him from whom the Nymphs were not estranged.
    Muses, forgo, forgo the pastoral song.

Whatever the worth of a man, yet poverty can bring him
   Lower than burning ague, or grey senility.
Sooner than bear it, Cyrnus, better a man should fling him
   From crags that no foot can clamber, or down the gulfs of
                       sea.

He dare not do a deed, he cannot utter sound,
   Once penury has chained him. His very tongue lies bound.

Theognis (translated by F. L. Lucas)

One is the race of Gods and men; and yet, though
                    Earth,
One common Mother, brought them both to birth,
Man is a thing of nothing, and Theirs the eternal sky,
In brazen strength for ever. But in us too can lie
Some godlike touch of heart or soul,
Though day and night we wander, powerless to descry
Where Fate hath drawn our goal.

Pindar (translated by F. L. Lucas)

Who, in his tenderest years,
   Finds some new lovely thing,
   His hope is high, and he flies
   On the wings of his manhood:
   Better than riches are his thoughts.
—But man's pleasure is a short time growing
   And it falls to the ground
   As quickly, when an unlucky twist of thought
   Loosens its roots.

Man's life is a day. What is he?
What is he not? A shadow in a dream
Is man: but when God sheds a brightness,
Shining light is on earth
And life is sweet as honey.
      Aegina, dear mother,
Keep this city in her voyage of freedom:
You, with Zeus and Lord Aiakos,
Pêleus, and noble Télamon, and Achilles.

Pindar (translated by
H. T. Wade-Gery and C. M. Bowra)

To be a good man, without blame and without
                    question,
foursquare founded hand and foot, mind also
faultless fashioned, is difficult.

Thus the word of Píttakos, but it does not
run right, though it was a wise man who said it:
that it is difficult to be excellent. Not difficult;
only a god could have this privilege; it is not *possible*
for a man not to go bad
when he has more bad luck than he can handle.
Any man is good while his luck is good,
bad when bad, and for the most part they are best
whom the gods love.

Therefore, I will not throw away my time and life
into unprofitable hope and emptiness, the search
for that object which cannot possibly be,
the Utterly Blameless Man among all of us who enjoy
man's food on the wide earth.
But if I find one, I will let you know.
No, I admire all, am a friend of any
who of his own will does nothing shameful. Against
necessity not even the gods can fight.

I do not like to find fault.
Enough for me if one is not
bad, not too unsteady, knows
what is right and good for his city,
a sound man. I will not
look out his faults. For the generation
of fools is endless. Take anything as **good**
which is not soiled with shame.

Simonides
(translated by Richmond Lattimore)

I heard the voice of that bird, son of Pólypas, whose piercing outcry
   and whose arrival announces to men the season when fields
are plowed, and the voice of her broke the heart that darkens within me,
   since other men possess my flourishing acres now,
and not for me are the mules dragging the plow through the grainland,
   since I have given my heart to the restless seafarer's life.

Theognis (translated by Richmond Lattimore)

Beware the month of Lênaion—foul days, all of them, of them, of sharp air that would flay an ox; beware the cruel hoar-frosts that Bóreas brings when he blows upon the face of the earth.

Hesiod (translated by T. F. Higham)

Over Thrace the land of horses he blows, and breathes upon the wide sea and lifts it up. Earth also and her forests bellow aloud.

On many a high-crested oak he falls, and on many a thick-set fir. In hollows of the hills he lays them low; they are brought to the earth's rich lap, and the huge wood is all in uproar.

Wild beasts shiver and set their tails between their legs. Some have pelts that are thick with fur; but even so the cold wind pierces their shaggy breasts.

Through hide of ox he goes, it does not stay him; and through the fine hairs of the goat, but not through fleeces of sheep. Because their wool is abundant, Bóreas, that mighty wind, pierces them not at all. But the old man is bent before him, like a wheel.

Neither does he pierce the tender skin of a girl, while yet she keeps to the house at her mother's side, unschooled by golden Aphrodîtê.

Carefully she bathes her gentle body and anoints it with olive oil; and so will go to her bed in a room withdrawn.

For then is the season of winter, when the Boneless One gnaws his foot in a fireless home and habitations of sorry comfort; nor does the sun beckon him forth where he may feed, but wheels about over the land and city of the Black Men and shines less readily upon the Hellene race.

Then too wild creatures of the woods, horned and hornless, whimper for misery as they flee through the forest dales. No thought is theirs but to find shelter in thick coverts or the hollow of a rock.

Feeble then as a three-legged mortal, as one back-broken and staring towards the ground, they go about to escape the white snow.

Then wrap yourself up, as I bid you, in a soft cloak and a tunic of body-length; and look to the making, that the weft be thick and the warp spare.

This take, and clothe yourself, that the hairs of your body may lie at rest and not start up on end.

And bind sandals upon your feet, cut to measure from the hide of a slaughtered ox, and stuffed with a lining of felt.

Take also, when the cold season comes, the skins of firstling kids, and stitch them together with ox-sinew, to shield your back against the rain.

And wear on your head a hat made up of felt, to keep your ears dry.

For morning strikes cold, once Bóreas is upon us; and at morning also a mist comes down from the heavens of stars.

Upon the fields of the rich it is spread, and nurtures the corn.

Sucked from the ever flowing rivers and raised high aloft by the stormy wind, sometimes it turns to rain towards evening; and sometimes to wind, when Thracian Bóreas packs cloud upon cloud.

All his days Hélios, the Sun, has hard work for his
                                  portion.

Mimnermus
(translated by Richmond Lattimore)

Never is there any pause for rest that is given to him,
either himself or his horses, once Dawn of the rosy fingers,
   leaving the Ocean waters goes on her way, up the sky.
For Hélios is carried across the sea-waves in a wondrous
   hollow cup for a bed, the work of Hephaístos' hands,
made of precious gold, and with wings. Over the sea's
                              surface
   it carries him, gratefully sleeping, from the Hespérides'
                               shore
to the Ethiopians' country. There he keeps his swift chariot
                          and horses
   waiting, until the Dawn, the early child, shall arrive.

Never man again may swear, things shall be as once they
                                were;

Archilochus (translation after J. H. Merivale)

Never more in wonder stare, since the Olympian thunderer
Bade the Sun's meridian splendour hide in shade of murky night;
While affrighted nations started, trembling at the sudden sight.
Who shall dare to doubt hereafter, whatsoever man may say?
Who refuse with stupid laughter credence to the wildest lay?
Though for pasture dolphins ranging leap the hills and scour
                             the wood,
And fierce wolves, their nature changing, dive beneath
                        th' astonished flood.

Solon (*translated by Richmond Lattimore*)

This city of ours will never be destroyed by the planning
    of Zeus, nor according to the wish of the immortal gods;
such is she who, great-hearted, mightily fathered, protects us,
    Pallas Athene, whose hands are stretched out over our heads.
But the citizens themselves in their wildness are bent on
                                            destruction
    of their great city, and money is the compulsive cause.
The leaders of the people are evil-minded. The next stage
    will be great suffering, recompense for their violent acts,
for they do not know enough to restrain their greed and
                                            apportion
    orderly shares for all as if at a decorous feast.
        .   .   .   .
    they are tempted into unrighteous acts and grow rich.
        .   .   .   .
    sparing the property neither of the public nor of the gods,
they go on stealing, by force or deception, each from the other,
    nor do the solemn commitments of Justice keep them in check;
but she knows well, though silent, what happens and what has
                                            been happening,
    and in her time she returns to extract a full revenge;
for it comes upon the entire city as a wound beyond healing,
    and quickly it happens that foul slavery is the result,
and slavery wakens internal strife, and sleeping warfare,
    and this again destroys many in the pride of their youth,
for from enemies' devising our much-adored city is afflicted
    before long by conspiracies so dear to wicked men.
Such evils are churning in the home country, but, of the
                                            impoverished,
    many have made their way abroad on to alien soil,
sold away, and shamefully going in chains of slavery . . .
        .   .   .   .
Thus the public Ruin invades the house of each citizen,
    and the courtyard doors no longer have strength to keep it
                                            away,
but it overleaps the lofty wall, and though a man runs in
    and tries to hide in chamber or closet, it ferrets him out.
So my spirit dictates to me: I must tell the Athenians
    how many evils a city suffers from Bad Government,
and how Good Government displays all neatness and order,
    and many times she must put shackles on the breakers of laws.

She levels rough places, stops Glut and Greed, takes the force
                                            from Violence;
    she dries up the growing flowers of Despair as they grow;
she straightens out crooked judgments given, gentles the swollen
    ambitions, and puts an end to acts of divisional strife;
she stills the gall of wearisome Hate, and under her influence
    all life among mankind is harmonious and does well.

Solon (*translated by Richmond Lattimore*)

My purpose was to bring my scattered people back
together. Where did I fall short of my design?
I call to witness at the judgment seat of time
one who is noblest, mother of Olympian
divinities, and greatest of them all, Black Earth.
I took away the mortgage stones stuck in her breast,
and she, who went a slave before, is now set free.
Into this sacred land, our Athens, I brought back
a throng of those who had been sold, some by due law,
though others wrongly; some by hardship pressed to escape
the debts they owed; and some of these no longer spoke
Attic, since they had drifted wide around the world,
while those in the country had the shame of slavery
upon them, and they served their masters' moods in fear.
These I set free; and I did this by strength of hand,
welding right law with violence to a single whole.
So have I done, and carried through all that I pledged.
I have made laws, for the good man and the bad alike,
and shaped a rule to suit each case, and set it down.
Had someone else not like myself taken the reins,
some ill-advised or greedy person, he would not
have held the people in. Had I agreed to do
what pleased their adversaries at that time, or what
they themselves planned to do against their enemies,
our city would have been widowed of her men. Therefore,
I put myself on guard at every side, and turned
among them like a wolf inside a pack of dogs.

ALPHA, BETA, GAMMA, DELTA...

Though archaeologists in recent years have opened new vistas of knowledge of early Mediterranean history by their decipherment of one of the puzzling Cretan and Mycenaean scripts—the one called Linear B—the classical Greek alphabet itself derives, not from this, but from the Phoenician. That alphabet, ancestor of most of those used in the world today, was introduced in Greece between the ninth and the eighth centuries. Early examples of Greek writing indicate that in borrowing the script the Greeks made the invaluable contribution of adding vowels, which the Phoenician alphabet lacked. The Greeks took five Phoenician consonants—*aleph, he, vav, yod,* and *ayin*—for which their language had no corresponding sounds, and used them to denote the vowels *alpha, epsilon, upsilon, iota,* and *omicron.* Another innovation was their invention of the letters *phi, psi, chi,* and *xi* to indicate Greek sounds that had no counterpart in the Phoenician language. By the seventh century there were three ways of inscribing alphabetic Greek: right to left; vertical; left to right on one line and right to left on the next. At first each region had its own local alphabet, but by the end of the fifth century they had all given way to the Ionic form, which we know as the classical Greek of Athens; this was the forerunner of the Cyrillic alphabet used in present-day eastern Europe. The Etruscans, however, had adapted the Chalcidian form, and it was to develop into the Roman alphabet, which we still use today.

| PHOENICIAN | | GREEK | | | ROMAN |
Name of Letter		Name of Letter	Ionic	Chalcidian	
ALEPH	𐤀	ALPHA	A	A	A
BETH	𐤁	BETA	B	B	B
GIMEL	𐤂	GAMMA	Γ	Κ	C
DALETH	𐤃	DELTA	Δ	D	D
HE	𐤄	EPSILON	E	F	E
VAV	𐤅	DIGAMMA		FϹ	F
ZAYIN	𐤆	ZETA	I	I	Z
CHETH	𐤇	ETA	日	日	H
TETH	𐤈	THETA	⊕	⊕	
YOD	𐤉	IOTA	I	I	I
KOPH	𐤊	KAPPA	K	K	K
LAMED	𐤋	LAMBDA	Λ	L	L
MEM	𐤌	MU	M	M	M
NUN	𐤍	NU	N	N	N
SAMEKH	𐤎	XI	Ξ	⊞X	X
AYIN	𐤏	OMICRON	O	O	O
PE	𐤐	PI	Γ	Γ	P
TSADE	𐤑	SAN		M	
QOPH	𐤒	KOPPA	Φ	Φ	Q
RESH	𐤓	RHO	PD	RP	R
SHIN	𐤔	SIGMA	ϟϚ	ϟ	S
TAU	𐤕	TAU	T	T	T
		UPSILON	V	Y	V
		PHI	Φ	Φ	
		CHI	X	Y↓	
		PSI	Y	Φϟ	
		OMEGA	Ω		

LEONARD VON MATT

EXPANSION
AND
ENERGY

About 750 B.C. the Greek world began to shake off the torpor that had settled over it after the Dorian invasions; Greek mariners and merchants once again explored the coasts of the Mediterranean and the Black Sea and brought back news of fertile ground and protected sites. Greek cities seeking markets for their goods, or food and land for overflowing populations, or motivated by a greed for territory, sent forth large numbers of colonists. Most of the settlers were men, and sometimes they intermarried with the natives of their new countries. There followed an inevitable exchange of ideas; but still in many ways the colonies remained essentially Greek. The greatest unifying force in the much enlarged Greek world was, of course, the existence of a common language, but almost as important were bonds of religion and shared ideals. Traders traveling back and forth between the mainland and the overseas settlements helped maintain cultural ties, and common traditions were renewed when Greeks forgathered at Panhellenic festivals such as those at Delos and Olympia. Western Mediterranean colonies were the most prosperous; the ruins of the temple of Hera at Acragas (a city settled early in the sixth century which became one of the richest and most populous towns in Sicily) are shown at left.

OVERLEAF: *Sixth-century marble lions stand guard over the island of Delos, sacred to Apollo, where pilgrims from the entire Greek world assembled annually to celebrate the god's festival.*

FRITZ HENLE, PHOTO RESEARCHERS

MUSEO NAZIONALE, NAPLES;
LEONARD VON MATT

LEONARD VON MATT

THE GREATER GREECE

Magna Graecia—the Greek colonies in Italy and Sicily—gave as much to the homeland as it had taken. Colonists in Africa and elsewhere also drew upon local societies, but it was only Italian and Sicilian settlers who made important cultural contributions; the prosperity that was derived from trade allowed their cities to encourage and support artists and thinkers. The school of Pythagoras arose in Croton. Greece found one of her finest musicians and poets in the Sicilian Stesichorus, one of her great doctors in Democides: indeed, no science or art was left unenriched by Magna Graecia.

The coin from Paestum, above, and the town's temples, right, illustrate two aspects of Magna Graecian character. Cities often spent the wealth they acquired from exports to erect magnificent sacred buildings.

GEORGE HOLTON, PHOTO RESEARCHERS

VITAL CROSSROADS

The establishment of colonies in the eighth century was largely responsible for the growth of trade and industry in the Greek world. New communities abroad had enough land to grow more food than they consumed, and they had raw materials that were scarce in Greece. The colonies' exports allowed an ever increasing number of men on the mainland to stop cultivating the land and turn to manufacturing; and overseas dwellers were hungry for manufactured products like the most important colonial import: decorated jars filled with wine and olive oil. To be sure, trade developed gradually and its beginnings were crude: farmers and artisans, producing a little more than they needed for themselves, hopefully packed their goods on mules or boats and set off; if they were lucky they found a buyer. But a commercial spirit had entered the Greek world, and by the fifth century the Greeks had developed such refinements as stabilized currencies and banks, wholesalers and retailers, factories and warehouses—in short, a working capitalistic system.

LOUVRE; GIRAUDON

Corinth took advantage of her unique position on the isthmus between the Aegean and western seas to establish important colonies. She became a major metropolis, or "mother city," and the liveliest, bawdiest, most popular stopping place in all Greece. Corinth excelled in shipbuilding and shipping; sixth-century Greek craft like those depicted in the vase painting above were probably built there. Ruins of the temple of Apollo, built at Corinth in the sixth century, are shown at right.

UNITY AT OLYMPIA

In the divided Hellenic world, with its squabbling and competitive city-states, athletics early became a major unifying force. By the eighth century the quadrennial games at Olympia had evolved into one of the most important Greek religious festivals. All wars were suspended during the games; all cities sent their best athletes to compete, participating in the quest for excellence that was one of the principal manifestations of the Greek spirit. Indeed, at times some cities were so eager to excel that they attempted to convince famous athletes to switch their citizenship or even bribed opponents to pretend defeat. Victors were given public honors and sometimes money; statues were dedicated to them, and their feats were commemorated with victory odes. From 776, the traditional date of the first festival, to the fourth century A.D. the games continued without interruption—a symbol to Greeks everywhere of the unique value of their civilization.

HARISSIADIS

AMERICAN SCHOOL
OF CLASSICAL STUDIES, ATHENS

The sixth-century temple of Hera at Olympia, the ruins of which are shown at right, was one of the oldest Doric structures. It was originally built with wooden columns which were gradually replaced with columns of stone offered by the pious. The games at Olympia, dedicated to Hera's husband Zeus, made the shrine the central meeting place of Greece. A vase at left represents a young athlete binding a fillet on his head as a sign of victory. At Olympia special sanctuaries displayed life-sized statues of victorious athletes.

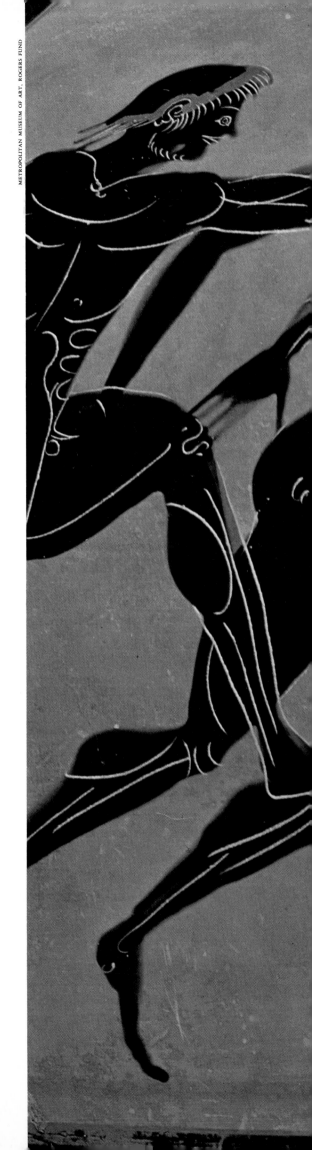

METROPOLITAN MUSEUM OF ART, ROGERS FUND

THE ATHLETIC IDEAL

"What a disgrace it is for a man to grow old without ever seeing the beauty and strength of which his body is capable," Socrates is reported to have said. For to the Greeks, training the body had long been as important as developing the mind. They prized the skills, the vitality, and most of all the style that were encouraged by athletics. The citizen had an obligation to the public as well as to himself to be trained, for he had to be prepared to serve his city in time of war. And so for all its youths the Greek state provided athletic training combined with military exercise—practice in wrestling and in javelin throwing, racing nude or dressed in armor. Athletes were taught competitiveness as well as form, competitiveness so relentless that only winners were applauded and losers were considered disgraced. It was their love for athletics that the Greeks felt distinguished them from barbarians. They alone were eligible to compete in the great periodic games at Olympia which, like those at Delphi, Corinth, and Nemea, were also religious festivals. Although all Greece acclaimed the athletic ideal, it failed to maintain it. By the middle of the fifth century professional athletes had become so prominent at Olympia that private citizens were no longer able to compete with them on equal terms.

An Athenian vase painting (right) depicts a spirited foot race.

VATICAN; ALINARI

TRAINING THE YOUNG

In most Greek cities the physical training of the young was under the direction of a public official placed in charge of the gymnasium, or sports ground. There instructors taught wrestling and ball playing, the use of weapons and the care of the body. The gymnasiums were attended mostly by youths from thirteen to nineteen who devoted their nineteenth year to military training; many adults came there regularly too, to exercise and enjoy the society of their friends. Younger boys received their training at the palaestrae, which were private establishments. In both the palaestrae and gymnasiums youths might be seen hitting punching bags, practicing wrestling holds on dummies, or running with hoops. Team sports were played too; yet, as elsewhere in Greek life, individual competition was emphasized.

A tombstone from Athens (opposite) shows a boy practicing with a hoop. Below, youths are shown in a palaestra; one folds a garment he has just removed, a second oils himself, a third searches for a thorn in a companion's foot. Two athletes at left clean themselves with iron scrapers.

STAATLICHE MUSEEN, BERLIN; HIRMER

NATIONAL MUSEUM, ATHENS; BOISSONNAS, GENEVA

MUSEO DELLE TERME,
ROME; ALINARI

MUSEUM OF FINE ARTS, BOSTON

LOUVRE

THE HARDEST TEST

The harmonious combination of beauty, skill, and strength, which the Greek athlete strove to attain, was displayed best in the pentathlon, a major contest of the Olympic festival. Unlike boxing or other contests such as chariot racing, which required the development of one skill over others, the pentathlon encouraged balance. Its five events—running, jumping, discus throwing, javelin throwing, and wrestling—all depended as much on co-ordination as they did on power. Indeed, boxing was not included among them because it gave an advantage to extremely strong or big men. Victory in the wrestling match went to the man who had achieved three falls, provided that the falls had been effected gracefully and according to the established canon of holds. If a wrestler threw his opponent clumsily, he was disqualified. Few athletes were ever able to win all five events of the pentathlon; victory in any three of them was probably enough to win a crown of olive leaves.

The five events of the pentathlon are shown on these pages. In the relief below two wrestlers are seen between a runner and a javelin thrower; one wrestler grasps his opponent's arm to swing him over a shoulder. Vase paintings show (at left) runners and (above) a jumper holding weights to increase his momentum. Opposite, a Roman copy of Myron's Discobolus *depicts the pentathlon's remaining event, the discus throw.*

MUSEUM, ATHENS; HOYNINGEN-HUENE, RAPHO-GUILLUMETTE

161

5

THE
RIVAL
CITIES

Go tell the Spartans, thou who passest by,
That here obedient to their laws we lie.

—*Simonides of Ceos: epitaph to the*
Spartan dead at Thermopylae

To sum up, I say that Athens is the school of
Hellas.
—*Pericles: funeral oration*
for the Athenian dead

What passes for Sparta today is a grubby, dusty provincial town of some 11,000 souls tucked away in the upland valley of the thin-flowing Eurotas, and neither the oleander blooming along the riverbank nor the reeds and rushes that sway handsomely with the wind can overcome, when you visit it, a general impression of torpor, oblivion, and gloom. The valley itself is not one of Greece's more favored ones. The surrounding heights are near and hard, yet not dramatic; the bottom lands are fertile, but dull: you miss the soaring mountainscape of Delphi, the splendid setting of Athens overlooking the spanking sea, the elegance of Epidaurus, poised between its well-shaped slope and pleasant water, and the enchantment of the curving vale of Olympia. You find yourself asking why, if the Greeks were so imaginative, a particularly vigorous tribe of them—the Dorian conquerors of the Peloponnesus—should have picked this landlocked, ordinary spot as the seat of their kingdom, when there was so much else to beckon them—sites as splendid as Mycenae, looming on its crags high over coastal plains and strategic bays. One answer is that there were many kinds of Greeks, and that imagination was the least of the qualities that distinguished those who became the Spartans of history—a breed that eventually became as dour and ingrown as Sparta's landscape.

Thucydides, an Athenian, was to write of the city that engaged his own in mortal combat: "If Sparta were laid waste and there remained nothing but the temples and the foundations of public buildings, posterity, I think, would find it difficult to believe that the power of this town corresponded to its fame." In the end Sparta was to be destroyed—not so much by others as by its own shortcomings—and if hardly a foundation stone survived, that was primarily because the Spartans had laid so few. While other cities built, Sparta drilled; what its people in fact constructed was little more than an armed camp surrounded by outposts and dependent villages, and sustained by a military code. Yet it was this barracks of a state that led almost all the Greek peninsula when Athens was still only a second-rate power, and that in the end succeeded in bringing down its rival from a zenith of Periclean brilliance and glory into humiliation and shame.

Athens and Sparta are not even one hundred fifty miles apart, separated by Attica's western slopes and the narrow isthmus of Corinth that leads down into the province of Argolis, but in their primes they moved at the opposite poles of Greek being and met chiefly to collide. There are few greater paradoxes in history: here were two communities of men settled on the same south-European outcrop, related by origin, speaking the same language, worshiping the same gods, linked by tales of common ancestral heroes, and equally proud of their Hellenic superiority over the *barbaroi*, or lesser breeds without the law; yet they were so diametrically different in their ways of living and thinking as to make each in effect the reverse of the other—though also, in another sense, the complement.

Fifth-century Athens stood at the cosmopolitan crossroads of the Greek world, bustling with trade, its Piraeus port lined with ships, its streets crowded with visitors from Asia Minor, Sicily, Egypt. Sparta sat in the hinterland as a self-sufficient commune of manorial soldier-lords who frowned upon trade, and foreigners too. It was as if Athens looked forward, and Sparta back. Athens, ever ready to try the new, for instance adopted from the Lydian kings of Asia Minor their seventh-century invention of currency of fixed weights as a convenient medium of exchange; and the drachma, probably first minted in Solon's day and later stamped with the Athenian owl, greatly helped expedite commerce. Gradually these became to Mediterranean trade what the British pound sterling was to become to world trade more than two millennia later: a stable unit in terms of which many-sided commitments could be made. Yet the Spartans, even through the fifth century, stuck obstinately to unwieldy, primitive iron bars as their only instrument of barter—a symbol of their suspicion not only of exchange but of any kind of change.

The Athenians prided themselves on their costly, richly painted and decorated temples, stoas, and gymnasiums; the Spartans, on their disinterest in outward show. The busy Athenians, when an outside challenge or danger reared, raised conscript armies led by amateur generals, each elected to serve for a year; the Spartiates— that is to say, the master class who controlled Sparta, descendants of the Dorian tribesmen who had won the land—were themselves a standing army, each soldier-citizen being permitted to do little more than dedicate his life to the profession of sword and spear. These prototypes of Prussians were the most skilled and devoted soldiery of the age, as King Xerxes of Persia was to learn when he attacked the Greeks early in the fifth century. Herodotus recalls that a deposed and renegade king of Sparta, Demaratus by name, who had placed himself in the service of the Persians, warned Xerxes that the Spartans, small as they were in number, would put up a phenomenal resistance against him: "when they fight singly, [they] are as good men as any in the world, and when they fight in a body, [they] are the bravest of all." And so they were to be, when three hundred of them faced the entire Persian host at the pass of Thermopylae in the year 480, dying to the last man. The

MUSEUM, SPARTA; BOUDOT-LAMOTTE

In 480 the Spartan king Leonidas, with his small force of 300 Lacedaemonians, fell in fierce battle at the pass of Thermopylae attempting to stop the invading Persian armies.

glory of the Athenian-led sea victory over Xerxes' fleet at Salamis in the same year was no greater than that of this self-sacrifice.

Although so bold in battle, the Spartans nevertheless remained fearful and recessive at home. Athens proceeded from early kingship through oligarchy and rule by tyrants to the world's first democracy. Sparta, though it managed to combine the rule of kings with oligarchs, went no further than that; on the contrary, while Athens was feeling its way forward, Sparta stuck fast in the extremes of oligarchy. In Athens a series of reforms, inspired by Solon's, broadened the franchise and steadily increased popular participation in government over the resistance of Athens' own class of eupatrids—the nobility, literally "the well-born"—but in Sparta nothing of the sort took place. In Athens, in due course, a tradesman or a blacksmith, provided he was of old local lineage and good repute, could not only vote but was encouraged to hold public office. In Sparta the very small elite minority withheld all political rights from the subjects whom they had conquered and whom they reduced to the state of either *perioikoi* (voteless freemen) or helots (bondsmen and agricultural serfs). While Athenians listened in the Agora to popular orators and reformers such as Cleisthenes in the late sixth century, the Spartans set up the unattractive system of Europe's first secret police, the *krypteia*. Under this system young Spartiates were yearly commissioned to put to the sword any helots they suspected of disaffection. The fears of their governing clans were only too well founded, since the Spartiates had set themselves so aloof from the subject populace that there was a constant danger of insurrection: Sparta's brave arms were first of all pointed against social upheaval at home.

Such Spartan preoccupation with maintaining discipline and class distinction was bound to lead to rigidity and even desiccation, while Athens by contrast experimented and expanded. This, Thucydides himself was to point out in a searching passage early in his history of the climactic struggle between the two states that broke out in 431. Shortly before the clash, as the rivals are girding and there is uncertainty in the Spartan camp as to whether the moment is ripe for assaulting Attica, Thucydides has a Corinthian spokesman friendly to the Spartans deliver them a lecture on their faults. "The Athenians," he says, "are addicted to innovation, and their designs are characterized by swiftness alike in conception and execution; you have a genius for keeping what you have got, accompanied by a total want of invention, and when forced to act you never go far enough. Again, they are adventurous beyond their power, and daring beyond their judgment, and in danger they are sanguine; your wont is to attempt less than is justified by

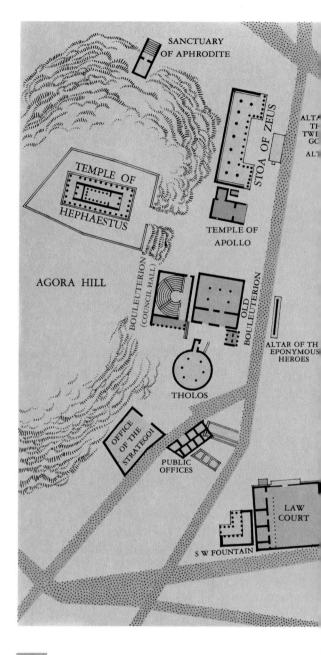

▮ BUILT BY 490 B.C.

▮ BUILT BETWEEN 489–401 B.C.

▮ BUILT BETWEEN 400–300 B.C.

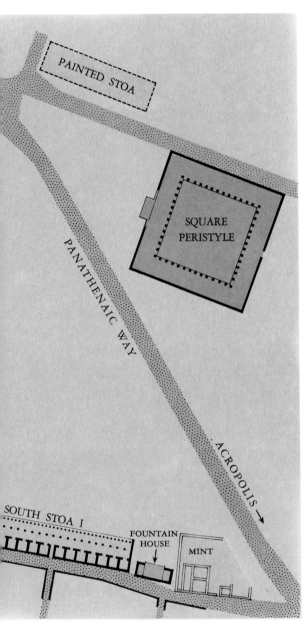

THE AGORA *For the Athenians the Acropolis was fortress and sanctuary; but the Agora, or market place, built up over the centuries, was the center of their daily lives. Philosophers debated on the colonnade of the Painted Stoa; and craftsmen's workshops located in the Agora were thronged with citizens who came to haggle and buy. Chairmen of the Council of 500 dined in the Tholos before a meeting; a citizen wishing to propose a new law posted it by the Altar of the Eponymous Heroes. The chief court of Athens (composed of citizen-jurors) met in the Law Court, while other courts assembled in the Square Peristyle. The administration of the city-state was carried out from offices in the Agora. The Panathenaic Way, the route for religious processions to the Acropolis, and the number of temples and sanctuaries indicate its function as a secondary religious center.*

your power. . . . Further, there is promptitude on their side against procrastination on yours; they are never at home, you are never away from it: for they hope by their absence to extend their acquisitions, you fear by your advance to endanger what you have left behind."

"A total want of invention": biting words, and true. Athens produced in statecraft a Solon, a Themistocles, a Pericles; in drama an Aeschylus, a Sophocles, a Euripides, an Aristophanes; in sculpture a Phidias, a Praxiteles; in architecture a Mnesicles, one of the builders of its new Acropolis; in history a Thucydides; in philosophy a Socrates, a Plato; whereas Sparta in its prime produced soldiers. Brave as they were, they were almost literally dumb; if in their "laconic" style of speech they cultivated brevity and silence, it was, as has been remarked, because they had little or nothing to say.

Athens' readiness to pursue a new idea can be seen prophetically developing throughout the sixth century—the era that established its character, as the fifth century was to bring about its leadership. Of Solon's innovations in his still simple and agricultural polis of the first decade of the sixth century, none was more telling than his scheme to introduce manufactures (chiefly smithing, pottery making, woodworking); and since Athens was wanting in craftsmen, he proposed that his fellow citizens invite many such men from abroad. Not only that, but he offered them full citizenship as an incentive to their coming. His countrymen agreed, even though this meant diluting their own franchise with the votes of foreigners and of the lower classes, and their reward was trade and prosperity.

If this was a milestone in Athenian economic growth, a comparable one in culture was the effort by Solon's long-ruling successor Pisistratus, in and out of power from the 560's to the 530's, to make Athens the spiritual center of the Attic communes that were grouped around it. Some of his work took the form of developing the first religious Panathenaic games in about 566; then, of bringing to Athens the annual festivals to the nature god Dionysus that had been held in the countryside for decades past, with their choral chants and dances. Finally, as there grew out of these festivals the rudimentary art of the drama, the first public contest for a tragic play was set up in Athens in the year 534—and with this event the history of the Greek theatre begins.

Militarily, too—for all its amateur methods under arms—sixth-century Athens showed verve and strategic insight when about 570 it seized from the neighboring city-state of Megara the off-shore island of Salamis, which dominated the western approaches

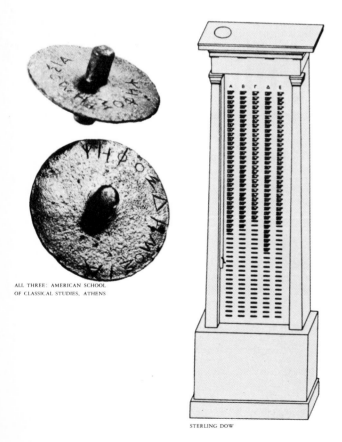

Unlike Sparta, Athens emphasized wide civic participation in government to safeguard democracy. A system of ostracism was instituted whereby a powerful individual could be exiled if enough citizens voted against him. The ostrakon above, inscribed "Out with Themistocles," was cast unsuccessfully in 483. Allotment machines such as the one in the drawing below were used to select jurors for the law courts. At the end of a case jurors cast their ballots. Those with a closed hub (below) brought acquittal; open ballots meant condemnation.

ALL THREE: AMERICAN SCHOOL
OF CLASSICAL STUDIES, ATHENS

STERLING DOW

to the Piraeus and thus threatened Athens' seagoing trade. By this shrewd stroke Athens made itself mistress of all its nearby waters, and soon a strong naval power was in the making.

Then just before the close of the century Athens took a revolutionary stride politically and socially in the reforms instituted by Cleisthenes, who identified himself with popular aspirations, as Solon and Pisistratus had. Not a great sage like Solon, not a benevolent tyrant like Pisistratus, Cleisthenes was an insurgent leader who, in the last decade of the sixth century, proved himself a superlative organizer of a liberal state.

Ironically, he had come to power with the aid of Sparta, in the course of a revolt of leading Athenian eupatrid families against the sons and heirs of Pisistratus, who had behaved privately in an unseemly fashion and publicly in an all too partisan one. Sparta had several designs in aiding the rebellion: one was to make Greece safe for oligarchy, and another was to gain a hold over Athenian affairs—which Sparta did by requiring Athenian aristocrats, as the price for its help, to join its own Peloponnesian League. Sparta miscalculated badly: Cleisthenes, emerging on top as a popular leader in this tortuous struggle, at once swung Athens into the opposite direction from oligarchy. It is with him that the city's working democracy actually begins.

For Solon, while curbing the exclusive power of the old nobles, had left many of their institutions more or less intact—chiefly their senate, the Council of the Areopagus, restricted to leading men who had once been archons of the state, and endowed with supreme authority to oversee the people and their officials. But he had created, below this, the Council of Four Hundred, which was known as the *boule*. This was carefully apportioned so that equivalent numbers of men would come from each of the four traditional Ionian tribes of free citizens. A second breakdown of the populace, based on a ladder of income—from the *pentacosiomedimni*, or affluent "five-hundred-bushel men," down to the *thetes*, those of small resource—determined who was eligible to hold office. Then, a general assembly, or *ekklesia*, of free citizens elected officials annually, but its choice was limited in that the highest—the archons and military commanders—could be chosen only from the top class; and the thetes were not eligible to hold any office at all, although they took part in the voting.

Cleisthenes, in his sweeping innovations of 507 or thereabouts, changed all this. First, he threw out the old structure of four tribes, dissolved several hundred clans led by entrenched families, and set up a new division of ten Athenian tribes, each of which included residents of the city, the coast, and the Attic countryside. At the same time he almost doubled the size of the electorate by further extending the right of citizenship. Then he took sovereign power from the old Council and vested it in the Assembly, to which all officeholders high and low were to be directly responsible. The Council, or *boule*, was to continue as a body preparing business for action by the Assembly, but its membership was now based on the ten tribes (each providing fifty men) without reference to income class; moreover, it was not to consider itself a superior representative branch of government but simply a high executive committee reporting to the Assembly of some twenty to thirty thousand citizens, which now was the legislature.

Eventually any citizen, whatever his station, was to be eligible for any public office; and it came to be expected that every citizen would serve at some time or another in at least one. This was achieved by a system of election by lot and the annual rotation of most major public offices, with a ban on re-election until many other men had had their chance to serve in turn; so that anyone might find himself chosen one of next year's magistrates or jurors or tax collectors or councilors. Then, if he had been picked for the Council from the roster of citizens, he might also suddenly find himself its presiding officer for a day: for the Council chose from its number, also by lot and turn, a different president for each day's session. Since the Council met some three hundred days a year, this meant that in a decade three thousand Athenians had sat in the highest chair—one that in view of the turbulence of Athenian politics was very often the hot seat.

The effect of this scheme of things, as it developed over the half century from Cleisthenes to Pericles, was to distribute firsthand experience of government among more and more people, with less and less reference to class. There was no bureaucracy, no hereditary caste of governors. To be sure, it was thought to be to the good that men of prominent lineage, wealth, and station devote themselves particularly to public life, they having the leisure and the means to do so, while others must think of earning a living. (Pericles later paid wages so that the poorer citizens could leave their daily labors to assist the state.) The idea of professionalism at the top became abhorrent to very many Athenians as they savored, even if only briefly, the challenges and pleasures of sharing in government. In theory every citizen was capable of filling any office for which he might be chosen—or, under this revolving system, he would soon learn how to be, for if he failed, there were serious penalties. Even Athens' ten yearly generals, the *strategoi*, were elected annually from the entire body of citizens, although in practice experienced military leaders were given preference again

HASSIA

From the speakers' platform on the hill called the Pnyx legislation was proposed three or four times each month to the Assembly, composed of all the Athenian citizens.

and again. The historian Thucydides was to find himself a general in the war with Sparta and was exiled for his failure to hold the city of Amphipolis. And Pericles himself, greatest of Greek statesmen, was to be heavily fined by the Assembly for what its strategists regarded as his miscalculations in the same war.

For those citizens not tapped by the lot, there was the drama of participation in the Assembly. It met outdoors, usually four times every month, on the slope known as the Pnyx, opposite the Acropolis, its session commencing at dawn with the sacrifice of a pig to Zeus. The order of business had already been prepared by the Council in its roofed chamber at one side of the Agora, where it had been reviewing legislative proposals and carrying on state affairs pending the Assembly's next meeting. Hard by the Council's building was the Tholos, the circular headquarters of the chief administrators, who were prepared to be called upon at any moment. The sun rises, the pig is killed, prayers are offered, the agenda is presented—and then, as like as not, disorder threatens. Though only some two or three thousand of the eligible assemblymen actually appear (most of those from outlying districts do not find the time to come), the mass is large enough to be difficult to handle. While there are no organized political parties as such, men of different factions seek to outshout, browbeat, and insult each other, to the whistles and foot stamping of a crowd that not only likes candor but relishes vituperation. Only when his time runs out on the water clock is the speaker stopped. By the late fifth century only a highly skilled orator—the professional of persuasion—can prevail above such a boisterous crowd as this one. Enter, finally, the demagogue.

So broad and bold and unpredictable a frame of rule inevitably did not sit well with the proudest old families. Class antagonism was to plague Athens throughout its history. The scheme also contained within itself obvious dangers of corruption, foolhardiness, incompetence in high office: all this, too, was to be visited upon Athens. Yet there were many of the gentry who swallowed their prejudices or memories and plunged in generously to help make the new system work: and in so doing, they lent to it the kind of grace that in America we associate with Jeffersonian democracy, of which the Athenian one was the distant model. Moreover, the exuberant participation of so many different kinds of men in their newly discovered self-government lent to the Athenians as a whole a style theretofore unknown.

Far removed from this stands the bleak, fixed world of Sparta. Although it may seem repugnant to us now and out of accord with all that we admire most in ancient Greece, we are repeatedly

STAATLICHE MUSEEN, BERLIN

Two small bronzes depict the costume of classical warriors. The spearman above, shield in hand, is dressed for battle. Over his short chiton he wears a decorated cuirass, and greaves cover his legs. The Spartan soldier opposite is shown wrapped in a cloak. Both warriors wear helmets of the Corinthian type which protect both the face and the head.

168

brought up against the fact that the Athenians themselves were by no means united in distaste for it. On the contrary, numbers of them—and in particular many of their chief philosophers—were strongly drawn to it, preferring it to the system of Athens. Socrates, ever the skeptic about Athens' ways and waywardness, may have been speaking half in jest when he remarked of the Spartans' "laconic" speech that it was really a sort of disguise: "But they conceal their wisdom . . . and pretend to be fools, so that their superiority over the rest of Greece may not be known to lie in wisdom, but seem to consist in fighting and courage. Their idea is that if their real excellence became known, everyone would set to work to become wise." Plato, however, was in earnest when in mapping his scheme for an ideal state in the *Republic* he modeled it largely on Sparta.

The Athenians pursued liberty, but there remained among many of them a fear—a partly justified fear, as it turned out—that too much liberty, or rather too little restraint, might lead to popular license. Among their eupatrids in particular there was a contrary impulse toward order, stability, hierarchy—and whatever else Sparta lacked, it most certainly had that. Dull or not, it had *eunomia*, or "the state of being well-lawed," which in turn was the embodiment of a rigorous ideal that required of everyone total, uncritical devotion to the state. Therefore Plato admired it, impatient at democracy's disorder and dreaming of a dedicated rule by only the best and most highly trained. Athens, he wrote, "is full of liberty and free speech and every one in it is allowed to do what he likes. This being allowed, it obviously follows that each man can plan his own life as he pleases." But it was just this that he found displeasing, enthralled as he was by the Spartan scheme of a firmly led band of brothers living like a garrison, eating at common mess tables, and thinking their thoughts in common.

With the Athenian Xenophon, Plato's contemporary and like him a pupil of Socrates, the attraction for Sparta became positively rapturous. Far-traveled and widely employed as a soldier of fortune (he went into both the Spartan and the Persian service, leading the famous march of the Ten Thousand to the Black Sea that he described in the *Anabasis*), he finally settled in Sparta and wrote a panegyric that not only acclaimed its system for its authoritarian virtues but agreed with the Spartans that it was divinely inspired. Much later still, the biographer Plutarch, a Greek who entered the Roman service in the first century A.D., was to produce in the life of the ancient Spartan lawgiver Lycurgus his own paean to the system that had humbled the Athenian state. "In general," he wrote approvingly, "Lycurgus made the citizens accustomed to

WADSWORTH ATHENEUM, HARTFORD, J. P. MORGAN COLLECTION

have neither the will nor the ability to lead a private life; but, like the bees, always to be organic parts of their community, to cling together around the leader, and, in an ecstasy of enthusiasm and selfless ambition, to belong wholly to their country."

This admiration for things Spartan on the part of some of the most distinguished men of Greece often outdid what some Athenians had to say in praise of their own. This was not the case with Pericles, the guiding spirit of his city's democratic party as well as of the polis as a whole during the high fifth-century era that bears his name. Always eloquent about Athens, he was to be at his proudest in the great funeral oration he gave in 431 in honor of the first Athenians to die in the great war with Sparta. Enumerating the virtues and blessings of his fellow citizens, he dwelled especially on their civil freedom and went on to say (as Thucydides reports it): "The freedom which we enjoy in our government extends also to our ordinary [i.e., private] life. There, far from exercising a jealous surveillance over each other, we do not feel called upon to be angry with our neighbor for doing what he likes, or even to indulge in those injurious looks which cannot fail to be offensive, although they inflict no positive penalty." In such an open society, a Plato or an Aristotle was to be free to call for a closed one. Conversely no Spartan of record had the wit or the daring to call for an open one. Athens was to betray its principles by resorting to banishment and assassination; but Sparta never even learned those principles. As the great Athenian orator Demosthenes in the fourth century remarked, "You are not allowed to praise the laws of Athens or of any other state; far from it, you have to praise what conforms with their institutions." All the contrast between the libertarian and the totalitarian spirit that has come down through history rings in such words as these.

The class divisions of Athens, its chronic upheavals, the corruption that finally overcame it, explain much of the Athenians' attraction toward Sparta; but there was more. Undoubtedly Sparta's emergence as a teaching state, bent on forming its citizens' characters into a cohesive mold, absorbed many of those taken up with the training of youth—narrow though its training was. Athens was long to wrestle with this problem of order versus individuality. It may well have been an awareness of the fascination for Sparta on the part of the Athenians that caused Pericles in his oration for the Athenian dead to claim for his own city (as against Sparta) the role of being "the school of Hellas." Significantly, the primary argument on which he based his claim was the following: "I doubt if the world can produce a man, who where he has only himself to depend upon, is equal to so many emer-

STAATLICHE MUSEEN, BERLIN; BOUDOT-LAMOTTE

A sixth-century funerary monument from Sparta shows a dead couple, with two tiny figures, probably their descendants, bringing offerings to them. During this period Sparta, unlike Athens, was neglecting the arts in order to concentrate all of its energies on military pursuits.

gencies, and graced by so happy a versatility as the Athenian."

However, as many an Athenian no doubt sensed, versatility alone was not enough to make a full man. The iron of order was needed too. Here we can detect a contrast of personality between the two main stems of the Greek race as it developed—on one hand the Ionians of Attica and Asia Minor, adventurous, imaginative, high-spirited, and on the other the Dorians of the Peloponnesus, sturdy, austere, conservative. There was an urge on the part of the livelier breed to strengthen itself with some of the steadying virtues of the other. The Spartan was one of the least pleasing of Dorians, when compared for instance to the many-sided Corinthians, his kin who dwelled closer to Athens; but he was certainly the most vigorous and, moreover, bred of the purest Dorian stock. The traveling bard Pindar of Thebes, who early in the fifth century wrote poems in praise of the best people of practically every city-state that harbored him—Athens, Syracuse, Aegina, Abdera, Corinth, and Sparta—liked to celebrate the ancient Dorians as the "fair-haired Danaeans" of the heroic age, and many Greek listeners seem to have regarded the Spartan as the embodiment of some superior strain from the North. (However, the myth that Greece owed its glory to Aryan blood, so attractive to Nordic racists, sprang up only when Germanic scholars went to work.) However, there was recognition among Ionian Greeks of a grave and potent Dorian (or Doric) style, which expressed itself most forcefully in thick-columned temples like that of Hera at Olympia —a style very different from the slender grace of Ionian buildings. The Athenians themselves were to adopt the Doric style for the Parthenon, the greatest shrine of their Acropolis.

Though Sparta itself was visibly a cultural desert during Greece's greatest centuries, there was a sense both north and south of the Gulf of Corinth that at some time in the past it had flowered in the arts no less than in war—indeed, that it had experienced its own "golden age." This, too, may have added to its lure. Finds such as gold and silver jewelry of the seventh century, well-carved work in ivory, and pottery tell of an early time of Spartan imagination as well as luxury. We also know that although all the arts save martial music (in the Doric mode) were discouraged in the Sparta of its martial prime, in earlier times the city had been as receptive to the lyre and the bard as other Greek cities were. Thus early in the seventh century, perhaps in response to advice from the oracle at Delphi, the Spartans imported the lyric poet and musician Terpander from the faraway Aeolian isle of Lesbos, presumably to stage a contest in choral singing. Terpander, so far as we can learn from this dimly recorded period, was a considerable innovator in

EGYPTIAN EXPLORATION SOCIETY

When they recited their works, Greek poets usually accompanied themselves on the lyre. The terra-cotta lyre player below comes from Thebes and dates from the sixth century. It is almost contemporaneous with the greatest of Theban poets, Pindar. The writing on the papyrus fragment seen at right identifies it as part of a label for a copy of that poet's complete works. The papyrus was found in Egypt; unfortunately, however, none of the missing works of Pindar were discovered with it.

LOUVRE

music. He was often regarded by the Greeks as the inventor of the lyre of seven strings, as well as the creator of the drinking song —a form without a future in the puritan Sparta to come.

Only a few fragments of his verses or songs survive: thus

> *Let us pour a libation*
> *To Memory's daughters,*
> *The Muses, and to the Muses'*
> *Leader, Leto's son.*

Soon after Terpander, the Spartans also gave harbor and audience to the amorous and romantic poet Alcman of Lydia, east of the Aegean, who in one of his surviving fragments wrote significantly, "The skillful playing of the lyre has equal rank with the sword," and then tuned his instrument to sing such a song as this:

> *No more, O maiden voices, sweet as honey, soft as love is,*
> *No more my limbs sustain me.*
> *A halcyon on the wing*
> *Flying o'er the foam-flowers, in the halcyon coveys,*
> *Would I were, and knew not the care,*
> *The sea-blue bird of spring!*

or this, one of the loveliest lyrical fragments of all Greek time:

> *The far peaks sleep, the great ravines,*
> *The foothills, and the streams.*
> *Asleep are trees, and hivèd bees,*
> *The mountain beasts, and all that dark earth teems,*
> *The glooming sea, the monsters in their deeps:*
> *And every bird, its wide wings folded, sleeps.*

With poetry and music and ornament, early Sparta appears to have developed very much as other Greek states did; then either late in the seventh century or early in the sixth an extraordinary change of course and character came over it. In the eighth, it had a working kingship and had enriched itself by conquering the neighboring Messenians in the fertile southwest; a few more steps of growth might have found it extending itself to become a trading power in the Aegean. But then came Lycurgus, the divinely inspired lawgiver who reformed luxurious Sparta and gave it a new code or constitution. Or so the Spartans later said, claiming that Lycurgus had received his edicts directly from the Delphic Apollo, god of law—somewhat as Moses had received his tablets from the great God of the Hebrews.

There is no historical proof that there ever was an individual named Lycurgus, any more than there is that there was a man named Moses. But there is abundant evidence that the change in

HARISSIADIS

Emissaries from all over Greece came to seek advice at Apollo's shrine, high on a mountainside at Delphi. Above, are remains of the god's fourth-century temple.

Sparta's life brought about in his name was immense, even though myth and mystery surround the process. Tyrtaeus, a late seventh-century chronicler, tells in a surviving fragment of an approach made by the Spartans to Apollo's oracle at Delphi and reports what they were told: "For thus the lord of the silver bow, far-working Apollo, the golden-haired, gave response from his rich shrine: There shall govern the Council [of Sparta] the Kings, honored of the gods, to whose care is entrusted the lovely city of Sparta, and the Elders ripe in years, and after them the men of the people, giving obedience in turn to just decrees. . . ." Later, in the fifth century, Herodotus, although he was usually anxious to get through the veils of legend to the core of truth, repeated another traditional Lacedaemonian tale: "Lycurgus, a man of distinction among the Spartans, had gone to Delphi, to visit the oracle. Scarcely had he entered into the inner fane, when the priestess exclaimed aloud:

'O thou great Lycurgus, that com'st to my beautiful dwelling,
Dear to Zeus, and to all who sit in the halls of Olympus,
Whether to hail thee a god I know not, or only a mortal,
But my hope is strong that a god thou wilt prove, Lycurgus.'"

Thereupon, having been so extraordinarily praised from on high (for it was of course Apollo who was speaking through the mouth of the priestess), he was presented with Sparta's "entire system of laws."

All this has every earmark of a piece of shrewd invention by the Spartans to strengthen the acceptance of their harsh new system by giving it an air of divine command. As the American scholar Moses Hadas observes: "The only reasonable deduction from the mass of conflicting evidence is that Lycurgus was not the inventor of the Spartan constitution, and that his name (which probably represented an ancient wolf god) was deliberately associated with the new legislation to enhance its credit." But of the particularly close ties that existed between the Delphic oracle and Sparta there is no doubt. As Dr. Hadas remarks, "Delphi was always against Athens and democracy"; and Thucydides himself wrote that at the start of the Peloponnesian War the oracle proclaimed that it would take Sparta's side. Spartan officials were constantly on the move to the holy precinct to obtain the latest advice on how to administer their state. At certain times on moonless nights the ephors, or overseers, of Sparta would search the sky, and if they saw a shooting star they would suspend their kings from office until they could get fresh counsel from Delphi.

The fact that there were two kings, and that the ephors could

ARCHAEOLOGICAL MUSEUM, FERRARA; HIRMER

In a detail from a vase painting, Apollo is depicted laurel-crowned, seated in his Delphi temple before the omphalos, the stone said to mark the center of the world.

THE RULERS OF SPARTA

THE EPHORS

MEMBERSHIP: Five supreme magistrates, one from each Spartan deme, or commune, elected annually by the Assembly.

FUNCTIONS: To initiate legislation, to summon and preside over both Assembly and Council, to control finance, and to act as a supreme civil court. The ephors had power to impeach the kings and directed the secret police (*krypteia*).

THE COUNCIL OF ELDERS (*Gerousia*)

MEMBERSHIP: Twenty-eight councilors, all over the age of sixty, chosen by lot from the nobility.

FUNCTIONS: To initiate legislation and to act as the supreme criminal court.

THE KINGS

NUMBERS: Two, hereditary.

FUNCTIONS: In peacetime, primarily ceremonial; in wartime, one king became commander-in-chief of the army in the field.

THE ASSEMBLY (*Apella*)

MEMBERSHIP: Every male citizen over thirty.

FUNCTIONS: To vote on the legislation proposed by the ephors and the Council of Elders.

---

suspend them at will, shows up the "reformed" Spartan system of government in all its incongruity. The kings, hereditary and two in number, were probably survivals of the circumstance that Sparta and its surrounding countryside had originally been conquered by separate tribes of Dorians. That so odd an arrangement was allowed to continue no doubt reflected an urge on the part of the leading families to have each king check the other, while they in turn through their elected ephors would check both. The kings, moreover, had been reduced to chiefly ceremonial status: they presided at processions, held certain priestly offices, and occupied the first seats at banquets, where they were entitled to a double portion of every viand served. However, when Sparta made war, one king went into the field as commander, his military powers then becoming absolute, while the other remained at home, watching him—no doubt jealously—from a distance.

Along with the ephors—the high magistrates of the city—there stood a council, or *gerousia*, of well-born elders who advised the dual kings and served as a high court. This council was literally a body of old men, since no one was admitted to this office until he had reached the age of sixty. Below them, in turn, came an assembly, or *apella*, of all Spartiate male citizens of the age of thirty and over. This was theoretically a public meeting empowered to vote on every issue confronting the state, but in practice it was hamstrung by having no right of initiative or debate. It was, as we would say, simply a "rubber-stamp" legislature like those maintained in totalitarian powers in later eras to lend applause to decisions already made; and one Spartan statute provided that if the councilors found a vote of the Assembly wrongheaded or "crooked," they could simply throw it out.

Below the electorate of 3,000 or 4,000 Spartiates lay a voiceless helot population over forty-six times greater in number. But above the whole creaking structure stood the five annually elected ephors (one for each old Spartan commune), who together acted as a directorate that oversaw the state in general and its kings in particular. Although most Greeks praised the Spartan state for its *eunomia*, actually no scheme of government more cumbersome or guaranteed to produce eventual paralysis could have been devised; and this precisely was to be the outcome.

Lycurgan "reform" also meant that hitherto common lands were divided into lots that were made hereditary, passing from Spartiate father to son. Their holders were forbidden to engage in trade or any commercial enterprise, all their support coming from the labor of serfs. Boys were taken from their homes at the age of seven to be trained in state schools for martial pursuits (with a little reading and writing thrown in) while girls of nubile age were prepared for marriage and motherhood by drilling nude in outdoor exercises (without the necessity of learning to read and write). Sickly infants were exposed—that is, ordered to be taken to a nearby mountainside and abandoned to slow death or the swift jaws of wolves. Youths were unmercifully hazed by being required to do servile attendance on their elders and to endure hunger and deprivation as tests for manhood. They were required to mess and bunk with other males until well on into their married life, visiting their wives only furtively.

Considerable sexual freedom was, to be sure, one of the few liberties granted in this disciplinary state, but in the first instance much of it was directed homosexually. It was understood that a young Spartiate would enter into a liaison with some elder friend or mentor of the armed squirearchy; then if he chose to play the field with discus-throwing girls who appeared in the arena as unclothed as himself—well and good. If children then resulted before marriage, no damage whatever was done to the girl's reputation—unless the offspring were weak or faulty and thus unworthy of the fatherland. Those who have studied the mores of the late Nazi Germany may be struck by certain correspondences.

If despite all this many Athenians romanticized Sparta, there have been reverse impulses in times since to romanticize the Athenians and to think of their state as somewhat more ideal than it actually was, democratically speaking. The splendors of the great age that lay ahead for Athens were prefaced by certain limitations. For all its spreading of political rights, Athenian democracy, while allowing more freedom than Sparta, did not mean that the great majority of adult males or anything like a majority were to obtain the franchise. Pericles, in fact, when leading the city in the mid fifth century, was to reduce the number of voters. Athens' ratio of enrolled citizens to total population may have been one to seven or eight—more than double that of Sparta; it was hardly a full democracy, if indeed there is such a thing. Several categories of men remained excluded: chiefly those who were employed by others (on the ground that, being so employed, they were not their own masters and free to lend their time to public service); resident foreigners, some of whose families had been established in Athens for generations (with an exception for those who had been granted citizenship by Solon's or Cleisthenes' dispensations); and, finally, the mass of slaves.

Just how many of the latter there were in Athens in a given generation can only be conjectured. One leading authority, A. W. Gomme, estimates that toward the end of the fifth century, when

THE RULERS OF ATHENS

THE ASSEMBLY *(Ekklesia)*

MEMBERSHIP: Every male citizen over eighteen.

FUNCTIONS: To formulate all policy, domestic and foreign; to declare war, conclude treaties, elect citizen-generals *(strategoi)* and all magistrates.

THE COUNCIL OF FIVE HUNDRED *(Boule)*

MEMBERSHIP: Citizens over thirty, chosen annually by lot, fifty from each of ten tribes. (In the fifth century the tribe consisted of citizens from geographically scattered communes.)

FUNCTIONS: To prepare agenda for the Assembly, to supervise the administration of domestic and foreign affairs, including finance and wars. Its executive committee was the *Prytanis*, whose fifty members changed every five weeks.

THE COURT *(Heliaea)*

MEMBERSHIP: Six thousand citizens chosen by lot.

FUNCTIONS: To sit as juries with wide civil jurisdiction; there were no judges.

THE ARCHONS

MEMBERSHIP: A board of nine citizens elected annually by lot.

FUNCTIONS: Originally the senior archon was chief of state; in the fifth century he was reduced to ceremonial and minor judicial duties.

DMITRI KESSEL, COURTESY *Life*

A relief from the Persian royal palace at Persepolis shows Darius I, sheltered by his royal umbrella. Darius' vast army marched into Greece to punish the Athenians for aiding their fellow Greeks of the Ionian coast in their rebellion against Persian power.

the full-grown Athenian state extended over some 1,000 square miles of Attica, their number may have reached 115,000 out of a total population of possibly 315,000 (of which, again possibly, some 43,000 by then were citizens). Of the slave population, perhaps a half were in domestic service, while the other half worked on the fields, in industries, and in the marble quarries of Mount Pentelicon or the silver mines of Laurium.

The Athenian slave was, to be sure, a different person from the one we think of when we use the term in the context of the West's seizure of black Africans on the Guinea coast. He was likely to be a fellow Greek or near Greek who had fallen into bondage by taint of birth or capture in war or default in payment of debt. Every Greek state—like the kingdoms of the East—followed this method of obtaining cheap, unfortunate, subjugated, and often highly talented manpower. Ironically it was Solon's own reform of abolishing bondage for debt at home that caused Athenians to seek slaves abroad by raiding the lands of the *barbaroi*. A few rich, landed families accumulated as many as a thousand; a middle-class household might have up to a dozen—Plato, we are told, had five, and Aristotle, thirteen. There are records of highly gifted slaves who served their masters as children's tutors, architectural draftsmen, business assistants or even associates, and educated intimates of the family. Since many a master worked hard too at trade or other enterprise, the system was relatively more decent than at Sparta, where the master did no work at all except with the sword; but it rarely occurred to the best Athenians to free their slaves as Aristotle was to do, and as Thomas Jefferson at Monticello did more than two millennia later.

Occasional amnesties were granted by the state—particularly when in an emergency Athens needed to swell its army or navy. (Slaves were not normally permitted to bear arms.) Such an instance arose in 490, a pivotal year in Greek history, when the mightiest attacking force yet known to Hellenes descended upon Euboea, the island strip just off the Attic coast. The generals of King Darius of Persia had come with possibly as many as 30,000 men, to burn its key city of Eretria, cross over to the mainland, and encamp at Marathon on the approach to Athens. Many nearby Greek states would not help fight off so formidable an invader, and the Spartans were slow to respond to Athens' appeal for aid (it was the time of the full moon, and they said they must complete their religious observances of it before taking to the field). Desperate for support, the Athenian commander Miltiades enlisted a considerable number of slaves as supporting infantry, and marched them along with his trained hoplites straight to Marathon.

The Persian assault upon mainland Greece was complex in origin. Its basis lay in three circumstances. The first was the decay of old empires in the Middle East; the second the fragility of the little Greek settlements and states that had arisen on the Asia Minor coast; the third, the awakening of a vigorous breed of tribesmen in the rough Iranian inland to the possibilities of extending themselves over richer country than their own. The Assyrian realm, long the chief power in the Near East, had sunk by the seventh century into torpor; the Babylonians and the Medes had revolted against it; and eventually the Persians gained control of the entire realm, while the kingdom of Lydia in Asia Minor— once an Assyrian tributary—rose in power. Lydia had shown itself hospitable to the Greek settlements strung along the Asia Minor shore; and Croesus, the fabulously wealthy king who ruled Lydia in the mid sixth century, had been anxious to ally himself to Greek ideas and institutions. This had taken him to the point of consulting the oracle at Delphi, which was to prove his undoing. Fearful of the rise and approach of Persian power from the East under King Cyrus, he asked Delphi for advice and received the counsel that if he crossed the river Halys, which lay between him and Cyrus' Persians, he would destroy an empire. The oracle however omitted to say which empire. Importunately he crossed the river and in doing so, did in battle destroy an empire—his own.

Profiting from Delphi's mischief, the Persians took over Lydia in about 546, and for the first time, Lydia's neighbors to the west, the Greeks, confronted a major expansionist power. Yet Lydia was only a minor element in Persia's emerging grand design: first the subjugation of all the Middle East, then expansion northward to the Caucasus, southward through Syria to Egypt, and eastward all the way to India. Far from being hostile to the Asiatic, or Ionian, Greeks, the Persians, like Croesus before them, felt considerable kinship with them and respect for their cultural attainments in such towns as Ephesus and Miletus, and many Ionians in turn willingly entered Persian service.

But the rule of satraps, even when benevolent, was bound to come into collision with the Greek political awakening, especially as the idea of self-rule spread from town to town and from island to island. A brilliantly gifted Persian ruler, Darius I, coming into power about 520, had set about reorganizing his empire into provinces and building new roads and canals. In 512 he extended his realm even into Europe, crossing the Bosporus to subjugate wild Thrace along the Black Sea coast, and then reaching west to Macedonia and north to the Danube. Shock and apprehension came over the Hellenes; and the bravest of these were the Ionians

Herodotus reports that King Croesus of Lydia was condemned to be burned on a funeral pyre after his defeat by the Persians. Croesus was saved when rain, sent by Apollo, extinguished the flame. The amphora above illustrates another version of the tale in which Croesus, having poured out a libation, voluntarily sacrifices himself upon a pyre.
LOUVRE; HIRMER

177

who in several Asia Minor cities revolted against the satraps, the Milesians going so far as to attack and sack the Persian-held city of Sardis, with help from Athens and Eretria.

In this sense the Greeks themselves instigated the Persian wars. For Darius, returning from his far triumphs, found himself with a domestic revolt on his hands that seemed to call for punitive action. And act he did, first crushing Miletus and the other rebellious cities and islands, and then sailing a great expedition westward to chastise the Greek mainland conspirators, of whom, we are told, he knew only dimly. "The Athenians," he is said to have remarked contemptuously, "who are they?" He was soon to learn.

The military task seemed simple. It was, after having reduced Eretria, to land upon the Attic coast and then proceed to invest presumptuous Athens, which lay thinly garrisoned and hemmed in between mountains and sea, protected only by the Acropolis heights. All might have gone well for Darius' commanders (aided by Sparta's deference to the full moon) save that Miltiades of Athens, a tactician of the first magnitude, elected not to await attack at the city's gates, but to deliver a counterattack of his own out of the hills upon the Persians who were forming up on their landing area at flat seaside Marathon, over twenty miles away. With only about 10,000 armed men at hand (Plataea alone, among Greek sister states, sent a contingent in time to be of help), his scheme was a master stroke, relying on the Greeks' familiarity with their own terrain, their aroused individual patriotism, their skill at man-to-man combat, and their readiness to charge in at the double against the flanks of a far superior host, throwing it off balance. As Herodotus writes, "The Persians, therefore, when they saw the Greeks coming on at speed, made ready to receive them, although it seemed to them that the Athenians were bereft of their senses, and bent upon their own destruction; for they saw a mere handful of men coming on at a run without either horsemen or archers. Such was the opinion of the barbarians; but the Athenians in close array fell upon them, and fought in a manner worthy of being recorded. They were the first of the Greeks, so far as I know, who introduced the custom of charging the enemy at a run, and they were likewise the first who dared to look upon the Median garb, and to face men clad in that fashion. Until this time the very name of the Medes had been a terror to the Greeks to hear.

"The two armies fought together on the plain of Marathon for a length of time; and in the mid battle, where the Persians themselves and the Sacae had their place, the barbarians were victorious, and broke and pursued the Greeks into the inner country; but on the two wings the Athenians and the Plataeans defeated the

THE PERSIAN EMPIRE *In the sixth century the Persian kings ruled the greatest empire the world had ever seen. Their domain reached from Greece to India and incorporated all the centers of the Middle Eastern civilization.*

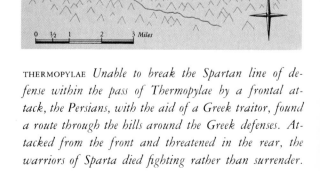

THERMOPYLAE *Unable to break the Spartan line of defense within the pass of Thermopylae by a frontal attack, the Persians, with the aid of a Greek traitor, found a route through the hills around the Greek defenses. Attacked from the front and threatened in the rear, the warriors of Sparta died fighting rather than surrender.*

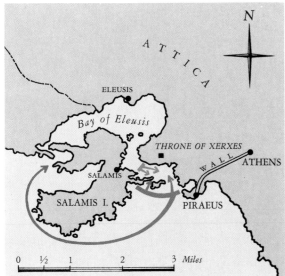

SALAMIS *The Persian fleet (in red) divided into three contingents, blockading the Greeks within the bay of Eleusis. As Xerxes watched from a hill overlooking the site, the Greek triremes (blue line) went forward to defeat the Persians in the narrow strait where the invaders' navy was not able to utilize its strong numerical advantage.*

enemy. Having so done, they suffered the routed barbarians to fly at their ease, and joining the two wings in one, fell upon those who had broken their own center, and fought and conquered them. These likewise fled, and now the Athenians hung upon the runaways and cut them down, chasing them all the way to the shore, on reaching which they laid hold of the ships and called aloud for fire."

The tardy Spartans, once the moon waned, arrived on the field too late to assist, and congratulated the victors. The day was Athens'—and so, it now seemed, was the Greek future. Among the many who found honor on the field that day was a rising Athenian leader, Themistocles, who was then perhaps only thirty, and a promising playwright, Aeschylus, about thirty-five. Phenomenal lives and works lay ahead of both.

Themistocles, supposedly of foreign origin on his mother's side, had made his first mark before Marathon, putting forth as a very young archon the challenging proposition that Athens had not been giving anywhere near enough attention to its fleet: its future, he claimed, lay on the sea, and it must build a force of triremes second to none, and fortify its harbors. Hard, unscrupulous, and later treacherous, he was nevertheless a spacious inspirer of a whole new Athenian military policy, and the years after Marathon proved him right. The Persians, having failed to humble Athens, might well come back; no conceivable land army alone could contain them if this time they came with all their force; but defensive walls would help, and a powerful navy could hack at their troop transports and supply ships on the wide Aegean. This was precisely what happened when Darius' successor, Xerxes, arrived in 480 with a much vaster armament for a second assault; though hugely outnumbered Greek troops died sacrificially at Thermopylae and Athens itself was sacked, the great Greek sea victory at Salamis decided the issue.

This time the Persian host, advancing by ship and foot from Asia Minor and Macedonia, was in Greek eyes all but numberless. There were Medes, Bactrians, Hyrcanians, Phoenicians, Thracians, Cissians, Egyptians, Ethiopians, Cypriotes, in the mass. Herodotus, in one of his most dramatic passages, says that some forty-six different peoples and tribes were included, and a computation of his highly imaginative listing comes out at a figure of 1,700,000 fighting men, in addition to sailors of the fleet and fresh contingents that joined as the horde advanced toward Attica. This wildly improbable estimate has been reduced by modern students such as J. B. Bury to a figure of 180,000 supported by possibly 800 triremes—still a stupendous force to hurl against so

179

lean a land in men and wealth as Greece. There has rarely been a greater force so poorly led against a much inferior one.

The polyglot host swarmed down over the northern Hellenic plains, state after state surrendering to it. But this time there was no matter of a full moon, and Athenian and Spartan and other leaders of marrow, knowing what was coming, met in conference and determined to try to hold off the horde at the pass of Thermopylae between the coastal hills and the sea—the gateway to Attica and thus to Athens. The honor of leadership went to King Leonidas of Sparta, who died along with his 300 picked Spartans rather than yield the pass, while betrayal led the Persians around his flank, to decimate several thousand troops gathered in support behind it. This threatened Athens with mortal danger, and Themistocles, rather than face a holocaust there, persuaded the Athenians to evacuate their capital, save for a small sacrificial garrison on the Acropolis, and to fall back upon the island of Salamis, where he had managed to concentrate a force of almost 400 triremes belonging to Athens and its allies.

The Spartans, being non-sailors and only too aware of Xerxes' vast fleet, argued that all defenders should draw back into the Peloponnesus itself. But Themistocles, the apostle of sea power, would have none of this, and argued against them that the Persian armada should be lured into the close waters off Salamis just west of the Piraeus, where the Greeks would have the advantage of fighting "in a narrow sea with few ships against many." As Herodotus has it, he added that "if things turn out as I anticipate, and we beat them by sea, then we shall have kept your Isthmus free from the barbarians, and they will have advanced no further than Attica, but from thence have fled back in disorder; and we shall, moreover, have saved Megara, Aegina, and Salamis itself, where an oracle has said that we are to overcome our enemies." Themistocles' summons prevailed, and the Greek captains delivered a smashing blow at the point he chose, while Xerxes reportedly sat on a nearby hillside watching his navy—his major means of retreat—being reduced to broken timber. The Persians fought bravely, the historian adds, and "each did his utmost through fear of Xerxes, for each thought that the king's eye was upon himself." But they were not equal to the Greek seamen.

Thus shaken, the main concern of many Persians was how to get home. Another land battle took place in 479 at Plataea in Boeotia, north of the Attic border, at which the Spartan king Pausanias highly distinguished himself and won the field, and upon which the army of the greatest empire dispersed and made its way eastward as best it could in what remained of its fleet.

MUSEUM, OSTIA

With his insistence that Athens base its defenses on naval power, Themistocles turned the Athenians from soldiers into mariners. His great tactical skills led the Greeks to victory at Salamis over a much larger Persian fleet.

There was now honor enough in Greece for all. Athens had been destroyed in substance—its temples toppled, its houses fired, its treasures looted—yet it was raised in spirit. Sparta had been confirmed in its extraordinary valor. A solemn pride came over both states. Yet it was Athens that responded most vigorously to it, rebuilding its templed city, constructing walls, and enlarging its fleet, making the Aegean waters safe for Athenian traders wherever they went. Moreover, island after island in the Aegean, fearful of a third assault by the massive Persians, turned for support to Athens, with its strong defenses and well-led ships. So the league that became known as that of Delos was founded, Delos being the sacred island of Apollo in mid Aegean and a symbol of the new-found unity of men ranging from Attica to Ionia. Though not a stronghold, it was to be the center of administration of fleets and funds for mutual defense. Indeed, a spirit not only of pride but of something approaching exaltation came over Athens as great creative energies were unleashed. Aeschylus, its poet who had fought both at Marathon and Plataea, was to embody this in his own symbolic way in a famous passage at the climax of his Orestes trilogy written about the year 458. He is telling of the final moment when the hero, pursued by the Furies, is granted trial and reprieve by Athena on the hill of Ares above the city, after which the avenging Furies are turned into benevolent Eumenides, helpers to new law and enlightenment. In a joyous invocation at the close of the *Eumenides*, the final play of the trilogy, the chorus chants:

BRITISH MUSEUM

Pericles governed Athens during the middle years of the fifth century, when the city stood at the height of its wealth and power; under his direction the citizens of Athens constructed the magnificent temples on top of the Acropolis.

χαίρετε χαίρετ' ἐν αἰσιμίαισι πλούτου.
χαίρετ' ἀστικὸς λεώς,
ἴκταρ ἥμενοι Διός,
παρθένου φίλας φίλοι
σωφρονοῦντες ἐν χρόνῳ.
Παλλάδος δ' ὑπὸ πτεροῖς
ὄντας ἄζεται πατήρ.

Joy to you, joy of your justly appointed riches,
Joy to all the people, blest
With the Virgin's love, who sits
Next beside her Father's throne.
Wisdom ye have learned at last.
Folded under Pallas' wing,
Yours at last the grace of Zeus.

Athenian youths—and many since—were to learn these lines by heart. Sparta, however, for all its victories, was not capable of such a speech as this, which so confidently foresaw a glorious future. Indeed, strong as it stood, it was highly suspicious of the Athenian alliance, which it was not invited to join. It preferred to go its own way, in any case. The two ways were tragically to collide.

BRITISH MUSEUM; F. L. KENETT

THE IDEAL FORM

Our knowledge of monumental Greek art is based primarily on sculpture in marble, such as the frieze of horsemen shown at left, which was carved to adorn the Parthenon. For of all the major works of Greek art, marble sculpture is what has come down to us in greatest quantity. Time has devoured most of the statues in bronze. It has destroyed all of the large paintings which the Greeks themselves held to be their noblest works; we can gain but a dim idea of their splendor from the many vase paintings that survive. Time has erased from the marbles the painting that covered them, which the Greeks considered so important that the painter of a statue was often paid as much as its sculptor; and Praxiteles could claim that his best statues were those the great painter Nikias had decorated. Many of the marbles we do have survive only in Roman copies. If these sculptures cannot give us an idea of the breadth of the Greek achievement, they can show us its principles—principles which were equally important to painter and sculptor. For sculptors also worked in the way Plato remarked painters did, fixing "their eyes on perfect truth as a perpetual standard of reference, to be contemplated with the minutest care before they proceed to deal with earthly canons about things beautiful." Even when it had become most technically skilled and more concerned with naturalism, the classical art of Greece continued to be based on this search for ideal forms.

ACROPOLIS MUSEUM; HASSIA

ACROPOLIS MUSEUM; HARISSIADIS

184

ACROPOLIS MUSEUM; HASSIA

THE ARCHAIC STYLE

Greek artists began carving life-sized statues in the seventh century B.C., at first working primarily with the standing male nude, or *kouros*, and his female counterpart, the *kore*, who was always shown clothed. Like the Egyptians from whom they drew their inspiration, archaic sculptors represented the figure in a rigid frontal stance with the left leg forward. But the Greeks were not content to copy the same formal style which the Egyptians had followed for thousands of years; they strove to make their statues more lifelike. To endow them with expression, sculptors added a subtle smile to the statues' faces; soon they learned to give figures depth and volume by replacing the flat surfaces with realistic rendering of musculature and detailed treatment of drapery. By the end of the sixth century the Greeks could portray the human form naturalistically.

The two maidens opposite are of the archaic period, as are the youth at left and Theseus shown carrying off Antiope, below.

MUSEUM, CHALKIS; HIRMER

185

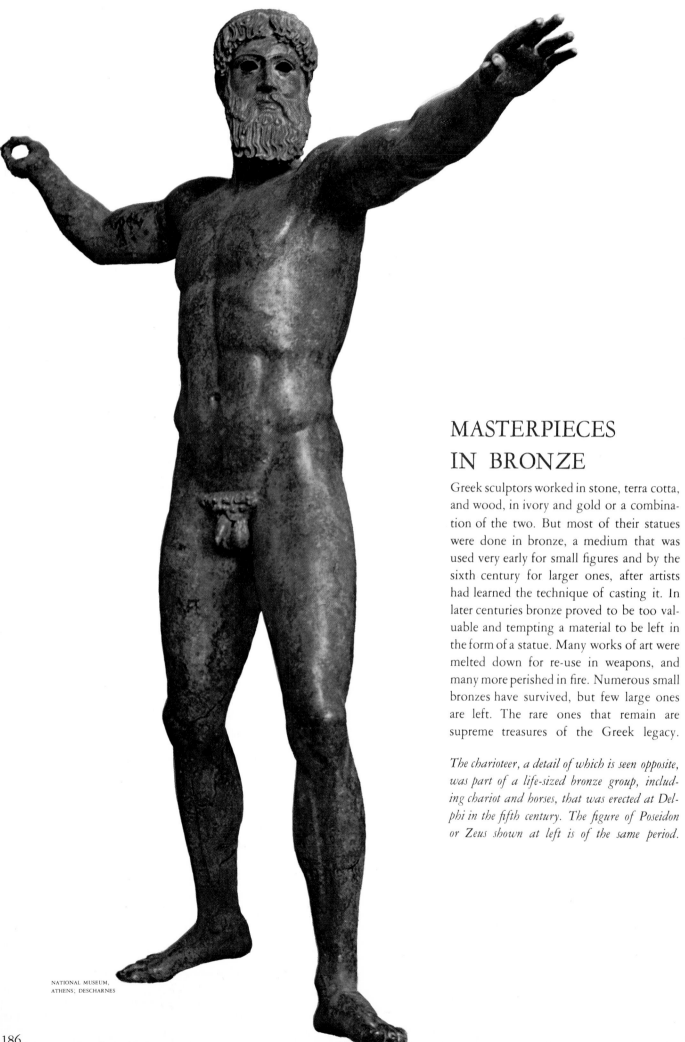

MASTERPIECES IN BRONZE

Greek sculptors worked in stone, terra cotta, and wood, in ivory and gold or a combination of the two. But most of their statues were done in bronze, a medium that was used very early for small figures and by the sixth century for larger ones, after artists had learned the technique of casting it. In later centuries bronze proved to be too valuable and tempting a material to be left in the form of a statue. Many works of art were melted down for re-use in weapons, and many more perished in fire. Numerous small bronzes have survived, but few large ones are left. The rare ones that remain are supreme treasures of the Greek legacy.

The charioteer, a detail of which is seen opposite, was part of a life-sized bronze group, including chariot and horses, that was erected at Delphi in the fifth century. The figure of Poseidon or Zeus shown at left is of the same period.

NATIONAL MUSEUM,
ATHENS; DESCHARNES

MUSEUM, DELPHI; DESCHARNES

GLYPTOTHEK, MUNICH; LEONARD VON MATT

MUSEO DELLE TERME, ROME; ALINARI

IMAGES FOR HIGH PLACES

Greek sculpture was primarily religious, used for the decoration of temples or for cult images within the temples. The colossal idols, which were probably the finest works, and certainly those on which most care was lavished, have all been lost. Much of the sculpture that remains comes from the pediments and from the friezes of temples. These statues show how Greek artists solved the problems that arise when a work of art is viewed from a distance. Many of the sculptures, which were to be placed high above the observer's head, are carved in deeper relief at the top than they are at the bottom, a technique that was carefully calculated to provide the figures with a lifelike appearance.

A warrior, opposite, from a temple pediment found in Aegina, raises his arm to strike. At one time the marble statue (which is partly restored) probably held a bronze spear. The nude flute-playing woman above, perhaps a courtesan, is carved in high relief on the side of an altar that may have been dedicated to the goddess Aphrodite.

ACROPOLIS MUSEUM; HANNIBAL

BRITISH MUSEUM; F. L. KENETT

PARTHENON STYLE

Under the direction of Phidias, who had been appointed to oversee the construction of the Parthenon, the sculptors of Athens carved hundreds of figures of gods and heroes, centaurs and citizens, to decorate the great temple of Athena. A sculptured frieze upon the building represented the Panathenaic procession, which every four years paraded through the streets of the city up to the Acropolis. Maidens and youths, on horseback and on foot, led cattle and sheep to sacrifice to the gods and brought a newly woven robe to clothe the cult image of Athena. This frieze was one of the few Greek temple sculptures to depict a contemporary scene instead of the customary mythological ones. Yet figures of the gods are on it too, awaiting the sacrifice at the procession's end. These sculptures of the Parthenon frieze, human and divine, like those that have come down to us from its pediments and metopes too, mark one of the summits of Greek classical art.

Two details from the Parthenon frieze depict, at right, a heifer being conducted to the sacrifice and, above, the goddess Artemis.

190

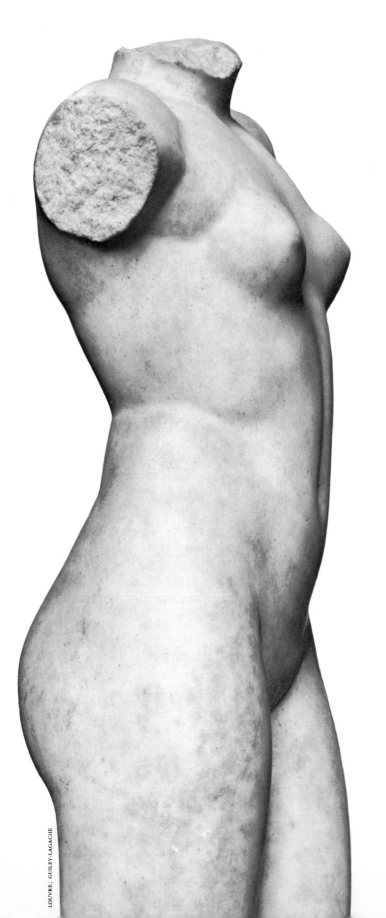

LOUVRE; GUILEY-LAGACHE

THE NUDE

Greek artists worked primarily from observing athletes rather than from models in the studio. In statue after statue dedicated in honor of Olympic victors they attempted to portray the musculature of the nude athlete in action. Their efforts led to a mastery of sculptural technique and to high development of the male portrait. The female image received less attention. At first women were shown clothed modestly, and then in a clinging and almost transparent robe, and finally nude. Eventually Greek sculptors carved female nudes as lifelike and beautiful as their male figures. But it was in the male body that artists searched for ideal proportions. Polycleitus labored as assiduously as his Renaissance counterparts were later to do in order to compose a treatise on symmetry and to devise a scheme by which a sculptor or painter might fix the perfect proportions for the human body. His system was so complex that it probably took into account the volume as well as the length of various parts of the body.

METROPOLITAN MUSEUM OF ART, FLETCHER FUND

In his Diadumenus, *seen at left in a Roman copy, Polycleitus tried to carve a body so perfect that athletes would be able to compare themselves to it in order to discover what their own flaws were. The* Esquiline Venus, *which is shown opposite, is a copy of a fifth-century Greek prototype.*

193

NATIONAL MUSEUM, ATHENS; DESCHARNES

THE INDIVIDUAL

Throughout the classical period, sculptors strove to show the ideal; for they believed that by representing the noblest type of the human body they could approach the depiction of divine beauty. Yet by the fifth century they had also begun to show emotion to differentiate individual sculptures from one another. By the time of Praxiteles in the following century, the classical ideal had been modified, so that faces became more expressive, figures more charged with movement. This foreshadows the great change that was to come in the Hellenistic period, when depicting an ideal became less important than portraying an individual or a momentary happening.

Praxiteles' Hermes with the infant Dionysus (left) is the only surviving original statue by one of the great Greek masters. But it has been suggested that the bronze opposite could also be the work of Praxiteles.

MUSEUM, OLYMPIA; ALINARI

KERAMEIKOS MUSEUM, ATHENS; HIRMER

MONUMENTS TO THE DEAD

The change that took place in Greek sculpture during the fourth century is most evident in the memorial carvings that were placed on graves. On them, features become less idealized and more human. Hundreds survive from the period following Athens' defeat by Sparta; indeed these monuments are almost the only Attic sculpture from an age when few public works were undertaken. At times it seemed as though even they would not be made, for the government objected to them when they became too ornate. Until 317 B.C., when their use was finally forbidden by sumptuary laws, the practice of erecting them was continued, providing sculptors with numerous opportunities to depict scenes of contemporary life.

Funerary monuments show a warrior (left) and a slave boy weeping for his master (opposite).

6

APOLLO
AND
DIONYSUS

*Now shall my song remember Apollo, Lord of
   the Bow,
At whom the Immortals tremble, what time they
   see him go . . .*
                    —*Hymn to the Delian Apollo*

*But I am Dionysus, Lord of the Revel—he
Whom Zeus begot on Cadmus' child, His own
   beloved Semele. . . .*
                    —*Hymn to Dionysus*

*Measured against the Apollonian idea, the Dionysian
one reveals itself as the eternal and basic wellspring
of art. . . . Yet wherever the Dionysian powers arise
in their impetuousness, Apollo also, wrapped in his
cloud, descends upon us.*
   —*Friedrich Nietzsche,* The Birth of Tragedy

The story is told that the philosopher Pythagoras, walking one day through the streets of the Greek settlement of Croton on the boot of Italy, passed a blacksmith's booth and was attracted by the diverse tones produced by different hammers striking the anvil. Pausing, he observed that the hammers ringing out at different pitch were of different weights, and that there seemed to be some regularity of scale between the notes. Might there not be some arithmetic progression governing the intervals of music?

He thereupon conducted an experiment—one of the first in the history of western science. Familiar with Greece's chief musical instrument, the seven-stringed lyre, he matched up two strings of equal length, thickness, and tuning, and found that when he "stopped," or clamped, one at its halfway point and plucked it, the string he had shortened by a half sang at precisely an octave higher than the other string. Similarly, if he "stopped" it at two thirds of its length, the shortened string sounded the fifth note of the octave above the first string. If he "stopped" it at three-quarter length, it sounded four notes higher than the first. He had found that there were numerical ratios between what we call the "concordant" intervals of scale (2:1, 3:2, and 4:3, to take the above). In terms of physics, he had shown that the vibration of two similar strings varies in inverse proportion to their length.

If some of this sounds abstruse and technical to the layman, it was not to Pythagoras and his disciples. On the contrary: in their eyes the recognition that music had a mathematical basis was one of transcendent import. For when considered together with other studies Pythagoras had been making in his absorption with number and form, it seemed to light up man's comprehension of the entire physical world around him, and of his own inner world of being as well. Greek art, architecture, ethics, religion, all were to be profoundly influenced by the numerical theories of the many-sided genius of sixth-century Croton.

That a discovery in music could exert so wide an impact upon Greek life was due in part to music's own role in that life, which was large and pervasive—perhaps more so than the role of music in any succeeding culture, even the Vienna of Haydn, Mozart, and Beethoven. Unhappily, we do not know with any certainty how it sounded. We do possess a few surviving fragments of ancient musical notation, with letters used to indicate the tones at which the given syllables of a chant were to be sung; but these letters cast no light on what the notes actually were in terms of any scale we know, and we have no idea of what Greek pitch actually was— that is, how a lyre's strings were tuned or a wind instrument such as the flutelike aulos was voiced. What we do know is that the

Greeks, quite apart from Pythagoras, had arrived at a highly developed system of harmonic series, or modes (one could call them "moods" more accurately than "keys"), and, moreover, that music making was an everyday activity among all classes. By "music" the early Greek also meant the dance and chanted poetry which were accompanied by the lyre or cithara or aulos. No wedding feast, no funeral rite, no harvest festival, no banquet or public ceremonial seems to have been complete without a gay or solemn music. We hear of the art very early, when in the *Iliad* a delegation of Agamemnon's men visit Achilles in his tent before Troy and find him singing lays of other heroes before him to the accompaniment of a lyre. By the time of the Panathenaic and Pythian games, devoted like those at Olympia to the celebration of spirit and body both, we find prizes being offered for performances on instruments and in song. Music became—partly as a result of Pythagoras' teachings—a subject of basic education; so great was the recognition of its importance that Plato, ever the puritan and moralist, laid down precepts as to which modes were to be taught to strengthen character, and which were not.

These modes, and the notion that each had its own ethical and emotional content, have fascinated and perplexed musicologists ever since, especially since no scholar can with any assurance reconstruct them on a western instrument. The Dorian mode was regarded as somber, virile, and warlike; the Lydian, lyric and plaintive; the Phrygian, passionate and unbridled; there were perhaps ten other modes, and all included quarter notes and other intervals that we associate with oriental music. Only the mind's ear can reconstruct in imagination the rise and fall of such music, its beat no doubt determined by stressed syllables of chant or movement of dancers, and its singers or players performing in monody without harmonic supports.

Immediate and stirring as music evidently was to the Greek, Pythagoras' study of it was part of a far greater search, namely that of the awakened Greek mind for central, governing principles that would reveal an underlying order amid the everyday diversities of nature. We have seen that Thales of Miletus thought he had found such a ruling principle or substance in water. His successor, the evolution-minded Anaximander, sensed a basic force in what he vaguely called "the Boundless." Another Ionian successor, Anaximenes, felt that the primordial unifying substance was air; still another, Heraclitus of Ephesus, identified it with fire, and further argued that the essence of all things lay in change: "Everything flows," he is said to have declared, "and nothing remains the same." All this, of course, was the sheerest guesswork—the

MUSEUM ANTIKER KLEINKUNST, MUNICH; HIRMER

The detail above from a wine jar depicts Dionysus, the god who gave wine to man; as patron of drama and passionate exuberance he stood as counterpart to the Apollo of reason and restraint.

imaginative young Greek mind striking out in many directions, ardently hunting for a more intelligible world than that provided by the random gods and their creation legends. Pythagoras, not satisfied with these explanations, turned from speculation to precise calculation. And his conclusion, based on what he had measured and counted, was that the root of all things was number.

He had found that musical relations can be explained by number. Ratio and symmetry could also be seen at the heart of many other manifestations around him: in the marvelous geometry of plants, in the relations of triangles, in the properties of individual numbers and series of numbers. Pythagoras, the first Greek scientist, was also the first man to pursue mathematics for its own sake rather than just as a practical aid. He became fascinated by the series or patterns that showed up when he represented given numbers by arrangements of rows of dots or pebbles. (This, as Bertrand Russell points out in his *Wisdom of the West*, "is a method of reckoning which in some form or other survived for a long time. The Latin word [for] 'calculation' means 'a handling of pebbles.'") Most fascinating was the number ten, which Pythagoras expressed thus:

Here, in what he called the *tetraktys*, was a perfect triangular series (note that it is the sum of its first four integers: $1 + 2 + 3 + 4 = 10$), and one whose pattern, moreover, was infinitely expandable. In the eyes of Pythagoras' followers the *tetraktys* had such transcendent properties that it became a mystical symbol by which they swore. Other numbers, when laid out geometrically by the same "pebble" method, were either "square" or "oblong." Some (4, 9, 16, etc.) were "square" in that they were the sum of successive odd numbers:

Others (like 6, 12, 20, etc.) were "oblong," being the sum of successive even numbers:

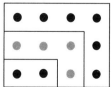

Still others, like the number five and its multiples, were asymmetri-

The singer above accompanies himself on a lyre, the favorite instrument of the ancient Greeks. The lyre was said to be invented by Hermes, who gave it to Apollo, and it became Apollo's chief attribute. With it, he represented all that was rational in the Greek spirit—adherence to harmony and respect for order—as well as gaiety and artistic sensitivity.

cal and "irrational," and were often expressed by the Pythagoreans in the form of the pentagram, or five-pointed star, which became a cabalistic symbol in the Middle Ages.

What is interesting in this to the mathematically inclined is that a series of integers (1 + 2 + 3 + 4) yields triangular numbers, while that of odd integers (1 + 3 + 5) yields square numbers, and that of even integers (2 + 4 + 6) yields oblong numbers. And while modern number theory has of course gone far beyond Pythagoras, it still uses his concept of the symmetrical numbers that satisfied his sense of order and progression as against the "irrational" ones that did not.

Ratio, consonance, rhythm, then, seemed to govern all things. To grasp the world about him, man must first find the number or proportion in things. Only when this is found can he truly distinguish the basic from the apparent, the permanent from the passing. Physical matter comes and goes and changes, and is perceived by the senses; but the forms, or "numbers," that underlie it are eternal, and these are perceived by the reasoning mind. The mind discovers the perfect, or the "ideal," and this is the only "real"; for that which is made known to the senses is transitory and imperfect. With this mighty leap of thought Pythagoras opens the way of Greek philosophy and prepares it for Plato, who (also beginning from mathematics) was to argue further the difference between the universal and the particular, between reality (which is one) and appearances (which are many), between what "is" and the objects of sense which are always "becoming" something else. Plato went on to argue that the highest reality is the Idea of The Good—which in turn, as we shall see, led to a new concept of a godhead.

Pythagoras' fifth-century followers were not ready to venture that further leap. Yet in their way they prepared for it. In their minds the result of their perception of the "real" through numbers and forms was a recognition of the entire world's unity or *harmonia*. At the highest level this was that harmonious "music of the spheres" which, they said, we failed to hear only because "the sound is with us right from birth and has thus no contrasting silence to show it up." The heavenly bodies, they claimed, gave out tones or vibrations at related intervals as they swung in orbit, and indeed every object "sang" or emitted some force of its own. (Was this some premonition of Newton's gravitational theory, or of ideas of radiation? Pythagoras is full of premonitions—he thought, for instance, twenty centuries before Magellan's ship finally proved it, that the world was round.)

While feeling his way toward the concept of some divine rule or

The bust above of Pythagoras is a Roman copy of a Greek work.

CAPITOLINE MUSEUM, ROME; SAVIO

THE RULE OF PYTHAGORAS

Mathematician, logician, musician, mystic, cult leader, and supposed magician all in one, the many-sided Pythagoras found time amid all his pursuits to found a school or brotherhood of his followers in Italy. This community, dedicated to self-purification and abstinence, adopted some taboos unique in the history of education and superstition. Among these were, in addition to abstention from meat:

To abstain from beans.
Not to pick up what has fallen.
Not to touch a white cock.
Not to break bread.
Not to step over a crossbar.
Not to stir the fire with iron.
Not to eat from a whole loaf.
Not to pluck a garland.
Not to sit on a quart measure.
Not to eat the heart.
Not to walk on highways.
Not to let swallows share one's roof.
When the pot is taken off the fire, not to leave the mark of it in the ashes, but to stir them together.
Not to look in a mirror beside a light.
When rising, to roll the bedclothes together and smooth out the impress of the body.

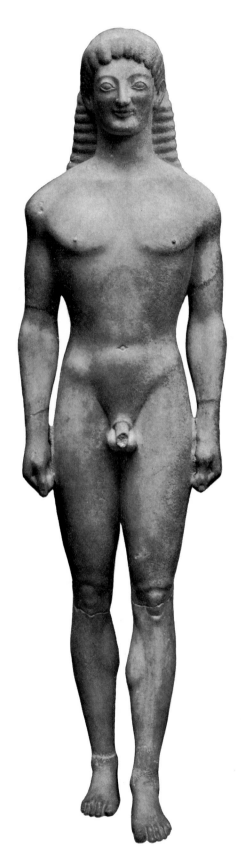

The kouros *above is representative of many Greek sculptures of the earlier archaic decades. The rigid posture and slightly extended left leg show the influence of Egyptian art.*
GLYPTOTHEK, MUNICH

Word or *logos* immanent in the numbers and proportions he saw about him, Pythagoras turned and peered deeply into the qualities of man himself. If man and nature were to be thought of as in concord, were not our individual beings ruled by number and *harmonia* also? What was the soul itself but a system of proportion? He asked the question, and his followers came forth with an answer. The soul, they argued, was made up of three parts as if on a scale—instinct and feeling (which we share with the animals) and reason (which is ours alone, and immortal). What was morality other than an effort to achieve balance and symmetry, and to pursue the just mean between extremes? Was not the healthy man (or, we would today say, the "well-adjusted" man) the one who was in a state of *harmonia*—quite literally "in tune"?

What was "well-adjusted" or well-proportioned or harmonious, then, was the ideal. It was also the most "real." It followed that whatever form or image a man himself created, that which had the most perfect proportions was the truest. In sculpture an ideal human shape carved in marble was "truer"—that is, more universal and relevant to the nature of man—than a representation that dwelt on the particular individuality of some one man, with all his imperfections or blemishes or departures from the ideal. In architecture a temple was most "true" (and this also in the literal, builder's sense of the word) when it stood in a just balance between vertical and horizontal, between thrust and support, between lift and weight, mass and interval. True proportion led to grace and beauty; indeed, the whole basis of beauty lay in proportion.

This was a thought many creative Greeks had been entertaining well before Pythagoras' time, expressing it in their own works. In every work of art, it was believed, there should be a harmonious ratio or relationship among all the elements: in architecture, for instance, so many units of length for so many of width or height. In Greek sculpture too, as it developed from its archaic forms, there was a similar search for ideal numerical ratios, the theory being that a figure not only required over-all balance and symmetry but a measurable relationship of each part to the rest. Polycleitus, one of Greece's greatest fifth-century sculptors (whose work, unhappily, we know only from Roman copies) was to be explicit about this, writing in a manual for students that "beauty consists in the proportions not of the elements but of the parts, that is to say, of finger to finger and of all the fingers to the palm and wrist, and of these to the forearm, and of the forearm to the upper arm, and of all parts to each other"; and he set out to codify certain rules of proportion—such as the height of a full figure equals seven and a half heads. This delight in discovering the "number," or inner order of things, was to continue and become central to the Greek legacy.

If we have been taken up here with highly intellectual concepts, it is because we are dealing with a people who discovered themselves in love with intellect as the way to truth, and found reality in abstraction. The very word *philosophia*, "the love of wisdom," may have been coined by Pythagoras; and this love, as Plato was to see it, led to knowledge of The Good—or God. There was one great god who best symbolized this Greek passion for the harmonious and true. Soon Greece was being beautified, on temple pediments like that at Olympia, with sculptures of Apollo, Pythagoras' patron and presumptive forebear. The divinity was carved in his cold majesty as the most perfect of gods, being in the shape of the most perfectly beautiful of men. And why was he the most beautiful? Because he embodied certain ideal laws of proportion, and thus the divine beauty of mathematics.

Yet Pythagoras' patron Apollo, as we have seen, was not only the lofty and luminous god of Greek reason and law. He was also a god of occult rite and eastern mystery and of the possessed priestesses at the oracle of Delphi which he shared with his supposed opposite, the unbridled and earthy Dionysus. And Pythagoras, the enlightened Apollonian, was like his patron half a Dionysian too, wedded to strange cult. Nothing illustrates more the contrasts and tensions in the Greek mind than the coexistence in it of the twin godhead images of Apollo, a god of reason, and Dionysus, a god of instinct and the irrational (indeed Apollo and Dionysus, when we come down to it, may well have been two sides of the same primordial image and thus, in the deep layers of Greek consciousness, one god divided). Again, nothing is more symptomatic of Greece than the presence on its earth of a Pythagoras, who in his person combined the varying strains of both, as geometer, mathematician, logician, magician, mystic, cult leader, healer, and soothsayer all in one.

Of the influences that shaped him we know little that is certain, though it seems clear that he absorbed a vast range of currents stirring in the Mediterranean world. (Like Thales before him and Socrates after him, he left not one word in writing; he simply talked, and his followers passed on his thinking.) Tradition has it that he was reared on the Aegean island of Samos, that he studied and traveled widely in Asia Minor and Egypt, and that he then quit his homeland as a man of about forty—perhaps in the year 530—to escape the oppressive tyranny of Polycrates and settled in Italian Croton, one of the many Greek daughter cities that had been established in the west. He appears to have come into direct

The free arms and individualized face of the Piombino Apollo (above), a bronze found in Italy, demonstrate the emerging naturalism in Greek sculpture of the late archaic age.

LOUVRE; GIRAUDON

contact with the Milesian thinkers of the school of Thales, as well as with Egyptian priest-stargazers and with the mystical sects of Orpheus then flourishing in mainland Greece and southern Italy; for echoes of each resound in his life's work.

Orphism, taking its name from the "divine musician," was a religious movement about whose origin, practices, and very nature there remains much obscurity as well as controversy. It may have sprung from eastern antecedents; it may have been not an organized cult at all, but simply a body of beliefs shared widely by people in the seventh and sixth centuries in the most diverse Greek places. However it may have arisen, its essence was a belief in the immortality of souls, in their transmigration, in personal redemption or purification through strict codes of abstinence, and in participation in rites or "mysteries" which the votary was not allowed to disclose. Some Orphic tales told that long before Homer's time Orpheus, a priest of Apollo, was killed by followers of Dionysus—from which the conclusion has been drawn that Orphism was an effort to redeem the Dionysian cult from this evil done. Others told of a proto-Dionysus himself being killed by Titans, to be resurrected as the Dionysus of the Olympians. Revelation from inspired texts supposedly received from Orpheus, as well as illumination through inspired healers, or *shamans*, in states of trance, figured in the worship, which centered not only about Dionysus as a symbol of rebirth but also about Apollo as a god of purification, or *katharsis*. (Again it can be seen how Dionysus and Apollo mix in the mists of early cult.) Now Pythagoras, when setting himself up as a teacher at Croton, seems to have brought with him not only an Ionian absorption with science and a mass of Egyptian priestly lore but much of Orphic faith and practice as well: for what he did was establish a religious brotherhood very much along Orphic lines, with himself its high priest.

This Pythagorean community was in a sense a monastic order, in which dedicated young postulants took vows of silence, abstinence, and retreat while they served a three- to five-year novitiate to prepare themselves for becoming *esoterici*—the initiates who would be admitted to the esoteric or secret knowledge of the Master. The community was open to women too, who were admitted under the same vows. Instruction emphasized mathematics and geometry. The doctrine of an afterlife was preached, but in the context of a belief in the transmigration of souls (therefore no eating of meat; the animal might have harbored the soul of some human predecessor). Together with philosophical enlightenment, purification was the goal of the Pythagorean fellowship, and this *katharsis* was believed to lie in the recognition of *harmonia*.

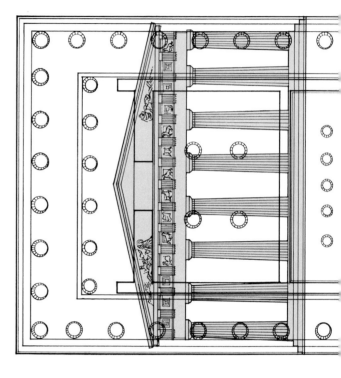

Although architects never developed a fixed canon of proportions for temples the way the sculptor Polycleitus did for the human body, they did follow certain rules for relating the parts of a structure to one another. Above, a floor plan of the Parthenon, with the façade plan superimposed upon it, shows that the space between columns was equal to half of each column's height. The number of columns along each side was double the number of those along the temple front, plus one. Early in the fifth century the sculptor Critios carved the statue of a youth shown at right; he probably followed a traditional scheme of proportions more flexible than the one which Polycleitus was to develop later in the century.

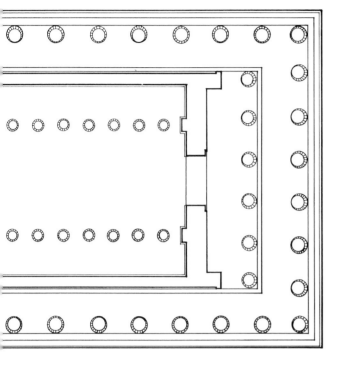

ACROPOLIS MUSEUM; HOYNINGEN-HUENE, RAPHO-GUILLUMETTE

Property was held in common, but this communistic society was at the same time markedly aristocratic, as members of leading educated families joined it. The fellowship was politically assertive too; under Pythagoras' leadership it tried to take over and run the city-state of Croton according to its ideals. For this it was persecuted by the local popular party; and as the order spread to other cities, its devotees were attacked or run out of town. They especially worshiped (as who of intelligence in the Greek world did not) the noble Apollo, but this hardly surpassed their veneration of Pythagoras himself, the white-robed master of vast and mysterious learning, of whose pronouncements or revelations they said in hushed tones αὐτὸς ἔφα—"He himself has spoken."

So compounded of contrasts, the sage of Croton is a central figure and symbol of Greek being, itself so divided between the rational and the irrational, between logic and instinct, between the scientific and the magical, between the state of self-possession and that of being possessed; and, one can continue, between symmetry and diversity, between order and abandonment, between the recognition of limits and the pursuit of the limitless, between restraint and vaulting ambition, or *hubris*. Pythagoras in all his wisdom could achieve no resolution or *harmonia* of all these diverse elements present both in himself and in those around him, any more than could Plato and Aristotle, who came after him. What was greatest in him and in Greece was the recognition of these conflicts for what they were and the belief that by grappling with them man might achieve a better order in his life.

The Greek arts most visibly embodied the contrasts. In those of form (architecture, sculpture, ceramics, vase painting), where men were the molders of supposedly enduring objects, it was natural for the Greek to lean to logic and make his shapes reflect ideals of harmony, perfection, and permanence. Here, one could say, the spirit of Apollo-Pythagoras was at work. But in another high art of Greece, the drama, in which the "clay" was human, another spirit—or another side of the Greek spirit—was paramount: the Dionysian. The stage play itself—a form unknown until the Greeks invented it—arose from magical and primitive rites connected with the worship of Dionysus. A sense of order, to be sure, was present even in the earliest Greek public performances designed to marry ancient ritual with the recital of lyric or epic poetry. But it was a different sort of order than that of the cold Apollo. A dynamic new structure emerged when a protagonist —supported by a chorus commenting, as if in the audience's behalf, on a stirring narration—was supplemented by a second and, then, a third speaker. As this prototype of drama evolved, it

The bronze tragic mask above was found in the ruins of an ancient warehouse in the Piraeus. Masks, tragic or comic, were used in Greek drama to suggest character and mood.

NATIONAL MUSEUM, ATHENS; HARISSIADIS

THE BIRTH OF TRAGEDY

Few lines in Greek drama so set the stage for dark fate to come than the opening ones in the Agamemnon, *the first play of Aeschylus' great Orestes trilogy. The audience knows from ancient tale what will happen: Agamemnon, returning from Troy, will be murdered by Clytemnestra and her lover Aegisthus. The watchman on the palace roof, awaiting the ships' return, begins in ironic simplicity:*

"I've prayed God to deliver me from evil
Throughout a long year's vigil, couched like a dog
On the roof of the House of Atreus, where I scan
The pageant of Night's starry populace,
And in their midst, illustrious potentates,
The shining constellations that bring men
Summer and winter, as they rise and set.
And still I keep watch for the beacon-sign,
That radiant flame that shall flash out of Troy
The message of her capture. . . ."

---

took on both a serious religious aspect that led to tragedy and a boisterous lewdness that led to comedy. In either case the concern was with the ever-changing and problematic condition of individual man—in tragedy, with his *hubris*, violent passions, and ill chance; in comedy, with his vulgarities and follies.

Yet, though Greek fine arts and drama may often seem far apart in the languages they speak—on one hand a Phidias carving man in gleaming perfection, on the other a Sophocles exploring his individuality and dolor—the extremes do meet. Though Greek drama deals with lawlessness, excess, and seemingly fortuitous circumstance, its tragic playwrights see some moral order behind all that. Perhaps the playgoer in the great Theatre of Dionysus at Athens, sharing the righteous wrath of Orestes that led him to kill his murderous mother Clytemnestra or pitying the innocent Oedipus for his unwitting parricide and incest with his mother Jocasta, found it hard to comprehend the justice of the fate meted out to these unhappy heroes. But an underlying law and design there must be, the dramatists said, even though it might be inscrutable. As if to emphasize the very shape of the design, they expressed their intimations of it in mighty symmetries or cycles of action and reaction, of guilt and consequence—in the Orestes plays a crime is punished by an avenging crime that in turn must be punished. So, immutable law and logic—Shall we say "number"?—govern each individual, who is only an offspring or shadow of the universal: and with this we once again move back from Dionysus to Pythagoras in his pure white robe and to Apollo.

Dionysus is also present in the Greek fine arts (he is always nearby wherever Apollo is), for the arts are not all serenity and sublimation by any means. The very siting of the temples of Delphi amid vertiginous cliffs and wild gorges suggests a linkage that Greek men felt between the reasoned and orderly and the tumultuous energies of nature. Apollo peers down coldly from many a pediment—or rather today from many a museum wall—but close by there may be vase paintings of maenads, Dionysus' handmaidens, swaying in ecstatic dance, their bodies possessed by some irrational power. One block of marble results in a sublimely composed Athena; another in a grotesque Gorgon's head, her tongue stuck out in a primeval grimace, recalling earlier earth powers or demons. The center relief on the pediment of one of the earliest major Greek temples, that of Artemis on the island of Corcyra—modern Corfu—dating from the early sixth century, is a gigantic representation not of an Olympian god but of such a weird Gorgon, grimacing and writhing. Naturalistic or "storytelling" representation of the incidental and anecdotal belongs, for the most part, to a much later day; but the appetites and joys of earth are celebrated even from early Greek time in drinking cups figured with prancing satyrs, in the posts raised before householders' doors as votives to Hermes, protector of the home, and each fronted with a phallus, and in vase paintings displaying sexual activity in so explicit a way that many museums turn them to the wall or keep them in rooms reserved for scholars.

When the arts of form in Greece began to revive in the late eleventh or early tenth century after generations of silence following the death of Mycenae, it was with pottery and pottery-painting that they commenced. The clay jug served as both a religious and a domestic vessel, bearing libations to the gods and the dead, as well as water and wine to the household, and to it the early Greek designer-artists devoted the best of their invention. They made long-necked ceremonial jars, often more than four feet high, which were turned on the wheel in sections and then joined before firing. It was as if in these outsized shapes of fragile material, which required perfect balance and stability, they were already exploring those major questions of proportion and scale that were to absorb the Greek mind. They decorated their work with figures in brown glaze—and what they put there were not images of man or beast or god, but a great variety of abstract and geometric patterns: parallel lines, triangles, concentric circles, semicircles, zigzag lines, and, next, the swastika and the meander line.

Artists went on in this way for perhaps two centuries. Only then does the human figure appear in paint: on the thick rotundities of vases we find rows of silhouetted shapes, schematic and triangular, rhythmic but rigid, and embedded in an over-all geometric scheme of which they are just a part. In their rudimentary appearance these figures bear no comparison with the sophisticated work that had been done by the Minoan painters almost a millennium before, nor are they the equal of the lifelike shapes drawn at an even earlier time on the tomb walls of Egypt. Yet these very modest Greek beginnings or re-beginnings in art presage what was to come; they continued and expanded the emphasis on symmetry and fundamental form—a form moreover determined to a considerable degree by function. The little men banded in a tight, convex procession between the handles of an early amphora are the precursors of the figures sculptured on the rigidly apportioned rectangular panels, or metopes, allotted to decoration along the frieze of a Doric temple, or on the far more difficult triangular space of the pediments at its ends.

Both metope and pediment—the great testing grounds of the Greek ornamental sculptor—were themselves forms created by the

According to popular belief, Gorgons turned all who looked on them to stone; terrifying Gorgon heads like the one above were used as protective images on buildings and armor.

ACROPOLIS MUSEUM; HANNIBAL

THE HORROR OF PURSUIT

In Aeschylus' next play, Agamemnon's son Orestes avenges his father's death by slaying both his mother and her paramour. For this he is pursued by the Furies, and in his fevered imagination there arises the image of monstrous Gorgons' heads. Thus Aeschylus writes in the Choephoroe, *or* Libation Bearers, *the second play of his trilogy:*

CHORUS: *Thou hast done well, bend not thy lips to such*
Ill-omened sayings and wild talk of woe.
Thou art deliverer of the land of Argos,
With one light stroke lopping two dragons' heads.

ORESTES: *Ah!*
What are those women? See them Gorgon-like,
All clad in sable and entwined with coils
Of writhing snakes! Oh away, away!

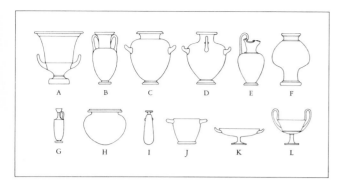

Among the most common Greek vase types were: (A) calyx krater, *used for mixing wine and water;* (B) amphora, *or storage jar;* (C) stamnos, *wine jar;* (D) hydria, *for water;* (E) oinochoe, *for pouring wine;* (F) psykter, *wine cooler;* (G) lekythos, *for oil;* (H) lebes, *mixing bowl;* (I) alabastron, *perfume bottle; and various drinking cups,* (J) skyphos, (K) kylix, *and* (L) kantharos.

NATIONAL MUSEUM,
ATHENS; HIRMER

geometry of structural engineering, forms in which the practical designer dictated to the artist. The metope was the response to a problem created by intervals between ground supports; the pediment, the result of raising a pitched roof. Egyptian and Mycenaean prototypes had suggested to Greeks the idea of a ceremonial walled chamber fronted by a "porch" consisting of eaves that extended over shafts, or columns. Gradually the idea of carrying these columns around the sides as well as the rear of the building emerged, making of them a structural colonnade carrying much of the weight of the pitched roof, which now extended over them, increasing the dignity and elegance of the structure. A longitudinal beam ran along the tops, or capitals, of these columns to give the roof foursquare support (this became the architrave); but athwart and above it, huge crossbeams were laid at intervals atop each capital, providing the building with rigidity. Proceeding from wood to stone, the Doric designer preserved the memory of his beam ends in the form of projecting stone blocks, or triglyphs, carved to simulate them. But this still left the question of what to do with the successive spaces between them. Simply leave them open, as gaping holes under the eaves? The Greek sense of order and fitness was not satisfied with that. So the answer was found to fill these spaces with panels (in some early instances of terra cotta) that made a virtue of their freedom from thrust and weight by being decorative. The ornament, however, a design contained within a strictly limited rectangle, had to be in a relief high enough to be clearly distinguishable to the viewer below.

The pediment, in turn, destined to house the splendors of the marbles of Olympia, Aegina, and the Parthenon, appears to have owed its shape in large part to the increasingly common use of roofing tiles in the seventh century. Cretan, Mycenaean, and very early Greek roofs were generally flat (there were some high-pitched roofs of thatch); but when tile, an efficient device for achieving drainage, came into use, it permitted—even dictated—a low-pitched roof and stimulated the shift to gable construction (and because of its weight, to stone construction too). This resulted in a broad and massive triangle above the entablature at either end of a rectangular building. This triangle had extremely acute angles at the base: and how to fill it became the most challenging of problems for the Greek sculptor, since the figures at its ends had to be low or prone, while those midway under the ascending limb had to be in a crouching or sitting position, leaving only those near or under the apex to stand tall and free.

Although small cult images and statuettes (mostly of wood or bronze) had been made previously, large-scale Greek stone sculpture begins presumably late in the seventh century with the stiff, ritualistic figure—particularly the life-sized, nude young male, or *kouros*, derived from Mesopotamian and Egyptian prototypes. With an abstract stare and usually a fixed archaic smile, he stood foursquare, without any bend or twist, arms rigidly at his side and left foot advanced slightly forward: if not a god or a god-man, then in any case an ideal. How to make him bend, or rather unbend? How to make him assume a more natural—one might say, more functional—human posture, without losing sight of the ideal? How to express movement, tension, gesture, individuality, personality, in lasting stone without at the same time expressing only the fleeting moment? This was the core of the sculptor's test, and it took generations to resolve it—a resolution that has left many modern admirers of the strict and archaic in Greek art wishing that the Greeks had not gone quite so far.

The sculptor working in relief—chiefly in the relatively small form of the metope—went at the challenge of motion first and by the middle of the sixth century was producing some vivid if crude depictions of action and struggle, using the labors of Heracles in particular as his subjects. In one such metope, from what is known as Temple C at Selinus in Sicily, the hero is shown with the two Cercopes, whom he has just vanquished and is carrying slung upside down from a pole on his shoulders (see illustration on page 211). The whole design is at the same time a shrewd construction of verticals, squares, and right angles, to which the metope's carver evidently gave much thought.

But his problem was relatively simple, since he was dealing with figures carved only frontally or in profile, with a minimum of modeling, and not intended to stand independently in any case. Meanwhile in large and free-standing sculpture the tradition of the rigid *kouros* went on for another half century or so. The form was a departure from Egyptian ones, to be sure, in that the youth was naked: his predecessors had either been robed or at least girt with a loincloth. (While his nakedness told of the emerging Greek cult of the body, his female partner in sculpture, the maiden, or *kore*, remained fully draped throughout the sixth century; it is not until the fifth that her garment begins to slip or become transparent— or in a few rare exceptions, disappear—and not until the fourth that she sheds it it altogether.)

A few harbingers of humanizing change and of relaxation of ritual stance do appear early in the sixth century in large sculpture —none more engaging, perhaps, than the life-sized figure found on the Acropolis of a man bearing a calf on his shoulders (see illustration on page 212). Is he carrying his burden for ritual sacri-

LOUVRE; GUILEY-LAGACHE

Pottery painting evolved within a century from the geometric lines of the amphora opposite (c. 750 B.C.) to the freer style of the one above, alive with men, plants, and beasts.

fice, for home consumption, or just to put out to pasture? One does not know. Some lovingly executed *korai* emerge also, their long tresses elegantly coiffed, their jewels gay, and their raiment rippling down in colorful folds that suggest the height of fashion. Yet these figures, winning as they are, are still highly stylized, impersonal, stiff, a little more than human, and thus somewhat remote. Ages before, the Egyptians and Cretans had been producing images as polished and handsome as these. It is only at the start of the fifth century—the one that was to be Greece's greatest—that there is a basic change, and then it rapidly takes on the scope of a major artistic revolution.

Most of what was built, carved, and painted particularly in and around Athens in those heady first decades of the fifth century was to perish at the hands of the Persian invader. Yet enough survives to tell of marvelous invention breaking out, without the loss of a sense of restraint. Perhaps no single work of art of that period ("transitional," some art historians call it, while others see it as "late archaic" about to go over into "early classical") conveys more of the sense of new perception and feeling astir than the statue of a youth attributed to Critios, and now housed in the Acropolis Museum close by the rubble from which it was unearthed (see illustration on page 205). For here is a man standing not as a ceremonial image but as a man himself stands, some muscles taut, others relaxed, shoulders slightly uneven, head slightly turned, weight more on one foot than on the other—ease and grace in his bearing rather than just stark erectness, yet repose and nobility informing his whole presence. Before, all was strength and schematic simplicity of form; but with the *Ephebe*, or youth, of Critios we have, if you agree with the eminent contemporary critic Sir Kenneth Clark, "the first beautiful nude in art."

Agree or not, here is a figure that stands at the threshold of a new era; the eye of the Greek artist has shifted from the far to the near, from the abstract to the concrete, from the symbolic to the "natural" (in which, however, he seeks to find an embodiment of the perfect). Greek art, in short, has proceeded part of the way to the study of what is of the earth, earthy, whereas Greek philosophy and science proceeded from physical manifestations close at hand to a consideration of what might lie behind or beyond them —that is, some governing rules or principles to be perceived only by the mind. The artist and the philosopher-scientist were both making great leaps of exploration. It took courage for a Critios (if it was he who carved the *Ephebe*) to abandon the tradition of a ceremonial image abstracted from man and replace it by a "real" man, just as it had taken courage for a Pythagoras to identify

A primitive terra-cotta figurine of a woman, probably a funerary offering, is decorated with birds and the imaginative geometric designs characteristic of eighth-century pottery.
MUSEUM OF FINE ARTS, BOSTON

"reality" with what was most abstract, that is, number. Here, one might argue, were Apollonian and Dionysian drives at work again and commingling—on one hand the pursuit of the perfect or ideal, and on the other the desire to be the witness and interpreter of everyday man, with all his earthly passions.

At about the time the Athenian *Ephebe* was made (say around the year 480) there was also carved in nearby Eleusis a figure of a running girl, body leaning as if into the wind, head turned back over her shoulder, drapery flowing with her current of passage— her complex motion a complete departure from convention and her whole air one of bounding grace (see illustration on page 213). Yet she, too, like the *Ephebe*, is in her way still "transitional": many problems of form in movement have not yet been solved; the pose, technically daring as it is, is not quite "natural"; and the girl still suggests more a generalized presence than any specific one. At about the same time, also, there were raised on the pediments of the Doric temple sacred to the local goddess Aphaia on the island of Aegina, just off the Athenian and Eleusinian coast, the extraordinary marbles found in 1811 by C. R. Cockerell and his party. Here we have "threshold" work in its greatest array: a massive group of warriors, some lunging, some prone and dying, others kneeling and arching their bows, their tutelary goddess standing above them—and all together, despite their battling movements, still inexpressive of individuality, aloof and cold. The execution of these marbles is rough and angular, compared with what Phidias was to accomplish when he designed the flowing figures of the Periclean Parthenon half a century later, with all their anatomical perfection and emotional finesse. Yet many a modern eye sees some special glory in such early sculptures as these from Aegina, the work of artists who had learned much but not yet so much that their chisels could tell everything—that is to say, perhaps too much.

In the intervening years enormous gains were made in sculptural mobility, naturalness, and refinement, while little was lost of the sense of the timeless and universal. The advances were greatly assisted by the use of bronze as a medium, to which artists increasingly turned; they were thereby able to work in malleable materials for molding and casting, instead of having to chip away at resistant rock. Even before the turn of the fifth century an unknown sculptor had cast an over-life-sized figure of a supple and seemingly reflective *kouros* that was recovered only in 1959 at the Piraeus to be acclaimed as both the earliest and one of the finest large Greek bronzes known to us. The decades before midfifth century produced two more advanced masterworks in bronze

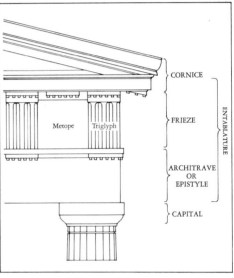

The entablature of a Doric temple, as exemplified by the northeast corner of the Parthenon (top) is shown diagrammatically in the drawing above. When temples began to be built of stone, they still retained elements of their wooden prototypes; the ends of wooden beams were symbolically represented by carved triglyphs. The spaces between them became metopes—stone rectangles which provided repeated opportunities for the Greek genius for decoration. The metope below, depicting Heracles carrying two dwarfs, is an early one, from a temple at Selinus, Sicily.

The Calf-bearer, *or* Moschophoros, *found on the Athenian Acropolis, was carved over a century before the Parthenon was built. It shows much of the stylization of other sculpture of the archaic period, but at the same time the statue suggests the beginning of a change in the direction of graceful human portrayal and movement. Man and calf are harmoniously unified, as if there were some understanding between them, and archaic rigidity gives way to a subtle play of form and balance.*
ACROPOLIS MUSEUM; ALISON FRANTZ

that have survived—the imperious, bearded Zeus or Poseidon, now in Athens' National Museum, superbly balanced in the act of hurling a thunderbolt or a trident, and the elegantly poised and robed charioteer at Delphi (both illustrated on pages 186–187).

Though the fifth-century maker of free-standing sculpture preferred bronze to stone and no doubt thought of it as equally durable, it proved singularly vulnerable to the ravages of man. For it was a substance of such value and convertibility that almost all bronze statues of ancient Greek times, as well as Roman ones, were melted down by subsequent generations simply to recover the metal for other uses. (Horace proved to be highly prophetic when he began his famous ode proclaiming the immortality of his poetry with the words "*Exegi monumentum aere perennius*"—"I have finished a memorial more lasting than bronze.") The major Greek bronzes that have survived owe their existence to having been either accidentally or intentionally buried from prying eyes or to having been sunk at sea—presumably on their way to eastern or Roman collectors. Thus the splendid Zeus or Poseidon mentioned above was brought up in fishermen's nets from the sea bottom off the coast of Euboea in 1928, having gone down with some transport in ancient times. The bronze *kouros* found in 1959 came to light with other bronze trove when workmen repairing a sewer in the Piraeus hit upon what seemed to be the burned-out remains of a warehouse for storing loot taken from Athens by the Romans in the first century B.C.

Three of the greatest Greek sculptors who are known to us by name, Myron, Phidias, Polycleitus, flourished in the middle of the fifth century. They worked for the most part in bronze, though no originals of theirs in metal remain. With these three, Greek art reaches a brief summit of balance in every sense of the word. Polycleitus, the measurer and codifier, is profoundly taken up with the problem of how to combine repose with life-giving movement, and resolves it in his own intellectual way. He evolves the figure of a broad-shouldered, massive athlete who is not quite standing still, nor yet in distinct motion, but poised as if about to walk—balanced, you could say, in a timeless moment of suspension between rest and action. Though we know this Polycleitan figure only through Roman copies of two of its versions, the *Doryphorus* and the *Diadumenus* (see page 193), the crudity of the imitations cannot distort the fundamental brilliance of the conception—one that was to become canonized in western art.

Myron, on the other hand, whose work we also know only through replicas, was evidently a sculptor absorbed with rendering strong motion, at the risk of becoming "momentary"; but he solved his problem by subordinating the action to a strict, geometric pattern. His masterwork, the *Discobolus*, shows us an athlete at the instant of extreme flection and tension in the act of twisting about to hurl a discus; yet, though nothing could be more fleeting than this, everything in the design is governed by an idea of equilibrium of lines and forces (see page 160). As Kenneth Clark remarks, it is "like some Euclidean diagram of energy."

In Phidias, meanwhile, the master of the Parthenon, we come to a man engaged with both grace and grandeur. We do not know just which sculptures and reliefs mounted on the new structure he himself executed. We do know that by 447 Pericles had made him artistic overseer of the Athenian polis' building program as a whole, and we believe that Phidias' mind and designing hand were present throughout the ornamenting of the great new temple, even though we cannot identify his actual chisel on pediment or frieze. We believe this because we sense a powerful unifying spirit at work throughout the Parthenon, shattered and despoiled and scattered among the world's museums though its relics now are.

It was a spirit dedicated to flowing rhythms, as in the frieze procession of lightly draped maidens now in the Louvre, or in the reliefs of harmoniously seated gods and goddesses, some now seated in the British Museum; to elegance of action, as in the groups of horsemen who once pranced handsomely on the frieze; to naturalism, as in such figures as a surviving horse's head from the east pediment, nostrils distended, veins bulging, as if at the moment of snorting charge; to exuberance of spirit, as in a lively mask or waterspout here and there; to ease of bearing, as in the gracefully reclining male pediment figure sometimes called the *Ilissus*. Above all, it was dedicated to the expressive mood, most expressive and most haunting of all in the reclining pediment group known as the *Three Fates*, headless and armless long before they were shipped away in Lord Elgin's sailing vessels, yet—through the brooding poise of their bodies and the drapery that ripples over them as if touched by some distant air—eloquent now as before of nobility and the mysterious loom of a divine presence.

For, "natural" as he likes to be, Phidias is majestic too. Indeed, he is the most majestic sculptor in all antiquity. Though his chisel on the Parthenon lintel eludes us, we do know that he himself did carve (with assistance, surely) three of the mightiest and most hallowed statues of classical times: first, the colossal bronze image of Athena, thirty or more feet high, that was erected about 456 near the highest point of the Acropolis, the gleaming tip of her spear visible far out at sea; next, the equally colossal gold and ivory figure of Athens' patroness erected within the sanctuary of the

Sculpture rapidly became more naturalistic when the Greeks had learned to impart motion to it. The lively Running Maiden *of Eleusis is an early attempt to express action in stone.*
MUSEUM, ELEUSIS; GERMAN ARCHAEOLOGICAL INSTITUTE, ATHENS

213

BRITISH MUSEUM; MANSELL

The Parthenon metopes, one of which appears above, were carved about forty years after the Eleusis maiden and show the advances that had been made in depicting emotion and action. They illustrate a mythological battle between Greeks and centaurs which occurred when the centaurs drank too much at a wedding and tried to rape the Greek bride.

Parthenon and dedicated in the year 438; third, at Olympia, to which Phidias appears to have removed his studio shortly thereafter, the statue of Zeus, seven times human size, acclaimed as his culminating masterwork. Ironically, all three have perished, and we know of them only through travelers' descriptions, representations on ancient coins, and a few poor scaled-down and hand-me-down later adaptations and statuettes.

In these immense figures—all difficult to visualize today—Greek impulses toward order and clarity on one side, and toward the wild and incommensurable on the other, were inextricably mixed (Apollo and Dionysus again, if you will). Hear Pausanias, a worldly second-century A.D. traveler, as he confronts the glittering Phidian Athena in her dark Parthenon sanctuary: "On the middle of her helmet is placed a likeness of the Sphinx . . . and on either side of the helmet are griffins in relief. . . . Athena stands erect, with a tunic reaching to the feet, and on her breast the head of Medusa is worked in ivory. She holds a statue of Victory about four cubits [some six feet] high, and in the other hand a spear; at her feet lies a shield and near the spear is a serpent. . . ."

The statue of Zeus at Olympia—a site until then peopled chiefly with severe sculptures in the late archaic tradition—must have been even more overpowering. Pausanias describes the statue as a magnificent figure in golden robes, holding a scepter gleaming with precious metals and seated on a mighty throne adorned with gold and ivory, ebony and precious stones; richly painted screens surrounded the image. To us today this may suggest an image more oriental or Byzantine than Greek, or at least wholly unlike the spare and strict Apollo erected on the west pediment at Olympia less than a generation before. Because time has eroded the painting, we often forget that the Greeks liked to color their sculpture as well as their buildings. Yet, knowing of Phidias' other accomplishments, if only through fragment and echo, we can be fairly certain that even in such a splendid display he never lost a sense of harmony and wholeness.

That sense continues well into the next century, though one could argue that in Praxiteles, who flourished about 350, it begins to become precarious. His glorious Hermes (illustrated on page 194) is at the same time a gentle Hermes, a bit exquisite in his sinuous twist and extreme good looks, and almost on the verge of sentimentality in the way he holds the infant Dionysus in his arm. Praxiteles' god, in his perfection, is a very human one. Is he near the point of becoming almost too human to remain a god, too immediate to be an ideal? Subsequent generations, taking Praxiteles rather than his forebears as their model, were to slip swiftly down into the intimate and anecdotal and "naturalistic" in art. The accomplished sculptor of the Hellenistic age knew how to design a figure in every conceivable posture and with any conceivable expression on his face; and at the culmination of that age he delighted in showing his mastery of the moment in such works as the writhing Laocoön group (see page 392). But the question remained: Between the permanent and the passing, what is "real"?

In architecture, by its very nature inclined to be the most durable and stable of arts, this problem presented no like difficulties to the Greek. Innovator and experimenter though he was in many things, in his formal building the Greek went just so far and no farther. He developed a few basic types; he improved, refined, elaborated on them, and then stuck with them, intent on achieving ideal proportions between all their elements, great and small, rather than reaching for some radical departure in design. From Egyptian prototypes and Mycenaean palace architecture, as we have seen, he derived the idea of a rectangular, porched temple. He developed as well the *tholos*, a circular chamber, perfecting it in the round shrines at Delphi and Epidaurus and the council chamber in the Athenian Agora. From very ancient hillside ceremonies of devotees of Dionysus he may also have conceived the idea of the semicircular outdoor theatre, built against the lean of a steep, concave slope, and which led to the masterwork at Epidaurus (see illustration on pages 238–239). Later he added the invention of the long, roofed gallery, or stoa, usually walled on one side, always colonnaded on the other, which served both as a covered market place for stalls, a promenade for citizens, and a particular meeting place for philosophers and their students—so much so that a whole school became known as the Stoic.

These forms, with their clarity and rhythm, sufficed for the architect. Different areas of the Greek world of course produced their own variations of style. To support their roofs, Ionian designers across the Aegean developed a system of columns culminating in capitals with voluted extensions along the lintel, as against the bluff, square capitals topping the Doric type. These extensions may have encouraged builders to space their columns more widely apart than before. Moreover, Ionic shafts were more slender, and this made them far less obstructive and lent a new sense of airiness to the structure. The effect was heightened by the alternating flutes and smoothly polished ridges that soon appeared on the Ionic column and by the graceful volutes of its capital; it was a winning response to the period's impulse toward greater refinement, and by the mid fifth century it was widely used by mainland architects, especially in Athens. The Corinthian order, with

Phidias' masterwork—the colossal ivory and gold cult image of Athena that stood inside the Parthenon—disappeared in later ancient times. This is a clumsy Roman copy of it.
NATIONAL MUSEUM, ATHENS; HANNIBAL

The cup painting above depicts a maenad, one of the mythical followers of Dionysus who wandered the countryside with the satyrs, honoring the god with wild orgiastic rites.

MUSEUM ANTIKER KLEINKUNST, MUNICH; HIRMER

its even more complex capital, was a later variation of the Ionic.

Here were technology and aesthetics in accord; and to this the Greek builder added some shrewd studies in applied psychology. A column with straight vertical lines gave an optical illusion of concavity; this he corrected by enlarging the diameter of the center section of the column (entasis). Then he also learned that to make it seem truly straight and just to the human eye on the ground, he should make a few other small but key corrections: he should have his columns lean inward slightly, and make the whole foundation, along with the entablature above it, rise at the center, dipping imperceptibly at the ends. As the architect Ictinus applied these refinements to the Parthenon, here was supreme calculation at work. (The slight· and subtle bend of the building can still be observed by taking a line of sight from one end of its stylobate, or base, to the other: there is a rise and fall of about four inches along the course of 228 feet.)

Yet, though he studied and improved continually, the Greek architect did not revolutionize. Though for instance he created within the Ionic scheme a running frieze that overcame the strict intervals of triglyph and metope, and though he painted his temples richly and piled more and more decoration upon them—from egg-and-dart moldings and dentils to carved rainspouts and figures atop the eaves—he never let this affect or distort the basic rule and reason of his inherited design. He left it almost entirely to the Romans after him to pursue the engineering of the high vault, the arch, the dome, and the grand façade. Indeed, though the Mycenaeans long before him had created an early masterpiece of vaulting in the subterranean "Treasury of Atreus," the Greek himself was content to live for the most part with the post-and-lintel system handed down, with improvements, from old timber-construction days—but he insisted upon striving to perfect the relationship of post to lintel.

Not that the temple and its precinct became just one fixed and rigid symmetry. Its often wild or precipitous site, its winding processional path which followed the course of an earlier one to reach some ancient altar, the accident of a sacred spring—all this kept the geometry from becoming too dry. The Acropolis complex as a whole—like that of the sacred precinct at Olympia, whose construction in large part preceded it—is quite asymmetrical; an accumulation of elements of different origins, styles, and purposes, it is built along no central axis and is collectively beautiful because of the very ease and "naturalness" of the placing of the elements, as against, for example, the parade-ground rigidity of Versailles. At the peak stands the perfect form of the Parthenon, corrected for all illusions or "appearances," and pure in every proportion. Yet obliquely opposite on the cliff, as a sort of counterweight, stands the highly irregular Erechtheum, completed half a century later and built on several levels with three porches of widely differing heights, two gabled and the third and smallest with a flat roof upheld by maiden figures, or caryatids. A profusion of steps leads to several chambers (the temple was dedicated to several gods) and to a crypt or basement below, over the well of Poseidon that was rumored to lie far beneath. For Greece, the Erechtheum is an unbridled building—all impulse and diversity, you could say, whereas the Parthenon is all unity—and it suggests a counterweight to its greater sister not only in its siting but in the Greek mind. Many a student has remarked that the two structures, with all their contrasts or perhaps because of them, together form an admirable composition, or whole.

Recrossing to the south edge of the cliff, you peer down into the semicircular bowl of the theatre sacred to Dionysus—those stones not far below the Parthenon's sunswept eaves that echoed to boundless passion and daemonic outburst. Here Aeschylus' Agamemnon first shouted his terrible death cry; here Sophocles' Aegisthus, thinking a covered corpse before him to be that of Orestes, discovered Clytemnestra slain instead; here the hill resounded to the frenzied shrieks of Euripides' Medea, betrayed by Jason and advancing to kill their children. Here scenes of the natural, the unnatural, and the supernatural piled horror upon horror. There were no ruminating Hamlets here, only the fiercest or most pitiful of men and women driven to their fates. And yet a sense of moral order governed these blood-drenched dramas, as did a sovereign sense of dramatic order, unified theme, and spare rigor in the telling.

Greek drama was an exploration of human faults, passions, and excesses. Yet it presumes the irony of fate, and the justice (or the injustices) of the gods. It tells of heroes overtempted by *hubris*, and yet, like the marble balance above the Dionysian slope, of order, plan, restitution, law. Its very violence is a complement to the immobile grandeur above, yet is part of it. Aristotle, the world's first dramatic critic, was to identify in Attic tragedy the three basic unities of time, place, and action—a way of saying that a great play was built like a temple too. As one of Greece's most searching minds, Aristotle was uniquely qualified to judge between Dionysian extremes and Apollonian restraints, and so to state his doctrine of the Mean.

Greece hardly needed to wait upon great Aristotle to publish this. It had been pursuing this thought all along.

Apollo, guardian of order, was not above disorderly love affairs; the painting may depict a scene between the god and Cassandra, who failed to keep a promise to give herself to him.
MUSEUM OF FINE ARTS, BOSTON

REMAK RAMSAY

THE NOBLE STRUCTURE

In the architecture of the fifth century—generally symmetrical, often severe, always stately, and sometimes light —the Greeks came closest to realizing the ideals of balance and perfection for which they had been striving ever since their emergence from the dark age that followed the death of Mycenaean culture. Increasing wealth from colonial enterprises and commerce gave them the means for adorning their cities with splendid temples to the gods, along with civic structures such as colonnades and outdoor theatres. In all these buildings the Greeks concentrated their skill and creativity, not on inventiveness and variety of form, but on the pursuit of harmony, proportion, and nobility in a few simple plans—the rectangular temple, the lengthy stoa, the hillside theatre. One architectural order followed another; but the fundamental design remained the same. From wood, the Greeks turned to stone for building; and as they became more familiar with it, they learned that its adaptability was as great as its limitations. By the fifth century they could perform fantastic tricks of optical illusion in shaping it, and were able to erect imposing buildings that seemed to be supported only by graceful columns. The Parthenon, standing atop the Athenian Acropolis, represents the peak of Greek architectural attainment; millions of viewers have approached it, as the picture at left does, from the eaves of the Propylaea, gateway to the holy precinct.

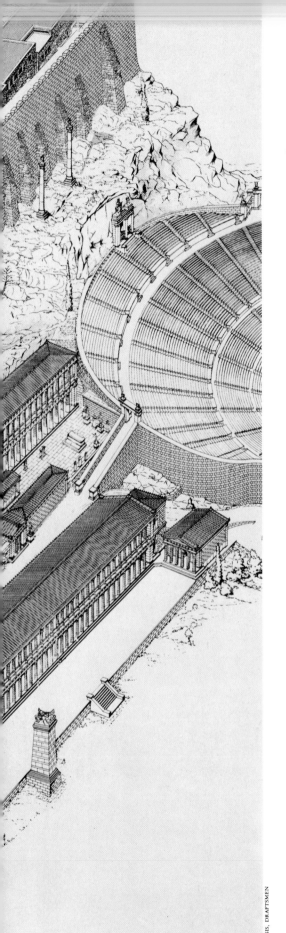

ATHENA'S HEIGHTS

In prehistoric times its steep crags made the Acropolis (meaning in Greek "the high citadel") a stronghold and place of refuge for the Athenians. In more peaceful days it became a religious sanctuary dedicated to the city's patron goddess. Persian invaders razed its shrines in 480 B.C. The world is fortunate in that Pericles' decision to rebuild them in mid-century coincided with the period of Greece's greatest artistic achievement. At left a reconstruction shows the Acropolis as it may have looked in late classical times (some subsequent buildings appear). Each major structure is numbered in the key below. Because the citadel was all rebuilt within fifty years, the relationship of each building to the other was well planned; one of the earliest constructions was the temple of Athena Nike (1), ingeniously perched in front of the Propylaea, or sacred gateway (2), whose north wing, the Pinakotheke (3), was used for exhibiting pictures. Next to the precinct of Artemis Brauronia (4), the bear goddess worshiped by young women, was the Chalkotheke (5), which may have been a storage place for treasures, especially bronzes; it had its own propylon (6). The Parthenon (7) was built as a dwelling for Athena, patroness of Athens. A shrine to a legendary king of Athens was located where a modern museum (8) now stands. Just opposite the little round temple (9) that the Romans added, Zeus was honored with a temple precinct (10). Behind Phidias' gigantic outdoor statue of Athena (11) was the altar (12) where rites to the goddess were performed. The Erechtheum (13) was the Athenians' favorite temple. Each year four young girls from noble families spent several months in the House of the Arrephoroi (14) working in the service of Athena. Against the north wall was another precinct of Zeus (15). Most of the edifices on the south slope of the Acropolis are Hellenistic: the Odeum of Herodes Atticus (16) was constructed about A.D. 167. The Stoa of Eumenes (17) served as a promenade for spectators at the Theatre of Dionysus (18), originally built in the fifth century B.C. and rebuilt many times; next to the theatre was the sanctuary of Asclepius (19).

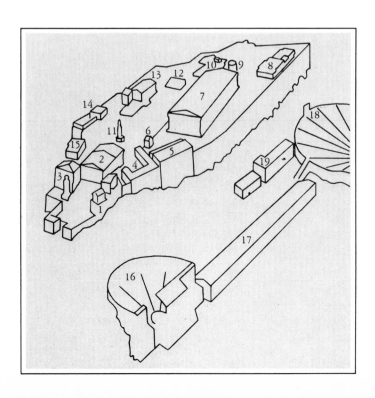

AL. N. OIKONOMIDES, ARCHAEOLOGIST; N. & K. GOUVOUSSIS, DRAFTSMEN

DESCHARNES

HARISSIADIS

SPLENDOR THROUGH TRIBUTE

It was only after Pericles had reconstructed the Long Walls connecting and fortifying Athens and the Piraeus that he undertook the task of erecting a glitter of new temples atop the ruined Acropolis. Tribute, reluctantly paid by Athens' allies in the Delian League, met the immense costs of the project. The Parthenon, begun in 447, was completed within fifteen years under Phidias' direction. He asked its architects, Ictinus and Callicrates, to build within the structure a sanctuary large enough to accommodate his tremendous statue of Athena, faced with ivory and gold (and costing about 850 talents, more than $10 million in today's money—a widely criticized extravagance). To do so, they used eight instead of the customary six Doric columns at each end of the temple and lengthened the sides proportionately. Their engineering skills enabled them to produce the illusion that the lines of the building were completely straight, though not one of them actually was: the columns lean inward a few inches, and the floor, frieze, and pediment are curved slightly. Such perfect proportions are united in the Parthenon that men are still trying to fathom the reckonings of the temple builders.

The Parthenon, the crown of Athena's city, is shown opposite, its marble floor swept by rain. Above, a view of the Acropolis taken from the west shows the Parthenon façade and the gateway approach to Athens' hilltop citadel.

ALISON FRANTZ

THE VIEW AT THE TOP

When the Parthenon was finished, the Athenians turned to the task of erecting the Propylaea, or sacred gate-building, as the entrance to the Acropolis. Traditionally such gateways had templelike façades; to this Mnesicles, the architect of the Athenian Propylaea, added sheer-walled wings which rose directly out of the Acropolis cliff. His concept of deliberately joining two building types was revolutionary; perhaps even more revolutionary was the fact that the Propylaea was designed to please people as well as the gods. The entrance was purposely shaped in the form of a U as if to enfold worshipers, who were greeted with a splendid vista of Athena's sanctuary as they stepped into the forecourt. Near the Propylaea stood the temple of Athena Nike, on the cliff's edge. Designed twenty years before it was finished in 423, this Ionic temple gave brightness and charm to the solemn citadel.

HARISSIADIS

HARISSIADIS

At far left, a view of the western slope of the Acropolis shows the slight Athena Nike temple beside the mass of the still imposing Propylaea. The temple appears again at left framed by two columns of the porch of the Propylaea and silhouetted in the sunset. The east façade of the temple, above, shows its well-preserved Ionic columns and frieze.

OVERLEAF: *The Erechtheum was unique in Greek architecture. Instead of a surrounding colonnade, the temple has porches on three sides, each of different dimensions and each rising from a different level. On the south side (right) stands the most beautiful of the porches, its roof supported by a row of graceful caryatid maidens.*

RAY MANLEY, SHOSTAL

225

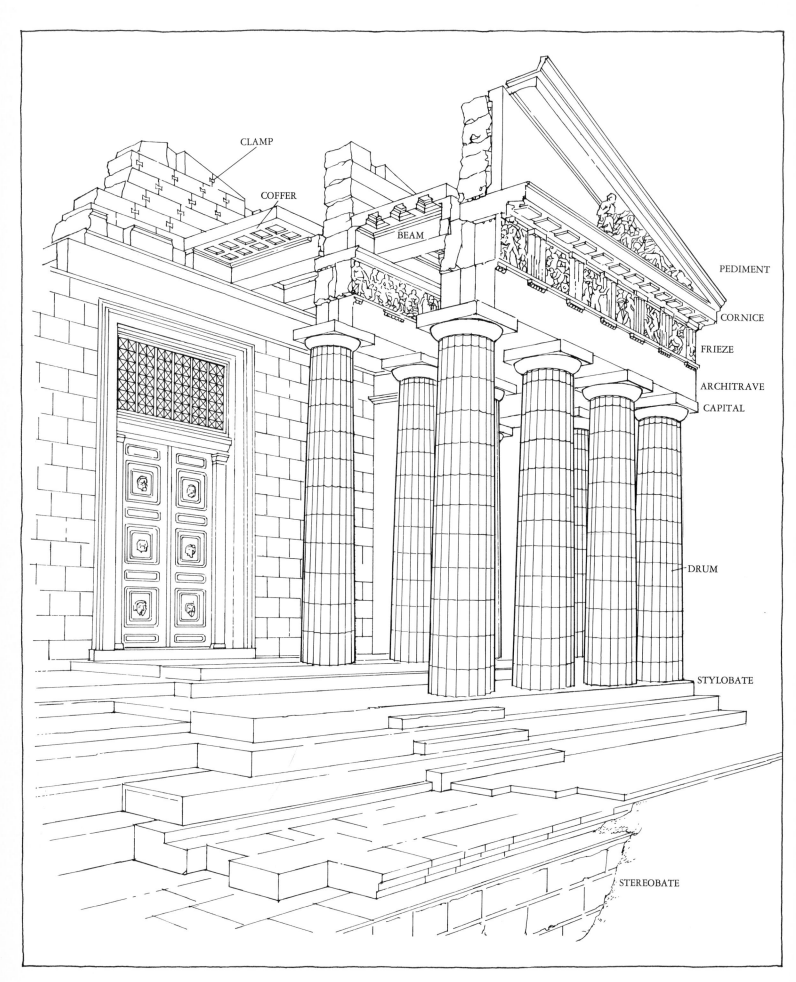

CLAMP

COFFER

BEAM

PEDIMENT

CORNICE

FRIEZE

ARCHITRAVE

CAPITAL

DRUM

STYLOBATE

STEREOBATE

The cutaway drawing of the Parthenon, above, shows the structure of a temple. The top of the sty-
lobate forms the floor. Walls and columns carry crossbeams or architrave; these in turn support
a coffered ceiling, gables across which beams for roofing will be laid, and frieze and pediment.

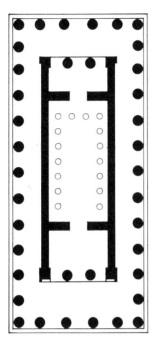

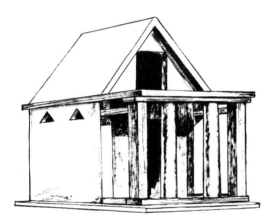

HOYNINGEN-HUENE, RAPHO-GUILLUMETTE

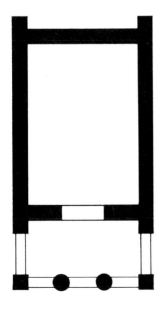

THE FINE ART
OF TEMPLE BUILDING

The great stone temples of ancient Greece were closely related to their mud-brick and timber prototypes, translating many structural elements, such as the thick wall, the pitched roof, the hewn beam, and the column, into limestone or marble. Basic design was carried over, too, and developed. A ninth-century B.C. hut-temple (drawing and floor plan at lower left) and the Hephaesteum, built at Athens in about 450 (floor plan and photograph above), both show essentially the same features: a columned porch leading to an inner chamber.

In classical times stone blocks quarried by slaves were slid down mountainsides in chutes and hauled to the building site in wagons pulled by thirty or forty oxen. The site swarmed with hundreds of workmen hired by the state, divided into small groups, and directed by master masons. Some crews laid a substructure (stereobate) of rough blocks, and on top of it, the stylobate—more carefully prepared stone recessed in steps. Others, with exquisite precision, dressed stones for the walls, using tools not unlike those of a modern sculptor; as the blocks were laid they were fastened together with metal clamps. All heavy building materials were lifted by derricks rigged with block and tackle, and guided into place by workmen atop wooden scaffolding. While the walls were being raised, other crews were at work on the columns. Rough stone was turned on lathes to make column drums, the bottom and top ones being fluted on the ground to provide guidelines for the rest of the fluting, which was done after the entire column was up. Then trained workmen spent many days polishing the columns and walls with oil and grinding stones.

DMITRI KESSEL, COURTESY *Life*

ROLOFF BENY

DORIC SEVERITY

The development of the architectural orders—those standard styles of column and entablature—aided the Greeks in the search for harmonious perfection, which they pursued in their buildings as in everything else. The use of the orders discouraged major innovations; but to work within a prescribed form, which remained essentially the same in every structure, encouraged refinement of the form and an infinite number of changes in proportion and size. The first order to arise on the mainland was the Doric; it originated in the seventh century when architects tried to reproduce in stone the wood-columned and mud-brick structures with which they were familiar. After the middle of the seventh century Doric temples remained virtually unchanged in both plan and structure. The Doric was the simplest and heaviest of the three Greek orders; but its very solidity and strength, when modified by the subtleties and refinements that developed in the working of stone, enabled the Greeks to bring the classical temple to its height.

The architects who built the limestone temple of Bassae (above) on an isolated Peloponnesian mountainside in the fifth century combined elements of all three architectural orders—Doric, Ionic, Corinthian. The glory of Bassae, however, resides in the ruggedness and power of its Doric exterior columns (opposite).

ORKALATIS, PHOTO RESEARCHERS

IONIC AND LATER GRACE

After the Doric and the Ionic forms, another architectural order, which came to be called Corinthian, was developed. In classical times almost every major building was made according to the specifications of one of the three. The Ionic order originated, probably in the seventh century, in Asia Minor, where the league of twelve Ionian cities had given rise to a cultural homogeneity that fostered a common architectural style. Ionic buildings varied in their floor plans, but their columns and entablatures were always fundamentally the same. Unlike the Doric, the Ionic column had a base and, instead of a plain round capital, elongated carved volutes. The Corinthian order, despite its name, seems to have originated at Bassae late in the fifth century and was subsequently developed by Athenian stoneworkers. Its capital of stylized acanthus leaves was designed to give an impression of added height.

MUSEUM, EPIDAURUS; HASSIA

HARISSIADIS

The Corinthian capital from Epidaurus (above) has the characteristic acanthus leaf pattern. Opposite, a picture of the porch of the temple of Athena Nike in Athens shows how stoneworkers altered the Ionic volutes when they appeared on a corner column. The base of an Ionic column is at right.

OVERLEAF: *After it was destroyed by the Persians, Poseidon's marble temple at Cape Sounion at the tip of Attica was rebuilt by Pericles at the same time as the Acropolis. Doric in style, but with unusually elongated columns, its prominent position made it in effect a lofty lighthouse to mariners.*

DANIELL, PHOTO RESEARCHERS

MARTIN VON WAGNER MUSEUM, WÜRZBURG

ORCHESTRA

PARADOS

PARADOS

RAMP

PROSKENION

RAMP

SKENE

At left is a floor plan of the theatre built at Epidaurus in about 350 B.C.; it is the best preserved of all those of ancient Greece. The stone building called the skene provided a permanent architectural background for the proskenion to which wooden sets, like that shown on the vase fragment above, were attached. The ramp and walkway (parados) were entrances for the actors and for the chorus, which always performed in the orchestra.

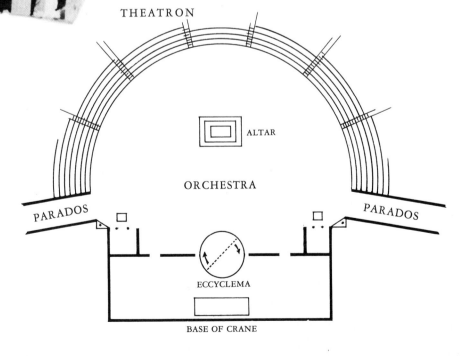

CRANE

DEUS
EX
MACHINA

BASE
OF
CRANE

The schematic drawings above and below demonstrate how some classical props were used. A deus ex machina *(an actor playing a god who resolved a complex dramatic situation) was floated out over the* skene *by a crane like that above; its location is indicated on the plan below. The* eccyclema *(below) was a platform that revolved, usually to display an event occurring "off stage."*

THEATRON

ALTAR

ORCHESTRA

PARADOS

PARADOS

ECCYCLEMA

BASE OF CRANE

THE THEATRE TAKES SHAPE

Greek drama evolved out of rites performed in honor of Dionysus by masked worshipers who danced and sang themselves into a frenzy in order to lose their own identity and merge with nature and the god. As drama slowly emerged from these ceremonies, becoming more and more formal in the process, the place where it was performed developed as well. The very earliest *orchestra* ("dancing place") was probably a threshing floor, worn smooth by the oxen who trod grain upon it; this was a logical site for Dionysian harvest celebrations. Around it the *theatron* ("seeing place") developed to accommodate those who came to watch. Theatres were placed on hillsides, wherever possible, to enable the greatest number of spectators to see clearly. For the earliest tragedies and satyr plays, actors probably costumed themselves in a tent (*skene*) in a sacred wood nearby. As plays grew more complex the actors were required to enter and leave the *orchestra* more quickly; eventually a wooden *skene*, containing dressing rooms and storage space, was built for them directly behind the theatre. In time, painted props were placed in front of this building to represent scenery; they became more and more intricate with the evolution of the *proskenion*, or central set, and the scene-building itself became merely a background structure. By the fourth century the Greek theatre had assumed a form that was not to change greatly thereafter—an *orchestra* faced by rows of seats carved out of a hillside, a stone scene-building with projecting wings between which was the open area of the *proskenion*, where most of the action took place.

OVERLEAF: *The surviving theatre at Epidaurus, one of the finest in the ancient world, gives evidence of the stone* skene *that once rose behind the* orchestra, *and the altar that occupied its center.*

DESCHARNES

DRAMATISTS AT THEIR HEIGHT

A perfect tragedy should . . . imitate actions which excite pity and fear . . . the change of fortune presented must not be the spectacle of a virtuous man brought from prosperity to adversity: for this moves neither pity nor fear; it merely shocks us. Nor, again, that of a bad man passing from adversity to prosperity . . . it neither satisfies the moral sense, nor calls forth pity or fear. Nor, again, should the downfall of the utter villain be exhibited. A plot of this kind would . . . inspire neither pity nor fear; for pity is aroused by unmerited misfortune, fear by the misfortune of a man like ourselves. . . . There remains, then, the character between these two extremes —that of a man who is not eminently good and just, yet whose misfortune is brought about not by vice or depravity, but by some error or frailty. He must be one who is highly renowned and prosperous—a personage like Oedipus . . .

Aristotle, Poetics *(translated by S. H. Butcher)*

Greek drama was born as a religious experience, and it was to remain religious in character throughout classical times. The action of each play began as the chorus entered, singing and performing a ceremonial dance; throughout the play it remained in sight of the audience, commenting on the unfolding drama like a divinely appointed voice. Its performance was always ritualistic. Sometimes it divided into two groups and sang alternately; sometimes the leader, or coryphaeus, and the chorus sang in turn; sometimes the chorus leader performed alone to further the action of the play. The characters that were brought to life by the great tragic playwrights were profoundly human, and it was expected that the audience would identify itself with them. Yet to the audience, they appeared more imposing than life size, for the actors wore elevated boots during the performance and were made more awesome by the masks that covered their faces.

Using mythic tales, the tragedians dealt with problems that for the Greeks were within the realm of religion. Their concern was the interconnection between man and the gods. Men's actions were judged in conformity with the divine laws that governed the universe, and tragedy occurred whenever these laws were broken. When Oedipus wed his mother, or Orestes murdered his, they were punished by the goddess of divine retribution, Nemesis, whose workings were inscrutable. Man's relation to man also found a place in drama. The comedies of Aristophanes, such as *Lysistrata,* mocked the leaders of the Athenian government; tragedies such as Euripides' *Hecuba* deplored the cruelties of war; and Aeschylus' tragedies about Orestes pleaded for men to leave retribution to the state rather than to individual revenge. On the following pages, passages from plays on each of these themes are presented in recent translation, to give some idea of the scope of Greek dramatic genius. As in the preceding anthology in this book, spellings, usages, rhythms vary widely according to preferences of individual translators writing for today's audience.

CLYTEMNESTRA'S CRIME

from Aeschylus' *Agamemnon*

(translated by Richmond Lattimore)

Upon his return from the Trojan War, the Mycenaean king Agamemnon was slain by his wife Clytemnestra and her lover Aegisthus, as Cassandra, the captive Trojan princess, had predicted. Clytemnestra felt justified in committing the crime, for Agamemnon had sacrificed their own daughter in order to obtain a fair wind to sail for Troy. The murder takes place off stage. What the audience sees, in this passage from the first play of the Oresteia, *is the chorus' reproachful debate with Clytemnestra.*

CHORUS

High fortune is a thing slakeless
for mortals. There is no man who shall point
his finger to drive it back from the door
and speak the words: "Come no longer."
Now to this man the blessed ones have given
Priam's city to be captured
and return in the gods' honor.
Must he give blood for generations gone,
die for those slain and in death pile up
more death to come for the blood shed,
what mortal else who hears shall claim
he was born clear of the dark angel?

(Agamemnon, inside the house.)

Ah, I'm struck a deadly blow and deep within!

CHORUS

Silence: who cried out that he was stabbed to death within the
house?

AGAMEMNON

Ah me, again, they struck again. I am wounded twice.

CHORUS

How the king cried out aloud to us! I believe the thing is done.
Come, let us put our heads together, try to find some safe way out.

*(The members of the Chorus go about distractedly,
each one speaking in turn.)*

Listen, let me tell you what I think is best to do.
Let the herald call all citizens to rally here.

No, better to burst in upon them now, at once,
and take them with the blood still running from their blades.

I am with this man and I cast my vote to him.
Act now. This is the perilous and instant time.

Anyone can see it, by these first steps they have taken,
they purpose to be tyrants here upon our city.

Yes, for we waste time, while they trample to the ground
deliberation's honor, and their hands sleep not.

I can not tell which counsel of yours to call my own.
It is the man of action who can plan as well.

I feel as he does; nor can I see how by words
we shall set the dead man back upon his feet again.

Do you mean, to drag our lives out long, that we must yield
to the house shamed, and leadership of such as these?

No, we can never endure that; better to be killed.
Death is a softer thing by far than tyranny.

Shall we, by no more proof than that he cried in pain,
be sure, as by divination, that our lord is dead?

Yes, we should know what is true before we break our rage.
Here is sheer guessing and far different from sure knowledge.

From all sides the voices multiply to make me choose
this course; to learn first how it stands with Agamemnon.

*(The doors of the palace open, disclosing the bodies of Agamemnon
and Cassandra, with Clytaemestra standing over them.)*

CLYTAEMESTRA

Much have I said before to serve necessity,
but I will take no shame now to unsay it all.
How else could I, arming hate against hateful men
disguised in seeming tenderness, fence high the nets
of ruin beyond overleaping? Thus to me
the conflict born of ancient bitterness is not
a thing new thought upon, but pondered deep in time.
I stand now where I struck him down. The thing is done.
Thus have I wrought, and I will not deny it now.
That he might not escape nor beat aside his death,
as fishermen cast their huge circling nets, I spread
deadly abundance of rich robes, and caught him fast.
I struck him twice. In two great cries of agony
he buckled at the knees and fell. When he was down
I struck him the third blow, in thanks and reverence
to Zeus the lord of dead men underneath the ground.
Thus he went down, and the life struggled out of him;
and as he died he spattered me with the dark red
and violent driven rain of bitter savored blood
to make me glad, as gardens stand among the showers
of God in glory at the birthtime of the buds.

These being the facts, elders of Argos assembled here,
be glad, if it be your pleasure; but for me, I glory.
Were it religion to pour wine above the slain,
this man deserved, more than deserved, such sacrament.
He filled our cup with evil things unspeakable
and now himself come home has drunk it to the dregs.

CHORUS

We stand here stunned. How can you speak this way, with mouth
so arrogant, to vaunt above your fallen lord?

CLYTAEMESTRA

You try me out as if I were a woman and vain;

but my heart is not fluttered as I speak before you.
You know it. You can praise or blame me as you wish;
it is all one to me. That man is Agamemnon,
my husband; he is dead; the work of this right hand
that struck in strength of righteousness. And that is that.

CHORUS

Woman, what evil thing planted upon the earth
or dragged from the running salt sea could you have tasted now
to wear such brutality and walk in the people's hate?
You have cast away, you have cut away. You shall go homeless
                                                          now,
crushed with men's bitterness.

CLYTAEMESTRA

Now it is I you doom to be cast out from my city
with men's hate heaped and curses roaring in my ears.
Yet look upon this dead man; you would not cross him once
when with no thought more than as if a beast had died,
when he ranged pastures swarmed with the deep fleece of flocks,
he slaughtered like a victim his own child, my pain
grown into love, to charm away the winds of Thrace.
Were you not bound to hunt him then clear of this soil
for the guilt stained upon him? Yet you hear what I
have done, and lo, you are a stern judge. But I say to you:
go on and threaten me, but I know that I am ready,
if fairly you can beat me down beneath your hand,
for you to rule; but if the god grant otherwise,
you shall be taught—too late, for sure—to keep your place.

CHORUS

Great your design, your speech is a clamor of pride.
Swung to the red act drives the fury within your brain
signed clear in the splash of blood over your eyes.
Yet to come is stroke given for stroke
vengeless, forlorn of friends.

CLYTAEMESTRA

Now hear you this, the right behind my sacrament:
By my child's Justice driven to fulfilment, by
her Wrath and Fury, to whom I sacrificed this man,
the hope that walks my chambers is not traced with fear
while yet Aegisthus makes the fire shine on my hearth,
my good friend, now as always, who shall be for us
the shield of our defiance, no weak thing; while he,
this other, is fallen, stained with this woman you behold,
plaything of all the golden girls at Ilium;
and here lies she, the captive of his spear, who saw
wonders, who shared his bed, the wise in revelations
and loving mistress, who yet knew the feel as well
of the men's rowing benches. Their reward is not
unworthy. He lies there; and she who swanlike cried
aloud her lyric mortal lamentation out
is laid against his fond heart, and to me has given
a delicate excitement to my bed's delight.

CHORUS

O that in speed, without pain

and the slow bed of sickness
death could come to us now, death that forever
carries sleep without ending, now that our lord is down,
our shield, kindest of men,
who for a woman's grace suffered so much,
struck down at last by a woman.

Alas, Helen, wild heart
for the multitudes, for the thousand lives
you killed under Troy's shadow,
you alone, to shine in man's memory
as blood flower never to be washed out. Surely a demon then
of death walked in the house, men's agony.

CLYTAEMESTRA

No, be not so heavy, nor yet draw down
in prayer death's ending,
neither turn all wrath against Helen
for men dead, that she alone killed
all those Danaan lives, to work
the grief that is past all healing.

CHORUS

Divinity that kneel on this house and the two
strains of the blood of Tantalus,
in the hands and hearts of women you steer
the strength tearing my heart.
Standing above the corpse, obscene
as some carrion crow she sings
the crippled song and is proud.

CLYTAEMESTRA

Thus have you set the speech of your lips
straight, calling by name
the spirit thrice glutted that lives in this race.
From him deep in the nerve is given
the love and the blood drunk, that before
the old wound dries, it bleeds again.

CHORUS

Surely it is a huge
and heavy spirit bending the house you cry;
alas, the bitter glory
of a doom that shall never be done with;
and all through Zeus, Zeus,
first cause, prime mover.
For what thing without Zeus is done among mortals?
What here is without God's blessing?

O king, my king
how shall I weep for you?
What can I say out of my heart of pity?
Caught in this spider's web you lie,
your life gasped out in indecent death,
struck prone to this shameful bed
by your lady's hand of treachery
and the stroke twin edged of the iron.

CLYTAEMESTRA

Can you claim I have done this?

Speak of me never
more as the wife of Agamemnon.
In the shadow of this corpse's queen
the old stark avenger
of Atreus for his revel of hate
struck down this man,
last blood for the slaughtered children.

CHORUS

What man shall testify
your hands are clean of this murder?
How? How? Yet from his father's blood
might swarm some fiend to guide you.
The black ruin that shoulders
through the streaming blood of brothers
strides at last where he shall win requital
for the children who were eaten.

O king, my king
how shall I weep for you?
What can I say out of my heart of pity?
Caught in this spider's web you lie,
your life gasped out in indecent death,
struck prone to this shameful bed
by your lady's hand of treachery
and the stroke twin edged of the iron.

CLYTAEMESTRA

No shame, I think, in the death given
this man. And did he not
first of all in this house wreak death
by treachery?
The flower of this man's love and mine,
Iphigeneia of the tears
he dealt with even as he has suffered.
Let his speech in death's house be not loud.
With the sword he struck,
with the sword he paid for his own act.

CHORUS

My thoughts are swept away and I go bewildered.
Where shall I turn the brain's
activity in speed when the house is falling?
There is fear in the beat of the blood rain breaking
wall and tower. The drops come thicker.
Still fate grinds on yet more stones the blade
for more acts of terror.

Earth, my earth, why did you not fold me under
before ever I saw this man lie dead
fenced by the tub in silver?
Who shall bury him? Who shall mourn him?
Shall you dare this who have killed
your lord? Make lamentation,
render the graceless grace to his soul
for huge things done in wickedness?
Who over this great man's grave shall lay
the blessing of tears

worked soberly from a true heart?

CLYTAEMESTRA

Not for you to speak of such tendance.
Through us he fell,
by us he died; we shall bury.
There will be no tears in this house for him.
It must be Iphigeneia
his child, who else,
shall greet her father by the whirling stream
and the ferry of tears
to close him in her arms and kiss him.

CHORUS

Here is anger for anger. Between them
who shall judge lightly?
The spoiler is robbed; he killed, he has paid.
The truth stands ever beside God's throne
eternal: he who has wrought shall pay; that is law.
Then who shall tear the curse from their blood?
The seed is stiffened to ruin.

CLYTAEMESTRA

You see truth in the future
at last. Yet I wish
to seal my oath with the Spirit
in the house: I will endure all things as they stand
now, hard though it be. Hereafter
let him go forth to make bleed with death
and guilt the houses of others.
I will take some small
measure of our riches, and be content
that I swept from these halls
the murder, the sin, and the fury.

ORESTES' VENGEANCE

from Aeschylus' *The Libation Bearers*
(*translated by Richmond Lattimore*)

Clytemnestra's crime was avenged by her son Orestes, who killed her along with her lover. His deed, in turn, was avenged by the inexorable Furies, who torment him to madness. The Libation Bearers is the second of three surviving tragedies that Aeschylus wrote about the family of Agamemnon. Other Greek playwrights also treated this theme. This passage begins after Orestes has murdered his mother and continues until the end of the play.

(*The doors of the house open, to show Orestes standing over the bodies of Clytaemestra and Aegisthus. His attendants display the robe in which Clytaemestra had entangled Agamemnon and which she displayed after his murder.*)

ORESTES

Behold the twin tyrannies of our land, these two
who killed my father and who sacked my house. For a time
they sat upon their thrones and kept their pride of state,
and they are lovers still. So may you judge by what
befell them, for as they were pledged their oath abides.
They swore together death for my unhappy sire
and swore to die together. Now they keep their oath.

Behold again, o audience of these evil things,
the engine against my wretched father they devised,
the hands' entanglement, the hobbles for his feet.
Spread it out. Stand around me in a circle and
display this net that caught a man. So shall, not my
father, but that great father who sees all, the Sun,
look on my mother's sacrilegious handiwork
and be a witness for me in my day of trial
how it was in all right that I achieved this death,
my mother's: for of Aegisthus' death I take no count:
he has his seducer's punishment, no more than law.

But she, who plotted this foul death against the man
by whom she carried the weight of children underneath
her zone, burden once loved, shown hard and hateful now,
what does she seem to be? Some water snake, some viper
whose touch is rot even to him who felt no fang
strike, by that brutal and wrong daring in her heart.

And this thing: what shall I call it and be right, in all
eloquence? Trap for an animal or winding sheet
for dead man? Or bath curtain? Since it is a net,
robe you could call it, to entangle a man's feet.
Some highwayman might own a thing like this, to catch
the wayfarer and rob him of his money and
so make a living. With a treacherous thing like this
he could take many victims and go warm within.

May no such wife as she was come to live with me.
Sooner, let God destroy me, with no children born.

CHORUS

Ah, but the pitiful work.
Dismal the death that was your ending.
He is left alive; pain flowers for him.

ORESTES

Did she do it or did she not? My witness is
this great robe. It was thus she stained Aegisthus' sword.
Dip it and dip it again, the smear of blood conspires
with time to spoil the beauty of this precious thing.
Now I can praise him, now I can stand by to mourn
and speak before this web that killed my father; yet
I grieve for the thing done, the death, and all our race.
I have won; but my victory is soiled, and has no pride.

CHORUS

There is no mortal man who shall turn
unhurt his life's course to an end not marred.
There is trouble here. There is more to come.

ORESTES

I would have you know, I see not how this thing will end.
I am a charioteer whose course is wrenched outside
the track, for I am beaten, my rebellious senses
bolt with me headlong and the fear against my heart
is ready for the singing and dance of wrath. But while
I hold some grip still on my wits, I say publicly
to my friends: I killed my mother not without some right.
My father's murder stained her, and the gods' disgust.
As for the spells that charmed me to such daring, I
give you in chief the seer of Pytho, Loxias. He
declared I could do this and not be charged with wrong.
Of my evasion's punishment I will not speak:
no archery could hit such height of agony.
And look upon me now, how I go armored in
leafed branch and garland on my way to the centrestone
and sanctuary, and Apollo's level place,
the shining of the fabulous fire that never dies,
to escape this blood that is my own. Loxias ordained
that I should turn me to no other shrine than this.
To all men of Argos in time to come I say
they shall be witness, how these evil things were done.
I go, an outcast wanderer from this land, and leave
behind, in life, in death, the name of what I did.

CHORUS

No, what you did was well done. Do not therefore bind
your mouth to foul speech. Keep no evil on your lips.
You liberated all the Argive city when
you lopped the heads of these two snakes with one clean stroke.

ORESTES

No!
Women who serve this house, they come like gorgons, they
wear robes of black, and they are wreathed in a tangle
of snakes. I can no longer stay.

CHORUS

Orestes, dearest to your father of all men
what fancies whirl you? Hold, do not give way to fear.

ORESTES

These are no fancies of affliction. They are clear,
and real, and here; the bloodhounds of my mother's hate.

CHORUS

It is the blood still wet upon your hands, that makes
this shaken turbulence be thrown upon your sense.

ORESTES

Ah, Lord Apollo, how they grow and multiply,
repulsive for the blood drops of their dripping eyes.

CHORUS

There is one way to make you clean: let Loxias

touch you, and set you free from these disturbances.

ORESTES

You can not see them, but I see them. I am driven
from this place. I can stay here no longer.

(*Exit.*)

CHORUS

Good luck go with you then, and may the god look on
you with favor and guard you in kind circumstance.

Here on this house of the kings the third
storm has broken, with wind
from the inward race, and gone its course.
The children were eaten: there was the first
affliction, the curse of Thyestes.
Next came the royal death, when a man
and lord of Achaean armies went down
killed in the bath. Third
is for the savior. He came. Shall I call
it that, or death? Where
is the end? Where shall the fury of fate
be stilled to sleep, be done with?

(*Exeunt.*)

HECUBA'S CRY FOR PITY

from Euripides' *Hecuba*

(*translated by William Arrowsmith*)

*After the fall of Troy, Queen Hecuba and the other Trojan
women were enslaved by the victorious Greeks. All but one of
Hecuba's numerous children had been slain or taken away from
her. As Euripides' tragedy begins, Hecuba learns that her remaining daughter Polyxena is doomed to die as a sacrifice on Achilles'
tomb. She pleads with Odysseus, whose life she had once saved,
to spare the girl, but he refuses. The guile which Greek tradition connected with his name is evident in this poignant scene.*

(*Enter chorus of captive Trojan women. They speak individually.*)

CHORUS

We come to you in haste,
Hecuba.

—   We left the tents . . .

—where the lot assigned us.

—Slaves, torn from home
    when Troy was burnt and sacked
    by the conquering Greeks!

—We bring you painful news.

—We cannot lighten your load.

—We bring you worse to bear.

—Just now, in full assembly,
    the Greek decree came down.

—They voted your daughter must die . . .

—to be slaughtered alive

—on the tomb of Achilles!

—The sails had been unfurled,
    and the fleet stood out to sea,
    when from his tomb Achilles rose,
    armor blazing, and held them back,
    crying:
    "Ho, Argives, where do you sail,
    leaving my grave unhonored?"

—Waves of argument broke loose,
    dividing Greek from Greek.
    If one man spoke for death,
    another spoke against it.

—On your behalf spoke Agamemnon,
    lover of your daughter,
    poor, mad Cassandra.

—Then the two sons of Theseus,
    twin shoots of Athens, rose and spoke,
    but both with one intent—
    to crown Achilles' grave
    with living blood, asking
    if Cassandra's love meant more
    than the courage of Achilles.

—And so the struggle swayed,
    equally poised—

—   Until *he* spoke—
    that hypocrite with honeyed tongue,
    that demagogue Odysseus.
    And in the end he won,
    asking what one slave was worth
    when laid in the balance
    with the honor of Achilles.

—He wouldn't have the dead
    descending down to Hades
    telling tales of Greek
    ingratitude to Greeks
    who fell for Hellas
    on the foreign field of Troy.

—And he is coming here
    to tear your daughter from your breast
    and wrench her from your arms.

—Go to the temples!

—   Go to the shrines

—Fall at Agamemnon's knees!

—Call on heaven's gods!

—Invoke the gods below!

—Unless your prayers prevent her death,
   unless your pleas can keep her safe,
   then you shall see your child,
   face downward on the earth
   and the stain in the black earth spread
      as the red blood drops
   from the gleaming golden chain
   that lies broken at her throat.

HECUBA

O grief!
         What can I say?
What are the words for loss?

O bitterness of age,
slavery not to be borne,
unendurable pain!
To whom can I turn?
Childless and homeless,
my husband murdered,
my city stained with fire. . . .
Where can I go?
What god in heaven,
what power below
will help me now?
O women of Troy,
heralds of evil,
bringers of loss,
this news you bring is my sentence of death.
Why should I live? How live in the light
when its goodness is gone,
when all I have is grief?
Bear me up,
poor stumbling feet,
and take me to the tent.

         (She stumbles painfully to Agamemnon's tent
         and then cries out in terror to Polyxena within.)

O my child!
         Polyxena,
step from the tent!
Come and hear the news
your wretched mother brings,
this news of horror
that touches your life!

         (Enter from the tent Polyxena, a beautiful young girl.)

POLYXENA

That terror in your voice!
That cry of fear
flushing me forth
like a bird in terror!

HECUBA

O my child! My baby. . . .

POLYXENA

Again that cry! Why?

HECUBA

I am afraid for you—

POLYXENA

Tell me the truth, Mother.
No, I am afraid. Something
in your face frightens me.

HECUBA

O my child! My child—

POLYXENA

You *must* tell me, Mother.

HECUBA

A dreadful rumor came.
Some Greek decree
that touches your life—

POLYXENA

Touches my life how?
For god's sake, Mother,
speak!

HECUBA

         —The Greeks,
in full assembly,
have decreed your death,
a living sacrifice
upon Achilles' tomb.

POLYXENA

O my poor mother!
How I pity you,
this broken-hearted life
of pain!
         What god
could make you suffer so,
impose such pain,
such grief in one poor life?
Alive, at least
I might have shared
your slavery with you,
my unhappy youth
with your embittered age.
But now I die,
and you must see my death:—
butchered like a lamb
squalling with fright,
and the throat held taut
for the gashing knife,
and the gaping hole
where the breath of life
goes out,
         and sinks
downward into dark
with the unconsolable dead.

It is *you* I pity,
Mother.
         For *you* I cry.
Not for myself,

not for this life
whose suffering is such
I do not care to live,
but call it happiness to die.

CORYPHAEUS
Look, Hecuba. Odysseus is coming here
himself. There must be news.

(*Enter Odysseus, attended by several soldiers.*)

ODYSSEUS
By now, Hecuba,
I think you know what decision the army has taken
and how we voted.
But let me review the facts.
By majority vote the Greeks have decreed as follows:
your daughter, Polyxena, must die as a victim
and prize of honor for the grave of Achilles.
The army has delegated me to act as escort.
Achilles' son will supervise the rite
and officiate as priest.
There matters rest.
You understand your position? You must not attempt
to hold your daughter here by force, nor,
I might add, presume to match your strength with mine.
Remember your weakness and accept this tragic loss
as best you can.
Nothing you do or say
can change the facts. Under the circumstances,
the logical course is resignation.

HECUBA
O gods,
is there no end to this ordeal of suffering,
this struggle with despair?
Why do I live?
I should have died, died long ago.
But Zeus preserved me, saved me, kept me alive
to suffer, each time to suffer worse
than all the grief that went before.
Odysseus,
if a slave may put her question to the free—
without intent to hurt or give offense—
then let me ask you one brief question now
and hear your answer.

ODYSSEUS
Ask me your question.
I can spare you the time.

HECUBA
Do you remember once
how you came to Troy, a spy, in beggar's disguise,
smeared with filth, in rags, and tears of blood
were streaming down your beard?

ODYSSEUS
I remember
the incident. It left its mark on me.

HECUBA
But Helen penetrated your disguise
and told me who you were? Told *me* alone?

ODYSSEUS
I stood, I remember, in danger of death.

HECUBA
And how humble you were? How you fell at my knees
and begged for life?

ODYSSEUS
And my hand almost froze on your dress.

HECUBA
And you were at my mercy, *my* slave then.
Do you remember what you said?

ODYSSEUS
Said?
Anything I could. Anything to live.

HECUBA
And I let you have your life? I set you free?

ODYSSEUS
Because of what you did, I live today.

HECUBA
Then can you say your treatment now of me
is not contemptible? To take from me
what you confess you took, and in return
do everything you can to do me wrong
and ruin me?
O gods, spare me the sight
of this thankless breed, these politicians
who cringe for favors from a screaming mob
and do not care what harm they do their friends,
providing they can please a crowd!
Tell me,
on what feeble grounds can you justify
your vote of death?
Political necessity?
But how? And do your politics require
the shedding of human blood upon a grave,
where custom calls for cattle?
Or is it vengeance
that Achilles' ghost demands, death for his death,
and exacts of her? But what has she to do
with his revenge? Who ever hurt him less
than this poor girl? If death is what he wants,
let Helen die. He went to Troy for *her;*
for *her* he died.
Or is it merely looks
that you require, some surpassing beauty in a girl
whose dying loveliness might appease the hurt
of this fastidious ghost? Then do not look
for loveliness from us. Look to Helen,
loveliest of lovely women on this earth

by far—lovely Helen, who did him harm
far more than we.
                    So much by way of answer
to the justice of your case.
                    Now, Odysseus,
I present my claim for your consideration,
my just demand for payment of your debt
of life.
        You admit yourself you took my hand;
you knelt at my feet and begged for life.
                    But see—

(Hecuba kneels at the feet of Odysseus and takes his hand.)

now I touch you back as you touched me.
I kneel before you on the ground and beg
for mercy back:
                    Let her stay with me.
Let her live.
            Surely there are dead enough
without her death. And everything I lost
lives on in her. This one life
redeems the rest. She is my comfort, my Troy,
my staff, my nurse; she guides me on my way.
She is all I have.
            And you have power,
Odysseus, greatness and power. But clutch them gently,
use them kindly, for power gives no purchase
to the hand, it will not hold, soon perishes,
and greatness goes.
                I know. I too was great
but I am nothing now. One day
cut down my greatness and my pride.
                    But I implore you,
Odysseus, be merciful, take pity on me!
Go to the Greeks. Argue, coax them, convince them
that what they do is wrong. Accuse them of murder!
Tell them we are helpless, we are women,
the same women whom they tore from sanctuary
at the altars. But they pitied us, they spared us then.
Plead with them.
            Read them your law of murder. Tell them how
it applies to slave and free without distinction.
But go.
    Even if your arguments were weak,
if you faltered or forgot your words, it would not matter.
Of themselves that power, that prestige you have
would guarantee success, swelling in your words,
and borrowing from what you are a resonance and force
denied to less important men.

CORYPHAEUS
                    Surely
no man could be so callous or so hard of heart
he could hear this mother's heartbroken cry
and not be touched.

ODYSSEUS
            Allow me to observe, Hecuba,
that in your hysterics you twist the facts.
                    First,
I am not, as you fondly suppose, your enemy,
and my advice, believe me, was sincerely and kindly meant.
I readily admit, moreover, the extent of my debt—
everything I am today I owe to you.
And in return I stand ready and willing
to honor my debt by saving your life. Indeed,
I have never suggested otherwise.
                    But note:
I said *your* life, not your daughter's life,
a very different matter altogether.
I gave my word that when we captured Troy
your daughter should be given to our best soldier
as a prize upon request. That was my promise,
a solemn public commitment which I intend to keep.
Besides, there is a principle at stake
and one, moreover, in whose neglect or breach
governments have fallen and cities come to grief,
because their bravest, their most exceptional men,
received no greater honor than the common run.
And Achilles deserves our honor far more than most,
a great man and a great soldier who died greatly
for his country.
            Tell me, what conduct could be worse
than to give your friend a lifetime of honor and respect
but neglect him when he dies?
                    And what then,
if war should come again and we enlist our citizens
to serve? Would we fight or would we look to our lives,
seeing that dead men get no honor?
                    No:
for my lifetime give me nothing more than what I need;
I ask no more. But as regards my grave,
I hope for honor, since honor in the grave
has eternity to run.
            You speak of pity,
but I can talk of pity too. Pity *us,*
pity our old people, those old men and women
no less miserable than yours, the wives and mothers
of all those brave young men who found a grave
in the dust of Troy.
            Endure; bear your losses,
and if you think me wrong to honor courage
in a man, then call me callous.
                    But what of you,
you foreigners who refuse your dead their rights
and break your faith with friends? And then you wonder
that Hellas should prosper while your countries suffer
the fates they deserve!

CORYPHAEUS
                    This is what it means
to be a slave: to be abused and bear it,
compelled by violence to suffer wrong.

THE AGONY OF OEDIPUS

from Sophocles' *Oedipus the King*

(*translated by David Grene*)

Oedipus, married to Jocasta, widow of the slain king Laius, reigns in Thebes. But the city is visited by a plague brought down, the oracle says, by Laius' unsolved murder. To save his people, Oedipus orders a hunt for the killer, only to grow fearful that a man he himself had slain at a crossroads may have been the king. Worse is to come: uncertain of his own parentage, he questions one of Laius' retainers and learns that he himself was born of the royal pair but was given away in infancy. Having unwittingly killed his father and wed his mother, he blinds himself.

OEDIPUS

Old man, look here at me
and tell me what I ask you. Were you ever
a servant of King Laius?

HERDSMAN

            I was,—
no slave he bought but reared in his own house.

OEDIPUS

What did you do as work? How did you live?

HERDSMAN

Most of my life was spent among the flocks.

OEDIPUS

In what part of the country did you live?

HERDSMAN

Cithaeron and the places near to it.

OEDIPUS

And somewhere there perhaps you knew this man?

HERDSMAN

What was his occupation? Who?

OEDIPUS

            This man here,
have you had any dealings with him?

HERDSMAN

            No—
not such that I can quickly call to mind.

MESSENGER

That is no wonder, master. But I'll make him remember what he does not know. For I know, that he well knows the country of Cithaeron, how he with two flocks, I with one kept company for three years—each year half a year—from spring till autumn time and then when winter came I drove my flocks to our fold home again and he to Laius' steadings. Well—am I right or not in what I said we did?

HERDSMAN

You're right—although it's a long time ago.

MESSENGER

Do you remember giving me a child
to bring up as my foster child?

HERDSMAN

            What's this?
Why do you ask this question?

MESSENGER

            Look old man,
here he is—here's the man who was that child!

HERDSMAN

Death take you! Won't you hold your tongue?

OEDIPUS

            No, no,
do not find fault with him, old man. Your words
are more at fault than his.

HERDSMAN

            O best of masters,
how do I give offense?

OEDIPUS

            When you refuse
to speak about the child of whom he asks you.

HERDSMAN

He speaks out of his ignorance, without meaning.

OEDIPUS

If you'll not talk to gratify me, you
will talk with pain to urge you.

HERDSMAN

            O please, sir,
don't hurt an old man, sir.

OEDIPUS (*to the servants*)

            Here, one of you,
twist his hands behind him.

HERDSMAN

            Why, God help me, why?
What do you want to know?

OEDIPUS

            You gave a child
to him,—the child he asked you of?

HERDSMAN

            I did.
I wish I'd died the day I did.

OEDIPUS

            You will
unless you tell me truly.

HERDSMAN

            And I'll die
far worse if I should tell you.

OEDIPUS

              This fellow
is bent on more delays, as it would seem.

HERDSMAN

O no, no! I have told you that I gave it.

OEDIPUS

Where did you get this child from? Was it your own or did you
get it from another?

HERDSMAN

              Not
my own at all; I had it from some one.

OEDIPUS

One of these citizens? or from what house?

HERDSMAN

O master, please—I beg you, master, please
don't ask me more.

OEDIPUS

              You're a dead man if I
ask you again.

HERDSMAN

              It was one of the children
of Laius.

OEDIPUS

              A slave? Or born in wedlock?

HERDSMAN

O God, I am on the brink of frightful speech.

OEDIPUS

And I of frightful hearing. But I must hear.

HERDSMAN

The child was called his child; but she within,
your wife would tell you best how all this was.

OEDIPUS

She gave it to you?

HERDSMAN

              Yes, she did, my lord.

OEDIPUS

To do what with it?

HERDSMAN

              Make away with it.

OEDIPUS

She was so hard—its mother?

HERDSMAN

              Aye, through fear
of evil oracles.

OEDIPUS

              Which?

HERDSMAN

              They said that he
should kill his parents.

OEDIPUS

              How was it that you
gave it away to this old man?

HERDSMAN

              O master,
I pitied it, and thought that I could send it
off to another country and this man
was from another country. But he saved it
for the most terrible troubles. If you are
the man he says you are, you're bred to misery.

OEDIPUS

O, O, O, they will all come,
all come out clearly! Light of the sun, let me
look upon you no more after today!
I who first saw the light bred of a match
accursed, and accursed in my living
with them I lived with, cursed in my killing.

              (*Exeunt all but the Chorus.*)

CHORUS

  STROPHE

O generations of men, how I
count you as equal with those who live
not at all!
What man, what man on earth wins more
of happiness than a seeming
and after that turning away?
Oedipus, you are my pattern of this,
Oedipus, you and your fate!
Luckless Oedipus, whom of all men
I envy not at all.

  ANTISTROPHE

In as much as he shot his bolt
beyond the others and won the prize
of happiness complete—
O Zeus—and killed and reduced to nought
the hooked taloned maid of the riddling speech,
standing a tower against death for my land:
hence he was called my king and hence
was honoured the highest of all
honours; and hence he ruled
in the great city of Thebes.

  STROPHE

But now whose tale is more miserable?
Who is there lives with a savager fate?
Whose troubles so reverse his life as his?

O Oedipus, the famous prince
for whom a great haven
the same both as father and son
sufficed for generation,
how, O how, have the furrows ploughed
by your father endured to bear you, poor wretch,
and hold their peace so long?

  ANTISTROPHE

Time who sees all has found you out

against your will; judges your marriage accursed,
begetter and begot at one in it.

O child of Laius,
would I had never seen you.
I weep for you and cry
a dirge of lamentation.

To speak directly, I drew my breath
from you at the first and so now I lull
my mouth to sleep with your name.

(Enter a second messenger.)

SECOND MESSENGER
O Princes always honoured by our country,
what deeds you'll hear of and what horrors see,
what grief you'll feel, if you as true born Thebans
care for the house of Labdacus's sons.
Phasis nor Ister cannot purge this house,
I think, with all their streams, such things
it hides, such evils shortly will bring forth
into the light, whether they will or not;
and troubles hurt the most
when they prove self-inflicted.

CHORUS
What we had known before did not fall short
of bitter groaning's worth; what's more to tell?

SECOND MESSENGER
Shortest to hear and tell—our glorious queen
Jocasta's dead.

CHORUS
                            Unhappy woman! How?

SECOND MESSENGER
By her own hand. The worst of what was done
you cannot know. You did not see the sight.
Yet in so far as I remember it
you'll hear the end of our unlucky queen.
When she came raging into the house she went
straight to her marriage bed, tearing her hair
with both her hands and crying upon Laius
long dead—Do you remember, Laius,
that night long past which bred a child for us
to send you to your death and leave
a mother making children with her son?
And then she groaned and cursed the bed in which
she brought forth husband by her husband, children
by her own child, an infamous double bond.
How after that she died I do not know,—
for Oedipus distracted us from seeing.
He burst upon us shouting and we looked
to him as he paced frantically around,
begging us always: Give me a sword, I say,
to find this wife no wife, this mother's womb,
this field of double sowing whence I sprang
and where I sowed my children! As he raved
some god showed him the way—none of us there.
Bellowing terribly and led by some

invisible guide he rushed on the two doors,—
wrenching the hollow bolts out of their sockets,
he charged inside. There, there, we saw his wife
hanging, the twisted rope around her neck.
When he saw her, he cried out fearfully
and cut the dangling noose. Then, as she lay,
poor woman, on the ground, what happened after,
was terrible to see. He tore the brooches—
the gold chased brooches fastening her robe—
away from her and lifting them up high
dashed them on his own eyeballs, shrieking out
such things as: they will never see the crime
I have committed or had done upon me!
Dark eyes, now in the days to come look on
forbidden faces, do not recognize
those whom you long for—with such imprecations
he struck his eyes again and yet again
with the brooches. And the bleeding eyeballs gushed
and stained his beard—no sluggish oozing drops
but a black rain and bloody hail poured down.

So it has broken—and not on one head
but troubles mixed for husband and for wife.
The fortune of the days gone by was true
good fortune—but today groans and destruction
and death and shame—of all ills can be named
not one is missing.

CHORUS
Is he now in any ease from pain?

SECOND MESSENGER
                            He shouts
for some one to unbar the doors and show him
to all the men of Thebes, his father's killer,
his mother's—no I cannot say the word,
it is unholy—for he'll cast himself,
out of the land, he says, and not remain
to bring a curse upon his house, the curse
he called upon it in his proclamation. But
he wants for strength, aye, and some one to guide him;
his sickness is too great to bear. You, too,
will be shown that. The bolts are opening.
Soon you will see a sight to waken pity
even in the horror of it.

(Enter the blinded Oedipus.)

CHORUS
This is a terrible sight for men to see!
I never found a worse!
Poor wretch, what madness came upon you!
What evil spirit leaped upon your life
to your ill-luck—a leap beyond man's strength!
Indeed I pity you, but I cannot
look at you, though there's much I want to ask
and much to learn and much to see.
I shudder at the sight of you.

OEDIPUS
O, O,

where am I going? Where is my voice
borne on the wind to and fro?
Spirit, how far have you sprung?

CHORUS

To a terrible place whereof men's ears
may not hear, nor their eyes behold it.

OEDIPUS

Darkness!
Horror of darkness enfolding, resistless, unspeakable visitant sped
   by an ill wind in haste!
madness and stabbing pain and memory
of evil deeds I have done!

CHORUS

In such misfortunes it's no wonder
if double weighs the burden of your grief.

OEDIPUS

My friend,
you are the only one steadfast, the only one that attends on me;
you still stay nursing the blind man.
Your care is not unnoticed. I can know
your voice, although this darkness is my world.

CHORUS

Doer of dreadful deeds, how did you dare
so far to do despite to your own eyes?
what spirit urged you to it?

OEDIPUS

It was Apollo, friends, Apollo,
that brought this bitter bitterness, my sorrows to completion.
But the hand that struck me
was none but my own.
Why should I see
whose vision showed me nothing sweet to see?

CHORUS

These things are as you say.

OEDIPUS

What can I see to love?
What greeting can touch my ears with joy?
Take me away, and haste—to a place out of the way!
Take me away, my friends, the greatly miserable,
the most accursed, whom God too hates
above all men on earth!

CHORUS

Unhappy in your mind and your misfortune,
would I had never known you!

OEDIPUS

Curse on the man who took
the cruel bonds from off my legs, as I lay in the field.
He stole me from death and saved me,
no kindly service.
Had I died then
I would not be so burdensome to friends.

CHORUS

I, too, could have wished it had been so.

OEDIPUS

Then I would not have come
to kill my father and marry my mother infamously.
Now I am godless and child of impurity,
begetter in the same seed that created my wretched self.
If there is any ill worse than ill,
that is the lot of Oedipus.

CHORUS

I cannot say your remedy was good;
you would be better dead than blind and living.

OEDIPUS

What I have done here was best done—don't tell me
otherwise, do not give me further counsel.
I do not know with what eyes I could look
upon my father when I die and go
under the earth, nor yet my wretched mother—
those two to whom I have done things deserving
worse punishment than hanging. Would the sight
of children, bred as mine are, gladden me?
No, not these eyes, never. And my city,
its towers and sacred places of the Gods,
of these I robbed my miserable self
when I commanded all to drive *him* out,
the criminal since proved by God impure
and of the race of Laius.
To this guilt I bore witness against myself—
with what eyes shall I look upon my people?
No. If there were a means to choke the fountain
of hearing I would not have stayed my hand
from locking up my miserable carcase,
seeing and hearing nothing; it is sweet
to keep our thoughts out of the range of hurt.

Cithaeron, why did you receive me? why
having received me did you not kill me straight?
And so I had not shown to men my birth.

O Polybus and Corinth and the house,
the old house that I used to call my father's—
what fairness you were nurse to, and what foulness
festered beneath! Now I am found to be
a sinner and a son of sinners. Crossroads,
and hidden glade, oak and the narrow way
at the crossroads, that drank my father's blood
offered you by my hands, do you remember
still what I did as you looked on, and what
I did when I came here? O marriage, marriage!
you bred me and again when you had bred
bred children of your child and showed to men
brides, wives and mothers and the foulest deeds
that can be in this world of ours.

Come—it's unfit to say what is unfit
to do.—I beg of you in God's name hide me,
somewhere outside your country, yes, or kill me,

or throw me into the sea, to be forever
out of your sight. Approach and deign to touch me
for all my wretchedness, and do not fear.
No man but I can bear my evil doom.

A STRATAGEM OF SEX

from Aristophanes' *Lysistrata*

(translated by Douglass Parker)

In this comedy the women of Greece, led by Lysistrata, set out to force their husbands to end the prolonged war between Athens and Sparta by vowing not to make love with them until peace is made. The resolution is a difficult one for them to keep. Their men, however, find the situation even more distressing; not only are they deprived of their accustomed pleasures, but women seem to be taking over the conduct of the government. In this passage, Lysistrata faces down the angry men, and some of the women too.

KORYPHAIOS OF MEN

The symptoms are clear. Our birthright's already nibbled. And
     oh, so
daintily: WOMEN ticking off troops for improper etiquette.
WOMEN propounding their featherweight views on the
     fashionable use
and abuse of the shield. And (if any more proof were needed)
     WOMEN
nagging us to trust the Nice Laconian, and put our heads
in his toothy maw—to make a dessert and call it Peace.
They've woven the City a seamless shroud, bedecked with the
     legend
DICTATORSHIP.
                    But I won't be hemmed in. I'll use their weapon
against them, and uphold the right by sneakiness.
                              With knyf under cloke,
gauntlet in glove, sword in olivebranch,

          (Slipping slowly toward the Koryphaios of Women.)

                              I'll take up my post
in Statuary Row, beside our honored National Heroes,
the natural foes of tyranny: Harmodios,

                    Aristogeiton,

                              and Me.

                                        (Next to her.)

Striking an epic pose, so, with the full approval
of the immortal gods,
                    I'll bash this loathesome hag in the jaw!

          *(He does, and runs cackling back to the Men.
          She shakes a fist after him.)*

KORYPHAIOS OF WOMEN
Mama won't know her little boy when he gets home!

          (To the Women, who are eager to launch a full-scale attack.)

Let's not be hasty, fellow. . . hags. Cloaks off first.

          *(The Women remove their mantles, disclosing tunics
          very like those of the Men, and advance toward the audience.)*

CHORUS OF WOMEN
We'll address you, citizens, in beneficial, candid,
     patriotic accents, as our breeding says we must,
since, from the age of seven, Athens graced me with a splendid
     string of civic triumphs to signalize her trust:
               I was Relic-Girl quite early,
               then advanced to Maid of Barley;
in Artemis' "Pageant of the Bear" I played the lead.
               To cap this proud progression,
               I led the whole procession
at Athene's Celebration, certified and pedigreed
               —that cachet
               so distingué—
               a *Lady!*

KORYPHAIOS OF WOMEN

                                        (To the audience.)

I trust this establishes my qualifications. I may, I take it, address
the City to its profit? Thank you.
                              I admit to being a woman—
but don't sell my contribution short on that account. It's better
than the present panic. And my word is as good as my bond,
because I hold stock in Athens—stock I paid for in sons.

                                        (To the Chorus of Men.)

—But you, you doddering bankrupts, where are your shares in the
     State?

          (Slipping slowly toward the Koryphaios of Men.)

Your grandfathers willed you the Mutual Funds from the Persian
     War—
and where are they?

                                        (Nearer.)

                    You dipped into capital, then lost interest . . .
and now a pool of your assets won't fill a hole in the ground.
All that remains is one last potential killing—Athens.
Is there any rebuttal?

          *(The Koryphaios of Men gestures menacingly. She ducks down,
          as if to ward off a blow, and removes a slipper.)*

                    Force is a footling resort. I'll take
my very sensible shoe, and paste you in the jaw!

          (She does so, and runs back to the women.)

CHORUS OF MEN
          Their native respect for our manhood is small,
          and keeps getting smaller. Let's bottle their gall.
          The man who won't battle has no balls at all!

KORYPHAIOS OF MEN
All right, men, skin out of the skivvies. Let's give them a whiff
of Man, full strength. No point in muffling the essential Us.

          (The men remove their tunics.)

CHORUS OF MEN

    A century back, we soared to the Heights
        and beat down tyranny there.
    Now's the time to shed our moults
        and fledge our wings once more,
    to rise to the skies in our reborn force,
        and beat back Tyranny here!

KORYPHAIOS OF MEN

No fancy grappling with these grannies; straightforward strength.
  The tiniest
toehold, and those nimble, fiddling fingers will have their foot
in the door, and we're done for.
                  No amount of know-how can lick
a woman's knack.
           They'll want to build ships . . . next thing we
  know,
we're all at sea, fending off female boarding parties.
(Artemisia fought us at Salamis. Tell me, has anyone caught her
yet?)
       But we're *really* sunk if they take up horses. Scratch
the Cavalry:
         A woman is an easy rider with a natural seat.
Take her over the jumps bareback, and she'll never slip
her mount. (That's how the Amazons nearly took Athens. On
  horseback.
Check on Mikon's mural down in the Stoa.)
                    Anyway,
the solution is obvious. Put every woman in her place—stick her
in the stocks.
        To do this, first snare your woman around the neck.

(He attempts to demonstrate on the Koryphaios of Women. After
a brief tussle, she works loose and chases him back to the Men.)

CHORUS OF WOMEN

    The beast in me's eager and fit for a brawl.
    Just rile me a bit and she'll kick down the wall.
    You'll bawl to your friends that you've no balls at all.

KORYPHAIOS OF WOMEN

All right, ladies, strip for action. Let's give them a whiff
of *Femme Enragée*—piercing and pungent, but not at all tart.

                (The women remove their tunics.)

CHORUS OF WOMEN

    We're angry. The brainless bird who tangles
        with *us* has gummed his last mush.
    In fact, the coot who even heckles
        is being daringly rash.
    So look to your nests, you reclaimed eagles—
        whatever you lay, we'll squash!

KORYPHAIOS OF WOMEN

Frankly, you don't faze me. *For* me, I have my friends—
Lampito from Sparta; that genteel girl from Thebes, Ismenia—
committed to me forever. *Against* me, *you*—permanently
out of commission. So do your damnedest.
                   Pass a law.
Pass seven. Continue the winning ways that have made your name
a short and ugly household word.

                  Like yesterday:
I was giving a little party, nothing fussy, to honor
the goddess Hekate. Simply to please my daughters, I'd invited
a sweet little thing from the neighborhood—flawless pedigree,
  perfect
taste, a credit to any gathering—a Boiotian eel.
But she had to decline. Couldn't pass the border. You'd passed a
  law.
Not that you care for my party. You'll overwork your right of
  passage
till your august body is overturned,
                and you break your silly neck!

(She deftly grabs the Koryphaios of Men by the ankle and upsets
him. He scuttles back to the Men, who retire in confusion.)

(Lysistrata emerges from the citadel, obviously distraught.)

KORYPHAIOS OF WOMEN

                   (Mock-tragic.)

Mistress, queen of this our subtle scheme,
why burst you from the hall with brangled brow?

LYSISTRATA

Oh, wickedness of woman! The female mind
does sap my soul and set my wits a-totter.

KORYPHAIOS OF WOMEN

What drear accents are these?

LYSISTRATA

             The merest truth.

KORYPHAIOS OF WOMEN

Be nothing loath to tell the tale to friends.

LYSISTRATA

'Twere shame to utter, pain to hold unsaid.

KORYPHAIOS OF WOMEN

Hide not from me affliction which we share.

LYSISTRATA

In briefest compass,

            (Dropping the paratragedy.)
      we want to get laid.

KORYPHAIOS OF WOMEN

                By Zeus!

LYSISTRATA

No, no, not HIM!
         Well, that's the way things are.
I've lost my grip on the girls—they're mad for men!
But sly—they slip out in droves.
             A minute ago,
I caught one scooping out the little hole
that breaks through just below Pan's grotto.
                One
had jerry-rigged some block-and-tackle business
and was wriggling away on a rope.
             Another just flat

deserted.

Last night I spied one mounting a sparrow,
all set to take off for the nearest bawdyhouse. I hauled
her back by the hair.

And excuses, pretexts for overnight
passes? I've heard them all.

Here comes one. Watch.

(*To the First Woman, as she runs out of the Akropolis.*)

—You, there! What's your hurry?

FIRST WOMAN

I have to get home.
I've got all this lovely Milesian wool in the house,
and the moths will simply batter it to bits!

LYSISTRATA

I'll bet.

Get back inside.

FIRST WOMAN

I swear I'll hurry right back!
—Just time enough to spread it out on the couch?

LYSISTRATA

Your wool will stay unspread. And you'll stay here.

FIRST WOMAN

Do I have to let my piecework *rot?*

LYSISTRATA

Possibly.

(*The Second Woman runs on.*)

SECOND WOMAN

Oh dear, oh goodness, what shall I do—my flax!
I left and forgot to peel it!

LYSISTRATA

Another one.
She suffers from unpeeled flax.

—Get back inside!

SECOND WOMAN

I'll be right back. I just have to pluck the fibers.

LYSISTRATA

No. No plucking. You start it, and everyone else
will want to go and do their plucking, too.

(*The Third Woman, swelling conspicuously,
hurries on, praying loudly.*)

THIRD WOMAN

*O Goddess of Childbirth, grant that I not deliver
until I get me from out this sacred precinct!*

LYSISTRATA

What sort of nonsense is *this?*

THIRD WOMAN

I'm due—any second!

LYSISTRATA

You weren't pregnant yesterday.

THIRD WOMAN

Today I am—
a miracle!

Let me go home for a midwife, *please!*
I may not make it!

LYSISTRATA

(*Restraining her.*)

You can do better than that.

(*Tapping the woman's stomach and receiving a metallic clang.*)

What's this? It's hard.

THIRD WOMAN

I'm going to have a boy.

LYSISTRATA

Not unless he's made of bronze. Let's see.

(*She throws open the Third Woman's cloak,
exposing a huge bronze helmet.*)

Of all the brazen . . . You've stolen the helmet from Athene's
statue! Pregnant, indeed!

THIRD WOMAN

I am *so* pregnant!

LYSISTRATA

Then why the helmet?

THIRD WOMAN

I thought my time might come
while I was still on forbidden ground. If it did,
I could climb inside Athene's helmet and have
my baby there.

The pigeons do it all the time.

LYSISTRATA

Nothing but excuses!

(*Taking the helmet.*)

This is your baby. I'm afraid
you'll have to stay until we give it a name.

THIRD WOMAN

But the Akropolis is *awful*. I can't even sleep! I saw
the snake that guards the temple.

LYSISTRATA

That snake's a fabrication.

THIRD WOMAN

I don't care *what* kind it is—I'm *scared!*

(*The other women, who have emerged from
the citadel, crowd around.*)

KLEONIKE

And those goddamned holy owls! All night long,
tu-wit, tu-wu—they're hooting me into my grave!

LYSISTRATA

Darlings, let's call a halt to this hocus-pocus.
You miss your men—now isn't that the trouble?

(*Shamefaced nods from the group.*)

Don't you think they miss you just as much?
I can assure you, their nights are every bit
as hard as yours. So be good girls; endure!
Persist a few days more, and Victory is ours.
It's fated: a current prophecy declares that the men
will go down to defeat before us, provided that *we*
maintain a United Front.

THE GREEKS HAD A WORD FOR IT

The Greek language was as inventive as the people who spoke it. Some terms have survived in modern tongues; others have disappeared, yet they recall the distinctive make-up of the Greek mind.

When we use such words as *philosophy*, *biology*, or *physics*, we are in effect speaking Greek, since all these terms derive directly from Greek origins (*philos* plus *sophia* meaning a lover of, or the love of, wisdom). When we use such terms as *love, order, honor, fate,* or *happiness*, we are not leaning on derivatives from the Greek language, but we are using concepts taken from the Greeks. Far more concerned with the spoken word than the written one, the Greeks gave many variant shadings to a relatively small number of key words that were highly flexible and dependent on the context in which they were used. Translators have struggled for centuries with them, only to learn that the Greek way of thought cannot literally be rendered. Here are some examples of one-word Greek concepts that defy one-word translation but that are basic to Greek being.

aidos—religious respect, reverence, conscience, awe; also modesty of spirit, sense of honor, compassion.

ananke—fate, destiny, "what has to be" (related to *moira*, denoting the share allotted by the gods to man).

arete—personal excellence, valor, all-round strength of character, virtuous bravery.

charis—graciousness, kindness to one's fellow man, goodwill; also thankfulness, gratitude, favor.

demos—the people of a state as a whole; also, in a political sense, the common people as opposed to the aristocrats.

eros—passionate, physical love; yet also spiritual love, attachment to the beautiful; the inspiring spirit of the arts.

eunomia—civil order under good law, the well-run state.

hamartia—error, unintentional sin, or fault, in the sense of the "tragic flaw."

hubris—pride, overweening ambition inviting disaster.

logos—proportion, calculation, reason, the ultimate rationality in things; also the spoken word.

paideia—education; the shaping of good character, especially in the young.

philia—friendship, affectionate regard; also, in its earliest sense, blood kinship.

physis—the "stuff" of which things are made, nature, the physical basis of the universe.

polis—a community of self-governing men; earliest meaning, "citadel," but later the collective life — political, religious, and cultural—of the people of the state.

psyche—the soul, the emotional rather than the rational self, the wellspring of courage as well as conscience.

sophia—wisdom; yet also cleverness, practical skill and dispatch.

sophrosyne—wisdom; chiefly in the sense of prudence, self-control, moderation.

7

LIFE
AND
LOVE

Health is the best that Heaven sends;
Next, to be comely to look upon;
Third is riches, justly won;
Fourth, to be young among one's friends.
                        —Simonides of Ceos

While his thinkers and artists wrestled with the questions of the ideal and the real, of harmony and diversity, the typical Greek citizen of the fifth century was chiefly concerned with getting the most out of a life that had become increasingly pleasant for the favored and gradually less austere for those who were not. This easing of existence had the soundest psychological and economic bases, for it rested upon the final breaking of the Persian threat. Vanquished on the peninsula and its close-in waters in the years 480 and 479, Xerxes' retreating warriors were pushed across the Aegean by revolts in the Greek islands; eventually Greek pursuers cleared Cyprus and then liberated the Bosporus region and Byzantium of the invader, establishing strongholds along the wild Thracian coast as they advanced. The rolling-back campaign was not a swift thrust, but a process extending over ten years; finally the remaining Persian army and fleet were broken at the mouth of the Eurymedon River in southern Asia Minor in a land and sea battle brilliantly led by Cimon of Athens in 468. Minds were now free from fear of a return of the *barbaroi*, while the seas were free for a vast resurgence of commerce, with Athens, at the head of the Delian League, imposing upon the Aegean in effect a *pax athenica* by means of a fleet numbering as many as two hundred galleys.

Many Greek states shared in the vigor and prosperity that resulted from extensive trade. Corinth exported tiles and woolens; Chalcis its bronze utensils and arms; west Peloponnesian ports like Patrae (the modern Patras) their olive oil, wine, and lowland fruit. Athens itself, though drawing on the long hinterland of Attica, had no surplus of food to export; on the contrary, it needed constant and regular supplies of grain from the Black Sea region to feed its teeming populace. In exchange it offered the finished goods of its mines, quarries, tanneries, workshops in abundance— smelted zinc, refined silver, forged ironwork, polished marble, leather fashioned into shoes, harnesses, and saddles, household and ceremonial pottery of every description, furniture, resin and oil for the lamps of northerly coasts, and numberless trinkets to divert the *barbaroi*. Fifth-century Athens, the world's first strong commercial power, bears a marked resemblance to the England of the time of the industrial revolution: both were the leading importers of raw materials and the leading exporters of finished ones, with their naval squadrons cruising between far-flung bases to ensure safe passage.

This traffic above all required a reliable medium of exchange; the Athenians had been among the first to maintain a stable currency. Yet venture capital was still extremely limited: banks were rare, moneylenders usurious; often city temples themselves served as lending agencies, advancing funds from their treasuries to worthy individuals. These men were unlike the later-day merchant adventurers of Europe, with their Hanseatic League and East India companies; each was likely to be shipper and skipper all in one, somewhat like the shipowner-captains of early New England, going shares with a few friends to load their vessel with a mixed cargo of whatever might be salable abroad, and then setting off on a long voyage to seek out the best markets and to bargain for what they could most advantageously bring home in return.

Before long a rich variety of cargoes was being unloaded at the Piraeus. A minor playwright, Hermippus, writing in about 429, lists some typical imports: from daughter cities in Italy, sides of beef; from Cyrene, hides; from the Hellespont, dried fish; from Egypt, sails and cord; from Syracuse, hogs and cheese; from Syria, frankincense; from Rhodes, raisins; from Libya, ivory; from Phrygia, slaves. And there was more: rugs from Carthage; linens from Alexandria; dyes from Phoenicia; tin from faraway Britain.

One can reconstruct in imagination Athens' crowded port at that time: its basin no doubt encumbered then as now with flotsam and refuse of every sort; a flotilla of triremes of the Athenian-Delian fleet moored nearby, prepared for quick action in case of alarm; and the heavier mechant ships of burthen (broad-beamed, single-masted, carrying one immense sail to catch a favoring wind) tied up at dockside. Greek crews and polylingual sailors from the Levant, Africa, or as far away as Spain mingle with gangs of stevedores unloading a consignment of wheat from the Crimea or packing an outgoing shipment of amphorae in straw from dusty drays; municipal checkers are weighing incoming grain into the public warehouse (precautions are taken to prevent any middleman from cornering the supply); owner's agents are scurrying about the chandleries to provision a laden ship for sea; buyers, sellers, people with messages to send by the hand of the captain to a foreign port, are all milling along the waterfront with its creaking cordage, its fish smells, its pumpers flushing out casks and bilges; and, behind all this, fly-ridden little taverns are serving up wine-and-water and goat's cheese, while, in the farther alleys for which the Piraeus was already famous, prostitutes from many lands, in cheap paint and trinketry, are working their trade. Almost every kind of person and chattel of the ancient world passed through this entry port on the way to the great mart of Athens, so that Pericles in the pride and dignity of his famous funeral oration could justly say, "The magnitude of our city draws the produce of the world to our harbor, so that to the Athenian the fruits of other countries are as familiar a luxury as those of his own."

LOUVRE; GIRAUDON

A Greek man's house was not always his home. He relished drinking evenings with friends, often in the house of a hetaira, where men conversed while flute girls played and danced for them.

MUSEUM OF FINE ARTS, BOSTON

MUSEUM OF FINE ARTS, BOSTON

STAATLICHE MUSEEN, BERLIN

Three terra-cotta statuettes, probably made as grave offerings or shrine dedications, depict everyday activities: a barber trims his client's hair (top); a seated man prepares his dinner over an open fire (center); a woman peers into her oven (bottom).

Yet all these incoming products, along with those made at home, still did not endow the Athenian household with a visible air of abundance. Fortunes were made, but throughout the fifth century, at least, ostentation in one's domestic arrangements was frowned upon. Pericles reportedly owned a profitable *ergasteria*, or workshop, and became affluent, but so far as we know he remained modest in his house and appurtenances. In the next century the public orator Demosthenes (who owned a furniture workshop with twenty slaves) lamented the passing of frugality when he remarked: "The great men of old built splendid edifices for the use of the State, and set up noble works of art which later ages can never match. But in private life they were severe and simple, and the dwelling of an Aristides or a Miltiades was no more sumptuous than that of an ordinary Athenian citizien." (Aristides, well-born, wealthy, and talented both as statesman and a soldier, played a leading role at Marathon and Salamis and commanded the Athenian forces at the victory of Plataea; renowned for his rectitude, he appears to have died in poverty.) The self-indulgent, mercurial leader Alcibiades—protégé of Pericles, leader in the war against Sparta, and owner of a manufactory as well—marked the change at the end of the fifth century when he had the interior of his house decorated with wall paintings, an extravagance for which he was widely criticized.

One reason why the fifth-century Athenian—and, one can say, the town-living Greek citizen in general—kept a simple house was that he spent so little time in it. It was his dormitory, his seat for occasional attendance on his wife and for an evening meal with male companions—not much more. His sunny climate invited him to live as much as possible outdoors. His gregarious disposition led him to spend the better part of the day in the busy market place and under the eaves of its stoa, walking, talking, doing business with friends; his propensities for male company and for exercise led him to frequent his public gymnasiums and baths in afternoon; his other male propensities, to seek out the company of a female friend for the evening, before returning home.

The structure and furnishing of the Greek house reflect its master's lack of preoccupation with it. It is built of the simplest materials—sun-dried brick, hardened clay—and usually consists of a low, dun-colored oblong cluster backing away from streetside without any conspicuous portal to mark it, save that a stone Herm, with its head of Hermes and its phallus, is posted outside the door as a good-luck and fertility symbol. Inside, a number of small rooms front upon a central court dedicated to domestic pursuits; the women's quarters are at the rear, or if the house is large, under the low rafters of an upper story. Its flooring may consist simply of hard-packed earth covered by rush mats; then cement begins to be used, and before long, wealthier families indulge themselves in tile mosaics and a few rugs from Asia Minor or Carthage. Walls are stucco and whitewashed; interior doorways are often just curtained apertures; window glass is unknown. Cooking is done on an open fire, though some houses possess baking ovens; winter heating is achieved not by a hearth, but by movable braziers; lighting, by small and somewhat perfunctory oil lamps; sanitation, by terra-cotta bathtubs and latrines sometimes flushed by a jug of water sluiced down a drain. Toward the end of the century some wealthy famiíes build into their houses a paved bathroom, with water piped in; but for the most part flowing water is a luxury, and personal cleanliness consists in an oil rubdown, followed by a jug of cooling water from the rain-catch or the public well.

In the rooms a functional simplicity of furniture reigns. The chief articles are wood-frame couches, with a webbed seat of cords or leather thongs, that do the double duty of serving as beds at night and as reclining seats for men at meals. (The custom of eating and drinking in a longitudinal posture is restricted to men; the women of the house sit upright on chairs and do not take their meals with the men if guests are present.) Small, low three-legged tables called *trapezai*—remote precursors of the modern coffee table—are set individually before each couch for the service of food and drink: the huge, groaning banquet board mentioned in Olympian and Homeric myths, and later to figure again in the history of conviviality, seems in fifth-century Greece to have disappeared. In one of the rooms there is often something resembling what Americans of former generations called a "Grandfather's chair"—one big armchair of honor for the patriarch of the family, appropriately called the *thronos*. There are a few other armless chairs and stools, gracefully turned, as we know from numberless representations of them on vases and reliefs, but with these—apart from a storage chest here and there—the furnishing of the Greek citizen's house is virtually complete.

Occasionally there is a decorated mirror or a painted wall like the one in rich Alcibiades' house; but only one form of ornament is pervasive in the Greek house—figures painted on the sides of the everyday bowl, jug, pot, or vase. The craft of vase painting had evolved into a considerable art, and into a diverting portraiture of daily life as well. Nameless artists had both refined the shapes of pottery and, letting their imaginations run free, peopled the pottery with scenes of verve and exuberance far removed from

MUSEUM OF FINE ARTS, BOSTON

MUSEUM OF FINE ARTS, BOSTON

MANDRALISCA MUSEUM, SICILY; ANDERSON

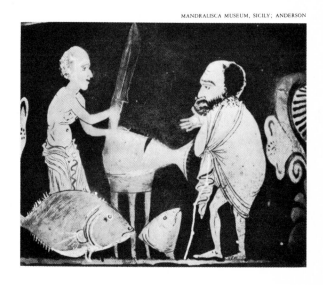

Details from vase paintings show tradesmen at work: (top) a butcher and his assistant carve a hindquarter of beef; (center) a carpenter puts finishing touches on a chest he is making; (bottom) a fishmonger slices a tuna as a customer watches him.

NATIONAL MUSEUM, ATHENS; SKIRA

A soldier's wife, seated on a typical Greek chair, watches her husband's departure from home. (His helmet can be seen in the detail reproduced here.) The objects shown hanging on the wall include a red hood, a mirror, and a jug.

the geometric patterns and the little stylized figures of centuries before. Reversing their technical process along the way (in the sixth century they painted black figures on a clay that turned reddish or orange when fired, and in the fifth they blacked out the background, leaving silhouetted figures to stand forth in the warm color of the clay) and displaying increasing mastery of drawing, they depicted not only the familiar mythic figures in action—gods disputing, heroes battling, satyrs indecently prancing—but also contemporaries going about their work and play, harvesting, hunting, spinning, cooking, bathing, sporting, fighting, marrying, worshiping, begetting, dallying, and dying. Each house, otherwise so bare, contained some share of this social autobiography on jugs, and the vase painters were restrained by no limits as to what they might represent.

These artists tell of a society that is male-centered in most respects—lean, naked youths out exercising, adult men sharing in their sports, sometimes caressing their favorites, or reclining and bibbing at male drinking-parties, or *symposia*, while women go about the household duties of weaving, minding the children, and directing the servants. Yet they tell of strong heterosexuality too, with scenes of amorous pursuit, youths embracing their mistresses, and flute girls and dancers regaling their middle-aged hosts. They tell us also, and with more homely detail than sculpture can do, of the nature of Greek dress—or rather the limitations of it—a topic most pertinent to Greek mores.

A millennium and more before, the elegant court women of Crete had worn multicolored robes with flounces and a tight-fitting bodice that left their entire breasts provocatively exposed. But this had long been forgotten; now man and woman alike wore one basic garment, shapeless in itself except insofar as it was pinned together and girdled—the *chiton*, or tunic, which was nothing more than a rectangular piece of material, often linen, brooched at the shoulders and sewn down part of the side, and then, in the case of women, taken up at the waist and left to hang down to the ankles, while men wore it to the knee. The girdle, apart from being the garment's one concession to revealing form and causing a pleasant scheme of folds or pleats, also had its erotic meaning as a symbol of virginity: Homer and other Greek poets speak often of "loosing the maiden's girdle." Yet the girdle and the ankle-length chiton were sometimes worn by men, too.

Men wore no underclothing, while many women did wear a slip and a breastband, or primordial brassiere; their bare feet stood in sandals, their head was covered only when on dusty travel by a felt hood of sorts; and, since the chiton left the forearms bare, the woman of good position generally tossed about her shoulders a light cloak, or *himation*, when she ventured from her house. The man often donned such a himation too, sometimes even dispensing with the chiton underneath—a departure that caused some scandal, particularly when the cloak stopped well above the knee and led, especially in a reclining posture, say at a banquet, to what Greek guardians of morals considered indecent exposure.

In general, while Greek men felt a minimum of clothing to be best—for men—and while they stripped for games and baths whenever opportunity offered and made a cult of the beautiful young male over the centuries, they were equivocal about the showing of the female body. We have seen with what diffidence the Greek sculptor proceeded to render the nude female, long after he had portrayed the virile *kouros* in full anatomical detail. A sense of restraint—even a sort of puritanism, if you will—came over the Greeks at the thought of bared breasts or the all too specific revelation of the womanly form. Few things caused greater scandal among right-thinking men or served more to alienate Sparta morally from many a community to the north of it than its girls' practice of wearing their version of the chiton (the Dorian *peplos*) quite unsewn and open on the side where its ends met, with the result that when walking, their whole left thigh would come into view—and then, as if this were not enough, of dropping their peplos altogether to go into the arena to engage naked in contests with men. Critics assailed these girls as "thigh-showers" (we would say "exhibitionists") and accused them of sexual profligacy, in which charge the critics were generally right; and one of the sharpest of them, Euripides, in his *Andromache*, written in Athens during the struggle with Sparta, snorts in disdain: "Wish as you might, a Spartan girl never could be virtuous. They gad abroad with young men with naked thighs, and with clothes discarded, they race with 'em, wrestle with 'em, Intolerable!"

The daily vesture and appearance of the proper Greek was not necessarily severe and drab. Far from it. Having laid a foundation of generally subdued good taste, the Greek then proceeded to embroider it, very much in the way he painted and ornamented his temples (and the relationship of the simple, flowing lines of the chiton to the fluted column has often been pointed out). Thus the tunic did not have to be a bleached white; it could be, and often was, a brilliant saffron or red or purple. Though women adhered to its basic form, they burst out over it with bracelets, amulets, necklaces, earrings, diadems, lockets, and chains, and hung jewels and ribbons in their dressed hair. Men, too, affected ornaments and rings (Aristotle wore several) and went each morning to the

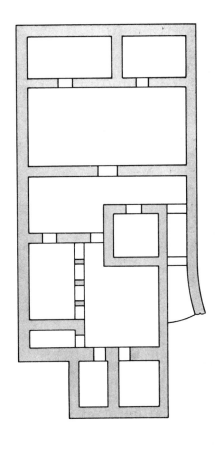

Houses were simple and sparsely furnished, partly because men spent little time at home, returning from the agora or palaestra only in the evening. The floor plan of a house (above) shows the entrance hall leading past the porter's room into the main courtyard; the large room just beyond is probably the dining room where the master of the house received his guests. Below, a woman arranges clothing on a bed in the women's quarters, which were customarily separated by a strong door from the remainder of the house.

COURTESY ANDRE EMMERICH GALLERY

263

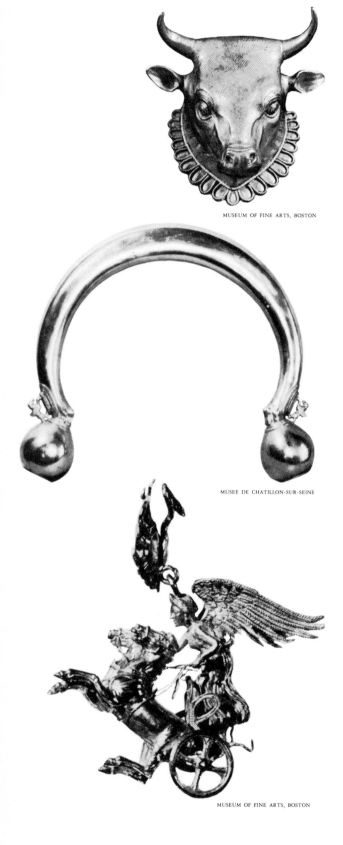

MUSEUM OF FINE ARTS, BOSTON

MUSEE DE CHATILLON-SUR-SEINE

MUSEUM OF FINE ARTS, BOSTON

Despite the simplicity of their dress, Greek women loved ornament. At top is a bull's head pendant; in the center, a diadem found in France and thought to be of Greek workmanship. The intricate earring that is shown at bottom may have been intended originally for the statue of a goddess.

barber to be groomed and to have their locks braided or curled. Scented unguents, dyes, depilatories, perfumes, were all in daily use among women and testify that the supposedly "natural" Greeks were not so different from other breeds in wishing to put on their best face. In a text fragment that survives, Aristophanes gives a long and sardonic list of some specific aids to Athenian beauty, ranging from clippers, scissors, grease paint, hair nets, sea-weed paint, and pumice stone to beauty plasters and false hair.

The women who made the most elaborate recourse to these aids were, to be sure, those who did so for sound professional reasons —the higher courtesans, or *hetairai* (meaning "companions"), often as gifted as they were seductive and altogether the most interesting (and sometimes the most dangerous) women of Greece. These were the unconventional females in a society in which the position of woman generally was limited—as was man's relationship with her. Demosthenes is said to have expressed the accepted male attitude of his time when he remarked in a matter-of-fact way: "We have courtesans for the sake of pleasure, concubines for the daily health of our bodies, and wives to bear us lawful offspring and be the faithful guardians of our homes"—not a word about love, romantic or other, nor about passion either. The poet Hesiod long before him had been equally matter-of-fact when he said: "A house, a wife, and an ox to plow with are the first needs of life"—in that order. (Aristotle, who liked the order of Hesiod's listing, picked it up and made it central to the theory of the good life he set forth in his *Politics*.) Pindar in his odes and Plato in his dialogues, both of whom saw in women chiefly a source of sensual gratification, celebrated the ardor of young men for one another as being both more noble and more natural than that between male and female. Yet enlightened companionship, head-strong passion, and on occasion a complete love did occur between Greek man and woman, though most of this took place outside of marriage. Its chief beneficiaries on the female side could range from a clever dancing girl of the demimonde to a woman who was the precursor of a Marquise de Montespan, cultivated, dashing, skillful, and a great lady in all but reputation.

In the period of the Persian invasions, the Ionian courtesan Thargelia—"a great beauty, extremely charming, and at the same time sagacious," as Plutarch describes her—had affairs with many a Greek leader while herself beholden to the court of Xerxes, and in so doing is thought to have forwarded many secrets from her bed to his at the Bosporus. Later, the brilliant libertine Aspasia of Miletus so entranced Pericles both by her body and her wit that soon she held the greatest public figure of Greece in thralldom, and his enemies came near destroying him by accusing him of being in her power. The stunning Phryne of Thespiae posed for, loved, and inspired Praxiteles and the painter Apelles as well, and became somewhat of a patroness of arts in her own right when she offered Delphi a statue of Aphrodite for which she had sat for her lover. Leontis of Boeotia is recalled as having helped the elderly thinker Epicurus to a practical understanding of the philosophy of pleasure. A wry comment has it that Lais of Corinth kept pompous Demosthenes virtuous by demanding 10,000 drachmas for an evening with him, though, liking the company of philosophers, she gave herself gratis to indigent Diogenes, the inhabitant of a barrel. Thais of Athens, believed to have been mistress of Alexander the Great, was not only to exert great influence upon his political affairs but to become, after his death, the wife of Ptolemy I of Egypt, and thus a queen.

STAATLICHE MUSEEN, BERLIN

The history of social customs presents problems to those wishing to draw clear borderlines between the vocations of the courtesan, the concubine, and the prostitute—and nowhere more than in ancient Greece did these roles meet and mingle with innumerable shadings. Prostitution in the ordinary, indiscriminate sense was not only recognized but regularized, the common women, or *pornai*, who filled the brothels of the Piraeus for instance being taxed on their receipts. Sacred, or temple, prostitution came to be accepted and appreciated, but only in Corinth, as an aspect of that robust city's cult of its patroness, the love goddess Aphrodite. Her cult had come to Corinth in the eighth century from the island of Cyprus, near which she had supposedly first risen from the sea and where every Cypriote girl of whatever class was required to give herself once in her life to a stranger in the temple precinct, in obeisance to the goddess and the fertility principle. By the time the cult reached Corinth, hundreds of female devotees of Aphrodite were ready to offer themselves not just once but continually, as career priestesses of her order, so to speak— a dedication for which they won considerable respect among Greeks. Some were free citizens of good birth; others were slaves who could win citizen status simply by being manumitted by their owners to the priests of the goddess' temple on Acrocorinth.

STADTISCHE MUSEEN, FRANKFURT/MAIN

MUSEUM, COS; HIRMER

One fifth-century Corinthian citizen named Xenophon (not to be confused with the Athenian Xenophon, the author of the *Anabasis*) pledged twenty-five such girls to the temple should he win two contests at the Olympic games—which he thereupon did. The proceeds of his "fillies"—so Pindar called them in an ode—went, we are told, into the collection plate. Enhanced by such generous endowments as Xenophon's, the number of Aphrodite's

Both men and women wore simple lengths of linen or wool wrapped about the body to hang in graceful folds. The peplos (above, left) was attached at the shoulders and often belted at the waist. At top a man dons a himation, or cloak. Another himation is shown on the statue above.

HOSPITALITY AT CORINTH

Temple prostitution was unknown in Greece—with the notable exception of Corinth, where a rich citizen named Xenophon presented a gift of twenty-five obliging girls to the temple in thanks for his victories at the Olympic games, and furthermore commissioned the poet Pindar to write an ode to celebrate them. Pindar, himself no lover of women, unbent and wrote an erotic chant that was apparently widely sung and danced to. Only its opening stanzas survive:

Young hospitable girls, beguiling creatures in
    wealthy Corinth,
You who burn the amber tears of fresh frankincense
Full often soaring upward in your souls to Aph-
    rodite,
Heavenly Mother of lovers;

To you girls she has granted
Blamelessly upon lovely beds
To cull the blossom of delicate bloom;
For under love's necessity all things are fine.

Yet I wonder whatever the lords of Corinth will
    be saying
Of me—!
Devising as I am a prelude to sweet song
All for the pleasure of anybody's girls!
But we've tested their gold with a pure touchstone.

O Lady of Cyprus! Hither to your sanctuary
Xenophon has brought fillies—
A hundred limbs of girls—
Glad for the fulfillment of his vows.

handmaidens at Corinth eventually exceeded one thousand, if the historian Strabo is to be believed, and the rich trading city became the bawdiest in Greek antiquity. A proverb soon arose to warn the visitor: "A journey to Corinth does not profit every man," meaning that its costs and vices might ruin both his purse and health.

Several steps above the waterfront *pornai* and the devoted temple girls—though how many steps, it is difficult to judge—stood such a popular *hetaira* as Metiche of Athens, who was engaging enough to become the heroine of a comedy (since lost) by the minor playwright Eubulus, and who acquired the nickname "Clepsydra" (meaning "water clock") because she received her lovers on the hour. What was she—a stylish courtesan or just another harlot? Her history is unclear: perhaps she was both. And what of the woman in Greece who carried on another very ancient tradition, that of the concubine, or "minor wife," more or less permanently attached to an otherwise married male? Here we are on even more uncertain ground. According to *Iliad*, in that early time most men of rank kept in their households one or more assistant consorts. In classical times in Attica it appears this was no longer socially accepted—though there is a puzzling reference in an oration of Demosthenes that lumps mother, wife, sister, daughter, and concubine together in one breath. In Sparta, always apart and on its own, a special form of concubinage was allowed in that men could acquire other women to supplement their own progeny in the interests of the state, while wives could also roam afield for the same purpose: the lending or borrowing of helpmeets among Spartan males for this or other aims was quite common.

Among such irregular mates of many categories, Pericles' own Aspasia stands out as the most talented, the most highly placed, yet also the most mixed in her roles. Coming from her Milesian home to Athens at mid fifth century, at a time when the education of girls was confined to elementary reading and writing along with domestic crafts and some music, she emerged as a proponent of more education and freedom of movement of women—an early feminist, no less. To this end she opened a school in which she taught the arts of discourse and rudiments of philosophy, inviting citizen wives to attend along with their husbands, and to bring along their daughters too. From her lecture courses there appears to have developed the world's first salon, frequented by Pericles and Socrates and probably also by Euripides, Phidias, Anaxagoras, and Alcibiades, and many other prominent men of the time. Yet she may also have added to her school an establishment of girls gifted in other arts; at least so Plutarch, the favorite gossip of antiquity, suggests when he writes that "her occupation was anything but creditable, her house being a home for young courtesans."

Just what the truth of this is, remains conjectural. What is known is that Pericles became infatuated with her, abandoned his wife for her, and openly lived with her in what Plutarch describes as "wonderful affection." Yet Aspasia, though the statesmen and philosophers of Athens flocked around her as she became the glass of fashion and the embodiment of the New Woman, was regarded by many as a menace to the state and an offense to its morals. It was widely said that Pericles had been enticed into making war against hitherto friendly Samos at the behest of his foreign paramour, her home city of Miletus having had a long-standing feud against the Samians. He was accused of squandering public funds, and hostility reached the point where he was traduced on the stage as a whorekeeper in such lines as these:

> To find him a Hera the goddess of lust
> Bore that harlot beyond shame,
> Aspasia by name.

In the end, the conservative faction in Athens brought in a charge of impiety and indecency against her. Pericles eloquently defended her before the city's massed jurors and won her acquittal, but his reputation as peerless leader was damaged.

Compared to the life of Aspasia, that of the well-born, respectable women of Greece whose sights she had sought to raise was dull and confined. Or so a long consensus of information and opinion has taught us, though modern scholars have raised searching questions as to whether, as the fifth century wore on, it was always quite as confined as has been represented. In legal status, to be sure, the Greek woman was hardly more than a chattel, as women had long been in the oriental world; it was only through the variety and imagination of Greek experience that she gradually became "interesting." The main social unit, before and after, was the family. Its basic function was to provide continuity through the production of legitimate children and, through them, the orderly handing on of property. In a day of small population and of much loss by death, the production of such children was the first necessity, if polis and order were to survive. Marriage, then, was an obligation, a fulfillment of duty to the gods: in Greece celibacy was forbidden by law in some cities and condemned by custom in all, and not to have children was not only a misfortune but an impiety.

It followed that marriage was a function not of love but of social economics. Matches were arranged by contract, the bride and her dowry passing from her father's into her husband's keep-

LOUVRE; GUILEY-LAGACHE

METROPOLITAN MUSEUM OF ART, FLETCHER FUND

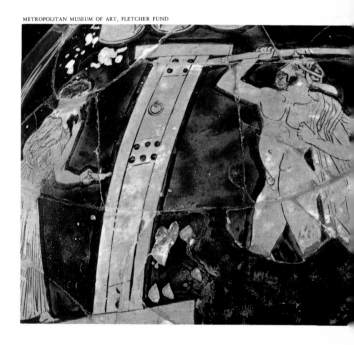

Dancers, such as the girl with castanets shown at top, entertained at festivals. Above, a reveler returning late from a festival in honor of Dionysus pounds on the door as his wife approaches timidly, lamp in hand, to let him in.

BRITISH MUSEUM

AMERICAN SCHOOL OF CLASSICAL STUDIES, ATHENS

A statuette from Tanagra (top) shows a mother with a baby in her lap. When school or household tasks were done, children amused themselves with toys and pets (above) or such games as hide-and-seek and leapfrog.

ing to do with as he saw fit. If she failed him in any way— particularly in the production of children—the husband could divorce her without so much as stating his reasons. She could neither hold property nor claim to inherit it from him nor bring suit against him or anyone else, nor make a contract of any kind. She remained throughout her life in the charge of some male; if widowed, she returned into the guardianship of her father or next of male kin. Her husband could maintain concubines without giving her cause for redress; but adultery on her part, under the Greek double standard of morality, was a grave offense against him. If a man in turn committed adultery, his offense was not against his victim, but against the man who was her guardian.

The place of the good Greek child-bearing wife was not only the home, but particularly the women's quarters of the home; she should not mix with the public affairs of men, nor even appear frequently in the streets (shopping being done by her husband or the family servants in any case). Xenophon, friend of Socrates and author of the *Anabasis*, declares sententiously in an essay entitled *Oeconomicus*, or *Economics*: "The god has ordained and the law approves that each should follow his own capacity. It is not so good for a woman to be out of doors as in, and it is more dishonorable for a man to stay in than to attend to his affairs outside." Yet he also gives an engaging glimpse of Greek domesticity in this portrait, cast in form of a dialogue between Socrates and a country squire, Ischomachus, who has taken a young bride. The author Xenophon—a soldier returned from the wars, who disdained the pleasures of Athens while cultivating his lands—no doubt patterned Ischomachus after himself.

Socrates, who in the dialogue has gone into the country to explore for himself the question of whether it may not afford more of the good life than do the jaded cities, delivers himself of a panegyric on the virtues of husbandry and the blessings of the soil as the mother of occupations and of kindly qualities in man as well. Ischomachus tells Socrates how he arranges the life of his country wife and manages his estates. He tells how his wife was not yet fifteen when he married her, and had spent her girlhood in strict seclusion, knowing "no more than how, when given wool, to turn out a cloak, and had seen only how the spinning is given out to the maids." He had told her when taking her to wife that he wanted her to be the best possible superintendent of his household and the begetter with him of creditable children. Finding her "docile and sufficiently domesticated to carry on conversations," he proceeded with her practical education, instructing her in the importance of arranging furniture and utensils in an orderly fashion, of keeping the flour dry and the wine cool, of supervising work at the loom, of making inventories, and of maintaining accounts of income and expense—and gave her some advice, as well, as to how healthy, natural color in the cheeks is superior to cosmetics, when he found her applying paint too thickly. All this, apparently, his girl-wife accepted with dutiful grace. He himself rode out each morning to manage his field hands, put his horse through its paces on a cross-country canter, and possibly visited with neighbors before returning for his first meal of the day.

Housebound as she was, a wife so active, shouldering so many responsibilities, bears little resemblance to an odalisque on a divan. She stands somewhere in that long vale between primordial times when woman was exalted as earth mother, life-giver, and matriarch and a later day when she was to emerge to be recognized freely as man's full partner if not his full equal—the day that Aspasia in her way sought to herald. The wedding ceremony that the Greek bride underwent tells of her position: it was simply an act of property conveyance, with an evening procession from her father's house to her bridegroom's (the scene of a ceremonial meal at which men and women were segregated in separate rooms or at separate tables) and the groom's gesture of carrying her bodily over his doorstep (a symbol of sexual seizure preserved even now in the West). But gradually, late in the classical period, Greek woman began to rise and to be regarded as something more than either chattel or diversion or the object of sudden passion—notwithstanding the lingering opinions of Plato in the fourth century to the contrary.

It remained the rule that a wife could not attend her husband's banquetings (and we have from the same Xenophon an account of one of the most exuberant of these stag affairs, Socrates and eight other male guests being regaled by jesters, flute girls, acrobats, and quantities of wine), but she found herself, like Penelope in the legendary past, managing a great household. Though no unmarried woman, save one resident priestess, was permitted to attend the Olympic games, women were eventually allowed to have their own Olympics. Spartan girls, of course, had long since been parading bare in the stadiums, and the lusty commentator Athenaeus writes, ignoring the moral objections that had been raised, "The Spartan custom of displaying the young girls naked before strangers is highly praised; and in the island of Chios it is delightful just to walk to the gymnasiums and running tracks to see the young men wrestling naked with the young girls, who are also naked.") The young girls of Athens too were allowed to come out from under their wraps, at least

MUSEUM OF FINE ARTS, BOSTON

BRITISH MUSEUM

BRITISH MUSEUM

A wife's days were spent in the home performing domestic chores. She would have to teach her daughter how to cook (top) and she would probably have to grind flour for daily bread (center). Later she could relax in the bathtub (bottom).

Small molded figurines known as Tanagra statuettes, after the town where many of them were found, became popular throughout Greece in Hellenistic times. They often depicted an elegantly dressed lady such as the one above.

LOUVRE; GUILEY-LAGACHE

figuratively and occasionally: the greatest of the city's processions, at the opening of the quadrennial Panathenaic games—with young athletes forming up at the city gates with their chariots and javelins to march across the Agora and up the steep incline—was led by a bevy of maidens.

The Greek woman of the fifth century could not participate as an actress in the emerging theatre of her time (any more than a woman of Shakespeare's time was permitted to participate in that of his, all parts being taken by men or youths), but she was allowed and encouraged to attend it, and there she found much of it to be written about herself and her relations with man, sometimes tragic, sometimes comic, on occasion ribald. She saw portrayals of such tender heroines of the mythic past as Antigone, Alcestis, Iphigenia, and of such tormented, brutal ones as Hecuba and Medea. She also saw jocular portraits of herself and her fellow women in her own time—none more pungent than in Aristophanes' celebrated satire *Lysistrata*, written during the long-drawn-out war between Athens and Sparta, and in which the heroine proposes to her fellow wives that the way to end it would be for them to deny themselves to their husbands until they stopped fighting. The farce of the situation develops around the anguish in the minds of Lysistrata's friends concerning such extreme self-denial for so worthy a cause.

Nothing could better demonstrate a brilliant playwright's recognition of the power of woman and of man's abiding weakness for her. Nothing, in short, could be more human, adult, and witty. But while Aristophanes is mocking women, he is also mocking their dense, war-driven men, who would be far better off savoring home pleasures than marching about. And Aristophanes, for all his laughter, is not antifeminist either: on the contrary, in 411, the year that saw the premiere of *Lysistrata* at the Lenaean, or winter, festival in Athens, he also brought forth the comedy entitled *Thesmophoriazusae* (sometimes translated as *The Festival Women*), which was a direct personal attack on the tragedian Euripides for the unfavorable portraits of women given in *his* plays. In its first act Athenian women assemble to vow to punish the tragedian for his insults to their sex. After hearing a chorus leader deliver a speech prizing the virtues of women over those of men, Euripides disguises himself in the costume of a woman—in specific, that of an old bawd—in order to escape retribution; and on this note, complicated by the intervention of the police and the presence of a transvestite father-in-law, the farce ends.

At the outset of *Lysistrata* Aristophanes has one of the wives who has been summoned to the heroine's sexual protest meeting complain, "but it's not easy, you know, for women to leave the house. One is busy pottering about her husband; another is getting the servant up; a third is putting her child asleep or washing the brat or feeding it." Later he has her ask what sensible thing she could possibly do, dwelling as she does "in the retirement of the household." Yet the very fact that a playwright could present such protest and complaint—and that the Greek theatre audience thought it plausible—tells us that women of position were coming forth from their limited world behind the courtyard and the stairs. We have already seen the gradual emergence of the female nude in Greek art; what is more significant is the gradual emergence of Greek woman as a complete personality.

The exquisite marble relief known as the *Birth of Aphrodite* (illustrated on pages 66–67), carved in the fifth century and exhumed in the nineteenth A.D. in Rome, tells of an artist as preoccupied with feminine spirit as form. The goddess, fully shaped, yet very young and delicately and discreetly draped, rises from the sea assisted by supporting maids or goddesses, to one of whom she looks up in an almost diffident way, aware of her own beauty but perhaps not yet quite certain of how to use it—a sensitive image of woman on the threshold, but seen without the slightest sentimentality. Just as expressive in their way are the numerous memorial tablets, or steles, that begin appearing in the fifth century to mourn the passing of a beloved woman. These shafts, carved in low relief, generally show the departed (she may be mature wife or young girl; in at least one instance a slave girl is memorialized) seated in the presence of those who love her or clasping hands with them as she leaves for the world of the shades; and often an inscription recalling her name and circumstance is still legible. Thus on one stele Damasistrate and her husband join hands at parting; they are attended by a child and a kinswoman but have eyes only for each other. An epitaph surviving in *The Greek Anthology* reads: "In this stone Marathonis laid Nicopolis, and bedewed the marble chest with tear. But it was of no avail. What profit hath a man whose wife is gone, and who is left solitary on earth?" Men who could know and remember women in this fashion had obviously learned both to understand and prize them.

Yet, despite all this, Greek attitudes toward the opposite sex remained ambivalent—as did their attitudes toward sex in general. To discover this has sometimes come as a shock to philhellenes of later centuries, who were anxious to erect an image of a culture so much sunnier and presumably freer than that of the constricted Christian West. Many a man, repelled by the frost that descended upon sexuality when Saint Paul so effectively linked it to sin, and

This stylish woman portrayed in a Roman replica of a fifth-century statue is considered to be the beautiful Milesian courtesan Aspasia; she was for years the mistress of Pericles, who left his wife to live with her.
LOUVRE; GUILEY-LAGACHE

271

Grave steles and vase paintings give evidence of the strong bonds of affection that existed between husband and wife. The tombstone above, which the Athenian Ktesileos commissioned for the grave of his deceased wife Theano, shows him parting from her with devotion and grief.

NATIONAL MUSEUM, ATHENS; HIRMER

by the alternate seizures of prudery, smuttiness, shame, and compulsive ostentation that have come over it since, has looked back nostalgically to a warm-blooded people apparently free from all obsession with the subject one way or the other, and to whom sex was just a healthy natural function, as everyday as eating, and to be enjoyed very much as one enjoys eating. Or so the myth goes. It was strengthened by knowledge of Spartan girls publicly wrestling their males in the nude, of erotic scenes painted like any others on household pottery, or of Aristophanes being as broad and funny about sexual functions as he was about other functions of the body. But while the Hellenes widely savored all this as much as the philhellenes, it was only one side of their view of a subject that for them had its troubling obverse. What could be more frank than the spectacle of maidens carrying a huge phallus in procession, often accompanied by a symbol of their pudenda too? But such processions were religious, dating back to prehistoric times, and combined a worship of the miracle and joy of procreation with a sense of awe and mystery concerning the process. And though the fifth-century educated Greek felt he was sophisticated about the biological facts of life, there stayed with him an awareness of the generative power as being something larger than his life—a gift of the gods or of nature that could be beneficent and yet potentially dangerous too. It could provide stalwart sons as the ancient corn goddess had provided ample fields, yet it could also bring forth demons and disasters, and the Greek had only to look back through his tales and dramas to the Mycenaean Helen or Clytemnestra to remind himself how fatal the sexual lure could be. Dionysian and priapic rites, sacred prostitution along with sacred virgins, excesses here, taboos there, and the pursuit of the cult of male *paiderasteia* in particular, all speak of a people beset as much by sexual uncertainty as by attraction.

Physically intimate friendship among men, it should be said, was so far as we know primarily concentrated in the upper class of citizens (in Sparta, the pioneer in this respect, the warrior class), while the lesser orders remained conventionally heterosexual. It should also be said that the homosexual, as the man whose erotic impulses are directed only toward males, was universally scorned: what was accepted and practiced in the leading circles was bisexuality—a man siring possibly a large number of offspring and heading the family while engaged with a male lover as well.

In this equivocal area of Greek life, so difficult to comprehend in a modern age unaccustomed, at least publicly, to such a mixture, the sorriest figure was often the handsome youth from abroad who had fallen into this or that city's hands by capture and then into those of some citizen by purchase, and who, as his attraction waned, declined from the role of companion or male concubine into that of a common slave. The loftiest figure in it was none other than Plato himself, after Socrates the most illustrious mind of Greece, intent on exploring the farthest reaches of the human psyche; he was evidently wedded to male relationships with only a shadowy interest in the female.

Plato in his *Symposium*—perhaps the most absorbing of the twenty-five dialogues on which his lasting fame as a thinker chiefly rests—suggests his predilections and those of the highly cultivated Athenian elite in which he moved and taught. The work is a remarkable tour de force altogether, full of surprises, lively exchanges, and poetic ascents. Set down in about the year 384, when Plato was in his mid-forties and had just taken to lecturing outside the city's walls in the grove of Academus (from which arose the name of his Academy), it purports to recall a convivial evening's talk of almost a generation earlier, supposedly in 416, when a group of bright spirits had forgathered with Socrates to eat, drink, and discuss the subject of Love. Those present included the playwright Aristophanes, the two young literary men Phaedrus and Pausanias, and the physician Erixymachus; later in the evening, long after the guests have agreed to dismiss the flute girls and to drink sparingly in order to pursue their talk in good order, the wine-flushed Alcibiades breaks in with a band of revelers and disrupts the proceedings. But before this happens each of the guests reclining about Socrates has delivered himself of an encomium on *eros*, by which, it rapidly becomes apparent, he means primarily friendship or love among men.

Then Socrates takes over with a brilliant discourse that lifts the evening to another level. He proposes that Love exists not for the sake of the self but for that of an object; that Love is higher as the object is higher; and that at best, Love lifts man from the passions of earth to a vision of absolute beauty, or God.

At least such are the thoughts that Plato puts into the mouth of the master who died a decade and a half earlier, representing them as having been uttered about a decade and a half before that at a party at which Plato himself was not present in any case (he would have been thirteen at the time). To try to unravel the problem of what the aging, earthy Socrates himself may have said on this or any other topic as against what his pupil in his dialogues said he did, has long frustrated students. In any event the two remain what might be called the Siamese twins of philosophy, since the first never wrote and the second professed, even long after his master's death, that he chiefly listened. In the case of the *Sympo-*

MARTIN VON WAGNER MUSEUM, WURZBURG; HIRMER

LOUVRE; HIRMER

The varied pleasures of extramarital love were celebrated in numerous vase paintings. One at top shows a bearded gentleman wooing a complaisant youth. Another, above, depicts a reveler, who is almost nude, with his arm thrown about the shoulder of an elegantly dressed courtesan.

sium there is hardly a doubt that the Socrates speaking is not Socrates at all, but the Plato who wishes to be identified with him. What is all the more puzzling, then, is that Plato-as-Socrates, in the great argument that takes the dialogue to its peak, claims that his full insight into Love came not from manly wisdom but from a woman, one Diotima of Mantinea, "who was deeply versed in this and many other fields of knowledge . . . and it was she who taught me the philosophy of Love." What was a woman doing instructing Plato particularly in this subject, especially since he appears to have disdained the sex or at least to have been highly equivocal in his feelings toward it? True, in the *Republic*—his scheme for an ideal society—he argues that some women are superior and, as wives and helpmeets of the Guardians of the state, should receive the same education as men. Yet he seems to feel that the female mind is weaker; in his *Laws* there is reference to woman's "disposition" as being "inferior to man's."

Students will go on, no doubt, investigating and debating the identity of this mysterious Diotima. Did she indeed ever exist outside Plato's own imagination? We shall probably never know the answer to this. What we do know is that in the *Symposium* she exists as a kind of sybil confounding Socrates (or rather Plato-Socrates) with leading questions, seeming to turn the tables of argument on him, and on occasion making open fun of him: "Don't you know that holding an opinion which is in fact correct, without being able to give a reason for it, is neither true knowledge . . . nor ignorance?" ("Yes," is the lame response of Plato-Socrates, "that's perfectly true.") And then this curious high priestess of Love seems to turn into Plato himself when she says, in a passage that marks the summit of the evening, "And now, Socrates, there bursts upon [man] that wondrous vision which is the very soul of the beauty he has toiled so long for. It is an everlasting loveliness which neither comes nor goes, which neither flowers nor fades, for such beauty is the same on every hand, the same then as now, here as there. . . . Nor will his vision of the beautiful take the form of a face, or of hands, or of anything that is of the flesh. It will be neither words, nor knowledge, nor a something that exists in something else, such as a living creature, or the earth, or the heavens, or anything that is—but subsisting by itself in an eternal oneness. . . . And so, when his prescribed devotion to boyish beauties has carried our candidate so far that the universal beauty dawns upon his inward sight, he is almost within reach of the final revelation. And this is the way, the only way, he must approach, or be led toward the sanctuary of Love."

STAATLICHE MUSEEN, BERLIN

Plato's Diotima, however, hung somewhat in the rarified air

Paintings around the outer surface of a cup show a school in session. At top, youths are being instructed in the playing of the aulos, or double flute, and in writing on a wax surface with a stylus. On the other side of the cup, above, the students are shown learning to perform on the lyre and to recite poetry by reading from a scroll that is being held by one of the masters.

above and beyond the sights of the everyday intelligent Greek, whatever his aspirations. The Athenian himself was largely taken up with the everyday pursuit of what we would call the ideal of the all-round man. The ascetic or the specialist or the man of intellect who was exclusively an intellectual was generally not to his liking. Just as in the polis there was no priestly caste and no civil service, there were few other specialized professions either. There were schoolmasters, there were professional reciters of poetry to music, and, most prominently, there were physicians. Late in the fifth century these men began to emerge from their role as quasi-priestly healers working in the name of Asclepius (considered by some to be Apollo's son), with a secret lore of herbs, potions, and ointments; now they became scientific practitioners, followers of Hippocrates, the first Greek man of medicine who was not at the same time a medicine man. Many doctors, in addition to learning from Hippocrates' careful study of bodily symptoms, appear also to have abided by the famous oath of ethical conduct ascribed to the physician of Cos, which marks what could be called the beginning of the professional outlook.

But meanwhile a building engineer was likely to be his own architect, civic organizer, arranger of sculpture and decoration as well. The playwright or historian might find himself commanding troops: Sophocles led Athenian infantry during the Samian revolt, as Thucydides did in the Peloponnesian War. Toward the end of the century, a group of full-time specialist instructors in higher education emerged, coaching aspiring young men for a fee in the arts of rhetoric and oratory—skills most valuable in the highly vocal society of the agora. Yet these teachers, though they let themselves be called *sophistai*, meaning "men of wisdom," and though they included such brilliant masters of persuasion as Protagoras, Gorgias, and Isocrates, were far removed from Socrates, who was never a professional man of wisdom himself, never accepted so much as an obol for his teaching, and rather despised these Sophists for making a business of showing how to influence people. His own area was simply talk—good talk—and he once remarked that his possessions did not exceed five drachmas in value (say ten dollars in today's equivalent).

Unlike the professionals, this robust and earthy individual—in his day a soldier, a president of the Athenian Assembly, and at all times the irreverent gadfly about all that was going on in the polis—was not interested in smoothing anyone's way to fortune but rather in sharpening wits by inquiry. You joined Socrates at the colonnade or under some friend's roof, not to hear a magisterial brain hold forth ex cathedra, but because, in either a

SOCRATES AND THE SOPHISTS

Usually genial in his talk, Socrates enjoyed letting fly at his chief foes, the Sophists, with barbs of wit. Looking upon them as sheer manipulators of argument, skilled in making bad reasons seem good ones, he accused them of being men of little wisdom out to mislead those who had less. Thus he pursues his point with his young follower Phaedrus:

SOCRATES: *Suppose I tried to persuade you to acquire a horse to use in battle against the enemy, and suppose that neither of us knew what a horse was, but I knew this much about you, that Phaedrus believes a horse to be that tame animal which possesses the largest ears.*

PHAEDRUS: *A ridiculous thing to suppose, Socrates.*

SOCRATES: *Wait a moment. Suppose I continued to urge upon you in all seriousness, with a studied encomium of a donkey, that it was what I called it, a horse, that it was highly important for you to possess the creature, both at home and in the field, that it was just the animal to ride on into battle, and that it was handy, into the bargain, for carrying your equipment and so forth.*

PHAEDRUS: *To go to that length would be utterly ridiculous.*

SOCRATES: *Well, isn't it better to be a ridiculous friend than a clever enemy?*

PHAEDRUS: *I suppose it is.*

SOCRATES: *Then when a master of oratory, who is ignorant of good and evil, employs his power of persuasion on a community as ignorant as himself, not by extolling a miserable donkey as being really a horse, but by extolling evil as being really good, and when by studying the beliefs of the masses he persuades them to do evil instead of good, what kind of crop do you think his oratory is likely to reap from the seed thus sown?*

PHAEDRUS: *A pretty poor one.*

serious or a lighthearted mood, he had invited you as one whom he liked. There might be flute girls and wine, or there might not; the old fellow might be slightly awash and full of jokes, or quite sober; but in either state he was likely to be bent on drawing you out, on hearing every argument, and then on bringing you to discover their difficulties or contradictions and to attain the truth yourself. He would start a conversation that was far less a debate or a dispute from prepared positions than it was a joint probing among friends, testing ideas by questioning them—one could say, a dialogue of the mind with itself. What was the nature of virtue? friendship? beauty? Socrates was ready to listen to any line of thought almost endlessly, coaching it along by a searching question here and there, until the persons about him sometimes found themselves still talking at the approach of dawn. If the outcome of so many hours' exchange was not agreement, it was at least illumination. Even the hours of Socrates' last day and evening— spent with friends while in prison awaiting the fatal potion of hemlock that was to be administered to him for his offenses against the state—are full of good-humored discourse, Socrates weighing with Phaedo and other young men devoted to him the subject of the soul and immortality. The soul is immortal, he gets his followers to agree, because it can perceive and partake of a truth, a goodness, and a beauty that are eternal. Man knows God to the extent that he has in himself some inkling of these eternals. Then Plato's curtain descends upon this marvelous dialogue and life with Socrates saying in high irony to Crito, another pupil, as he takes the poison, "Crito, we ought to offer a cock to Asclepius"—that is, a thank-offering to the god of healing.

The kind of young man able to converse with Socrates had to be educated and ready of wit. Yet the formal schooling of an Athenian was, at least by modern lights, quite limited. Indeed, outside Sparta, where all teaching was a state prerogative, there appears to have existed nowhere in Greece what we would call an educational system. There were no public schools or colleges. While Greek states other than Sparta prided themselves on being the patrons of their people's arts, they felt that schooling itself should be left almost entirely in private hands. A girl in any case, as we have seen, received household training and the rudiments of reading and writing at home. A boy citizen, once he had been "accepted" by his family in a religious rite ten days after his birth (in Athens no less than in Sparta, a parent had the right to expose a faulty infant upon a hillside to slow death or a speedy one by wild animals), might have an attendant slave or *paedagogus* to oversee him during his school days. At the age of six he was likely to be placed in a private school where a *grammatistes* drilled him in elementary language and arithmetic, while a *kitharistes*, or harpist, taught music and recitation of poetry.

At about the age of fourteen this basic fifth-century schooling ceased, save for the fortunate few whose parents could afford to pay a *sophistes* to carry them on or to find some other advanced school or tutor able to inculcate geometry and philosophy. The curriculum seems brief and sparse when compared with today's—there was no teaching of Civics, Social Studies, or General Science, any more than of Home Economics, or Mass Communications Techniques. Vocational training of any sort was avoided: the Greek evidently felt that just as manners should be taught at home by parental precept, trades should be taught under a tradesman's roof by apprenticeship. Limited as his schools were, they were there to inculcate the fundamental disciplines of word and number. If you mastered these, you could probably move ahead on your own to mastering others. In short, the school was thought of as an early preparation for life, not for a livelihood.

Yet while his schoolrooms remained under private auspices, the Greek delighted in spending large sums of public money on the building of stadiums, gymnasiums, and theatres—the games, festivals, and performances that took place in them being thought of not as recreation but as exercises deeply tied to ethical precept and religion. So, in the broadest sense, in Greece education was public after all; one might even say that it has never been more public. The nude wrestler in palaestra, the chanter on the hillside stage reciting from Homer, the thousand or so men and boys who sometimes took part in a single Athenian festival or drama, the girls who led the solemn Panathenaic procession—all were figures in a scheme of communal participation in cultural experience. And throughout this, from the bout in the local palaestra to the exalted contests at Olympia and the rivalry of playwrights for the prize in the Theatre of Dionysus, runs the strong Greek sense of peaceable competition as a way of proving one's excellence, or *arete*.

The very concept of athletics—from *athlos*, meaning "contest" and signifying the idea of training, testing, and perfecting the body as a unity with the mind—is a Greek one. Organized contests, as distinguished from death-dealing duels, go far back in Greek consciousness—to Heracles, regarded as the first athlete and the founder of sports; to Homer, who in the *Iliad* describes the ceremonial contests that were held following the funeral of Patroclus before Troy, and which included boxing and chariot and foot races. (In the *Odyssey*, in a lighter mood he has the princess Nausicaa and her maidens play a game of ball and subsequently

MUSEO NAZIONALE,
ROME; ANDERSON

This portrait of Socrates is a Roman copy of a famous work by Lysippus, who was the court sculptor of Alexander the Great. The original statue was made of bronze and showed the great philosopher seated, instructing his followers.

277

Two men are shown sacrificing a pig on an altar in a detail from a sixth-century Athenian cup. It was customary for every athlete to offer a sacrifice to the gods before competing in any of Greece's great periodic athletic festivals.

LOUVRE; ARCHIVES PHOTOGRAPHIQUES

the hospitable Phaeacians regale their visitor with a feast and a meet that includes wrestling, dancing, and heaving a great stone—precursor of the discus.) Martial Sparta overdid the cult of the body—or rather distorted it by giving little heed to the mind—but Athens and other Greek cities regarded physical training as a vital branch of education.

It was one that could best be served by erecting public facilities open to all, comprising athletic grounds, baths, and possibly a lecture hall or colonnade for relaxation and talk as well—something beyond the means of a private school. Thus there were three large gymnasiums in fifth-century Athens alone, and their layout provided pleasant centers for philosophers too. Plato frequented one of them in the grove of Academus before he withdrew to his own garden nearby. His pupil Aristotle was to meet his students, often fresh from workout and rubdown, in another called the Lyceum.

Such public establishments, to be sure, were not on the scale of those at Olympia and Delphi, the chief shrines of what were in effect sports-pilgrimages. Every few years visitors from all over Greece arrived to perform in or attend championship matches, to worship particular gods, to witness spectacles and parades, and to enjoy something of the excitement of a fairground as well, with local and foreign products and souvenirs being hawked along the approaches to the precinct. Boisterous Corinth biennially celebrated its Isthmian games in honor of Poseidon, and mountainous Delphi staged its quadrennial Pythian games in honor of Apollo in a rock-strewn enclave almost in the clouds above its temples.

But the greatest of these assemblies was the quadrennial one at Olympia—so meaningful a meet that heralds went forth to every town and to the countryside to announce it, proclaiming a general truce among all Greek states so that their young men could join to compete in the pentathlon of jumping, discus throwing, javelin hurling, wrestling, and running; in boxing, chariot racing, and other events. The scene at Olympia—in its prime a vast religious-athletic camp crowded with temples, memorial steles, columns, fountains, statues, dormitories, hostels, individual city treasuries, practice grounds, and shaded paths leading to the grass-banked arena—seized the general Greek imagination. Processions, public prayers, sacrifices, orations, receptions of dignitaries opened the festival, along with the swearing-in of contestants, each youth emerging from his training tent to attest to the judges that he was of proper Greek birth, properly trained, and as such would not cheat in the contests. The award of a crown of olive leaves to the victor culminated it, followed by more religious observances and a banquet to Greece's new heroes in the

Prytaneum, the sanctuary in which the sacred fire was kept.

Not everyone in Greece was wholly in accord with the immense adulation bestowed upon the winners of the Panhellenic games, many of whom, after receiving their wreaths, became the subjects of hymns and public statuary and recipients of large donations besides. Euripides, for instance, in deploring what he feared to be a trend toward cult and professionalism, remarked that athletic prowess alone does not fit a man for leadership in war any more than in peace, and that "It is the wise and good man who should be crowned with leaves, the temperate and just ruler of the city who frees it from evils." In Athens itself, that most festive of cities, the basis of competition—and adulation—was broader. Observing some sixty holidays a year in honor of this god or that victory, the Athenians took many days and evenings off to celebrate every form of contest. No less than four major annual festivals were staged honoring Dionysus, and these were exceeded in splendor only by the great quadrennial feasts. One honored Demeter; the other, honoring the patron goddess Athena, was marked by musical competitions, torchlit ceremonies, and boat races.

Yet of all these, the most unique were the spring Dionysian contests or "games" at which the competitors were not athletes, but dramatists, each one chosen by the city's archon to enter the rivalry with a new script, and among whom the chief heroes were Aeschylus (with thirteen annual prizes), Sophocles (with twenty), and Euripides (with four). Fifteen thousand or more persons sat on the slope of the Acropolis to look down at the bare circular platform, or *orchestra*, on which choruses in robes and players in masks moved to the long lines of strophe and antistrophe, interrupted by quick, hard exchanges in everyday speech. The plays they saw, in broad daylight, with a minimum of scenery, were ancestral and religious (in the case of Aeschylus), polished and formal (Sophocles), or highly emotional and critical (Euripides); but in any case, whether invoking old memory and morality or exploring the new, the plays were smashing good theatre—as the people of the polis showed by flocking to them. The squire, the ordinary citizen, the educated slave of Athens, all attended them as the highest voice of competition and imagination as well. Here were stories of dark destinies overtaking the all-too-proud or the unfortunate; yet here also, amid the mirror of fate and adversity, was the recognition of man's strength, his passing joy, his urge to fulfillment, his delight at having friends, and his sorrows at having lost them. "If a man is good, he is happy; if he is happy, he is good," so runs an old Greek saying. This was not necessarily true; but at least it was said and believed.

A fifth-century vase painting represents a victorious athlete being crowned with a fillet by a winged figure who symbolizes victory. Athletic prowess also brought civic honors and, on some occasions, great financial rewards as well.
METROPOLITAN MUSEUM OF ART, FLETCHER FUND

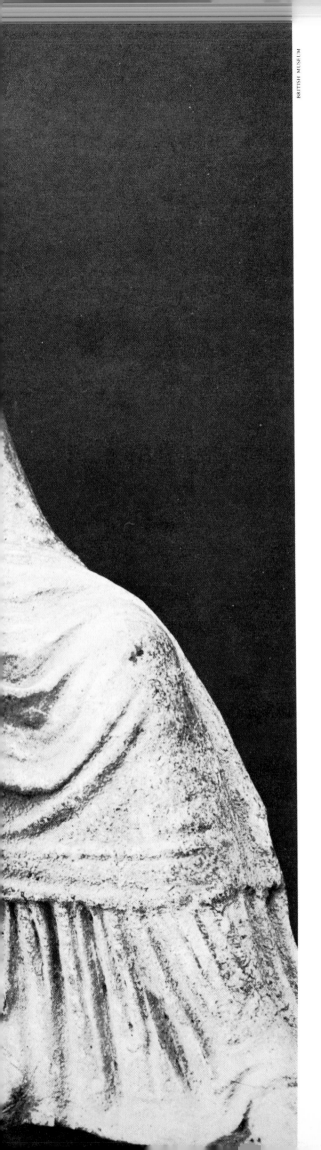

THE GREEKS
AT HOME

When walls were built around Athens in the year 479, the entire population was conscripted for the task; women, even those as elegant as those shown gossiping at left, old men and children, the rich and the poor, labored side by side on its construction. The city was a unit. Within it there were divisions, of course, but they were far less strong than in later, more complex societies. During the classical period, in Athens at least, snobbery was not exaggerated. Traders were looked down upon, but artisans were not, and in the artisans' workshops, master and slave worked side by side. The difference between town and countryside was not great; the Greek word for "farmer" had not yet evolved into a synonym for "boor," as it was later to do. Craftsmen and farmers dwelling near the city lived lives not dissimilar to those of townsmen. All were usually as interested in living pleasantly as in making money; all made sure they had time for the gymnasium and, in democracies, the assembly. Women's lives too did not vary much, for even the artisan owned a slave or two who did the marketing and most of the household work; and the wife of a rich man was expected to spin wool and weave. The manual worker—sculptor or stonemason—was paid the same as a doctor or teacher; the ideal society, the Greeks believed, was the communal one that Plato described, in which "friends have all things in common."

BOTH: ARCHAEOLOGICAL MUSEUM, HERAKLEION; HASSIA

BOTH: MUSEUM OF FINE ARTS, BOSTON

REWARDS OF TRADE

By the year 500 most of Greece had begun to use silver coinage; and certain cities—Corinth, Athens, and Aegina—maintained a currency reliable enough to serve as standard in international trade. Greek mariners sailed throughout the Mediterranean and Black Sea in search of markets and commodities. In the western reaches of the Mediterranean they were ousted by Carthaginian and Etruscan rivals, but elsewhere they maintained supremacy. Some Greek cities considered commerce unimportant, however. Sparta discouraged it by using unwieldy iron bars instead of coins. Other cities used coins as a form of internal taxation; they cut down their silver content and then called them in and paid for them, not at face value, but according to the actual weight of the silver they contained. Although the average Greek enjoyed the benefits of commerce, he still looked down on it. He preferred to bury his money for safekeeping rather than circulate it in trade.

Athena and her owl are shown at upper left on the obverse and reverse of an Athenian four-drachma coin; the Syracusan decadrachma below depicts the goddess Arethusa and a racing chariot. The classical drachma was equivalent to about two present-day American dollars. At right, the monarch of Cyrene, a Greek colony in Africa, watches men weighing and storing sacks of what may be wool.

ASHMOLEAN MUSEUM, OXFORD

MILAN, PRIVATE COLLECTION; FELBERMEYER, ROME

ARTISANS AT WORK

During the classical period there were a few factories in Athens, but most of the city's workshops were small, run by a master and a few relatives or employees, slave or free. The pottery industry, the most important in the city, was conducted along these simple lines, even though the export of vases, containing wine or olive oil, was carefully developed to bring in great wealth. Most craftsmen did not invest in raw materials, but worked on leather, metal, textiles, or wood that were provided by their customers. Workmen labored from dawn to dusk, taking time off at midday for a nap or a visit to the gymnasium, but about one day in every six was a holiday, marked by a religious celebration or a political assembly.

Details of vase paintings show artisans at work. At left, above, a shoemaker cuts a pattern to fit a boy's foot; below, potters are finishing bowls. Opposite, an artist paints a statue of Heracles while his assistant heats an iron that is used for smoothing paint.

METROPOLITAN MUSEUM OF ART, ROGERS FUND

METROPOLITAN MUSEUM
OF ART, ROGERS FUND

LOUVRE

TILLERS OF THE SOIL

It was only in Thessaly and Sparta that farmers were serfs;
elsewhere in Greece they were small freeholders, working their
own land. They were considered equals of the townsmen, politically and socially, and their economic independence was en-
sured by laws forbidding any one man to own too much land.
Farmers plowed the stony earth to raise grain and cultivated the
vine, olive, and fig—those staples of the Greek diet. Their
counterparts in the uplands herded sheep and goats, for milk,
meat, and wool. Only the most valuable crops were sent to
market in the towns, for, throughout Greece, the roads were so
poor that it was very expensive to transport goods upon them.

286

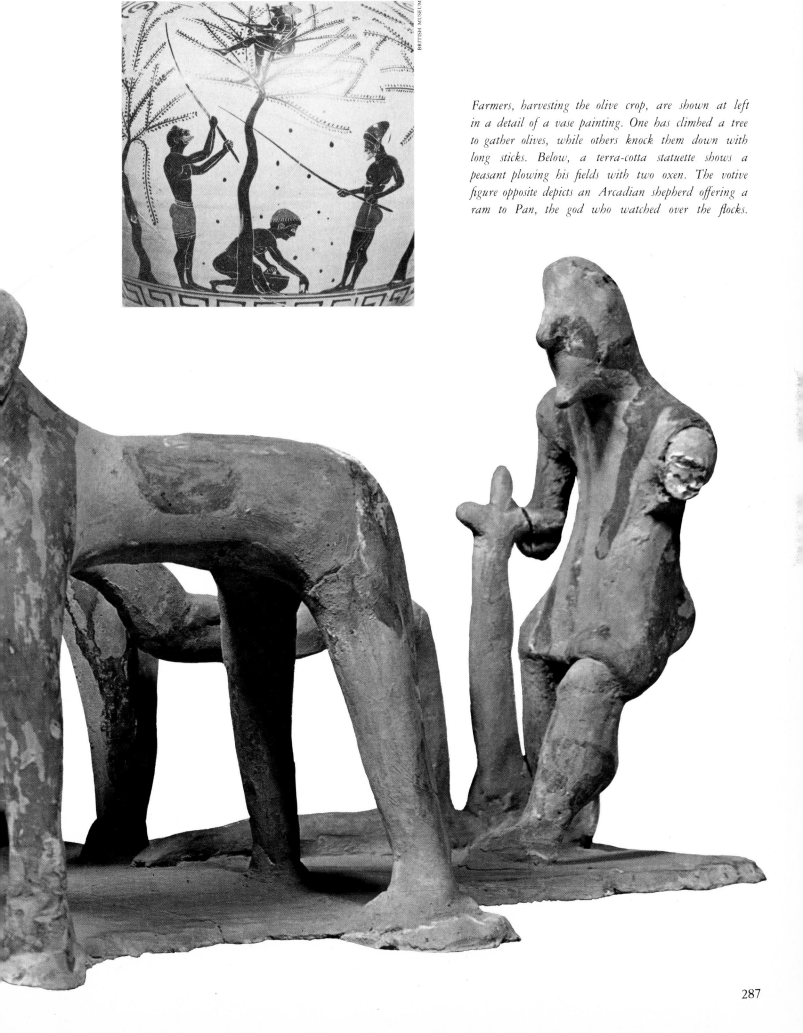

Farmers, harvesting the olive crop, are shown at left in a detail of a vase painting. One has climbed a tree to gather olives, while others knock them down with long sticks. Below, a terra-cotta statuette shows a peasant plowing his fields with two oxen. The votive figure opposite depicts an Arcadian shepherd offering a ram to Pan, the god who watched over the flocks.

BRITISH MUSEUM

THE GOOD WOMEN OF GREECE

Wedding attendants chanted aphrodisiac songs as the bride and bridegroom marched through the streets from her house to his. Outside the bridal chamber guests waited noisily until the marriage was consummated. After the wedding, however, the Greek woman received a good deal less attention, just as she had before it. She was never to look a strange man in the face nor speak before being spoken to. She was required only to run her household and provide the children her husband desired.

A circular vase painting from the fourth century shows a bride being adorned for her wedding. Above, a maiden places a wreath or diadem upon her long, curled hair. Opposite she is shown with another attendant who holds up a mirror in which she can inspect herself. The small winged figures are erotes, or cupids, representing love.

STATE HERMITAGE MUSEUM, LENINGRAD

OVERLEAF: *A detail from a fourth-century vase, made in one of the Greek settlements in Sicily, depicts a symposium, or drinking party. Revelers reclining on couches are attended by courtesans, who provide them with music as well as more intimate entertainment. On the floor is a large krater, a vessel used for mixing wine.*

MUSEO NAZIONALE, NAPLES

8

TRIUMPH AND TRAGEDY

Thucydides, an Athenian, wrote the history of the war between the Peloponnesians and the Athenians, beginning at the moment that it broke out, and believing that it would be a great war, and more worthy of relation than any that had preceded it.

—Thucydides, opening lines of his History

The year 431 found Athens at its zenith, though no Athenian would have recognized it as such, since a zenith implies a descent to follow. He was aware that year, as in years before, of brilliant advances in his arts, of mastery in his statecraft, and of a general sense of civic well-being around him. Why should all this not lead to even greater achievements and rewards?

In his physical setting he had much to look upon with pride. The shining new Parthenon, Pericles' magnificent memorial to his city's victory over the Persians, had just been completed even to its last pediment sculptures, after barely fifteen years of intensive effort. Phidias' great gold and ivory statue of Athena had been dedicated several years earlier. The Propylaea, that awesome new gateway raised on the Acropolis from the rubble of past assault, had also been constructed to serve as the ceremonial entrance for long processions winding up the Sacred Way. Pericles' building program was so rousing that centuries later Plutarch was to recall it in these words: "As the buildings rose stately in size and unsurpassed in form and grace, the workmen vied with each other that the quality of their work might be enhanced by its artistic beauty. Most wonderful of all was the rapidity of construction. Each one of them, men thought, would require many successive generations to complete it, but all of them were fully completed in the heyday of a single administration."

The Long Walls, built to replace those razed by the Persians, stood secure against any new threat of siege. Such neighboring maritime rivals as Megara and Aegina had been brought under Athenian sway; the Delian League had been converted into what was in effect an organization of tributary states. All this, coupled with the making of a final peace with a frustrated Persia in 448, left Athens the undisputed mistress of the Aegean. By the year 431 no ship of whatever homeland could safely traverse the waters from Egypt to Thrace, from Crete to the Crimea, without the benevolence of the lords of trade and admiralty ensconced at Athens, and few captains were of a mind to challenge them.

Pericles had also been striving to surmount another obstacle to the growth and mastery of Athens. The most dubious gift of the gods and nature to the men of Attica was the narrow isthmus, controlled by Corinth, that connected them with the Peloponnesus— a fine overland communications route, to be sure, but also a causeway for any land army from the peninsula bent on taking maritime Athens from the side or rear, as well as a barrier to the entry of Athens' ships into the westward-facing Gulf of Corinth, unless the land approaches to it could be secured. To win command not only of these approaches but of the whole gulf had become Pericles' master plan. In this he had almost—but not quite—prevailed.

The extraordinary Corinthian sea corridor, which runs westward for about eighty miles between the mainland and the peninsula before it opens onto the Ionian Sea under the lee of offshore islands, had long tantalized Athenian sailors. It was the natural, direct avenue for traffic to Greek settlements on the Adriatic and in Italy, Sicily, and beyond. Yet the Athenians, being harbored northeast of the forbidding isthmus, had had no recourse when setting sail for, say, Acragas or Syracuse, other than to strike far south and double around the capes of the Peloponnesus, as Odysseus' men had done, before making their westing. (Light coastal vessels, it is true, were portaged across the isthmus, at its narrowest point, Corinth permitting; but what was needed was a safe landing area at the head of the gulf so that Athenian ships could take on cargo that had been hauled across the isthmus and thus avoid returning home for it.) The gulf was also strategic internally: whoever controlled it could control much of the traffic between states of the mainland and those of the Peloponnesus. Since rich Corinth, sitting comfortably at its apex, was of no mind to share control of it with anyone, Pericles felt he must flank and isolate the troublesome city. In a series of brilliant strokes in the early 450's he had brought the entire northern coast of the gulf under Athenian dominion, including the outpost of Naupactus, which guarded the gulf's narrow western entrance—a Gibraltar if held by a strong power. Moreover, Pericles had built ties of friendship with provincial Achaea, far out along the gulf's southern shore, with its port of Patrae just across the strait from Naupactus. Now Corinthian craft could pass the strait only upon the say-so of Athens and its friends. On the other hand, Athenian or allied vessels could fairly safely traverse the length of the gulf, which seemed to be on its way to becoming another Athenian lake, like the Aegean to the east.

It was never fully to become that—or if indeed it was that for a few years, the condition was not to remain. Athens' extension, and the vigor and imagination that went into it, had stirred men of nearly every Greek state and tribe, some to throw themselves under its protection, others to gather around its foes. An uneasy balance of power prevailed while the rival leagues—the Delian of Athens and the Peloponnesian headed by Sparta—jockeyed and maneuvered to win a new confederate here or gain a further foothold there. Corinth, humiliated and embittered by Athenian encirclement, drew close to its ally Sparta with thoughts of a war of revenge against Pericles' empire—for that was what his demesne now was. Although during the decades following the Persian wars

BIBLIOTHEQUE NATIONALE, PARIS; GIRAUDON

Among the philosophers and dramatists who crowded Athens at the peak of its brilliance, none voiced Greek concepts of man and his fate with more depth and poignance than Pericles' friend Sophocles, here shown reading from one of his tragic plays.

DESCHARNES

The fertile, wooded island colony of Corcyra (Corfu), shown above, became strong enough to challenge its mother city Corinth. Their rivalry inaugurated a chain of events that embroiled the entire Greek world in the Peloponnesian War.

an uneasy balance had existed between the leagues, averting major collision, the 450's saw an increasing number of border clashes, struggles at the periphery, and defections of subject states from one camp to the other. Local revolts among Athens' new-found subjects in particular showed that Pericles had spread himself too far too fast to be able to consolidate his gains; finally the door which he thought he had slammed shut on the Corinthian corridor swung ajar, and out streamed the Corinthian fleet.

The occasion that took these galleys out into the Adriatic in 435 was a colonial conflict that soon threatened to become a general one. The actual quarrel was between Corinth and its own daughter city of Corcyra on what today is known in the West as the island of Corfu. The settlers of Corcyra, arriving from Corinth in the eighth century, had built themselves a hardy island stronghold and then decided to sunder ties with the mother city and preserve "complete political isolation" (so Thucydides describes it, citing their spokesmen) while girding themselves with a fleet second only to that of Athens (Thucydides credits them with 120 galleys in the year 435). About the year 625—such was the complexity of the Greek colonial system—the cities of Corinth and Corcyra jointly had spun off a settlement farther up the Adriatic at a place called Epidamnus, the present-day Durazzo on the Albanian coast; and it was over this remote spot that "mother" and "daughter" now went to war. The Corcyraeans beat off the Corinthians in a first round of battle, but wondered if they could do so if the men of Corinth were to return in greater force, with allies. So they abandoned their proud isolation and sought an ally—Athens.

The reporter-historian Thucydides, fated to be not only a witness of the vast struggle but also a participant in it, records the succinct arguments made by Corcyraean envoys when they arrived before Pericles and the Assembly asking for support. They apologized, in effect, for their past policy of isolation. They warned of the warlike designs of Sparta and Corinth upon Athens. They described their own naval strength and emphasized how great a help this would be to Athens in the event of a general conflagration. Finally they warned that if it should unfortunately happen that Corcyra were overrun in a second attack from Corinth, its fleet and bases would, of course, become part of the Peloponnesian power, which would then far outweigh that of Athens.

The envoys from opposing Corinth, also present in Athens, appeared before the Assembly with a warning against heeding the Corcyraean appeal. To enter into an alliance with the ungrateful Corcyraeans, they declared, would violate the treaty guaranteeing peace that had been signed by the two leagues in 445 and threaten the balance of power. Pericles was more impressed by Corcyraean naval power than by the Corinthian threat, and persuaded the Assembly to make a pact with the island state. The agreement was to be one for mutual defense only, against the attack of a third power, but its meaning was to tie Greece's two strongest fleets together, which unquestionably did shake the balance.

This was an ominous moment for all of Greece. One thinks by distant analogy of the world of Europe in the years just before 1914: the rival Great Power camps hardening, outlying "incidents" occurring with increasing frequency from Morocco to the Balkans, ministers initialing secret treaties (for "mutual defense" only), recurrent crises causing the lights of Downing Street, Quai d'Orsay, Wilhelmstrasse, and Ballhausplatz to burn late at night, armies growing and dreadnoughts deploying while daily life went on in a summer of security and contentment.

The Athenian world, as the fateful year 431 neared, had no glitter comparable to that of Europe of 1914, yet it was astir with a sense of fulfillment and promise. Its diversity, like its luxury, was limited; yet its intellectual range and richness were unprecedented. A spirit of originality, of readiness to re-examine all things past— myth, custom, ancestral order and belief—and to arrive at new values and insights, coursed not only through its artists and its scientists but through its public spokesmen as well. And in a real sense the dramatists and scientists of these years were themselves also public spokesmen, or at least public critics, voicing new views about society and taking issue with past ones in the theatre or agora. Pericles, significantly, was a particular friend of Sophocles, the great humanizer of Greek drama, of whom it was said that he "brought Tragedy down from the clouds." Pericles was also a patron and one-time pupil of Anaxagoras, a religious skeptic and an extraordinary prophet of new science.

Anaxagoras—born about the year 500 in Clazomenae, near present-day Izmir in Asia Minor—was only one of many of a school of thinkers bent on pursuing the quest begun back in the time of Thales of Miletus, to find rational principles or laws governing the physical world, thus pushing back superstition and ignorance. Empedocles of Acragas in Sicily, a combination poet, visionary, magician, and student of nature in the Pythagorean tradition, had come forth with hints of an evolutionary idea of growth and had also hit upon the thought that light requires a given time to travel from one point to another. Parmenides of Elea in southern Italy, who probably was an elderly man at mid-century when he visited Athens, had declared the earth to be round and observed that the moon always had its bright portion turned toward the sun. Leucip-

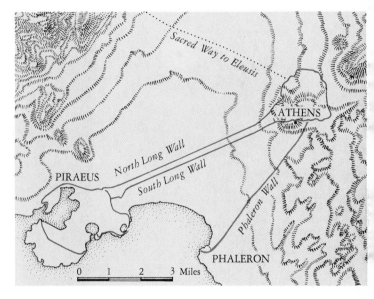

To connect Athens with the sea on which its life depended, the citizens, in the middle of the fifth century, constructed two walls—one to the Piraeus, the other to Phaleron, where the town's first harbor was situated. A few years later the Phaleron wall was abandoned, and the road to the Piraeus was made more secure by the addition of another wall parallel to the first.

The philosopher-scientist Anaxagoras, depicted on the coin above, was one of the great intellectuals who gathered in Periclean Athens. He taught that all things are made up of infinitesimal elements and were given their form by a supreme intelligence; and that man had evolved from the lower animals.
BRITISH MUSEUM

pus of Miletus, who flourished about 440, had speculated on the origin of stars and suggested that they had sprung from some central source or vortex. Democritus of Abdera in Thrace, who lived probably from about 460 to 370, set forth the theory that everything in the universe was made up of combinations of a basic physical unit that he called the atom. But of all these, Anaxagoras of Clazomenae was undoubtedly the most brilliant in his generation; at the age of twenty he came to Athens and began a splendid career. As many-sided as Pythagoras in the century preceding, he was astronomer, biologist, meteorologist, and philosophical pioneer alike. He correctly explained eclipses; he came forth with a rational hypothesis of planetary origin; he declared that the sun was an incandescent rock (somewhat larger than the Peloponnesus, he thought) from which the moon received its light. He studied tides and weather to the advantage of Greek mariners. He set up, to the distress of the materialists among Greek thinkers, the idea that Mind (*nous*) was the primal cause of all being and held power "over all things that have life." Turning to the study of man, he produced an astonishing evolutionary insight when he argued that the reason man had advanced beyond animals was that his erect posture had freed his hands for grasping and manipulating objects.

This was an amazing and precocious notion. Suggestions had long come from Ionian philosophers that all life—human and animal—could be traced back to a common origin, and that the Olympian stories of creation were just fables. But here a speculative thinker (not wholly speculative, though; he appears to have made some anatomical studies of animal brains) was hitting upon a very specific anthropological truth. It was not the whole truth, to be sure. He had probably never seen or even heard of the apes, and so was unaware of all that anthropology was to learn about human development from studying them. But the fact that Anaxagoras, in a time when propitiatory magic was still generally practiced, sensed a line of man's ascent or, if you will, of descent, makes him a startling Greek precursor of Darwin—just as in astronomy he was a precursor of Copernicus. He was accused of atheism for saying that the sun was not a god, but just a white, hot rock. One thinks of Galileo.

While Greek science forged ahead so daringly, Greek drama was not to be left behind. Nearly sixteen years lay between the triumph in the Athenian theatre of Aeschylus' sombre trilogy, the *Oresteia*, on the theme of the family of the god-cursed Orestes, and the flowering of a different sort of playwright, the polished Sophocles of the *Antigone* of about 441, forerunner of a long line of increasingly humane and poignant dramatizations that were to culminate in his masterly *Electra* and *Oedipus the King*. Euripides —younger than Aeschylus and Sophocles, a critic of Olympian religion and a brooding romantic to boot—entered the lists in 438 with his *Alcestis*, a haunting drama based on an old tale in which Apollo, having brought down upon himself the wrath of his father, Zeus, is condemned to serve for a while under a mortal master, King Admetus of Thessaly. He finds the king to be a model of human decency—only to learn that Admetus is doomed to an early death. Apollo prevails upon the Fates to spare the king. They agree, but only on condition that someone else die in Admetus' place. This his noble wife Alcestis agrees to do—she is both the heroine of the play and an exemplar of human character superior to that of the unconscionable deities.

In 431 Euripides, always critical, always turbulent, presented the *Medea*—his stormy adaptation of the story of the wife betrayed for another woman by the Argonaut Jason. Her vengeance upon this god-favored hero was to culminate in the murder of the children she had borne him. Yet, in this relentless drama of a human alone, bereft of protection, and without prospect of godly justice in sight, there appears an extraordinary interlude which is no less than a paean of the chorus to the high dignity of man— and to the proud and confident city of Athens:

Euripides, the last of Attica's great tragedians, is portrayed above in a Hellenistic sculpture. He was closely connected with Anaxagoras and Socrates, but unlike his friends he avoided public life. Both plot and character in many of his plays, however, show that he was influenced by the day's politics.
NY CARLSBERG GLYPTOTHEK

> *From of old the children of Erechtheus are*
> *Splendid, the sons of blessed gods. They dwell*
> *In Athens' holy and unconquered land,*
> *Where famous Wisdom feeds them and they pass gaily*
> *Always through that most brilliant air where once, they say,*
> *That golden Harmony gave birth to the nine*
> *Pure Muses of Pieria.*

This was spoken, or rather chanted, in 431 to admiring listeners in a city on the verge of disaster. For in that same year commenced the suicidal struggle between Athens and Sparta that was to leave Attica a shambles and all Greece in disarray. The handsome speech of Euripides in his *Medea* was to be almost the last in this vein. What came next, whether in Greek drama, Greek art, Greek politics or thought, though it still spoke with greatness, was to display the anguish of something lost. Less than thirty years divide Anaxagoras or the playwrights at their proudest from the reflections of the philosophers at their gloomiest and the behavior of politicians like Alcibiades at their shabbiest.

One great speech did still remain—that noble funeral oration in which Pericles mourns those fallen in the first winter of the war. In tones of exaltation he speaks of the unique gifts of the gods and of man's own intelligence to Athens; he praises the city's high civilizing mission, but he still recognizes its faults. While drawing no untoward comparisons, one is tempted to recall an utterance in a related vein two and a half millennia later; opening his memoirs, another chieftain of a proud and harried state, General Charles de Gaulle of France, speaks of his country as "dedicated to an exalted and exceptional destiny. Instinctively I have the feeling that Providence had created her either for complete successes or exemplary misfortunes." Complete successes and exemplary misfortunes: there could be no more perfect characterization of the triumph and tragedy of the Athenian state.

Historians, beginning with Thucydides himself, the eyewitness, have debated over the centuries the causes of the deadly collision. Had Pericles blindly overreached himself as the Athenian master builder, and so brought the whole structure toppling down? Many contemporary critics thought so, accusing him of waste, foolhardiness and worse—and indeed he was driven from office on a charge of embezzlement shortly after war's outbreak, to be reinstated for a brief period before his death. "Pericles made the war," Aristophanes was to say quite flatly, blaming him for having failed to rescind a harsh embargo against the people of Megara, an incident that had added flames to the crisis. Plutarch introduces a yarn that Pericles "kindled the war" with Sparta to distract the public from the accusation of embezzling public funds that had been made against him and his friend Phidias.

The slanders by Plutarch and by Pericles' contemporary enemies do not stand up under the general verdict of history, which finds no reason to doubt Pericles' probity, high dedication, and *arete*. Some doubts remain, though, as to his ultimate perspicacity. Was there in him a tragic flaw that led him from balanced judgment, or *sophrosyne*, in the direction of overweening pride, or *hubris*—that flaw which lies at the heart of so much Greek drama? Were there, more deeply, some flaws of character and behavior among the proud Athenians he led?

The Athenians on the eve of the war seemed to possess everything that mattered—political hegemony, adequate security, immense reputation, sovereign style, intellectual leadership, and a free and inquiring spirit. What went wrong? One primal danger lay in the jealousy aroused in other Greek states when they saw one of their number growing so great. Although the year 431 figures, so to speak, as the 1914 of the Hellenic world—the day the lights went out, not to be rekindled for a generation—a hardly less decisive date is that of 454. For that was the year in which Pericles and his party in power in Athens, hitherto the chief supporters and guarantors of the Delian League of defense against Persia, caused the

GLYPTOTHEK, MUNICH

The vase painting above represents a part of the action of Euripides' Medea. The enraged Medea, whose husband Jason had forsaken her to marry King Creon's daughter, impregnated a robe with poison and sent it to her rival; at top center Creon and his daughter are shown dying after having touched the robe; at lower center a chariot drawn by a serpent arrives to take Medea to Athens, where she has been promised asylum.

war chest or treasury that had been kept on the sacred mid-Aegean isle of Delos to be transferred to Athens itself, to be guarded solely by Athenian power. This bold action, taken on the ground that Delos was in an exposed position in the event of a renewed assault from the east, changed the shape of Aegean affairs entirely. What had been a confederation now became an Athenian empire. Allied states were no longer asked to contribute ships, they were asked to contribute money with which Athens itself would build and man and command the ships. Furthermore, island states within Athens' reach were not just invited to join and pay; they were compelled to do so. Many that formerly had been autonomous and regarded as friends were reduced to tributaries. Only Lesbos, Chios, and Samos retained their independence; Athenian garrisons moved in upon the others, while Athenian emissaries dictated their constitutions and laws of trade, to the point where Pericles enforced the use of Athenian coins, weights, and measures throughout many of them. It was imperial tribute money—there is no other word for it—that paid for the building of the Parthenon and many other noble Athenian monuments.

Did Pericles fail to perceive that his rising empire over the seas, coupled with his tenuous one on land, would draw Athens' enemies together for common resistance and counterstroke? Or, if he did perceive it, was he ready to risk a general encounter? As an empire-builder, he in some respects resembles Napoleon, who never did quite comprehend why so much growth and victory on his part could provoke such unquenchable antagonism in others. Yet with this, much of the analogy ends: Napoleon was strong on land, uncertain at sea; Pericles commanded a sea empire. As to character, Pericles, the statesman-philosopher, is hardly to be equated with the Corsican *condottiere* with a genius for browbeating men and an *arriviste*'s lust for the pompous and grandiose. Pericles was the scion of a cultivated family long devoted to the arts and civic responsibility, and most of his life was given to proposing and carrying through domestic reforms and improvements, promoting trade, or pursuing his beloved building program.

Over three decades, beginning in about 463, the Athenians had recognized the particular strength and quality of Pericles. After coming into prominence as one of the state prosecutors who succeeded in ostracizing Cimon, a brave Athenian leader who had strong pro-Spartan inclinations, Pericles rapidly became the recognized leader of the popular party, and from the year 443 on was annually re-elected one of the military commanders, or *strategoi*. His reforms and innovations brought down upon him the hatred of the party of landholding squires and other conservatives, very

On a tile discovered in Corinth, workmen are shown laboring in a clay pit. Corinth, grown prosperous from its pottery industry and its transit trade, attempted to maintain peace with both Athens and Sparta, but it finally went to war with Athens, alarmed by that city's growing power. Eventually Corinth fell under the domination of Sparta, at a time when most of the Greek cities, on both the mainland and the islands, had joined the rival leagues set up by the Athenians and the Spartans.

STAATLICHE MUSEEN, BERLIN

much as the reforms of one of his predecessors, Cleisthenes, half a century earlier, had also aroused the old guard. Many of these men identified Pericles' imperial moves with a dangerous scheme to extend and enforce democracy over all of Greece. Paradoxical as this may sound, in a sense this was what Pericles was out to do, hoping to set up popular governments on the Athenian model (under Athenian guidance, to be sure) as far as his fleets could reach. Many conservatives also thought he should not tangle with Sparta, whose oligarchic system they admired.

Others, living perhaps simply on their estates in Attica, and with mixed sensibilities, were antagonized by Pericles' costly visions of a beautified Athens. "Greece," one such voice said, "is surely suffering sore insult and manifest tyranny, when she sees that with the monies contributed perforce for the war we are gilding and adorning our city like a wanton woman, decking her with costly statues and offerings and thousand-talent temples." The more Pericles heard these objections, though, the more he seems to have been determined to push ahead and make of Athens, as he later declared, "the school of Hellas." The man who walked with Sophocles and Anaxagoras was no demagogue; yet he was a partisan, an expansionist, a believer in what we might call the Manifest Destiny of Athens—and this, while it inspired him and led to glory, invited catastrophe also.

To mention yet another paradox, perhaps this outward show of power would not have become so compulsive and great if Athens' own inner equilibrium had been greater. The glories of the Periclean age were mixed with uncertainties; perhaps there never was a supreme creative period so divided, often against itself. For all the posed perfection of a figure by Phidias, the Athenian mind of his generation seems to have been permeated by an increasing sense of flux. "*Panta rhei ouden menei*," ("All things flow, nothing remains the same"), the early philosopher Heraclitus of Ephesus is reported as saying, meaning that reality was something whose essence lay in "becoming," rather than in "being." This, again, was only a partial vision; all intelligent Greece had long been in search of lasting certainties, ideals, and laws amid the vagaries of change. But where to find them? By the latter half of the fifth century neither Olympian religion nor constituted moral codes seemed to provide them.

Religion? Attacks had been delivered not only upon the Olympian system but upon the very idea of gods in man's image, Xenophanes, a sixth-century Ionian philosopher, having remarked contemptuously that if donkeys had religion, they would no doubt imagine their gods in the shape of donkeys. Creation myths? To Anaxagoras, with his physics and metaphysics, they were a sheer laughingstock. Homeric legends and those of Hesiod and early bards came under sharp scrutiny also, and Euripides at one point was to go so far as to refer to myths and legends generally as "the wretched tales of poets"—as if he were not a poet too.

Ancient rules of tribal fealty and blood brotherhood of a rough chivalric sort had long persisted. Yet these, so often violated, were being brought into increasing question as well. Neighborliness, altruism, assistance to one's fellow man had never been among the particular Greek virtues; philanthropy, though the word is of Greek origin, was hardly practiced, beyond such customs as providing a free education to sons of soldiers killed in the wars. The good Greek was taught to love his friends and hate his enemies; to forgive an enemy was a sign of weakness. And now these old tribal loyalties were breaking down, too, amid the class and political conflicts of growing states. Was personal ambition or personal anger at a rebuff greater than devotion to the welfare of a polis? It often seemed so. Scheming for power, the Spartan chieftain Pausanias, victor at Plataea in 479, had entered into treasonable relations with the Persians. Themistocles of Athens, no lesser hero of the Persian wars than Pausanias, as well as the chief rebuilder of the city before Pericles, had fallen out with his people and deserted to the Persians, where he rounded out his life as a noble at the court of Artaxerxes. Whom could you trust? Pericles, it is known, had large sums at his disposal for secret uses, including bribery. "At no time," says the other Pausanias, the Greco-Roman historian, "was Greece wanting in people afflicted with this itch for treason."

So the years of Athens' highest fulfillment were lived under the sign of much uncertainty and an increasingly precarious balance. On one hand stood the man of oligarchic persuasion and guardian of traditional mores; on the other, the man of experiment and venture, exemplified at his best by Pericles and at his worst by Pericles' young friend and protégé, the demagogic and irresponsible Alcibiades (a mixture of genius and fraud, and one day—when he allegedly played a part in smashing the city's sacred Herms—to be quite literally the image breaker of Athens). On one hand Attica, like other areas of Greece, still saw the persistence of primitive cults with their magic rites; supposedly self-reliant leaders still hung upon the latest cryptic sign from Delphi. On the other hand, Athens was the center of the urban sophisticate, the skeptic, the searcher after new lights.

Yet Athens itself was not wholly committed to urbanity and new lights either. So bitter was the strife between religion and

PRIDE BEFORE THE FALL

In the celebrated oration which Pericles gave at the public funeral of the first Athenians to fall in the winter of 430 in the war against Sparta, he enumerated the strengths and virtues of his city, emphasizing the freedom and self-reliance of its citizens. He went on to declare:

"Nor are these the only points in which our city is worthy of admiration. We cultivate refinement without extravagance and knowledge without effeminacy; wealth we employ more for use than for show . . . in our enterprises we present the singular spectacle of daring and deliberation, each carried to its highest point, and both united in the same persons. . . . In generosity we are equally singular, acquiring our friends by conferring not by receiving favors. . . . And it is only the Athenians who, fearless of consequences, confer their benefits not from calculations of expediency, but in the confidence of liberality . . . Athens alone of her contemporaries is found when tested to be greater than her reputations, and alone gives no occasion to her assailants to blush at the antagonist by whom they have been worsted . . ."

science that at the height of the Periclean age, the study of astronomy was forbidden in Athens altogether, as threatening to lead to impiety—and this despite Pericles. Anaxagoras of Clazomenae was hailed before the Assembly on a charge of irreligion; and though Pericles saved his friend from what might well have been doom by arranging his escape, the leading scientific mind in fifth-century Greece had to set up school elsewhere.

Innovation in Athens had a way of leading to counterinnovation. Young Socrates, for instance, though a challenger of old dogmas, was inclined to dismiss science as an inferior concern; and, far from being an admirer of Periclean democracy, he was on his way to becoming one of the chief critics of it. The boisterous writer of comedy, Aristophanes, when setting out in his twenties to satirize all that he saw about him, did not pick tradition as the butt of one of his first important plays, *The Clouds*. Instead, he seized upon the new generation of fashionable doubters of religion, the followers of such men as Anaximander and Anaxagoras, whom he regarded as charlatans. In *The Clouds* he makes his assault all the funnier by presenting as chief charlatan and sophist an impersonation of Socrates, whose disdain of Sophists he blandly ignores. The character Socrates becomes increasingly pompous as he propounds his notions of an in inanimate, godless world. After a "Chorus of Clouds" has entered and the earthling Strepsiades cringes at a clap of thunder, we have this passage:

STREPSIADES
Name of Earth, what a voice! Solemn and holy and awful!

SOCRATES
These are the only gods there are. The rest are but figments.

STREPSIADES
Holy name of Earth! Olympian Zeus is a figment?

SOCRATES
Zeus? What Zeus? Nonsense. There is no Zeus.

STREPSIADES
*No Zeus?
Then who makes it rain? Answer me that.*

SOCRATES
*Why, the Clouds,
of course.
What's more, the proof is incontrovertible.
For instance,
have you ever yet seen rain when you didn't see a cloud?
But if your hypothesis were correct, Zeus could drizzle from an empty sky
while the clouds were on vacation.*

STREPSIADES
*By Apollo, you're right. A pretty
proof.
And to think I always used to believe the rain was just Zeus
pissing through a sieve.*

Greek comedy, emerging from primitive fertility rituals in honor of Dionysus, remained earthy and unconfined. The fourth-century terra-cotta figurine above depicts masked comic actors playing two drunken old cronies.
STAATLICHE MUSEEN, BERLIN

All right, who makes it thunder?
Brrr. I get goosebumps just saying it.
SOCRATES
                    The Clouds again,
of course. A simple process of Convection.
STREPSIADES
                         I admire you,
but I don't follow you.
SOCRATES
         Listen. The Clouds are a saturate water-solution.
Tumescence in motion, of necessity, produces precipitation.
When these distended masses collide—boom!
                    Fulmination.
STREPSIADES
But who makes them move before they collide? Isn't that Zeus?
SOCRATES
Not Zeus, idiot. The Convection-principle!

In his *Ecclesiazusae,* written several decades later, Aristophanes was to take on the radical democratic leaders, uplifters and utopians too, asking in effect the question, All right, who's going to do all the daily work?—and in his *Lysistrata* he was to make his unique sexual argument for achieving peace. All this was lively, bracing, and wonderfully diverting for a society so adult as to be openly self-critical—up to a point, that is. There was worry in Athens about so much criticism. Aristophanes was held in question no less than Socrates. The inquirer mixed with the scoffer, the idealist with the adventurer, the political scientist with the rabble-rouser, the poet with the propagandist: and the result, while phenomenal, was also parlous. Athens, although it had grown strong, was not so sure of its ways as to be totally secure, nor so rich as to become satisfied. Its very nature, on the contrary, had developed into a most volatile one. So abounding in diverse energies and drives, it had either to proceed or erupt.

If in all this turbulence there was anything around which Athenians could gather in common emotion, irrespective of party or faith, it was undoubtedly the world of the great living dramatists—that of the tragedians, not of the ribald and derisive Aristophanes. You did not have to believe, any more than Euripides himself did, in Olympian religion and all the ancient myths to share in what was said and chanted there under the hillside auspices of Dionysus. Most of the audience shared in drama as a public moral rite, as few playgoers since have done, except for the medieval townsmen attending so-called morality plays, performed before the doors of cathedrals or on platforms set up in the market square. The dramatists were increasingly concerned with human character and its attempts at grace under fateful pressure; but always they remained preoccupied with moral law. Punishment or

While comedies left little to the imagination, by the late fifth century, authors like Aristophanes were writing satires; biting, witty, they retained elements of ribaldry. Above, an actor wooing a maid almost falls off a ladder.

BRITISH MUSEUM; SKIRA

retribution follows flaw, or *hubris*, as the dark follows the day—except when skeptical Euripides helps resolve and relieve a dread situation with a *deux ex machina* (quite literally, a god who descends from above by means of a machine).

The lesson of pride and fate, as illustrated by stories ranging from Aeschylus' *Oresteia* to Sophocles' Oedipus plays, became more and more pertinent and urgent as Athens' own *hubris* grew, though perhaps few in the vast applauding audiences grasped an immediate application. The English philosopher Alfred North Whitehead was one day to remark that the Greek tragedians, because of their belief in immutable law, were themselves, more than the Greek philosophers, the founders of scientific thought. But their audiences, spellbound on seeing the self-blinded Oedipus or Medea splotched with the blood of her brood, were probably not thinking of scientific laws. They were experiencing the purge of "pity and fear"—the function, as Aristotle saw it, of tragedy. Presumably they were also being chastened by the thought of a will greater than their own, when for instance they heard the chorus in Sophocles' *Oedipus the King* intone:

> *May destiny ever find me*
> *Pious in word and deed*
> *Prescribed by the laws that live on high:*
> *Laws begotten in the clear air of heaven,*
> *Whose only father is Olympus . . .*
> *Insolence breeds the tyrant, insolence*
> *If it is glutted with a surfeit, unseasonable, unprofitable,*
> *Climbs to the roof-top and plunges*
> *Sheer down to the ruin that must be . . .*

Here, both in the lines and between them, could be heard the cautionary voice of a playwright who was also tutor and prophet, counseling restraint and the "holy fear" that runs through the Greek consciousness, though not calling for abject submission or passivity. For "I pray that the God may never abolish the eager ambition that profits the state," the chorus goes on to say; it is only that a man, like a state, should be prudent, recognizing limitations while exercising strengths:

> *If a man walks with haughtiness*
> *Of hand or word and gives no heed*
> *To Justice and the shrines of Gods*
> *Despises—may an evil doom*
> *Smite him for his ill-starred pride of heart!*

These lines of Sophocles, however, were probably first heard at the Great Dionysia in Athens, several years after the outbreak of the war with Sparta, when the holocaust of pride had already begun.

A vase painting above depicts Orestes (right) embracing the sacred omphalos at Delphi, hoping it will protect him from a Fury who pursues him because he killed his mother. Aeschylus, Sophocles, and Euripides all wrote about Orestes. Opposite, Oedipus, another tragic hero, ponders the riddle of the Sphinx: "What walks on four legs in the morning, two at noon, and three in the evening?" Oedipus' correct guess, that it referred to man in successive stages of life, saved Thebes from the scourge of the man-devouring Sphinx.

MUSEO NAZIONALE, NAPLES; HIRMER

VATICAN MUSEUM; ALINARI

It is difficult today, in a time when the theatre at its best is an adjunct to life rather than a monitor of it, to think of this most successful and admired of Greek dramatists in a quasi-priestly role. Handsome, dashing, an athlete in his youth, genial and witty in his middle years, a great befriender of young men, twice one of the *strategoi* under Pericles, and the holder of many other public posts as well, author of possibly more than 120 plays, and vigorous enough to console himself in his old age with a *hetaira* by whom he had children, Sophocles seems the model of the highly endowed Athenian in balance. For fully thirty years, between Aeschylus' death in 456 and the fulfillment of young Euripides' promise by the 420's, he ruled the Athenian stage as splendidly as Pericles ruled the state. Yet he was also the man who saw far ahead, alive with warning, and who lived on, as Pericles did not, to see the collapse of so much pride and hope. As the Peloponnesian War led Athens from defeat to defeat, he wrote his sorrowing sequel to *Oedipus the King*. In *Oedipus at Colonus* he narrates the end of a great man fallen, though ennobled by ordeal; and this play rings to some like a dirge to Athenian greatness. In it the chorus is moved to speak in astonishingly dark and personal tones:

> Though he has watched a decent age pass by,
> A man will sometimes still desire the world.
> I swear I see no wisdom in that man,
> The endless hours pile up a drift of pain
> More unrelieved each day; and as for pleasure,
> When he is sunken in excessive age,
> You will not see his pleasure anywhere.
> The last attendant is the same for all,
> Old men and young alike, as in its season
> Man's heritage of underworld appears:
> There being then no epithalamion,
> No music and no dance. Death is the finish.
> Not to be born surpasses thought and speech.
> The second best is to have seen the light
> And then to go back quickly whence we came.

This is a far cry indeed from the exuberant invocation to the promise of Athens that appears in the *Eumenides*, the culminating play of the Orestes trilogy. Aeschylus had written his paean to Athenian greatness and wisdom only fifty years earlier.

Equally dark is the tone of the aging Euripides, who in about 415 produced *The Trojan Women*, its legendary subject being the utter destruction of Troy and its more immediate theme the mindless ruination of war. He was writing at a parlous moment. Athens, already embroiled with Sparta, was about to send out a punitive expedition to Sicily that was to end ruinously. As if he sensed the

The inscribed fragment of stone above is a memorial to the Athenian soldiers who fell during the battle of Potidaea in 432. The revolt of this colony was one of the incidents leading to the Peloponnesian War.

BRITISH MUSEUM

The Roman bust, above, represents Alcibiades, the charming profligate of the Golden Age who convinced the Athenians to break a truce in the Peloponnesian War. Later he turned traitor and went over to the Spartan side.

VATICAN MUSEUM; ALINARI

outcome, he had Hecuba of Troy symbolically speak:

Ah, wretched me. So this is the unhappy end
And goal of all the sorrows I have lived. I go
Forth from my country and a city lit with flames.
Come, aged feet; make one last weary struggle, that I
May aid my city in its affliction. O Troy, once
So huge over all Asia in the dawn wind of pride,
Your very name of glory shall be stripped away.

For "Troy," read "Athens": the troubled and tormented mind of Euripides was putting out an impassioned plea for peace. He did not live long thereafter, but as a son of Greece's age of anxiety he lived long enough to see the worst of war. Upon his death in 406, the Athenians gave him a funerary ceremony in the Theatre of Dionysus, and the aged Sophocles was there to lead actors in a masque to mourn him. Aristophanes also paid handsome tribute to this man who had given so much to art and to the state.

Though there was no Sarajevo to set off the greatest conflict "yet known in history," as Thucydides called it, there had come in 432, just after the Corcyra crisis, a collision over an even more distant spot that led directly to the assize of arms. Potidaea was a remote outpost on the wild Macedonian coast of the Aegean. It had been settled by Corinthians and remained much under their influence, though it had also been made a tributary ally of Athens. Fearful that Corinth might try to extend its influence there, the Athenians ordered the Potidaeans to raze their city walls and dismiss their Corinthian magistrates. This the provoked men of Potidaea refused to do, and a general revolt against Athens broke out in the area, to which Athens responded by placing the city under siege (Socrates and young Alcibiades both taking part in the attack). Corinthian leaders in turn responded to this assault upon their colonists by trying to incite the whole Peloponnesus to war. With disorder fast spreading throughout the Greek world, Pericles took another aggressive step: he proclaimed harsh trade decrees against Corinth's ally Megara, on the nearby isthmus, excluding her from all the empire's markets. This only increased the tension. Parleys between Athens and the Peloponnesian League over the rescinding of those decrees led nowhere, with the result that the League presented an ultimatum requiring Athens to acknowledge the independence of all Greek cities—that is, dissolve her empire and thus humble herself.

The twenty-seven-year war that followed was actually a series of wars interrupted by truces that solved nothing, by treaties that were soon broken, by seasons of stand-off and peacemaking efforts that soon gave way to resumption of unbridled savagery. It was in part a tribal war, in the sense that the heirs of the age-old contenders for primacy in Greece, the Dorians and the Ionians, their ancient differences made more acute by big-state rivalries, now struck at each other with the ferocity of Teuton and Gaul in later ages. It was also a class war in the sense that fellow friends of oligarchy often crossed these tribal lines to help each other bring democracy down. It was in many of its stages as much a civil war inside Athens and its dominions as one among Greeks as a whole. It was a war for commerce and empire, fought with the usual military weapons of the time. Yet in its method it was also a distinctly psychological war, in which every device of emotional appeal, persuasion, prejudice, and threat was deployed to sustain morale on one side and undermine it on the other, and thus to augment iron blades with mental shafts to determine either side's staying power. It was the first modern war, and in some of its ramifications more akin to those of the twentieth century A.D. than those even, say, of the eighteenth.

It was a dirty war, as civil wars usually are: mass executions of prisoners, massacres of the disaffected, assassinations of public leaders who had taken the wrong course, were the order of the day. The Athenians slaughtered the adult citizens of Melos and sold their women and children into slavery; later, when the reviving oligarchic party of Athens routed the polis' democrats in the time of worst military defeat, perhaps fifteen hundred heads fell. For all the bravery of the hoplites and sailors on either side and the particular brilliance of the Spartan commander Lysander, much of the war's leadership was ignoble. Cleon of Athens, a rich and corrupt tanner's son who rose to power by his part in throwing out Pericles and who then turned demagogue, cynically warned his fellows against any softness toward wavering allies on the ground that "your empire is a despotism and your subjects disaffected conspirators, whose obedience is insured not by your suicidal concessions, but by the superiority given you by your own strength and not their loyalty." Indeed it had become a despotism, Cleon's faction having put over the outrageous notion that the war was not to be paid for by Athens itself, but by taxes imposed on its tributaries. Even more outrageous was the behavior of Cleon's rival, Alcibiades, the Periclean favorite—showman, adventurer, rabble-rouser, roisterer, lady-killer, good soldier, and traitor all in one—who became as much a menace to his own city as he ever was to Sparta, his unbridled ambition and personal instability ruining all of Pericles' designs.

Previous wars in historical times of Greek against Greek had generally been brief, local encounters—often just a single clash of

THE PLAYBOY OF ATHENS

Many stories are told of the pranks of Alcibiades, who became a ward of Pericles and a companion of Socrates. Both doted on him for his high spirits and seemed not to mind the fact that this outrageous fellow never quite grew up.

Xenophon recounts an evening when the ward engaged Pericles in a discussion of law. Pericles remarked, ending the talk: "At your age we used to be clever too in such questions. It was just such matters we used to practice our wits on, as you seem to be doing." Alcibiades retorted, "Too bad I couldn't have known you when your brain was at your best, Pericles!"

Plutarch tells of another kind of encounter: "He gave a box on the ear of Hipponicus, whose birth and wealth made him a person of great influence and repute. And this he did unprovoked by any passion or quarrel between them, but because, as a joke, he had agreed with his companions to do it. People were justly offended at this insolence . . . but early the next morning, Alcibiades went to his house, and knocked at the door . . . took off his outer garment, and . . . desired him to scourge and chastise him as he pleased." Hipponicus was so moved that he forgave the youth and offered him his daughter in marriage.

Extravagant and original in his tastes, he affected purple robes ("like a woman," says Plutarch); yet when addressing workers, he wore a laborer's sackcloth. He sent seven chariots to represent him at the Olympic games and cut off the tail of his costly dog to attract attention. His wildest extravagance yet was his participation, on the eve of the expedition to Sicily, in a drunken foray, smashing the sacred Herms posted in front of citizens' houses in Athens. "The matter was taken up the more seriously," says Thucydides, "as it was thought to be ominous for the expedition." Indeed it was. Though some mystery still surrounds Alcibiades' role in the desecration, enough anger was aroused to undermine his authority over the troops.

A statue of Victory by the sculptor Paionios was dedicated to Zeus at Olympia by the Messenian allies of Athens, probably to commemorate a battle against the Spartans. According to one tradition the Messenians, close neighbors of Sparta, refrained from placing an inscription naming their defeated enemies on the statue for fear it might inspire the Spartans to seek revenge.

MUSEUM, OLYMPIA; ALISON FRANTZ

arms between individual city-states, each mustering no more than a few thousand soldiers. The Persian wars of course had been of another character, with vast Asiatic hordes sent like dumb beasts against the superior skills of the Hellenes. Now these blooded Hellenes were out in full force against each other, league against league, tooth and claw, driven to furious commitment for almost a generation, their theatre of war eventually extending all the way from Sicily to the Bosporus.

The forces were formidable: Sparta, supported by almost its entire peninsula and by many states north of the Corinthian Gulf as well, could muster some 30,000 crack hoplites plus auxiliaries; Athens, on the other hand, had its strong fleet of possibly 300 triremes (with additional squadrons from the islands of Corcyra, Lesbos, Chios, in support) and a land force of some 13,000 first-line infantry, which were backed by a small cavalry and reserves of undetermined quality. The military problem was clear: a great congregation of land forces was confronting a sovereign sea power. (Among the Peloponnesian states, only Corinth could muster a fleet of strength, while not even the proudest Athenian could assume that his foot soldiers would be a match for Sparta's in a showdown.) Pericles, dictating strategy in the short time that remained to him before his death, saw the point entirely: let the Lacedaemónians attack us by land and wear themselves out by overrunning most of it, while we withdraw and stand securely behind our walls and bastions and at all costs preserve our command of the sea, its vital supply routes, its wealth, and in so doing, maintain the idea of an Athenian commonwealth. He had not forgotten Themistocles.

Pericles' strategy was wise, yet he did not live to execute it. In 430, just after the war's outbreak, an incalculable disaster struck Athens in the form of the plague, which decimated the masses of people drawn back behind the Athenian walls for safety and carried Pericles away too a year later. Athens did hold off Sparta to the point of a truce in the year 421, which even involved a fifty-year treaty of peace; but in 415, Alcibiades, taking advantage of this pause, promoted and made himself one of the leaders of a huge expedition to Sicily designed to subjugate strong, independent Syracuse and all the other Dorian settlements there as well. In this way the whole Peloponnesus would be outflanked and the Ionian Sea, between Greece and Sicily, converted into another Athenian lake. This was a complete reversal of Pericles, who had learned enough to know just how much Athens could safely attempt. Alcibiades' frivolous scheme involved, as Thucydides tells us, "by far the most costly and splendid Hellenic force that had ever been sent out by a single city up to that time" (4,000 Athenian heavy infantry, 300 horses, and 100 galleys, accompanied by 50 Lesbian and Chian vessels and many more besides). And it came to utter grief at Syracusan hands, its men—the elite of Athens' soldiery—all being either killed or enslaved. Meanwhile Alcibiades, who was recalled to account for his part in the affair of the smashed Herms, deserted to the Spartan side and made contact with the Persians as well, who stood waiting on the eastern sidelines with revenge in their minds.

This was the most bitter of hours yet for Athens, but worse was still to come. Sparta, seeing the empire of its enemy in such disarray, renewed the war. Syracuse joined in, and Persia lent a helping financial hand from afar. One by one the Athenian allies, like Alcibiades himself, deserted. The Athenian treasury, which only a decade before had been drawing close to 500 talents a year from its Delian tributaries, was all but bankrupt. Social revolts, both conservative and radical, swept the uncertain system which Pericles had sought to bring into some sort of equilibrium. Many of the slave workers of the Athenian mines of Laurium deserted, and the mines were closed. The reviving oligarchic party of Athens revolted also, abolishing the Assembly and setting up in 411 a Council of Four Hundred to liquidate the democrats and to make peace with Sparta on collaborationist terms. Soon thereafter a counterrevolution, led by surviving democrats in Athens, broke out. They in turn liquidated the Four Hundred, substituted a limited assembly of five thousand citizens—and called back Alcibiades with a promise of full amnesty!

Let Thucydides, who saw and endured all this, have the last word about its degradation: "Thus every form of iniquity took root in the Hellenic countries by reason of the troubles. The ancient simplicity into which honor so largely entered was laughed down and disappeared; and society became divided into camps in which no man trusted his fellow. To put an end to this, there was neither promise to be depended upon, nor oath that could command respect; but all parties dwelling rather in their calculation upon the hopelessness of a permanent state of things, were more intent upon self-defense than capable of confidence."

What was perhaps most surprising was that in these years of combined onslaught, division, and desertion, Athens held out as long as it did. Nearly ten more years were needed to break its power and spirit. In 407, after being pardoned, Alcibiades gained a round of victories in the eastern Aegean, but when a fleet under his command had been destroyed by the Peloponnesians, he went into exile. Now the last resources of Athens

BRITISH MUSEUM

A ten-drachma coin (above), which shows Victory crowning a charioteer, was struck by Syracuse in memory of the destruction of the Athenian army that came to attack the city during the Peloponnesian War. This costly and imprudent expedition, inspired by the young Alcibiades, did more than anything else to lose the war for Athens. Below, a detail from a memorial stele that was discovered in Attica depicts an Athenian warrior killing a Spartan.

METROPOLITAN MUSEUM OF ART, FLETCHER FUND

were mobilized to raise still another fleet to save the vital grain supply routes from the Bosporus. This armament of perhaps 180 vessels, incompetently led and indifferently manned, was caught off guard by Lysander's squadrons at Aegospotami on the Hellespont. Alcibiades, who in this disorder had tried once again to reinstate himself, soon after met a not undeserved death at the hands of the Phrygians.

This was the end. When news of the abject naval defeat reached Athens, Xenophon tells us, a sound of wailing rose along the Long Walls: "That night no one slept." Denuded of fleets, supplies, and allies, Athens behind its walls soon caved in under siege and signed a total surrender. The terms were that its empire be wholly dissolved, its Long Walls be razed, its remaining warhips be forfeited (although in the end Athens was permitted to retain twelve galleys), its numerous antidemocratic exiles be allowed to return (with the thought that they would assume power), and that the city become an ally (that is, a subordinate) of Sparta. Pro-Spartan turncoats, we are told, took joyfully to tearing down the walls hand in hand with their conquerors; and a new regime of oligarchs known as the Thirty Tyrants and led by the vindictive Critias declared a virtual holiday of judicial murder of many of the supporters of democracy.

In this turmoil of humiliation and betrayal, surviving Athenian patriots sought to strike back from exile. Led by Thrasybulus, they managed within a year to oust the Thirty (who had further dishonored themselves by calling in a Spartan garrison to man the Acropolis) and to restore the old constitution. Among the Athenians, filled with a sense of having been abandoned by their gods, there was also a hunt for scapegoats in the form of men who had failed them, or misled them.

Alcibiades was dead; cruel Critias had been killed in battle. The most vulnerable person remaining in the Athens of 400 B.C. was old Socrates, the perpetual critic and disrespecter of accepted beliefs—old-line ones on this hand and new democratic ones on the other. It was the returning democrats who hailed him into the dock on a charge of impiety and corruption of youth. The legend has long persisted, launched by Plato and Xenophon (both of them antidemocrats) that the old man was the victim of a political vendetta. This does not appear to be true. He was placed before a jury of 501 citizens chosen by lot from the annual roster of many thousands of talesmen representing the whole voting body politic, following the system developed by Pericles himself. What is true is that a majority of this vast people's jury found him guilty as charged, and so testified to their own fears and doubts and disarray.

The Hellenic world was at war throughout most of the fifth century. Above, a warrior, armed with a spear and protected by a helmet and greaves, is shown offering a sacrifice at an altar.

AMERICAN SCHOOL OF CLASSICAL STUDIES, ATHENS

So the wisest and shrewdest mind of Athens became the martyr for its failings, and in taking the hemlock ended its Golden Age. Still, by no means all was lost to the city. Vengeful Sparta, having won its victory under the slogans of liberation from Athenian oppression and self-determination of Greek states, proved a harder taskmaster than ever Athens was, posting garrisons as far as its arms could reach—and a far less capable one too, being ignorant of trade or of the management of any men other than soldiers. Athens had grown great partly through its leadership in the Persian wars and its championship of the Greeks of Asia Minor. Sparta, having accepted Persian gold to help vanquish Athens in the final stage, promptly abandoned the Ionian Greeks to the Persian realm. Soon Corinth and Thebes, its former allies, were to turn against it, as dubious of its hegemony as they had been fearful of Athens'. Athens, chastened in defeat and trying to revive itself, was to many Greeks a more attractive presence than semiliterate Sparta in triumph. The word must have traveled up and down the peninsula that, as Plato himself remarked in a letter, "In general, the restored democratic party of Athens behaved justly and equitably."

To be sure, shorn of empire, decimated, all but subjugated, Athens was never to be again what it had been. Thebes, Corinth, Sparta, Athens itself, were to contend along with lesser states in a kind of vacuum of which no one could be the master. If there were any victors of the Peloponnesian War, they were the Persians, who saw the Greeks in fratricidal chaos, and the rough Macedonians of the north, who were soon to be heard from in history. But Athens, though it had lost its glory and much of its spirit, still had its incomparable mind. It had Plato, only twenty-three when the war ended, who amid all his disillusionment gave forth over the next generation the most intricate and poetic body of high thought and reflection uttered in any autumnal age. It was next to have Aristotle, born twenty years after war's end, who trudged down from the northern hills to become at seventeen a disciple of Plato, then sixty-one, and who soon became Greece's precentor in logic, political science, general philosophy, biology, grammar, aesthetics, and morals: so versatile and lasting a precentor, in fact, that Dante, eighteen centuries later, spoke of him as "the Master of all we know." Yet Aristotle, born of Plato, who in turn was born of the light of Socrates, was also in his lifetime to become the personal teacher of young Alexander of the mountainous kingdom of Macedonia, who overran all the Greeks and most of the known world—though not according to Aristotelian principles. The Delphic oracle, devious and inscrutable, had foretold much. But it never foretold all that.

A vase, which probably commemorates the restoration of democracy in Athens after the oligarchy established by the Spartans had been overthrown, shows Athena carrying a shield adorned with a representation of the Athenian tyrannicides.
BRITISH MUSEUM; HIRMER

THE HIGH SHRINE AT DELPHI

Mount Parnassus towers in grandeur above Delphi; another cliff drops precipitously into dark green olive groves almost a thousand feet below the shrine, and winter snow crowns the rugged mountains that surround the vertiginous site. The very atmosphere of Delphi is charged with awe. Perhaps that is why Apollo slew the dragon Python who guarded Mother Earth's oracle there, and took it for himself. (At left the ruins of Apollo's temple are seen below the Delphic theatre.) From early historical times the priests of Apollo had collected information from petitioners and stored it away, so that by the seventh century Delphi had become Greece's central archive and seat of political intelligence. It was not only the most sacred place in Greece, it was also the most powerful, for the pronouncements and prophecies of Apollo's oracle were considered necessary to any individual or city-state about to undertake an important project. The oracle, as interpreted by the priests, usually favored the aristocracy, established law codes, and traditional forms of worship. It seems the priesthood genuinely wished to promote stability in government and religion, though it also encouraged the orgiastic cult of Dionysus, who occupied the temple as alternate god in winter, when Apollo was away. Despite curious lapses—such as favoritism for the Persian invaders —the Delphic oracle reflected a strong Apollonian urge to see all Greece living peacefully under the rule of law.

OVERLEAF: *Far below Apollo's temple stand the ruins of the fourth-century tholos in the precinct of Athena, who was the only other deity to have her own sanctuary at sacred Delphi.*

RAY MANLEY, SHOSTAL

313

THE VOICE
OF THE ORACLE

Although Delphi had many attractions, it was primarily the oracle that, century after century, drew people to the shrine. Seekers of advice arrived at the town wearing the woolen fillet of a suppliant; they made sacrifices and performed certain rituals while awaiting their turn to submit written questions to Delphic priests who in turn would present the queries to the oracle itself, when the time was propitious. Priests managed the shrine and assisted the priestess, or Pythia, through whom the invisible Apollo made known his advice. The Pythia was required to be at least fifty years old and a virgin. To answer most questions she wrote down alternate answers to the problem set before her, placed the papers in a bowl, and shook it; Apollo signified the correct answer by causing one piece of paper to fall out of the bowl.

Many problems, however, could not be solved so easily, and to deal with those the Pythia entered a small room beneath the floor of Apollo's temple, washed in the water of the sacred fountain, and seated herself on a bronze tripod. If Apollo had accepted the suppliant's sacrifice, the priestess fell into a deep trance. Its cause is not clear: the Greeks attributed it to fumes rising from the Python, which supposedly still lay decomposing centuries after Apollo had killed it; perhaps the priestess' trance was due to her emotional state or to the fact that she had inhaled or swallowed a laurel-leaf brew. The entranced priestess pronounced syllables that were gibberish to all but the priest who had accompanied her underground; this man, called a *prophetes*, translated her utterances into verse. When, instead of giving advice, the oracle made a prophecy—its rarest, most expensive, and most highly respected performance—the *prophetes'* verses were almost as abstruse as the Pythia's words, so, another priest was called upon to interpret both. Even his translation, however, was usually ambiguous.

STAATLICHE MUSEEN, BERLIN

MUSEUM, DELPHI; JEAN-PIERRE TROSSET

Above, a petitioner stands before a priestess who is seated on a tripod and holding a laurel branch; through her Apollo will provide answers to questions.

The Greeks considered the omphalos, shown at left, to be the center of the earth. The finely carved stone was located in Apollo's temple at Delphi.

The stadium at right was built at Delphi for the quadrennial Pythian games, a Panhellenic festival second in importance only to the one held at Olympia.

316

HARISSIADIS

The Sacred Way, above, was trod by countless petitioners who came to Delphi for advice from Apollo.

The Pythia bathed in the waters of the Castalian fountain (right) before entering the place of the oracle.

MELLA

VEILED PROPHECIES

Delphi's oracular prophecies were usually ambiguous or mischievous, but hopeful petitioners often only saw the interpretation that favored them and thereby unwittingly chose their doom, as in these few examples:

Lydia's king Croesus learned from the oracle at Delphi that if he crossed the Halys River he would destroy a great empire. Understanding this to mean that he would vanquish the Persians, he crossed it, was defeated, and so lost his own mighty empire.

Warned at Delphi that he would kill his father and marry his mother, Oedipus deliberately left Corinth where he had been raised as the son of King Polybus and his wife. In a dispute at a crossroads he killed a man. He went on to Thebes, where he won the hand of the queen because he rid the city of the Sphinx. Years later he learned the oracle was right, for the Corinthian rulers were not his real parents: his wife and the man he had slain were.

Aristodemus, who was leader of the Messenians, was told by the oracle that if he wished to defeat the Spartans he must sacrifice a Messenian virgin. He offered his own unmarried daughter; though he won the first battle, he eventually lost the war. Apparently his daughter was not what he had thought her to be.

HASSIA

THE TREASURE HOUSE
OF GREECE

The monuments and treasuries that lined its Sacred Way indicate that Delphi was the most important and influential religious sanctuary in the Greek world; although it was traditional to make a thank-offering to a god for victory gained or disaster averted, sumptuous presents in such great abundance had never been given elsewhere. Apollo's servants did nothing to discourage this; indeed, the oracle's chief weakness seems to have been avarice. The priests at Delphi were eager to arrange special hearings and advice for any petitioner, Greek or "barbarian," who proffered expensive gifts, and it appears that over the years many a bribe was accepted. Although the Delphic oracle sometimes mediated political disputes, clashes between the city-states continued unabated; by the fourth century it had become customary for a triumphant city to raise a monument at Delphi, whether or not the oracle had played a part in its victory. If that state was subsequently defeated, the new victor built a more ostentatious memorial nearby. The earliest treasury—a small templelike building used to store the most valuable gifts dedicated to Apollo—was erected at the beginning of the sixth century by Corinth. Eventually there were more than a score of magnificent treasuries; in time of need, the cities that had built them were able to borrow money, using their offerings as security.

MUSEUM, DELPHI; DESCHARNES

The costly treasury of Athens (right), situated at a turn on the Sacred Way which leads to Apollo's temple at Delphi, was the first Doric building made completely of marble. The Athenians offered it as thanks to Apollo after ridding their city of tyranny and establishing democracy. At left is a detail from the north frieze of the Siphnian treasury, an archaic masterwork that depicts the battle between the gods and Giants; here a lion is seen attacking a Giant.

DESCHARNES

PRIME MOVERS OF THOUGHT

. . . I owe a greater obedience to God than to you, and so long as I draw breath and have my faculties, I shall never stop practicing philosophy and exhorting you and elucidating the truth for everyone that I meet. I shall go on saying, in my usual way, My very good friend, you are an Athenian and belong to a city which is the greatest and most famous in the world for its wisdom and strength. Are you not ashamed that you give your attention to acquiring as much money as possible, and . . . give no attention or thought to truth and understanding and the perfection of your soul? . . .

Now if I corrupt the young by this message, the message would seem to be harmful, but if anyone says that my message is different from this, he is talking nonsense. And so, gentlemen, I would say, You can please yourselves . . . whether you acquit me or not. You know that I am not going to alter my conduct, not even if I have to die a hundred deaths.

Plato, "Socrates' Defense," *Apology*
(*translated by Hugh Tredennick*)

As epic tales and lyrics enlivened the Greek mind and as drama deepened it, the pursuit of philosophy, science, and history vastly enlarged it. A chief pleasure to be found in the company of Greek thinkers is the range of their curiosity and the variety of their findings. The age of specialization lay far ahead of them. Greece's first philosophers were also its first scientists. Its early scientists were also among its poets and moralists. Its historians, striking out from realms of myth and folklore, were pioneer students of sociology, geography, and political behavior (the Greek word *historia* itself means research, investigation), and they were brilliant descriptive writers as well.

The early thinkers of Ionia concentrated on efforts to define the nature of the physical world and discover first principles or forces governing it. Their successors soon found themselves also concerned with questions of human perception and knowledge. Only tantalizing fragments of pre-Socratic writings and sayings survive, but these convey the originality of the Greeks' evolving search for truth. Pythagoras left no recorded word at all, yet his influence as mathematician as well as ethical teacher and mystic was profound; Heraclitus, deeply concerned with the problem of motion and change in what some held to be a world of immutable matter, wrote in oracular riddles. Socrates, the greatest of inquirers, taught less by lecturing than by asking, with the aim of drawing men out to think for themselves—a dangerous method, for he aroused new, challenging thoughts.

Plato, the inspired heir to so much speculation and enlarger of it, was both political analyst and poet, metaphysician and utopian. Aristotle, the ancient world's greatest logician, was also an experimental biologist and the first drama critic. Epicurus, not "epicurean" at all in the modern sense, was the founder of a new, rigorous school of ethical thought. In these pages translators new and old address themselves to the works of many masters.

A homely, snub-nosed Socrates conveys an aura of freedom and strength in this statuette.

AWAKENERS OF THE GREEK MIND

Fragments of Pre-Socratic Philosophy

(translated by Kathleen Freeman)

Anaximander of Miletus

The Non-Limited is the original material of existing things; further, the source from which existing things derive their existence is also that to which they return at their destruction, according to necessity; for they give justice and make reparation to one another for their injustice, according to the arrangement of Time.

Anaximenes of Miletus

As our soul, being air, holds us together, so do breath and air surround the whole universe.

Xenophanes of Colophon

There is one god, among gods and men the greatest, not at all like mortals in body or in mind.

He sees as a whole, thinks as a whole, and hears as a whole.

But without toil he sets everything in motion, by the thought of his mind.

And he always remains in the same place, not moving at all, nor is it fitting for him to change his position at different times.

For everything comes from earth and everything goes back to earth at last.

All things that come into being and grow are earth and water.

The sea is the source of water, and the source of wind. For neither could (the force of the wind blowing outwards from within come into being) without the great main (sea), nor the streams of rivers, nor the showery water of the sky; but the mighty main is the begetter of clouds and winds and rivers.

Heraclitus of Ephesus

That which is in opposition is in concert, and from things that differ comes the most beautiful harmony.

This ordered universe (*cosmos*), which is the same for all, was not created by any one of the gods or of mankind, but it was ever and is and shall be ever-living Fire, kindled in measure and quenched in measure.

The hidden harmony is stronger (*or*, "better") than the visible.

To God, all things are beautiful, good and just; but men have assumed some things to be unjust, others just.

All men have the capacity of knowing themselves and acting with moderation.

The fairest universe is but a dust-heap piled up at random.

Positions of honour enslave gods and men.

Parmenides of Elea

For it is the same thing to think and to be.

One should both say and think that Being Is; for To Be is possible, and Nothingness is not possible. . . .

. . . How could Being perish? How could it come into being? If it came into being, it Is Not; and so too if it is about-to-be at some future time. . . .

Nor is Being divisible, since it is all alike. Nor is there anything (*here or*) there which could prevent it from holding together, nor any lesser thing, but all is full of Being. Therefore it is altogether continuous; for Being is close to Being.

But it is motionless in the limits of mighty bonds, without beginning, without cease. . . .

Before Socrates, Plato, and Aristotle made Athens the capital of philosophy, schools of Greek thinkers flourished in places as far apart as Ionia, Sicily, and the town of Abdera in the north. Much of their teaching was passed on verbally to pupils; most of what was set down has been lost and is known to us only through comments by later writers. The first Greek to write a prose treatise speculating on the nature of things was Anaximander, a pupil of Thales in early sixth-century Miletus—though only one fragment survives. What united the varied men represented here by brief passages was a hunt for non-mythical explanations of the powers controlling the universe. Ideas about the basic physical elements absorbed them, leading to Democritus' concept of atoms; Anaxagoras set forth his belief in an all-creating Mind. Some also set down aphorisms revealing their study of the ways of man.

Empedocles of Acragas

... But come, listen to my discourse! For be assured, learning will increase your understanding. As I said before . . . I shall tell you of a double process. At one time it increased so as to be a single One out of Many; at another time it grew apart so as to be Many out of One—Fire and Water and Earth and the boundless height of Air, and also execrable Hate apart from these, of equal weight in all directions, and Love in their midst, their equal in length and breadth. . . .

All these (*Elements*) are equal and of the same age in their creation; but each presides over its own office, and each has its own character, and they prevail in turn in the course of Time. And besides these, nothing else comes into being, nor does anything cease. For if they had been perishing continuously, they would Be no more; and what could increase the Whole? And whence could it have come? In what direction could it perish, since nothing is empty of these things? No, but these things alone exist, and running through one another they become different things at different times, and are ever continuously the same.

Anaxagoras of Clazomenae

Other things all contain a part of everything, but Mind is infinite and self-ruling, and is mixed with no Thing, but is alone by itself. If it were not by itself, but were mixed with anything else, it would have had a share of all Things, if it were mixed with anything; for in everything there is a portion of everything, as I have said before. And the things mixed (*with Mind*) would have prevented it, so that it could not rule over any Thing in the same way as it can being alone by itself. For it is the finest of all Things, and the purest, and has complete understanding of everything, and has the greatest power. All things which have life, both the greater and the less, are ruled by Mind. Mind took command of the universal revolution, so as to make (*things*) revolve at the outset. And at first things began to revolve from some small point, but now the revolution extends over a greater area, and will spread even further. And the things which were mixed together, and separated off, and divided, were all understood by Mind. And whatever they were going to be, and whatever things were then in existence that are not now, and all things that now exist and whatever shall exist—all were arranged by Mind, as also the revolution now followed by the stars, the sun and moon, and the Air and Aether which were separated off. It was this revolution which caused the separation off. And dense separates from rare, and hot from cold, and bright from dark, and dry from wet. There are many portions of many things. And nothing is absolutely separated off or divided the one from the other except Mind. . . .

Democritus of Abdera

Man is a universe in little (*Microcosm*).

When inferior men censure, the good man pays no heed.

Many whose actions are most disgraceful practise the best utterances.

Good breeding in cattle depends on physical health, but in men on a well-formed character.

Fame and wealth without intelligence are dangerous possessions.

In prosperity it is easy to find a friend, in adversity nothing is so difficult.

It is right that men should value the soul rather than the body; for perfection of soul corrects the inferiority of the body, but physical strength without intelligence does nothing to improve the mind.

Misers have the fate of bees: they work as if they were going to live for ever.

Poverty under democracy is as much to be preferred to so-called prosperity under an autocracy as freedom to slavery.

323

SOCRATES DISCUSSES FRIENDSHIP

from Plato's dialogue *Lysis*

(translated by J. Wright)

From the labors of early thinkers, seeking to fathom the nature of things, we emerge into the warm, expansive presence of the master whose object was to help men know themselves. In this talk, as set down by his great pupil, we have a perfect instance of Socrates' way as a teacher. He draws out two youths, Lysis and Menexenus, on the subject of their companionship. Professing ignorance, he leads them with grace and wit and paradox to re-examine one of the basic relationships of man to man.

From my earliest childhood I have had a particular fancy; everyone has. One longs for horses, another for dogs, a third for money, a fourth for office. For my part, I look on these matters with equanimity, but on the acquisition of friends, with all a lover's passion. . . . On seeing, therefore, you and Lysis, I am lost in wonder, while I count you most happy, at your being able, at your years, to acquire this treasure with such readiness and ease—in that you, Menexenus, have gained so early and true a friend in Lysis, and he the same in you—while I, on the contrary, am so far from making the acquisition, that I do not even know how one man becomes the friend of another, but wish on this very point to appeal to you as a connoisseur. Answer me this. As soon as one man loves another, which of the two becomes the friend—the lover of the loved, or the loved of the lover? Or does it make no difference?

None in the world, that I can see, he replied.

How? said I. Are both friends, if only one loves?

I think so, he answered.

Indeed! Is it not possible for one who loves, not to be loved in return by the object of his love?

It is.

Nay, is it not possible for him even to be hated—treatment, if I mistake not, which lovers frequently fancy they receive at the hands of their favorites? Though they love their darlings as dearly as possible, they often imagine that they are not loved in return, often that they are even hated. Don't you believe this to be true?

Quite true, he replied.

Well, in such a case as this, the one loves, the other is loved.

Just so.

Which of the two, then, is the friend of the other—the lover of the loved, whether or no he be loved in return, and even if he be hated, or the loved of the lover? Or is neither the friend of the other, unless both love each other?

The latter certainly seems to be the case, Socrates.

If so, I continued, we think differently now from what we did before. Then it appeared that if one loved, both were friends, but now, that unless both love, neither are friends.

Yes, I'm afraid we have contradicted ourselves.

This being the case then, the lover is not a friend to anything that does not love him in return.

Apparently not.

People, then, are not friends to horses, unless their horses love them in return, nor friends to quails or to dogs, nor again, to wine or to gymnastics, unless their love be returned—nor friends to wisdom, unless wisdom loves them in return. But in each of these cases, the individual loves the object, but is not a friend to it, and the poet is wrong who says: "Happy the man who, to whom he's a friend, has children, and horses/Mettlesome, dogs of the chase, guest in a faraway land." [Solon]

I don't think he is wrong, Socrates.

But do you think he's right?

Yes, I do.

The lover then, it appears, Menexenus, is a friend to the object of his love, whether the object love, or even hate him. Just as to quite young children, who are either not yet old enough to love, or who are old enough to feel hatred when punished by father or mother, their parents, all the time even that they are being hated, are friends in the very highest degree.

Yes, such appears to be the case.

By this reasoning, then, it is not the object of love that is the friend, but the lover.

Apparently.

And so, not the object of hatred that is the enemy, but the hater.

Clearly.

It frequently happens, then, that people are enemies to those who love them, and friends to those who hate them—that is, are enemies to their friends, and friends to their enemies—if it be true that the lover is the friend, but not the loved. But surely, my dear friend, it were grossly unreasonable, nay, rather, I think altogether impossible, for a man to be a friend to his enemy, and an enemy to his friend.

Yes, Socrates, it does seem impossible.

Well, then, if this be impossible, it must be the object of the love that is the friend to the lover.

Clearly.

And so again, the object of the hatred that is the enemy to the hater.

Necessarily.

But if this be true, we cannot help arriving at the same conclusion as we did in the former case—namely, that it often happens that a man is not a friend, but even an enemy to a friend, as often, that is, as he is not loved, but even hated by the man whom he loves—and often again, that he is not an enemy, but even a friend to an enemy, as often, in fact, as he is not hated, but even loved by the man whom he hates.

No, I'm afraid we can't.

What are we to do then, said I, if neither those who love are to be friends, nor those who are loved, nor, again, those who both love and are loved? Are there any other people besides these that we can say become friends to each other?

To tell you the truth, Socrates, said he, I don't see my way at all.

Is it possible, Menexenus, said I, that from first to last we have been conducting our search improperly?

I am sure I think it is, Socrates, cried Lysis. And he blushed as he said so. For the words seemed to burst from him against his will in the intensity of the interest he was paying to the conversation—an interest which his countenance had evinced all the time we were talking.

I then, wishing to relieve Menexenus, and charmed with the other's intelligence, turned to Lysis, and directing my discourse to him, observed, Yes, Lysis, you are quite right, I think, in saying that if we had conducted our search properly, we should never have lost ourselves in this manner. Let us proceed, however, on this line of inquiry no longer—for I look upon it as a very difficult sort of road—but let us go back again to that point at which we turned aside, and follow in the steps of the poets. For poets, I conceive, are as good as fathers and guides to us in matters of wisdom. Well, the poets, if I mistake not, put forward no slight claims for those who happen to be friends, but tell us that it is God himself who makes them friends, by leading them one to another. They express, if I remember right, their opinion thus: "Like men, I trow, to like, God ever leads," [Homer, *Odyssey*] and makes them known. You have met with the verse, have you not?

Oh, yes.

And also with the writings of those learned sages which tell the same story—namely, that like must of necessity be ever friendly with like. And these are they, if I mistake not, who talk and write on nature and the universe.

True, they are.

Well, do you think they are right in what they say? I asked.

Perhaps, said he.

Perhaps, I answered, in half—perhaps, too, even in all—only we don't understand. For, as it appears to us, the nearer wicked men come to each other, and the more they see of each other, the greater enemies they become. For they injure each other. And it is impossible, I take it, for men to be friends, if they injure and are injured in turn.

So it is, he replied.

By this, then, it would appear, that half of their assertion cannot be true, if we suppose them to mean that wicked men are like one another.

So it would.

But they mean to say, I imagine, that the good are like and friendly with the good, but that the bad, as is remarked of them in another place, are not ever even like themselves, but are variable and not to be reckoned upon. And if a thing be unlike and at variance with itself, it will be long, I take it, before it

becomes like to or friendly with anything else. Don't you think so too?

I do, he answered.

When, therefore, my friend, our authors assert that like is friendly with like, they mean, I imagine, to intimate, though obscurely enough, that the good man is a friend to the good man only, but that the bad man never engages in a true friendship either with a good or a bad man. Do you agree?

He nodded assent.

We know then now, I continued, who it is that are friends, for our argument shows us that it must be those who are good.

Quite clearly too, I think, said he.

And so do I, I rejoined. Still there is a something in the way that troubles me; so let us, with the help of heaven, see what it is that I suspect. Like men are friendly with like men, in so far as they are like, and such a man is useful to such a man. Or rather, let us put it in this way. Is there any good or harm that a like thing can do to a like thing, which it cannot also do to itself? Is there any that can be done to it, which cannot also be done to it by itself? And if not, how can such things be held in regard by each other, when they have no means of assisting one another? Can this possibly be?

No, not possibly.

And if a thing be not held in regard, can it be a friend?

Certainly not.

But, you will say, the like man is not a friend to the like man, but the good will be a friend to the good, in so far as he is good, not in so far as he is like.

Perhaps I may.

And I should rejoin, Will not the good man, in so far as he is good, be found to be sufficient for himself?

Yes.

And if sufficient, he will want nothing so far as his sufficiency goes.

Of course not.

And if he does not want anything he won't feel regard for anything either.

To be sure not.

And what he does not feel regard for, he cannot love.

Not he.

And if he does not love, he won't be a friend.

Clearly not.

How then, I wonder, will the good be ever friends at all with the good, when neither in absence do they feel regret for each other, being sufficient for themselves apart, nor when present together have they any need of one another? Is there any possible way by which such people can be brought to care for each other?

None whatever.

And if they do not care for each other, they cannot possibly be friends.

True, they cannot.

Look and see then, Lysis, how we have been led into error. If I mistake not, we are deceived in the whole, and not only in the half.

How so? he asked.

Once upon a time, I replied, I heard a statement made which has just this moment flashed across my mind. It was that nothing is so hostile to like as like, none so hostile to the good as the good. And among other arguments, my informant adduced the authority of Hesiod, telling me that, according to him, "Potter ever jars with potter, bard with bard, and poor with poor." And so, he added, by a universal and infallible law the nearer any two things resemble one another, the fuller do they become of envy, strife, and hatred—and the greater the dissimilarity, the greater the friendship. For the poor are obliged to make themselves friends of the rich, and the weak of the strong, for the sake of their assistance; the sick man also must be friendly with the physician, and, in short, everyone who is without knowledge must feel regard and affection for those who possess it. Nay, he proceeded with increased magnificence of position to assert that the like was so far from being friendly with the like, that the exact opposite was the case; the more any two things were contrary, the more were they friendly to each other. For everything, he says, craves for its contrary, and not for its like—the dry craves for moisture, the cold for heat, the bitter for sweetness, the sharp for bluntness, the empty to be filled, the full to be emptied. And everything else follows the same rule. For the contrary, he added, is food to the contrary; the like can derive no advantage from the like. And I can assure you I thought him extremely clever as he said all this. He stated his case so well. But you, my friends, what do you think of it?

Oh, it seems very fair at first hearing, said Menexenus.

Shall we admit then that nothing is so friendly to a thing as its contrary?

By all means.

But if we do, Menexenus, will there not spring upon us suddenly and uncouthly and exultingly those universal-knowledge men, the masters of dispute, and ask us, whether there is anything in the world so contrary to enmity as friendship? And if they do, what must be our answer? Can we possibly help admitting that they are right?

No, we cannot.

Well then, they will say, is friendship a friend to enmity, or enmity to friendship?

Neither one nor the other, he replied.

But justice, I suppose, is a friend to injustice, temperance to intemperance, good to evil.

No, I don't think this can be the case.

Well but, I rejoined, if one thing is friend to another thing in virtue of being its contrary, these things must of necessity be friendly.

So they must, he allowed.

It follows then, I think, that neither like is friendly with like, nor contrary with contrary.

Apparently it does.

Well, then, said I, let us look again, and see whether we be not still as far as ever from finding friendship, since it is clearly

none of these things I have mentioned, but whether that which is neither good nor evil may not possibly turn out, however late, to be friendly with the good.

How do you mean? he asked.

Why, to tell you the truth, said I, I don't know myself, being quite dizzied by the entanglement of the subject. I am inclined though, to think that, in the words of the old proverb, the beautiful is friendly.

THE SOUL AND THE UNSEEN
from Plato's dialogue *Phaedo*
(*translated by Hugh Tredennick*)

Though the Phaedo *purports to be a conversation between Socrates and his friends in the last hours before his death, much of its substance is believed to reflect Plato's own thinking, as inspired by his master. Here are many of the ideas that were to give Platonism its immense influence: the concepts of regeneration, of knowledge as recollection from an earlier life, of immortality of the soul, and of the transcendent reality of perfect Ideas of which earthly appearances are only passing shadows.*

Suppose that when you see something you say to yourself, This thing which I can see has a tendency to be like something else, but it falls short and cannot be really like it, only a poor imitation. Don't you agree with me that anyone who receives that impression must in fact have previous knowledge of that thing which he says that the other resembles, but inadequately?

Certainly he must.

Very well, then, is that our position with regard to equal things and absolute equality?

Exactly.

Then we must have had some previous knowledge of equality before the time when we first saw equal things and realized that they were striving after equality, but fell short of it.

That is so.

And at the same time we are agreed also upon this point, that we have not and could not have acquired this notion of equality except by sight or touch or one of the other senses. I am treating them as being all the same.

They are the same, Socrates, for the purpose of our argument.

So it must be through the senses that we obtained the notion that all sensible equals are striving after absolute equality but falling short of it. Is that correct?

Yes, it is.

So before we began to see and hear and use our other senses we must somewhere have acquired the knowledge that there is such a thing as absolute equality. Otherwise we could never have realized, by using it as a standard for comparison, that all equal objects of sense are desirous of being like it, but are only imperfect copies.

That is the logical conclusion, Socrates.

Did we not begin to see and hear and possess our other senses from the moment of birth?

Certainly.

But we admitted that we must have obtained our knowledge of equality before we obtained them.

Yes.

So we must have obtained it before birth.

So it seems.

Then if we obtained it before our birth, and possessed it when we were born, we had knowledge, both before and at the moment of birth, not only of equality and relative magnitudes, but of all absolute standards. Our present argument applies no more to equality than it does to absolute beauty, goodness, uprightness, holiness, and, as I maintain, all those characteristics which we designate in our discussions by the term "absolute." So we must have obtained knowledge of all these characteristics before our birth.

That is so.

And unless we invariably forget it after obtaining it we must always be born *knowing* and continue to *know* all through our lives, because "to know" means simply to retain the knowledge which one has acquired, and not to lose it. Is not what we call "forgetting" simply the loss of knowledge, Simmias?

Most certainly, Socrates.

And if it is true that we acquired our knowledge before our birth, and lost it at the moment of birth, but afterward, by the exercise of our senses upon sensible objects, recover the knowledge which we had once before, I suppose that what we call learning will be the recovery of our own knowledge, and surely we should be right in calling this recollection.

Quite so.

Yes, because we saw that it is possible for the perception of an object by sight or hearing or any of the other senses to suggest to the percipient, through association, whether there is any similarity or not, another object which he has forgotten. So, as I maintain, there are two alternatives. Either we are all born with knowledge of these standards, and retain it throughout our lives, or else, when we speak of people learning, they are simply recollecting what they knew before. In other words, learning is recollection.

Yes, that must be so, Socrates.

Which do you choose, then, Simmias? That we are born with knowledge, or that we recollect after we are born the things of which we possessed knowledge before we were born?

I don't know which to choose on the spur of the moment, Socrates.

Well, here is another choice for you to make. What do you think about this? Can a person who knows a subject thoroughly explain what he knows?

Most certainly he can.

Do you think that everyone can explain these questions about which we have just been talking?

I should like to think so, said Simmias, but I am very much afraid that by this time tomorrow there will be no one on this earth who can do it properly.

So you don't think, Simmias, that everyone has knowledge about them?

Far from it.

Then they just recollect what they once learned.

That must be the right answer.

When do our souls acquire this knowledge? It cannot be after the beginning of our mortal life.

No, of course not.

Then it must be before.

Yes.

Then our souls had a previous existence, Simmias, before they took on this human shape. They were independent of our bodies, and they were possessed of intelligence.

Unless perhaps it is at the moment of birth that we acquire knowledge of these things, Socrates. There is still that time available.

No doubt, my dear fellow, but just tell me, what other time is there to lose it in? We have just agreed that we do not possess it when we are born. Do we lose it at the same moment that we acquire it? Or can you suggest any other time?

No, of course not, Socrates. I didn't realize what nonsense I was talking.

Well, how do we stand now, Simmias? If all these absolute realities, such as beauty and goodness, which we are always talking about, really exist, if it is to them, as we rediscover our own former knowledge of them, that we refer, as copies to their patterns, all the objects of our physical perception—if these realities exist, does it not follow that our souls must exist too even before our birth, whereas if they do not exist, our discussion would seem to be a waste of time? Is this the position, that it is logically just as certain that our souls exist before our birth as it is that these realities exist, and that if the one is impossible, so is the other?

It is perfectly obvious to me, Socrates, said Simmias, that the same logical necessity applies to both. It suits me very well that your argument should rely upon the point that our soul's existence before our birth stands or falls with the existence of your grade of reality. I cannot imagine anything more self-evident than the fact that absolute beauty and goodness and all the rest that you mentioned just now exist in the fullest possible sense. In my opinion the proof is quite satisfactory.

What about Cebes? said Socrates. We must convince Cebes too.

To the best of my belief he is satisfied, replied Simmias. It is true that he is the most obstinate person in the world at resisting an argument, but I should think that he needs nothing more to convince him that our souls existed before our birth. As for their existing after we are dead as well, even I don't feel that that has been proved, Socrates. Cebes' objection still holds—the common fear that a man's soul may be disintegrated at the very moment of his death, and that this may be the end of its existence. Supposing that it *is* born and constituted from some source or other, and exists before it enters a human body. After it has entered one, is there any reason why, at the moment of release, it should not come to an end and be destroyed itself?

Quite right, Simmias, said Cebes. It seems that we have got the proof of one half of what we wanted—that the soul existed before birth—but now we need also to prove that it will exist after death no less than before birth, if our proof is to be complete.

As a matter of fact, my dear Simmias and Cebes, said Socrates, it is proved already, if you will combine this last argument with the one about which we agreed before, that every living thing comes from the dead. If the soul exists before birth, and if when it proceeds toward life and is born it must be born from death or the dead state, surely it must also exist after death, if it must be born again. So the point which you mention has been proved already. But in spite of this I believe that you and Simmias would like to spin out the discussion still more. You are afraid, as children are, that when the soul emerges from the body the wind may really puff it away and scatter it, especially when a person does not die on a calm day but with a gale blowing.

Cebes laughed. Suppose that we are afraid, Socrates, he said, and try to convince us. Or rather don't suppose that it is we that are afraid. Probably even in us there is a little boy who has these childish terrors. Try to persuade him not to be afraid of death as though it were a bogy.

What you should do, said Socrates, is to say a magic spell over him every day until you have charmed his fears away.

But, Socrates, said Simmias, where shall we find a magician who understands these spells now that you . . . are leaving us?

Greece is a large country, Cebes, he replied, which must have good men in it, and there are many foreign races too. You must ransack all of them in your search for this magician, without sparing money or trouble, because you could not spend your money more opportunely on any other object. And you must search also by your own united efforts, because it is probable that you would not easily find anyone better fitted for the task.

We will see to that, said Cebes. But let us return to the point where we left off, if you have no objection.

Of course not. Why should I?

Thank you, said Cebes.

We ought, I think, said Socrates, to ask ourselves this. What sort of thing is it that would naturally suffer the fate of being dispersed? For what sort of thing should we fear this fate, and for what should we not? When we have answered this, we should next consider to which class the soul belongs, and then we shall know whether to feel confidence or fear about the fate of our souls.

Quite true.

Would you not expect a composite object or a natural compound to be liable to break up where it was put together? And ought not anything which is really incomposite to be the one thing of all others which is not affected in this way?

That seems to be the case, said Cebes.

Is it not extremely probable that what is always constant and invariable is incomposite, and what is inconstant and variable is composite?

That is how it seems to me.

Then let us return to the same examples which we were discussing before. Does that absolute reality which we define in our discussions remain always constant and invariable, or not? Does absolute equality or beauty or any other independent entity which really exists ever admit change of any kind? Or does each one of these uniform and independent entities remain always constant and invariable, never admitting any alteration in any respect or in any sense?

They must be constant and invariable, Socrates, said Cebes.

Well, what about the concrete instances of beauty—such as men, horses, clothes, and so on—or of equality, or any other members of a class corresponding to an absolute entity? Are they constant, or are they, on the contrary, scarcely ever in the same relation in any sense either to themselves or to one another?

With them, Socrates, it is just the opposite; they are never free from variation.

And these concrete objects you can touch and see and perceive by your other senses, but those constant entities you cannot possibly apprehend except by thinking; they are invisible to our sight.

That is perfectly true, said Cebes.

So you think that we should assume two classes of things, one visible and the other invisible?

Yes, we should.

The invisible being invariable, and the visible never being the same?

Yes, we should assume that too.

Well, now, said Socrates, are we not part body, part soul?

Certainly.

Then to which class do we say that the body would have the closer resemblance and relation?

Quite obviously to the visible.

And the soul, is it visible or invisible?

Invisible to men, at any rate, Socrates, he said.

But surely we have been speaking of things visible or invisible to our human nature. Do you think that we had some other nature in view?

No, human nature.

What do we say about the soul, then? Is it visible or invisible?

Not visible.

Invisible, then?

Yes.

So soul is more like the invisible, and body more like the

visible?

That follows inevitably, Socrates.

Did we not say some time ago that when the soul uses the instrumentality of the body for any inquiry, whether through sight or hearing or any other sense—because using the body implies using the senses—it is drawn away by the body into the realm of the variable, and loses its way and becomes confused and dizzy, as though it were fuddled, through contact with things of a similar nature?

Certainly.

But when it investigates by itself, it passes into the realm of the pure and everlasting and immortal and changeless, and being of a kindred nature, when it is once independent and free from interference, consorts with it always and strays no longer, but remains, in that realm of the absolute, constant and invariable, through contact with beings of a similar nature. And this condition of the soul we call wisdom.

An excellent description, and perfectly true, Socrates.

Very well, then, in the light of all that we have said, both now and before, to which class do you think that the soul bears the closer resemblance and relation?

I think, Socrates, said Cebes, that even the dullest person would agree, from this line of reasoning, that the soul is in every possible way more like the invariable than the variable.

And the body?

To the other.

Look at it in this way too. When soul and body are both in the same place, nature teaches the one to serve and be subject, the other to rule and govern. In this relation which do you think resembles the divine and which the mortal part? Don't you think that it is the nature of the divine to rule and direct, and that of the mortal to be subject and serve?

I do.

Then which does the soul resemble?

Obviously, Socrates, soul resembles the divine, and body the mortal.

PLATO VERSUS ARISTOTLE

Though Aristotle studied at Plato's Academy for twenty years and owed perhaps as much to his teacher as Plato did to his, he emerged as Plato's first critic. Their differences of mind and temperament were profound. Here the elder, the poet and mystical believer in ideal forms, presents his religious view of the world's origin. He is followed by the younger, the shrewd, matter-of-fact logician, who emphasizes the primacy of substance and categorizes its ever-changing qualities and forms.

Plato on the Creation
from the *Timaeus*
(*translated by Benjamin Jowett*)

Let me tell you then why the creator made this world of generation. He was good, and the good can never have any jealousy of anything. And being free from jealousy, he desired that all things should be as like himself as they could be. This is in the truest sense the origin of creation and of the world, as we shall do well in believing on the testimony of wise men. God desired that all things should be good and nothing bad, so far as this was attainable. Wherefore also finding the whole visible sphere not at rest, but moving in an irregular and disorderly fashion, out of disorder he brought order, considering that this was in every way better than the other. Now the deeds of the best could never be or have been other than the fairest, and the creator, reflecting on the things which are by nature visible, found that no unintelligent creature taken as a whole could ever be fairer than the intelligent taken as a whole, and again that intelligence could not be present in anything which was devoid of soul. For which reason, when he was framing the universe, he put intelligence in soul, and soul in body, that he might be the creator of a work which was by nature fairest and best. On this wise, using the language of probability, we may say that the world came into being—a living creature truly endowed with soul and intelligence by the providence of God.

This being supposed, let us proceed to the next stage. In the likeness of what animal did the creator make the world? It would be an unworthy thing to liken it to any nature which exists as a part only, for nothing can be beautiful which is like any imperfect thing. But let us suppose the world to be the very image of that whole of which all other animals both individually and in their tribes are portions. For the original of the universe contains in itself all intelligible beings, just as this world comprehends us and all other visible creatures. For the deity, intending to make this world like the fairest and most perfect of intelligible beings, framed one visible animal comprehending within itself all other animals of a kindred nature. Are we right in saying that there is one world, or that they are many and infinite? There must be one only if the created copy is to accord with the original. For that which includes all other intelligible creatures cannot have a second or companion; in that case there would be need of another living being which would include both, and of which they would be parts, and the likeness would be more truly said to resemble not them, but that other which included them. In order then that the world might be solitary, like the perfect animal, the creator made not two worlds or an infinite number of them, but there is and ever will be one only-begotten and created heaven.

Aristotle on First Causes
from the *Metaphysics*
(*translated by W. D. Ross*)

The subject of our inquiry is substance; for the principles and the causes we are seeking are those of substances. For if the universe is of the nature of a whole, substance is its first part; and if it coheres merely by virtue of serial succession, on this view also substance is first, and is succeeded by quality, and then by quantity. . . . Further, none of the categories other than substance can exist apart. And the early philosophers also in practice testify to the primacy of substance; for it was of substance that they sought the principles and elements and causes. The thinkers of the present day tend to rank universals as substances (for genera are universals, and these they tend to describe as principles and substances, owing to the abstract nature of their inquiry); but the thinkers of old ranked particular things as substances, e.g. fire and earth, not what is common to both, body.

There are three kinds of substance—one that is sensible (of which one subdivision is eternal and another is perishable; the latter is recognized by all men, and includes, e.g., plants and animals), of which we must grasp the elements, whether one or many; and another that is immovable, and this certain thinkers assert to be capable of existing apart, some dividing it into two, others identifying the Forms and the objects of mathematics, and others positing, of these two, only the objects of mathematics. The former two kinds of substance are the subject of physics (for they imply movement); but the third kind belongs to another science, if there is no principle common to it and to the other kinds. . . .

One might raise the question from what sort of non-being generation proceeds; for "non-being" has three senses. If, then, one form of non-being exists potentially, still it is not by virtue of a potentiality for any and every thing, but different things come from different things; nor is it satisfactory to say that "all things were together"; for they differ in their matter, since otherwise why did an infinity of things come to be, and not one thing? . . .

There are three kinds of substance—the matter, which is a "this" in appearance (for all things that are characterized by contact and not by organic unity are matter and substratum, e.g. fire, flesh, head; for these are all matter, and the last matter is the matter of that which is in the full sense substance); the nature, which is a "this" or positive state towards which movement takes place; and again, thirdly, the particular substance which is composed of these two, e.g. Socrates or Callias. Now in some cases the "this" does not exist apart from the composite substance, e.g. the form of house does not so exist, unless the art of building exists apart. . . . And so Plato was not far wrong when he said that there are as many Forms as there are kinds of natural object (if there *are* Forms distinct from the things of this earth). The moving causes exist as things preceding the effects, but causes in the sense of definitions are simultaneous with their effects. . . . Evidently then there is no necessity, on this ground at least, for the existence of the Ideas. . . .

But if there is something which is capable of moving things or acting on them, but is not actually doing so, there will not necessarily be movement. . . . Nothing, then, is gained even if we suppose eternal substances, as the believers in the Forms do, unless there is to be in them some principle which can cause change. . . .

Yet if we follow the theologians who generate the world from night, or the natural philosophers who say that "all things were together," the same impossible result ensues. For how will there be movement, if there is no actually existing cause? . . .

This is why some suppose eternal actuality—e.g. Leucippus and Plato; for they say there is always movement. But why and what this movement is they do not say, nor, if the world moves in this way or that, do they tell us the cause of its doing so.

In his Republic *Plato set forth a utopia in which classes of soldiers and ordinary folk are led by an elite of selectively chosen guardians among whom families and property are held in common. Justice would reign if everyone knew his station and worked for the general good. In his* Laws *he modified his positions, expounding a second-best constitution. But Aristotle vehemently attacked the notion of common property, holding that men could best realize themselves with goods of their own.*

Plato's Ideal State
from the *Laws*
(*translated by A. E. Taylor*)

In fact, properties must be fixed by some system which excludes recriminations among their owners. . . . In persons who have, like ourselves at this moment, the providential opportunity to found a new society where there are as yet no internal hostilities, to introduce such hostilities by the distribution of land and houses would be a combination of sheer depravity with superhuman folly.

What, then, would be the right method of distribution? First we must fix the total number of the citizens at the suitable figure; next we must come to an agreement about their distribution, the number and size of the sections into which they should be subdivided; the land and houses should be partitioned among these sections as equally as may be. What would be a satisfactory total for the population is more than can be rightly said without consideration of the territory and the neighboring communities. The territory should be large enough for the adequate maintenance of a certain number of men of modest ambitions, and no larger; the population should be sufficient to defend themselves against wrongs from societies on their borders, and to assist their neighbors when wronged to some purpose. . . .

Let us assume—to take a convenient number—that we have five thousand and forty landholders, who can be armed to fight for their holdings, and that the territory and houses are likewise divided among the same number, so that there will be one man to one holding. Let this total be divided first by two, and then by three; in fact it will permit of division by four, five, and the successive integers up to ten. Of course anyone who is acting as a legislator must be at least familiar enough with figures to understand what number, or kind of number, will prove most useful in a given state. Accordingly we will select that which has the greatest number of immediately successive divisions. . . .

The first-best society, then, that with the best constitution and code of law, is one where the old saying is most universally true of the whole society. I mean the saying that "friends' property is indeed common property." If there is now on earth, or ever should be, such a society—a community in womenfolk, in children, in all possessions whatsoever—if all means have been taken to eliminate everything we mean by the word *ownership* from life; if all possible means have been taken to make even what nature has made our *own* in some sense common property, I mean, if our eyes, ears, and hands seem to see, hear, act, in the common service; if, moreover, we all approve and condemn in perfect unison and derive pleasure and pain from the same sources—in a word, when the institutions of a society make it most utterly one, that is a criterion of their excellence than which no truer or better will ever be found. If there is anywhere such a city, with a number of gods, or sons of gods, for its inhabitants, they dwell there thus in all joyousness of life. Whence for the pattern of a constitution we should look to no other quarter, but cleave to this and strive to come as near it as may be in our state. . . .

First, then, let them make a division of lands and houses among themselves, and not till the soil in common, for that were a project beyond their birth, breeding, and education. But let the division be made with some such thought as this, that he to whom a lot falls is yet bound to count his portion the common property of the whole society, and, since the territory is his fatherland, to tend it with care passing that of son for mother, the more that the land is the divine mistress of her mortal children, and to think likewise of all the gods and spirits of the locality. . . .

Our society, we pronounce, must have neither gold nor silver, nor yet much making of profits from mechanical crafts, or usury, or raising of sordid beasts, but only such as husbandry yields or permits, and of it only so much as will not force a man in his profit gathering to forget the ends for which possessions exist, that is to say, soul and body, which will never be of any account without bodily training and education at large. Wherefore we have said, and said more than once, that concern for possessions should take the lowest place in our esteem, for whereas the objects of universal interest to man are in all three, interest in possessions, rightly pursued, holds the third and lowest rank, the interest of the body is second, of the soul first.

Aristotle's Dissent
from the *Politics*
(*translated by A. E. Wardman*)

Property is a connected subject. We must consider how property is to be organized by those who are going to live in the best state. Should it be in common or not? This question may be regarded as a separate issue, apart from the legislation having to do with children and wives. The question is: even if there are separate families, as is now universally the case, would it be better for property and the management of property to be common? Or should there be a compromise system? For example, should the farms be owned separately and the produce contributed to a common pool? . . .

Now, if the laboring class consists of noncitizens, there may well be another system with fewer difficulties; but when citizens are working their own property, there may be considerable difficulties raised by ownership in common. If there is inequality both in the rewards and in the work done, there are certain to be complaints by those who get less but work more against those who do little but receive a large reward. In general, association and partnership in affairs is one of the most difficult things, especially when these concern property. . . .

These and similar difficulties occur when property is held in common. The present way of holding property, if improved by good customs and a good legal system, would be much better. It will have the advantages of both schemes, namely, the advantage of property being both common and private. Property *should* be common in a sense; but generally it ought to be private. If management is divided among individuals, there will not be mutual complaints; and the properties will be improved because each individual runs his own private section. As regards use and enjoyment, virtue will guarantee the fulfillment of the proverb "friends' goods are common goods." Even now such a scheme exists in outline in some communities, so that it is clearly not impossible. In states that are well run, some parts of the scheme are already working, and other parts could easily be put into operation. An individual owns property privately, but makes his property available to his friends and uses theirs as common property. This happens in Sparta, where people use one another's slaves as though they were their own; and similarly their horses and dogs. They take food, if they need it on a journey, from the farms in the country. Clearly, the best course is for property to be privately owned but open to common use and enjoyment. . . .

Thinking that you own something yourself makes an enormous difference in the pleasure that it provides. The love that each of us feels for himself is not just pointless, but rooted in nature. Self-love is rightly criticized, but that is not the same as love for oneself; it means loving oneself more than one should, in the same sense that we use it disparagingly of the "money lover," for feeling love for such things is found among all men.

It is a very great pleasure to do favors and to help friends, visitors, or associates. This can be done when property is privately owned, but not when people make the state too unified. Besides, that plainly ruins the activities of two virtues: one is self-control in relation to women, for it is morally good to keep away from someone else's wife because one is self-controlled; the other is generosity in matters of property. In these other systems, one will not be able to prove one's generosity or to do any generous action at all: the practice of generosity consists in the use made of money.

Such legislation as Plato's looks attractive and benevolent. He who hears of it welcomes the news with pleasure, thinking that everyone will have a wonderful feeling of universal brotherhood, especially when it is argued that the evils now existing in states are due to the absence of property held in common. . . . But in fact these are not caused by the absence of a system of common property but are due to the evil in man; we see many more disagreements among partners and property owners in common than among private owners, although we notice also that the number of those who quarrel because of partnership is relatively small compared with the large number of private owners. Also, it is fair to mention not only the evils of which men would be rid by a common system but also the advantages that they will lose. Life in such conditions seems to be quite impossible.

We should consider that the reason for Socrates' [i.e., Plato's] mistake is that his starting point is incorrect. There is a sense in which both the household and the state ought to be a unity; but neither should be an entire unity. In one way, by increasing in unity, the state will cease to be a state; in another way, as it gets near to not being a state, it will be an inferior state, just as if one turned a harmony into unison or a rhythm into a single foot. The right thing is for the state to be a plurality, as we said before, unified and integrated by education. It is absurd for a man who is about to introduce education, and who thinks that the city will thereby be made good, to suppose that he can set things right by such measures as those described, instead of by social customs, culture, and laws; consider Sparta and Crete, where the legislator introduced the idea of common property by means of public messes. . . . We would have a really clear picture if we could see Plato's state actually in operation. It would not be possible to found such a state without making divisions and parts—that is, messes, clans, and tribes. The only result of the legislation will be the exemption of the guardians from farm work, which is something that the Spartans are attempting to achieve, even as their regime now stands. . . .

The fact is that the mass of the other citizens will form the bulk of the state, although their position has not been defined. Will the farmers, too, have property in common, or own it individually? Will they have their own wives and children, or have them in common? If they have everything completely in common in the same way, how will they be different from the guardians? . . .

But if the farmers are to have the same institutions as are found in other states, what kind of partnership will there be between the two groups? There are bound to be two communities in the one state, opposed to each other. For Socrates makes the guardians a sort of police force, whereas the farmers, craftsmen, and the rest are citizens. . . .

Also, he deprives the guardians of happiness, but says that the legislator must make the state happy as a whole. It is impossible for the state to be happy as a whole unless most people or all the constituent parts are happy. "Happiness" is not the same kind of term as "even." "Even" can apply to a whole without its being true of any part; but this is impossible with "happiness." If the guardians are not happy, who is?

EPICURUS' RULES FOR LIVING
from the *Principal Doctrines*
(*translated by Cyril Bailey*)

Following the prime of Plato and Aristotle, fourth-century Athens saw rival schools teaching everyday ethical guidance. The Stoics argued that since the universe is good, there can be no evil, and therefore man should live according to nature and accept whatever occurs. Epicurus, more vigorous in spirit, set out to rid men of superstition and fear of death and to imbue them with a belief in the rewards of equanimity, moderation, and thoughtful self-control. Here are some of his chief maxims:

The blessed and immortal nature knows no trouble itself nor causes trouble to any other, so that it is never constrained by anger or favour. For all such things exist only in the weak.

Death is nothing to us: for that which is dissolved is without sensation; and that which lacks sensation is nothing to us.

The limit of quantity in pleasures is the removal of all that is painful. Wherever pleasure is present, as long as it is there, there is neither pain of body nor of mind, nor of both at once.

It is not possible to live pleasantly without living prudently and honourably and justly, nor again to live a life of prudence, honour, and justice without living pleasantly. And the man who does not possess the pleasant life, is not living prudently and honourably and justly, and the man who does not possess the virtuous life, cannot possibly live pleasantly.

To secure protection from men anything is a natural good, by which you may be able to attain this end.

No pleasure is a bad thing in itself: but the means which produce some pleasures bring with them disturbances many times greater than the pleasures.

If every pleasure could be intensified so that it lasted and influenced the whole organism or the most essential parts of our nature, pleasures would never differ from one another.

If the things that produce the pleasures of profligates could dispel the fears of the mind about the phenomena of the sky and death and its pains, and also teach the limits of desires and of pains, we should never have cause to blame them: for they would be filling themselves full with pleasures from every source and never have pain of body or mind, which is the evil of life.

If we were not troubled by our suspicions of the phenomena of the sky and about death, fearing that it concerns us, and also by our failure to grasp the limits of pains and desires, we should have no need of natural science.

A man cannot dispel his fear about the most important matters if he does not know what is the nature of the universe but suspects the truth of some mythical story. So that without natural science it is not possible to attain our pleasures unalloyed.

There is no profit in securing protection in relation to men, if things above and things beneath the earth and indeed all in the boundless universe remain matters of suspicion.

The most unalloyed source of protection from men, which is secured to some extent by a certain force of expulsion, is in fact the immunity which results from a quiet life and the retirement from the world.

The wealth demanded by nature is both limited and easily procured; that demanded by idle imaginings stretches on to infinity.

The just man is most free from trouble, the unjust most full of trouble.

The pleasure in the flesh is not increased, when once the pain due to want is removed, but is only varied: and the limit as regards pleasure in the mind is begotten by the reasoned understanding of these very pleasures and of the emotions akin to them, which used to cause the greatest fear to the mind.

He who has learned the limits of life knows that that which removes the pain due to want and makes the whole of life complete is easy to obtain; so that there is no need of actions which involve competition.

If you fight against all sensations, you will have no standard by which to judge even those of them which you say are false.

Of all the things which wisdom acquires to produce the blessedness of the complete life, far the greatest is the possession of friendship.

The same conviction which has given us confidence that there is nothing terrible that lasts for ever or even for long, has also seen the protection of friendship most fully completed in the limited evils of this life.

Among desires some are natural and necessary, some natural but not necessary, and others neither natural nor necessary, but due to idle imagination.

The justice which arises from nature is a pledge of mutual advantage to restrain men from harming one another and save them from being harmed.

Justice never is anything in itself, but in the dealings of men with one another in any place whatever and at any time it is a kind of compact not to harm or be harmed.

Injustice is not an evil in itself, but only in consequence of the fear which attaches to the apprehension of being unable to escape those appointed to punish such actions.

The man who has best ordered the element of disquiet arising from external circumstances has made those things that he could akin to himself and the rest at least not alien: but with all to which he could not do even this, he has refrained from mixing, and has expelled from his life all which it was of advantage to treat thus.

HERODOTUS, EXPLORER

from *The Persian Wars*

(*translated by George Rawlinson*)

Because he was the first to attempt to separate fact from myth in narrating past events (though he did not always succeed), Herodotus is known as the Father of History. He also realized that to complete a systematic explanation of the world of which he wrote, it was necessary to describe its countries, and the society and customs of their inhabitants. Thus he might suitably be called the Father of Geography and Ethnography as well. This section from Herodotus tells of the land of the Scythians and beyond.

With regard to the regions which lie above the country [Scythia] whereof this portion of my history treats, there is no one who possesses any exact knowledge. Not a single person can I find who professes to be acquainted with them by actual observation. Even Aristeas, the traveller of whom I lately spoke, does not claim—and he is writing poetry—to have reached any farther than the Issedonians. What he relates concerning the regions beyond is, he confesses, mere hearsay, being the account which the Issedonians gave him of those countries. However, I shall proceed to mention all that I have learnt of these parts by the most exact inquiries which I have been able to make concerning them. . . .

On the opposite side of the Gerrhus [River] is the Royal district, as it is called: here dwells the largest and bravest of the Scythian tribes, which looks upon all the other tribes in the light of slaves. Its country reaches on the south to Taurica, on the east to the trench dug by the sons of the blind slaves, the mart upon Lake Maeotis, called the Cliffs, and in part to the river Tanais. North of the country of the Royal Scythians are the Blackcloaks, a people of a quite different race from the Scythians. Beyond them lie marshes and a region without inhabitants, so far as our knowledge reaches. . . .

Adjoining . . . are the people who bear the name of Iyrcae; they also support themselves by hunting, which they practise in the following manner. The hunter climbs a tree, the whole country abounding in wood, and there sets himself in ambush; he has a dog at hand, and a horse, trained to lie down upon its belly, and thus make itself low; the hunter keeps watch, and when he sees his game, lets fly an arrow; then mounting his horse, he gives the beast chase, his dog following hard all the while. . . .

Passing over a great extent of this rough country, you come to a people dwelling at the foot of lofty mountains, who are said to be all—both men and women—bald from their birth, to have flat noses, and very long chins. These people speak a language of their own, but the dress which they wear is the same as the Scythian. They live on the fruit of a certain tree, the name of which is Ponticum; in size it is about equal to our fig-tree, and it bears a fruit like a bean, with a stone inside. When the fruit is ripe, they strain it through cloths; the juice which runs off is black and thick, and is called by the natives "aschy." They lap this up with their tongues, and also mix it with milk for a drink; while they make the lees, which are solid, into cakes, and eat them instead of meat; for they have but few sheep in their country, in which there is no good pasturage. Each of them dwells under a tree, and they cover the tree in winter with a cloth of thick white felt, but take off the covering in the summer-time. No one harms these people, for they are looked upon as sacred,—they do not even possess any warlike weapons. When their neighbours fall out, they make up the quarrel; and when one flies to them for refuge, he is safe from all hurt. They are called the Argippaeans. . . .

Thus far therefore the land is known; but beyond the bald-headed men lies a region of which no one can give any exact account. Lofty and precipitous mountains, which are never crossed, bar further progress. The bald men say, but it does not seem to me credible, that the people who live in these mountains have feet like goats; and that after passing them you find another race of men, who sleep during one half of the year. This latter statement appears to me quite unworthy of credit. . . .

The Issedonians are said to have the following customs. When a man's father dies, all the near relatives bring sheep to the house; which are sacrificed, and their flesh cut in pieces, while at the same time the dead body undergoes the like treatment. The two sorts of flesh are afterwards mixed together, and the whole is served up at a banquet. The head of the dead man is treated differently: it is stripped bare, cleansed, and set in gold. It then becomes an ornament on which they pride themselves, and is brought out year by year at the great festival which sons keep in honour of their fathers' death, just as the Greeks keep their feast of the dead. In other respects the Issedonians are reputed to be observers of justice: and it is to be remarked that their women have equal authority with the men. Thus our knowledge extends as far as this nation. . . .

Thus much, however, is clear: if there are men beyond the north wind, there must also be men beyond the south wind. For my part, I cannot but laugh when I see numbers of persons drawing maps of the world without having any reason to guide them; making, as they do, the ocean-stream to run all round the earth, and the earth itself to be an exact circle, as if described by a pair of compasses, with Europe and Asia just of the same size. The truth in this matter I will now proceed to explain in a very few words, making it clear what the real size of each region is, and what shape should be given them. . . .

For my part I am astonished that men should ever have divided Libya, Asia, and Europe as they have, for they are exceedingly unequal. Europe extends the entire length of the other two, and for breadth will not even (as I think) bear to be compared to them. As for Libya, we know it to be washed on all sides by the sea, except where it is attached to Asia. This discovery was first made by Necos, the Egyptian king, who on desisting from the canal which he had begun between the Nile and the Arabian gulf, sent to sea a number of ships manned by Phoenicians, with orders to make for the Pillars of Heracles, and return to Egypt through them, and by the Mediterranean. The Phoenicians took their departure from Egypt by way of the Red Sea, and so sailed into the southern ocean. When autumn came, they went ashore, wherever they might happen to be, and having sown a tract of land with corn, waited until the grain was fit to cut. Having reaped it, they again set sail; and thus it came to pass that two whole years went by, and it was not till the third year that they doubled the Pillars of Heracles, and made good their voyage home. On their return, they declared—I for my part do not believe them, but perhaps others may—that in sailing round Libya they had the sun upon their right hand. In this way was the extent of Libya first discovered.

Next to these Phoenicians the Carthaginians, according to their own accounts, made the voyage. . . . Sataspes went down to Egypt, and there got a ship and crew, with which he set sail for the Pillars of Heracles. Having passed the Straits, he doubled the Libyan headland, known as Cape Soloeis, and proceeded southward . . . at the farthest point to which he had reached, the coast was occupied by a dwarfish race, who wore a dress made from the palm-tree. These people, whenever he landed, left their towns and fled away to the mountains; his men, however, did them no wrong, only entering into their cities and taking some of their cattle. The reason why he had not sailed quite round Libya was, he said, because the ship stopped, and would not go any further. . . .

But the boundaries of Europe are quite unknown, and there is not a man who can say whether any sea girds it round either on the north or on the east, while in length it undoubtedly extends as far as both the other two. For my part I cannot conceive why three names, and women's names especially, should ever have been given to a tract which is in reality one, or why the Egyptian Nile and the Colchian Phasis (or according to others the Maeotic Tanais and Cimmerian ferry) should have been fixed upon for the boundary lines; nor can I even say who gave the three tracts their names, or whence they took the epithets. According to the Greeks in general, Libya was so called after a certain Libya, a native woman, and Asia after the wife of Prometheus. The Lydians, however, put in a claim to the latter name, which, they declare, was not derived from Asia the wife of Prometheus, but from Asies, the son of Cotys, and grandson of Manes, who also gave name to the tribe Asias at Sardis. As for Europe, no one can say whether it is surrounded by the sea or not, neither is it known whence the name of Europe was derived, nor who gave it name, unless we say that Europe was so called after the Tyrian Europa, and before her time was nameless, like the other divisions. But it is certain that Europa was an Asiatic, and never even set foot on the land which the Greeks now call Europe, only sailing from Phoenicia to Crete, and from Crete to Lycia. However let us quit these matters. We shall ourselves continue to use the names which custom sanctions.

THUCYDIDES, RECORDER
from *The Peloponnesian War*
(*translated by Benjamin Jowett*)

The second great historian of the Greeks was the first to write of them in an analytical, critical spirit, probing his sources and immersing himself in close study of political and other actions, to many of which he had been witness. Thus he helped teach generations of Greeks about themselves. Here he records the eloquent plea for lenience made by Diodotus to the Athenians, who, angered by the revolt of their allies in Mytilene, had almost been persuaded by Cleon to destroy the city and its inhabitants.

"I am far from blaming those who invite us to reconsider our sentence upon the Mytilenaeans, nor do I approve of the censure which has been cast on the practice of deliberating more than once about matters so critical. In my opinion the two things most adverse to good counsel are haste and passion; the former is generally a mark of folly, the latter of vulgarity and narrowness of mind. When a man insists that words ought not to be our guides in action, he is either wanting in sense or wanting in honesty: he is wanting in sense if he does not see that there is no other way in which we can throw light on the unknown future; and he is not honest if, seeking to carry a discreditable measure, and knowing that he cannot speak well in a bad cause, he reflects that he can slander well and terrify his opponents and his audience by the audacity of his calumnies. Worst of all are those who, besides other topics of abuse, declare that their opponent is hired to make an eloquent speech. If they accused him of stupidity only, when he failed in producing an impression he might go his way having lost his reputation for sense but not for honesty; whereas he who is accused of dishonesty, even if he succeed, is viewed with suspicion, and, if he fail, is thought to be both fool and rogue. And so the city suffers; for she is robbed of her counselors by fear. Happy would she be if such citizens could not speak at all, for then the people would not be misled. The good citizen should prove his superiority as a speaker, not by trying to intimidate those who are to follow him in debate, but by fair argument; and the wise city ought not to give increased honor to her best counselor, any more than she will deprive him of that which he has; while he whose proposal is rejected not only ought to receive no punishment, but should be free from all reproach. Then he who succeeds will not say pleasant things contrary to his better judgment in order to gain a still higher place in popular favor, and he who fails will not be striving to attract the multitude to himself by like compliances.

"But we take an opposite course; and still worse. Even when we know a man to be giving the wisest counsel, a suspicion of corruption is set on foot; and from a jealousy which is perhaps groundless we allow the state to lose an undeniable advantage. It has come to this, that the best advice when offered in plain terms is as much distrusted as the worst; and not only he who wishes to lead the multitude into the most dangerous courses must deceive them, but he who speaks in the cause of right must make himself believed by lying. In this city, and in this city only, to do good openly and without deception is impossible, because you are too clever; and, when a man confers an unmistakable benefit on you, he is rewarded by a suspicion that, in some underhand manner, he gets more than he gives. But, whatever you may suspect, when great interests are at stake, we who advise ought to look further and weigh our words more carefully than you whose vision is limited. And you should remember that we are accountable for our advice to you, but you who listen are accountable to nobody. If he who gave and he who followed evil counsel suffered equally, you would be more reasonable in your ideas; but now, whenever you meet with a reverse, led away by the passion of the moment you punish the individual who is your adviser for his error of judgment, and your own error you condone, if the judgments of many concurred in it.

"I do not come forward either as an advocate of the Mytilenaeans or as their accuser; the question for us rightly considered is not, what are their crimes? but, what is for our interest? If I prove them ever so guilty, I will not on that account bid you put them to death, unless it is expedient. Neither, if perchance there be some degree of excuse for them, would I have you spare them, unless it be clearly for the good of the state. For I conceive that we are now concerned, not with the present, but with the future. When Cleon insists that the infliction of death will be expedient and will secure you against revolt in time to come, I, like him taking the ground of future expediency, stoutly maintain the contrary position; and I would not have you be misled by the apparent fairness of his proposal, and reject the solid advantages of mine. You are angry with the Mytilenaeans, and the superior justice of his argument may for the moment attract you; but we are not at law with them, and do not want to be told what is just; we are considering a question of policy, and desire to know how we can turn them to account.

"To many offenses less than theirs, states have affixed the punishment of death; nevertheless, excited by hope, men still risk their lives. No one when venturing on a perilous enterprise ever yet passed a sentence of failure on himself. And what city when entering on a revolt ever imagined that the power which she had, whether her own or obtained from her allies, did not justify the attempt? All are by nature prone to err both in public and in private life, and no law will prevent them. Men have gone through the whole catalogue of penalties in the hope that, by increasing their severity, they may suffer less at the hands of evildoers. In early ages the punishments, even of the worst offenses, would naturally be milder; but as time went on and mankind continued to transgress, they seldom stopped short of death. And still there are transgressors. Some greater terror then

has yet to be discovered; certainly death is no deterrent. For poverty inspires necessity with daring; and wealth engenders avarice in pride and insolence; and the various conditions of human life, as they severally fall under the sway of some mighty and fatal power, lure men through their passions to destruction. Desire and hope are never wanting, the one leading, the other following; the one devising the enterprise, the other suggesting that fortune will be kind; and they are the most ruinous, for, being unseen, they far outweigh the dangers which are seen. Fortune too assists the illusion, for she often presents herself unexpectedly, and induces states as well as individuals to run into peril, however inadequate their means; and states even more than individuals, because they are throwing for a higher stake, freedom or empire, and because when a man has a whole people acting with him, he magnifies himself out of all reason. In a word then, it is impossible and simply absurd to suppose that human nature when bent upon some favorite project can be restrained either by the strength of law or by any other terror. . . .

"Think of another great error into which you would fall if you listened to Cleon. At present the popular party are everywhere our friends; either they do not join with the oligarchs, or, if compelled to do so, they are always ready to turn against the authors of the revolt; and so in going to war with a rebellious state you have the multitude on your side. But, if you destroy the people of Mytilenè who took no part in the revolt, and who voluntarily surrendered the city as soon as they got arms into their hands, in the first place to slay them would be a crime, since they were your benefactors; in the second place you will play into the hands of the oligarchic parties, who henceforward, in fomenting a revolt, will at once have the people on their side; for you will have proclaimed to all that the innocent and the guilty will share the same fate. Even if they were guilty you should wink at their conduct, and not allow the only friends whom you have left to be converted into enemies. Far more conducive to the maintenance of your empire would it be to suffer wrong willingly, than for the sake of justice to put to death those whom we had better spare. Cleon may speak of a punishment which is just and also expedient, but you will find that, in any proposal like his, the two cannot be combined.

"Assured then that what I advise is for the best, and yielding neither to pity nor to lenity—for I am as unwilling as Cleon can be that you should be influenced by any such motives—but simply weighing the arguments which I have urged, accede to my proposal: Pass sentence at your leisure on the Mytilenaeans whom Paches, deeming them guilty, has sent hither; but leave the rest of the inhabitants where they are. This will be good policy for the future, and will strike present terror into your enemies. For wise counsel is really more formidable to an enemy than the severity of unreasoning violence."

Thus spoke Diodotus, and such were the proposals on either side which most nearly represented the opposing parties. In spite of the reaction, there was a struggle between the two opinions; the show of hands was very close, but the motion of Diodotus prevailed.

POSERS OF PROBLEMS

To the Greek mind, in which philosophic inquiry went hand in hand with the study of physical sciences and mathematics, innumerable puzzles and questions presented themselves. Problems of the measurement of motion and of space, of the relation of symmetrical to asymmetrical forms, of the properties of numbers, challenged original thinkers from Pythagoras to the geometers and astronomers of the Hellenistic age, when Greek science reached its prime.

Mathematicians had always supposed it was possible to divide the longer of two rods into a certain number of smaller lengths in such a way that a sufficient number of these units would exactly equal the other rod in length. Practically, of course, such an operation always appears possible. Pythagoras showed, however, that the length of the side of a square and that of its diagonals precisely lack this property. No unit, however small, could serve to measure both exactly: they are incommensurable.

A generation after Pythagoras, Zeno of Elea devised the famous paradox of Achilles and the tortoise. Zeno proposed that if the tortoise had a start of a mile in a foot race and ran at one-tenth the warrior's speed, Achilles could never win. In the time in which Achilles would run the first mile, Zeno argued, the tortoise would cover one-tenth of a mile, thus remaining in the lead. Repeating the same argument indefinitely showed that Achilles could never overtake the tortoise, since when he reached its starting point, the tortoise would always be a little farther on. A full explanation of the paradox had to await the development of the modern theory of mathematical limits.

Equally astonishing was the research in pure and applied mathematics by Eratosthenes, the head of the Alexandrian library and a successor of Euclid. He estimated the circumference of the earth and its diameter; his figures approximate modern findings, and his estimates of distances to the sun and moon have proved comparably accurate.

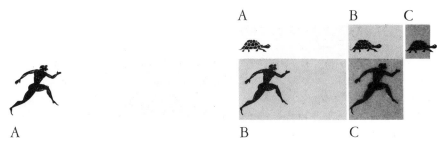

ZENO'S PARADOX: *According to this riddle, Achilles at A cannot in finite time win the race against the tortoise starting one mile ahead of him at its A and going at 1/10 his speed, since every time he moves from one point to the next, the tortoise moves from its point to the next (the tortoise's B being Achilles' C).*

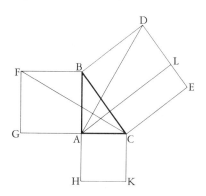

THE PYTHAGOREAN THEOREM: *The proposition that the sum of the squared lengths of the legs of a right triangle equals the squared length of the third side—the hypotenuse—appears to have been known to Chinese mathematicians possibly as early as 1100 B.C., and Egyptian surveyors made practical use of the theorem far earlier. We do not know if Pythagoras discovered its first rigorous proof, but his demonstration that the length of the hypotenuse could not be measured by fractional parts of the sides started a historic train of investigations. Among the dozens of known proofs, the one appearing in Euclid's Elements (third century B.C.) is most celebrated. An illustration of his method is shown above.*

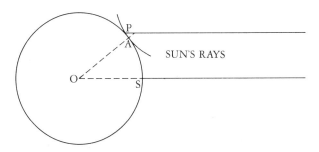

ERATOSTHENES' MEASUREMENT: *Using simple instruments and elementary geometry, Eratosthenes in the third century B.C. approximated the circumference and diameter of the earth to within 1.3 per cent of today's estimates. In his time it was commonly known that the noon sun of the summer solstice stood directly overhead at Syene (present-day Aswan, shown as s above), a city lying some 5,000 stadia— about 500 miles—south of Alexandria (A) and on the same meridian. At midday in Alexandria, Eratosthenes calculated the small angle (at P) formed by the sun's rays falling on a spherical sundial, and estimated the angle to be 1/50 of a circle. He knew that this quantity is in nearly the same proportion to the distance between the cities as is a circumference on the sundial to the distance around the earth.*

9

FINAL HARVEST

Until philosophers are kings, or the kings and princes of this world have the spirit and power of philosophy, and political greatness and wisdom meet in one . . . cities will never have rest from their evils—no, nor the human race, as I believe . . . —*Plato*, The Republic

Although few of us read Plato's Laws, *yet hundreds of thousands have made use of Alexander's laws and continue to use them.* —*Plutarch*, On the Fortune of Alexander

Greece, a land in which brilliant, high weather is usually prolonged through the month of September and then gives way abruptly to the coming of the rains and the darkening of the land, does not know the pleasures of autumn, as say, New England knows them. The Greek countryman sees the leaves fall, the vintage brought in, the furrows for winter sowing plowed; but he generally lacks the experience of that season when all the landscape is transfigured into a shimmering haze of final glow, the very weather standing still in a calm that is all the more poignant because everyone knows that any day the wind and frost will come and bring all color down. Yet Greece, without this annual interval of blazing life before the onset of the dark, experienced in its history a long, rich autumn of its own in the fourth century B.C.

It was a time, to be sure, of diminishing vitality. The sap, the essential Greek lifeblood, ran both thinner and slower than it had in the high summer of the fifth century. Until the final quarter of the fourth, it was not yet diluted by the Macedonian strain, but its traditional strength can be seen gradually declining almost decade by decade. This is most apparent in tragic drama and architecture, both of which came almost to a creative standstill, and in public mores, which even in victorious Sparta lost their old rigor. It is least apparent in sculpture and philosophy, which achieved triumphs of increasing refinement, though at the cost of a certain ruggedness of concept and contour. The sciences flourished while traditional religion shriveled, giving way to agnosticism on one hand and to mystery cults on the other. The old polis disintegrated as a viable institution, and there was no working ideal of another kind of community to replace it.

In the tragic drama, there was no successor to Aeschylus, Sophocles, and the ever-troubled Euripides—the latest of whose works, such as the *Iphigenia in Aulis* and the *Bacchae*, had portrayed a chaotic world without a moral order to help man find his way. After them, the fount dried up. In comedy Aristophanes, having exuberantly mocked the philosophers, the warriors, the moralists, and the amoralists alike, declined into rambling farce in his last known play, the *Plutus* of 388. He was followed by what is known to literary historians as the Middle Comedy; it was not until very late in the century that the New Comedy arose, its most talented playwright being Menander, whose witty commentaries on everyday mores were widely prized and were later adapted for the Roman stage by Plautus and Terence. (Of his plays, only portions of the originals had escaped oblivion until the discovery of an ancient papyrus of a complete comedy, the *Dyskolos*, in 1957.)

As epic poetry and tragic drama had withered away with the

passing of the gods, lyric poetry too declined in this mundane era. Skillful versifiers maintained the technique of amatory and reflective form, but there was no Hesiod or Sappho in the fourth century. The writing of history itself, so brilliantly begun by Herodotus and Thucydides, weakened in a time when there was very much to record. True, fourth-century historians were legion in Athens, and Ephorus was probably more widely read in the Hellenistic period than Thucydides; but the only chronicler comparable to the earlier masters was Xenophon, the stirring author of the *Anabasis*, describing the march of the Ten Thousand, which he led across Asia Minor.

In architecture there was no fourth-century successor to the virile Parthenon of the fifth. There were lesser temples in profusion, generally showing an absorption with the graceful Ionic style and its ornaments and motifs, but one would be hard put to single out any of those that have survived as equal in originality to the Ionian Erechtheum of the preceding century or in jewel-like balance to the little shrine of Athena Nike at the edge of the Acropolis. Indeed, apart from developing theatre construction in such superb hillside designs as that at Epidaurus or devising the leafy Corinthian capital, fourth-century Greek architects and engineers showed a marked decline in originality and enterprise.

Yet the face of Greece showed little change in the fourth century from the preceding one. The style of its sculpture, to be sure, did change rapidly in the hands of such masters as Praxiteles, Scopas, and Lysippus, peopling its temples and agoras with figures of increasing individuality and stir. In painting, a master of the first rank arose shortly after mid-century in the person of Apelles, whose portraits of living persons and panels of mythological scenes were considered to be the marvels of the age. Many anecdotes are told of this fashionable and engaging man—none more familiar than that concerning a day when Alexander of Macedonia posed for a portrait with his royal steed Bucephalus. Alexander, apparently not happy with the rendering of his horse, had Bucephalus brought into the studio for a closer look. Bucephalus, the story says, whinnied with approval at the sight of the panel, and the artist turned to Alexander to say, "Your horse seems to know more about painting than you do." Yet, great as Apelles' reputation was, his art suffered the ravages of time, and not one trace of it survives.

To many a man today, fourth-century Greece is more ambiguous and difficult to assess than is Greece of the classical age. Amid its curious declines or lapses in some areas and its high achievements in others, however, several things stand out. Greece,

ISTANBUL ARKEOLOJI MUZELERI

With his conquest of a vast empire, the Macedonian king Alexander the Great, who is shown above, disseminated Hellenic culture throughout the eastern Mediterranean and western Asia.

as the century wore on, was a more cosmopolitan and relaxed place to live in than before. Its internecine struggles had not devastated it; they had simply sapped and modified it. Though many of the best men of Athens had been killed or banished, the Greeks had learned not to make a holocaust of civil strife. The Spartans themselves, for all their severity as taskmasters, grew so prosperous from the tributes they exacted from vanquished states that they began to take on many of the worldly ways of their victims; wealthy Spartan families enjoyed creature comforts undreamed of by Lycurgus or the austere Leonidas. The Athenians, for their part, having seen their state battered and shamed, were of a mind to doubt its old virtues. All over Greece the old, strict sense of obligation of each citizen to his polis waned, and men of substance withdrew more and more into private pursuits and pleasures, leaving the conduct of public affairs to professionals.

It was an age of the political manager, the public rhetorician, the intellectual specialist, the hired attorney, the dawning civil servant, and the mercenary soldier as well—all employments which the old Greek polis had either deplored or hardly envisaged in its unique and imaginative notion that all qualified citizens should participate on every level in affairs of state. To be sure, the polis idea had often been nobler in thought than in realization. In Athens, for instance, it had not been helped by the gradual introduction of daily pay for civic duties that had originally been regarded as freely given. That scheme, applied first to jurymen in Pericles' time, had been extended by about 400 to provide a daily fee to any citizen willing to take the trouble simply to attend the sessions of the Assembly. The intention of the democratic party, then in command, was understandable enough: it was to ensure that citizens of small means, hard put to take time off from their regular employments, would not suffer when joining in public activity, and that they would appear in such numbers as not to be outvoted by those of ampler means. Its result, though, was to amass on the Pnyx and around the law courts hordes of hangers-on and petty job-seekers, many of them of meager qualifications and out for a government dole of a drachma or more a day. Such an environment itself lowered the tone of public life and caused increasing numbers of better qualified citizens to turn away from it in disdain. The philosopher Isocrates, a severe critic of what he felt to be the excesses of democracy in his home city of Athens, remarked that if the Assembly was to be paid, it ought to be paid by Athens' enemies, since it made so many blunders.

Yet while Isocrates worried and Plato sought to do away with popular government entirely, by substituting rule by the "best,"

Most of the works of Menander, the great playwright of Athenian New Comedy, have disappeared. Only one complete play of his has been found, the Dyskolos, *or* The Curmudgeon, *whose beginning and ending lines are shown on the papyrus leaves at right. The comedy, like so many others of its genre, revolves about a young lover pursuing a maiden against her father's wishes. Below, an ancient marble relief shows Menander holding the mask used by the actor who plays the lover; on the table are masks for the father and the daughter.*

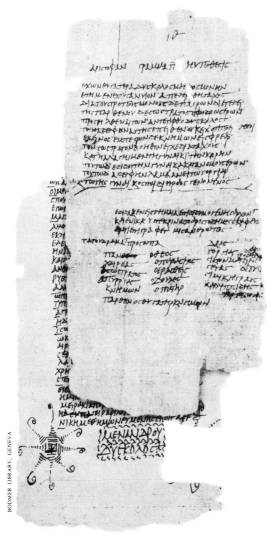

BODMER LIBRARY, GENEVA

PRINCETON UNIVERSITY ART MUSEUM

the weaknesses of the polis idea lay much deeper; for the polis had been overtaken not so much by spoilsmen and incompetents as by history. Devised in a simpler age, it was proving itself no longer adequate to the demands of a far more complex one, with the increasing intricacies of Greek alliances and counteralliances that extended over the entire Mediterranean area. The day called for the amalgamation of small squabbling Greek states into one great design; but for all the sharpness and breadth of the Greek mind, no genius arose who could achieve that, even though Isocrates preached it. On the contrary, Plato and Aristotle, the leading political philosophers, went on praising the small, independent polis as the ideal state, while deploring its Athenian democratic form in practice. Many city-states had banded together, intermittently, to resist the Persian invader; but now, a century later, the idea of effective Greek unification was as remote as ever.

Instead, particularism and feuding went on, first Sparta exerting hegemony, then Athens reviving, then Thebes coming to the fore, and faraway Syracuse extending its own sway. The Greek states remained as obstinately divided and parochial as ever, but the traditional pride and patriotism of the individual citizen withered away. During the Peloponnesian War Sparta had accepted Persian aid against Athens; in 393 or thereabouts a humbled Athens in turn accepted Persian assistance in rebuilding the Long Walls, pulled down by Spartan order. In Athens, moreover, a principle particularly cherished under the constitutions of Cleisthenes and Pericles had been abandoned with ill effects upon the cohesion of the state. Under the old polity, it was assumed that a citizen chosen for office would stand ready to serve in a civilian and military capacity both. But during the long years of the Peloponnesian War, the demand for soldiers had been so great that city-states were forced to recruit mercenaries to augment their citizen armies. The result was a caste of paid warriors whose purpose was more the pursuit of arms than patriotism as such, and the old concept of the citizen-soldier and of the unity of civil and military functions dissolved.

The end of the Peloponnesian War left many of these professionals without employers. They then hired themselves out to foreign states, sometimes taking with them whole contingents of the best hoplites into alien pay. All told, during the first quarter of the fourth century at least 25,000 Greeks were probably in active mercenary service somewhere, and the total may later have reached 50,000. Their achievements in fields abroad added luster to Greek arms, but not stature to their states.

Of these mercenaries, one of the most famous and successful was a young Athenian noble, Xenophon, who in 401 went into

341

The leading spokesman against Macedonian encroachment on Greece's independence was Demosthenes, one of antiquity's greatest orators, who delivered a series of fierce denunciations of King Philip II before the Assembly of Athens.

VATICAN MUSEUM; ALINARI

Persian service with the Ten Thousand, an army of Greek soldiers employed to assist one royal side in a dynastic struggle against another. For the Persians, under the line of kings following Cyrus, Darius, and Xerxes, who came to grief at Salamis, were undergoing internal strife too. When Darius II, monarch during the time of the Peloponnesian War, died, he left two sons: the younger was a prince named Cyrus, who was a satrap in Asia Minor and a strong friend of Sparta; the other was an elder brother who took the throne under the name of Artaxerxes II. To help oust Artaxerxes and install the young pretender Cyrus was the mission of these Greek soldiers of fortune. In his *Anabasis* Xenophon vividly described the concentration of the Greek mercenaries in Mesopotamia, their smashing victory over Artaxerxes' forces at Cunaxa, the tragic death of Cyrus in battle, and the collapse of his cause. When the Greek generals were treacherously murdered by their Persian employers, the isolated soldiers elected Xenophon to lead them on the long, hard march homeward across arid, hostile Asia Minor. After weeks of struggle they finally, with unbounded joy, caught sight of the sea, the Black Sea. Thus Xenophon describes the climactic moment of his emaciated men:

"They came to the mountain on the fifth day, the name of the mountain being Thekes. When the men in front reached the summit and caught sight of the sea there was great shouting. Xenophon and the rear guard heard it and thought that there were some more enemies attacking in the front, since there were natives of the country they had ravaged following them up behind. . . . However, when the shouting got louder and drew nearer, and those who were constantly going forward started running towards the men in front who kept on shouting, and the more there were of them the more shouting there was, it looked then as though this was something of considerable importance. So Xenophon mounted his horse and, taking Lycus and the cavalry with him, rode forward to give support, and, quite soon, they heard the soldiers shouting out 'The sea! The sea!' and passing the word down the column."

There are few passages in all the chronicle of struggle and adventure that surpass the graphic force and vividness of this one.

Yet, just what was Xenophon struggling for? He was a restive Athenian attracted to Persia for pay and also, perhaps, because of the lure of the sheer vastness of its realm compared to the smallness of Greece. Like many other Athenians, he was also attracted to Sparta and its authoritarian ways. Later, he joined a Spartan expedition against the Persians and became an honored resident of Sparta, recipient of a rich estate and busied with writing apologetics in succinct prose in defense of his latest adopted city. Athens banished him for his wandering loyalties, as it had condemned his master Socrates for his supposedly subversive teachings. Yet there was a fundamental difference: Socrates, while as disenchanted with Athenian democracy as Xenophon, was wedded to an integrity of his own; Xenophon, for all his individuality and literary gifts, was basically a soldier of fortune—the Greek precursor of the Renaissance *condottiere*.

So able and brave, yet in his way unstable, Xenophon characterizes much of this equivocal age. In it, patriotism mixed with betrayal; hard rationalism, with Orphic cult or with Eleusinian mysteries; ancestral ties, with disdain of them; new science, with disdain of that too; idealism, with gross hedonism or self-interest; learned philosophy, with what one might call anti-philosophy, in the form of the Cynics' mockery of Plato and his school.

The Cynic persuasion arose among thinkers who were dubious of high-flown metaphysical speculations and particularly of Plato's teaching that physical appearances were merely "shadows," and that only the "ideal" was "real." (The Greek term "cynic" had the connotation of "doggishness," not that of over-all doubt and sneering, as we use it today; the school probably took its name from the nickname applied to one of its leaders, Diogenes, "The Dog.") Against the aristocratic Plato's lofty disdain of the material world, the Cynics set forth their own concept: divest yourself of earthly needs and possessions, but do this for the purpose of getting back to nature and its illumination, not away from it. The Cynic school was founded by Antisthenes, an Athenian philosopher, who argued that most pleasures are treacherous and do not contribute to happiness; his goal, which he realized in his own life, was to find self-fulfillment in ascetic poverty. Diogenes, his pupil, took this "back-to-the-natural" doctrine to the extreme, holding that happiness is reached by satisfying only one's natural needs and by doing so in the most natural way, even as animals do. To exemplify this, he himself lived almost literally like a dog in the streets, sheltered only in a cask, or clay storage jug, and relieving himself in public. Repellent as he may have been in person, he was obviously a winning wit. Once, when a threat of war aroused the rich and comfortable Corinthians to drill and train, he took his cask and rolled it back and forth across their agora, explaining, "When everybody is so busy, I thought I should contribute something." Later, in one of the most familiar anecdotes of Greek history, the conquering Alexander of Macedonia paid a call on Diogenes. He found the old shaggy man lying in the gutter near his cask; when he asked if there was any service he could render, Diogenes' curt response was, "Stand out of the sunlight."

A Macedonian coin depicts a king, probably Philip II, astride a prancing horse. Philip's Macedonian kingdom came to dominate the Greek land to the south, whose numerous independent city-states had exhausted themselves through a century of struggle with one another.
BRITISH MUSEUM

The young and warlike Alexander is shown in a Roman cameo, probably with his mother, Olympias, who claimed that a god, Zeus Ammon, and not King Philip had been the boy's real father.
KUNSTHISTORISCHEN MUSEUM, VIENNA

Plato maintained that an ideal presence lay behind everything, and that the material world in which man dwelt was only one of appearances —it was the ideal alone that was the "real."

NY CARLSBERG GLYPTOTHEK, COPENHAGEN

The great logician and analyst Aristotle taught that the best way for man to understand the universe was by using his own five senses and not by searching for truths behind each phenomenon.

MUSEO NAZIONALE, NAPLES

This was undoubtedly less philosophy than it was pose—indeed, it was outright exhibitionism. Showmanship, though of a more decorous kind, appeared also in the craft of a new kind of performer—the *rhetor*, or professional public speaker, as trained to his calling as any masked actor of Aeschylus' plays. He was often a skilled lawyer (it was only recently that Athens had accepted the notion of the paid attorney, its old principle having been that any accused man should stand up on his own in court and defend himself in his own words as best he could). Drama being in decline, oratory became a sort of art form and a source of entertainment in itself: rhetors were known on occasion to rehearse their speeches before mirrors in order to gauge gestures and possible effects, and became renowned as they delivered themselves of scathing attacks on their opponents—the more violent the assault and the more pungent the reply, the better the show all around.

The art, or rather craft, of forensic advocacy (which the Greeks were to hand on to the Romans, and the Romans to us) arose in large part from Sophist teachers and their techniques of persuasion and of outpointing opponents. Occasionally it produced a major figure, as in Isocrates, a brilliantly gifted pamphleteer and polemicist who founded his own school of rhetoric in Athens about 392. Though a critic of Athenian democracy, this forceful and articulate man was sincerely dedicated to the cause of Athenian revival and moreover to Greek unity as a whole. He lived to the age of ninety-eight, always talking, always writing, always summoning his fellow citizens to action. It was perhaps largely under his goading influence that the city aroused itself from a certain lethargy to create a new maritime league designed chiefly to curb further Spartan extension—only to be overtaken by neighboring Thebes, which under the highly effective general Epaminondas threw the Spartans out of central Greece at the battle of Leuctra in 371. This was a decisive victory, which, with Epaminondas' consequent invasion of Sparta's own home valleys, marked the breaking of Sparta's power for all time. But it left the whole question of leadership among the Greeks in abeyance once again.

A second Athenian master of the public mind then came forth in the person of Demosthenes, the greatest orator to arise before the Roman Cicero, and one of the most stirring flayers of public morals to arise before Savonarola, and also one of the most successful practicing attorneys of all time. He was brilliant, yet shot through with contradiction; he lived self-indulgently and collected enormous fees, yet spoke with a stern tongue of prophecy and died bravely. Born to wealth and schooled in rhetoric, he early made himself a master in complex topics of civil suit—estate, inheritance, and the whole area of what we call the law of torts. A superb trial lawyer (it was said of him that he could prepare briefs for either party with equal ease) and a lobbyist in the Assembly for measures in behalf of his clients, he also served as a strict public prosecutor out to trap those who had done the state some wrong. Personally relaxed in morals—he apparently had liaisons with a large number of youths and women alike over the four decades of his prime—he nevertheless upbraided his fellow citizens for their laxity and lack of probity. Apparently in foreign pay at one point (the charge was made and never denied that he had accepted Persian money to arouse the Athenians against Macedonia), he stood out as the first leading Athenian to recognize the rising Macedonian threat for what it was.

Philip II, a highly virile, lusty, and shrewd chieftain from Macedonia, had in 359 made himself the feudal master of the rough tribesmen of the mountains and plains of northern Greece. He then had begun to conceive a scheme of aggrandizement against the Greek states themselves, planning to place his kingdom at their head, as Athens had once led the Delian League. Soon he also conceived the idea of a joint expedition against the Persians at the Bosporus and beyond. A bold and original organizer of fighting men, he improved on the old Greek system of close-ranked spearmen by devising a more open and mobile scheme: his phalanxes, bearing long spears, were supported by well-armored swordsmen, by archers who shot over the swordsmen's heads, and by cavalry sweeping around the flanks. Thus armed, he seized several northern Greek cities but was momentarily blocked by the resistance of Athens. But soon he was able to take advantage of a war among Greek states that had broken out over the seizure of the sanctuary of Apollo at Delphi and its treasury by the Phocians. Amid the turmoil a number of states called on Philip for help, and he was swift to respond, descending from the northern passes to be welcomed by many Greeks as a liberator and protector of the shrine. Not by Demosthenes, however, who as patriot, democrat, and leader of the resistance party, launched in 351 an extraordinary series of trumpet calls to his compatriots, warning them that the liberator might well be an enslaver. What he said, in the ringing orations known as *Philippics*, was that the new rising power in Macedonia was a threat to the Athenians, that Athens should consolidate all its forces to stand ready to meet it, that the city should seek allies, but that in any case it might have to bear the brunt of a Macedonian attack itself and thus must stand forth to lead as it had led in earlier days—if need be, alone. In the midst of his rolling periods, reminding

The remains of a gear wheel, shown above, come from a mechanism that was used for calculating the motions of the heavenly bodies; it was made during the first century B.C., *probably in Rhodes. The machine, a distant ancestor of the clocks we use today, shows the refinements reached by Hellenistic scientists, whose mechanical and mathematical skills laid the groundwork for much of the knowledge that dominated science until modern times. Their pride and talents are exemplified in Archimedes' statement: "Give me a place to stand on and I can move the world."*
NATIONAL MUSEUM, ATHENS; DEREK J. DE SOLLA PRICE

Athenians of their past greatness, he did not hesitate to pour obloquy on what he felt to be their latter-day decay, crying out that the old Athenian courage had given way to cowardice, discipline to disorder, ancient decency to corruption.

While the Athenians listened to their great tribune thundering against both Philip and their own fallen ways, they also heard other orators arguing that, far from fearing or resisting the Macedonians, the Greeks should accept their leadership. Aged Isocrates in 346 sent an open letter to Philip encouraging him to unite the quarrelsome city-states of Greece and to lead them against the Persians, still overlords of the Greeks on the Ionian coast. Alternately accommodating and opposing the aggressive hillmen of the north, the Athenians did make a strong military stand against Philip at Chaeronea in Boeotia in 338. But by now the time was very late. With little support other than that of Thebes, they were soundly trounced by Philip's phalanxes, his eighteen-year-old son Alexander leading the cavalry that helped sweep the field. The dismayed and divided Greeks now stood in the presence of what was in effect the first European nation—that is, a whole people spread over many provinces, but centrally administered—and their leaders accepted victorious Philip's call to meet with him for what could be called a "unity" conference at Corinth. The following year he set forth a plan for a joint expedition against Persia (as Isocrates had counseled); with it he gave an assurance that the individual Greek states' autonomy would be preserved, provided they followed him as their commander in chief. This summons, backed by Macedonian lancers, appealed to many a Greek—though it did not move so stalwart a patriot as Demosthenes, for all the deference Philip voiced to Athens as the torchbearer of Hellenic civilization. He had already paid his respects to it: anxious to acquire an Athenian gloss for his royal house, he had engaged Aristotle as his son Alexander's tutor when the boy was only thirteen.

Events now moved with gathering rapidity. In 336 Philip was murdered by one of his own retainers in a palace conspiracy, which led to uprisings both among northern tribes and in Greek cities against the suzerainty of his house (Demosthenes again being the chief Athenian agitator). But Alexander, barely twenty, at once seized the throne, although his legitimate claim to it had been disputed, and proclaimed his phenomenal mastery of men by subduing outlying tribes in lightning raids and descending upon the disaffected Greek states like a wolf upon the fold. He knew there had been conspiracy between some Greeks and Persia against Macedonia after his father's death; he razed Thebes as an example, yet spared Athens on receiving its submission. With

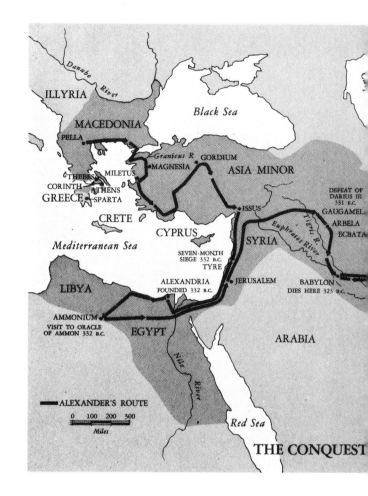

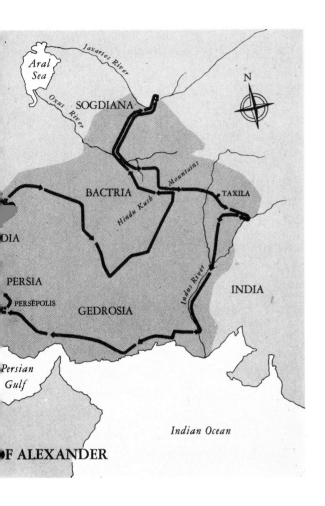

In 334 Alexander led his army out of the Macedonian capital of Pella. Marching through Asia Minor, he defeated the Persians at the Granicus River, and, according to legend, cut the famous Gordian knot; then he won another victory at Issus. After besieging Tyre he advanced into Egypt, where he founded the city of Alexandria and visited the oracle of Ammon, which hailed him as the son of Zeus. His greatest victory over the Persians took place at Gaugamela, near the Tigris River; from there he traveled to Babylon and the Persian capitals of Susa and Persepolis. Pursuing the Persian king Darius III, he marched his troops over the deserts and mountains of western Asia and into the heart of the continent. In India, within sight of the Himalayas, Alexander finally turned back. The young conqueror never returned home to Macedonia, however, for he died on his way back, at Babylon, in the year 323.

the allegiance of almost all shaken Greece in hand, he embarked in 334 on the venture that exceeded the furthest dreams of Philip —not just the reduction of the Persian power, but the subjugation of as much of the eastern world as possible to Hellas, of which this astonishing and possessed spirit now felt himself to be the leader. In this mighty march of empire, many heads had to fall: among them was the brave Demosthenes, whom Athenian collaborationists delivered into Macedonian hands soon after Alexander's death; doomed to the fate usually meted out to resistance leaders, he forestalled his enemies by committing suicide.

During the long period of erosion of Greek faith and pride, and the emergence in its stead of a union of force led by northern chieftains whom the Greeks themselves considered barbarians, the two greatest living minds in Greece itself had been hard at work, building structures of their own—in the abstract. Of the two, one thinks of Plato as the more lofty, the more poetic, the more imaginative, and certainly the more readable; of Aristotle as the more systematic, the more didactic, the more encompassing in the vast range of his investigations, and since he lacked Plato's grace of discourse, as the more forbidding today. Over the centuries, a special, almost mystical aura has surrounded Plato, the pupil and interpreter of Socrates, as perhaps the strongest spiritual presence in the Western world before the coming of Jesus of Nazareth. To many minds Aristotle, Plato's pupil, is, on the other hand, the hard dialectician who cast a confining spell over an entire Christian era, because medieval theologians accepted his teachings without question, at the expense of freedom and advance of thought.

Though Plato at first reading may seem by far the more palatable of the two, it can be argued (and it has often been argued, particularly in modern times) that he was one of the most reactionary, inhibited, and authoritarian minds to arise in the spaciousness of ancient Greece. For, although highly revered as the embodiment of Greek humanism, he was also profoundly at odds with it—alienated, we might say today. The problem of Plato is not simply that he deplored democracy, as we have seen, on the basis of its Athenian practice, and propounded in his Republic a utopia of a rigidly hierarchic state ruled by a specifically trained elite. The problem is much broader. He frowned not only on Homeric myths but also on the works of the tragedians and on much of the art and music of his own day as being unedifying, proposing for his ideal state a rigid censorship of art and literature to guard against what might seem to its governors to be unwholesome. This curious personality, who wrote poems and epigrams in

347

ALEXANDER AT THE WATER HOLE

While Xenophon's Anabasis, *chronicling the march of the Greek Ten Thousand in Persian service across Asia Minor and the Near East, remains widely read, probably few today encounter the work of Arrian, who in the second century* A.D. *also wrote an* Anabasis *(a generic title for a great adventure). Using the eyewitness accounts of Alexander's generals, Arrian (a general himself, under the Roman emperor Hadrian) produced antiquity's most complete and unbiased biography of Alexander the Great. Describing Alexander's retreat from India, and the deprivations of his men amid wasteland, drought, and the unknown, Arrian tells of the qualities of leadership in this revealing episode:*

"At this point I have not thought well to leave unrecorded the noblest achievement of Alexander. . . . The army was marching through sand and while the heat was already burning, since they were obliged to reach water at the end of the march; and this was some distance ahead. Alexander himself was much distressed by thirst, and with much difficulty, but still as best he could, led the way on foot; so that the rest of the troops should (as usually happens in such a case) bear their toils more easily, when all are sharing the distress alike. Meanwhile some of the light-armed troops had turned aside from the rest of the line to look for water, and had found some—just a little water collected in a shallow river bed, a poor and wretched water hole; they gathered up this water with difficulty and hurried to Alexander as if they were bringing him some great boon; but when they drew near, they brought the water, which they had poured into a helmet, to the king. He received it, and thanked those who had brought it; and taking it, poured it out in the sight of all the troops; and at this action the whole army was so much heartened that you would have said that each and every man had drunk that water which Alexander thus poured out."

his youth and was in maturity surely the most accomplished man of letters of his time, virtually banished poets from his ideal society; he even deplored reliance on books in Greece's existing society, fearing that this might weaken man's powers of memory. Moreover, he mistrusted all sciences save those of mathematics, geometry, and astronomy, fearing that they would place undue emphasis upon the evidences of the senses as against the ineffable, abstract truth that exists beyond the senses.

Behind all this lies his teaching (for the most part given as if through the voice of Socrates) that all impressions received by our senses are fragmentary and misleading, if not false, and tell us nothing of the true nature of things. Arguing that behind physical appearances and what he calls "the rabble of the senses," with their misshapen, passing images, there lies a realm of ineffable, perfect, eternal order which alone embodies "reality," he is preaching a doctrine of two worlds—one visible and one invisible. He is in effect saying that science, in its efforts to explore physical phenomena, is merely pursuing chimeras or "shadows." More than that, he is rejecting one traditional Greek ideal by arguing that man is in a state of disharmony between an evil, imperfect body and a divine spirit that enters into the body but is not part of it. Man, then, can attain fulfillment not by developing all his faculties of physical grace and intellectual insight together, but by divesting himself of all that is this-worldly and pursuing the transcendental light that lies yonder.

From this, in practical terms, it follows that man's leaders should be an aristocracy of philosophers or philosopher-kings who have clearly perceived such a light—unlike the rest of us who (to cite his famous metaphor) remain mentally imprisoned as if in a cave, seeing only shadows. Only a few elect can attain this illumination, which alone embodies truth and thus the idea of God, and they will give us the inspired Word. Plato was evidently infatuated with his concept of imprisonment in a cave, since it was figuratively such a confinement that he proposed for most of mankind: creative experiment in art, empirical studies of the world, and new movements in social organization were taboo unless specifically sanctioned by his philosopher-policeman. Rarely has a scheme been designed that is so rigid and so regardless of human capacities as this one evolved by the master of the grove of Academus. The inquiring Plato, born of skepticism, hardened into the absolutist who held that each man must fit into a preordained order of things (at top, the guardians, next the soldiers, below them the common people) and who thus projected Greece toward the acceptance of a dictator. In his ideal, the dictator to be accepted was a spiritualizing one, to be sure—which may help explain why so many men have considered Plato, in a distant sense, a prophet of Christ the King. But the dictator whom Greece actually received was of quite another character. He was the imperious, daemonic Alexander of Macedonia, half-wild, half highly cultivated, possessed by the notion that through his mother he was descended from Achilles and must outdo Achilles' deeds, ablaze with the ambition to conquer and unite the entire known world of the eastern Mediterranean and beyond, and ready, as his conquests succeeded, to have himself worshiped as an oriental god-king.

Plato died in 347; he could not possibly have forseen the revolutionary changes that Alexander, then only nine years old, would soon make in the Greek world. Plato's pupil Aristotle would live long enough to be able to ponder his own theories of the advantages of small communities over large ones in the light of historical developments; for his death did not come until 322, one year after the death of *his* pupil Alexander.

The young king who accomplished in a few years the incredible feat of not only uniting all men of Greek language but also of extending Greek influence as far as India did in many ways resemble the legendary Achilles, whom he strove to emulate. Just as Achilles had come from the very fringe of Achaean culture, so Alexander was a half outsider too. And indeed his Macedonia, despite its nationhood, was more akin in daily life to the pastoral, tribal ways of Homeric society than to those of urbane Athens. Like Achilles, he was phenomenal in personal beauty and unpredictable in behavior, one day chivalrous, kind, sunny, generous, and on the next possessed by frenzies of savage rage or withdrawn into brooding darkness. From his father Philip he no doubt inherited his lordly vitality and iron skill; from his mother, the fiery princess Olympias of northerly Epirus, who was rumored to have joined in Dionysian rites of the wildest sort, his uncontrolled temper and his instability. He loved his friend Hephaestion as dearly as Achilles had loved Patroclus; he loved women too; he also loved —or said he loved—philosophy, and he wrote to Aristotle: "For my part, I assure you, I had rather excel others in the knowledge of what is excellent, than in the extent of my power and dominion." But despite this protestation, his chief lust was for glory.

He had, or acquired as he advanced, a vision of cultural and political union of East and West under Greek, and particularly Macedonian, hegemony; and he took with him a retinue of court philosophers, surveyors, chroniclers, and engineers, as Napoleon was to do when entering Egypt. Yet he burned King Darius III's capital at Persepolis, killed or tortured the brave defenders of

One of the generals who inherited part of Alexander's empire was Seleucus. His share of the domain was the largest, and included Syria and much of Asia Minor, Mesopotamia, and the vast eastern territories that had belonged to Persia.
MUSEO NAZIONALE, NAPLES

349

The famous statue known as the Apollo Belvedere, *a Roman copy of a Greek original, showed the god holding a bow and a laurel branch; both his hair and the cloak over his arm were covered with gold.*

VATICAN MUSEUM; ANDERSON

Gaza to the last man, and in anger at Tyre's resistance had his levies slaughter 8,000 Tyrian soldiers and had the entire population sold into slavery. He paid gallant court to the fair kinswomen of beaten Darius, but Alexander's true method of persuasion was brute force brilliantly deployed: the high-speed march, sometimes covering forty miles of arid country in a day, the infantry phalanx tightly massed against superior numbers, the armored cavalry attacking on the flank, skirmishers fanning out to distract the enemy, and catapults used as field artillery.

Using such tactics, he was able in 333 to rout Darius' army of 100,000 men or more at Issus in the southeastern corner of Asia Minor, and an even larger host at Gaugamela near the Tigris River two years later. The most fortunate cities or states were those that submitted to him without a fight: the Ionian Greeks welcomed him, Damascus and Sidon bowed to him, somnolent Egypt not only received him but proclaimed him Pharaoh, gilded Babylon and Susa in the Persian heartland opened their gates. It was only when in his insatiate rush he struck across the wild back country of Bactria to the Hindu Kush to fight guerrilla actions against mountaineer tribesmen that he met diminishing returns of victory and loot. By 326, when he had crossed the Indus and decided to press on to the Ganges, his legionaries (though chroniclers tell us how they idolized him) had had enough and mutinied, forcing Alexander to return to Persia. There this possessed man, for all his dreams of Hellenizing the whole East, became more and more the prisoner of Eastern ways: he announced that he wished thenceforth to be worshiped as the divine son of Zeus, took to wearing Persian clothes and sitting on a golden throne, and asked his officers to prostrate themselves before him. In Babylon, at thirty-two, surrounded by sycophants and soothsayers, and ridden with drink and possibly with doubt, he died, leaving a stupendous empire without a royal heir, and his whole scheme of organizing and uniting it unrealized.

Apart from feats of arms, he had accomplished some great deeds. He had set up along his traverses of the Middle East a whole string of cities modeled along Hellenic lines, complete with columned temples, council chamber, gymnasium, agora, and stoa. Of these, great Alexandria in Egypt was to become a major East-West cultural and commercial meeting-ground (and Antioch in Syria, founded soon after in its image by one of his successors, was to be another). In addition, Alexander refurbished many existing cities to conform to the Greek model. He had brought in Greek and Macedonian traders no less than soldiers to intermingle and intermarry with the Eastern peoples, thus setting in motion a vast new migration in which eventually hundreds of thousands of men from the Hellenic mainland settled in the Middle East, Egypt, and Asia Minor, many of them repeopling the Ionian cities that other Greeks had once settled. Yet while he took with him the forms of Greek culture wherever he went, he had implanted little of its traditional substance: this was the tragedy of the conqueror who, for all of Aristotle's tutelage, had himself learned only its veneer, and (as his readiness to change himself into an oriental despot showed) had never penetrated its heart.

If the spirit of old Athenian Greece eluded him, it was even more remote to his chief Macedonian generals, who upon his death at once proceeded to carve up his empire among themselves, each making himself an absolute ruler of a share, some adopting Eastern god-king notions, setting up or attempting to set up dynasties, and then proceeding to attack his neighbor for a greater share, secure in the knowledge that no outside power remained to interpose itself in this in-fighting. This was an utter travesty of the unity Alexander had set out to achieve; the Macedonian had won, only to have his empire sundered and orientalized—the East revenging itself upon an overambitious West.

Three quarreling dynasties emerged: first, that of Alexander's boyhood friend and favorite general Ptolemy, who took over Egypt and passed it on to a line of heirs all also named Ptolemy (numbered II to XV) and most of them incompetent and decadent; second, that of Seleucus, another favorite, who acquired Mesopotamia, Persia, and eventually Syria and most of Asia Minor —all told, a dominion of some 1,500,000 square miles—in which Semitic, Persian, and Anatolian tongues and cultures persisted just under the Hellenized surface; third, that of still another general, Antigonus, who seized the Macedonian throne and whose successors exerted varying degrees of control over the old city-states of mainland Greece and the Aegean islands. Other kingdoms arose in this welter of imperial order and disorder, notably vigorous Pergamum in Asia Minor, which was to play a vital part in the eventual dissolution of Macedonian rule.

In commerce, the new lines opened to the East produced rich rewards. Goods from China and India now arrived fairly safely over the Afghan passes, skirted the Caspian shore to reach Mesopotamia, and so moved on to the coastal cities of the Mediterranean. A sea route brought spices, ivory, and gold from India to Arabian ports, from which they were hauled overland.

Most significant of all was the blaze of scientific study and discovery that was stimulated by Greek contact with the work of early astronomers and mathematicians of Babylon and Egypt

A winged figure of Victory, carved in the second century and discovered on the Aegean island of Samothrace, was designed to appear as if it stood on the prow of a ship heading into a strong wind.
LOUVRE

351

(a reverse effect of the Hellenizing process). Indeed, scientific achievement is the culminating splendor of Hellenistic civilization—a sprawling, self-doubting, morally and aesthetically declining but technologically brilliant culture that has been likened to our own. Sweeping theorems, now supported by close physical observations, engaged the minds of many of the ancient world's shrewdest investigators. Aristarchus of Samos in the third century set forth a theory that the earth moved orbitally around the sun, and calculated the length of the solar year. Hipparchus of Nicaea in Bithynia in the next century opposed this, setting forth a geocentric theory which was long to persist; he also—apparently drawing upon Babylonian records—figured out the precession of the equinoxes, made the first known chart of the heavens, and greatly improved instruments for making astronomical observations. Under Ptolemy I, Euclid opened in Alexandria a school at which he taught his theorems of plane and solid geometry that were to remain for two thousand years the bible of the subject. Archimedes of Syracuse studied in third-century Alexandria too, and became the author of many studies, including those on specific gravity, conic sections, and the principle of the lever, that were to make him, next to Pythagoras, the greatest scientist of antiquity.

Alexandria itself, a city laid out on a grid plan, with straight and transverse streets and squares to accommodate a population of perhaps nearly a half million Egyptians, Macedonians, Greeks, Jews, Syrians, Arabs, Persians, became the center of all this energy. It boasted the celebrated library and museum, a zoological garden, parks, gymnasium, stadium, hippodrome, beach resorts, the great harbor and lighthouse, and was the scene of diverse activities— scientists convening and teaching; doctors of medicine like Erasistratus and Herophilus pursuing studies of physiology and anatomy; scholars galore collecting and collating old papyri; merchants promoting new ventures and watching their ships come in. Wealth, leisure, culture, self-indulgence, reached a point there that caused the writer Herodas to call it "the house of Aphrodite," in which everything was to be found, from playgrounds and philosophers to fine wines and beautiful women.

Yet, amid all this, there could be no doubt that the beliefs and virtues that had once been essential to Greece were fast drying up. Men who thought they had outgrown Olympian religion and the worship of traditional city-gods were now being drawn to rationalism or reverting to old cults and to the occult; sometimes all these impulses combined. Astrology and alchemy— much of them of Eastern origin—and beliefs in chance and magic seized many a mind, undoing much that logical and scientific

This small and detailed bronze figure of an emaciated man is a Roman copy of a Hellenistic work; it was made during a period when artists no longer idealized their subjects but depicted them in a naturalistic or even grotesque manner.
DUMBARTON OAKS, WASHINGTON, D.C.

interpretations of the physical world had tried to bring about.

In the heterogeneous population of the Hellenistic world there was a prevalence of demons such as there had not been since pre-Homeric times. The universalism of Alexander had achieved an unexpected result—a kind of fatalism or quietism in which each subject, no longer an effective member of his own polis, now sought personal means of salvation. Some found it through asceticism, others simply through withdrawal and passivity. The Stoic philosophy, with its emphasis both on the brotherhood of man and on accepting one's station in the scheme of things and not trying to alter it, dominated and symbolized these years, with their pessimism and petrification. Moreover, Greek divinities often became blended with oriental ones. Thus on Delos, so long sacred to Apollo, there flourished the cult of Serapis, who combined some of the attributes of Zeus and other Olympians with those of Osiris, who in Egyptian belief was the representative of the departed Pharaoh and ruler of the dead. Isis, consort of Osiris, became identified in many Greek minds with Aphrodite and, thus assimilated, one of the great deities of the Mediterranean world. The cult of Mithras, a sun god of Indo-Iranian origin and connected with the religion of the Persian Zoroaster, in turn mingled with that of Apollo. Meanwhile Zeus became Zeus Ammon in Egypt and Zeus Hypsistos in Asia Minor. This tendency toward worship of a central god above all other gods increasingly exercised the imagination of the ancient world. The Hebrews had borne witness to Yahweh from the beginning; the new trend prepared the way for reception of a divine spirit such as man had not known before.

Politically, the Greeks were now near the end. The rising empire of Rome, blooded amid its duel with African Carthage, in which Greek Sicily had played an equivocal part, was not of a mind to suffer Greek opposition as its eyes turned from the western Mediterranean to the eastern. Macedonia, fearful of the Roman threat, had allied itself with Carthage—a poor decision, as it turned out, since after their victory over Hannibal the Roman legions descended upon Greece, in part in response to an appeal by Pergamum and Rhodes, which were being threatened by Macedonian ambitions. At first most Greeks received the Romans as liberators, especially upon receiving assurances from them that Greek independence would be restored. Later, particularly in 146 when the Roman general Mummius destroyed Corinth, they began to hate the Roman "liberators" as they had once hated the Macedonians. In 86 B.C., after feeble opposition, Athens submitted to Roman occupation and all was over. Or so it seemed.

A section of an Alexandrian treatise on astronomy depicts the planets' movements. Astronomy was but one of the sciences in which the Alexandrians excelled; they were famous as geographers, mathematicians, and physicians as well.
LOUVRE

AGORA MUSEUM, ATHENS; ROLOFF BENY

THE
AUTUMNAL
AGE

When Alexander the Great marched his army across the Hellespont and into the heart of Asia, he inaugurated an era that prided itself on its universal outlook. Philosophers had proclaimed that "all men are created alike by nature in all respects, both Greek and barbarian." As if to illustrate this, Alexander gave dowries to 10,000 of his Macedonian troops who intermarried with Persian women. Scores of Greek cities were founded throughout the vast domain that he had conquered; they were filled with Greek settlers and natives who eagerly adopted Greek ideals and ways of living. The Hellenic world moved eastward; in the centuries after Alexander's death its centers were Rhodes, Pergamum in Asia Minor, Alexandria in Egypt, and Antioch in Syria. Greece itself became a backwater, politically almost powerless, but still a center of art, as can be seen by the magnificent stoa, shown restored at left, that a Pergamene king donated to the Agora at Athens. In the foreground a stele, dating from 336 B.C., shows Democracy crowning a representation of Athens; the inscription is a law against tyrants which had been promulgated to forestall the possibility of revolt in favor of Macedonian control. The Greek city-states struggled fiercely to maintain their independence and traditions; but too often, despite their determined efforts, they were forced to be satisfied with only the memory of their former glories.

MUSEO NAZIONALE, NAPLES; ALINARI

356

A mosaic of the battle of Issus, at which Alexander broke Persian power in 333, shows the young conqueror at far left, mounted on his steed. The Persian king Darius, in his royal chariot, dominates the right half of the scene. The mosaic, which dates from the first century A.D., is a Roman copy of a Greek original.

STAATLICHE MUSEEN, BERLIN; HIRMER

GRANDEUR AT PERGAMUM

One of the successor states that arose on the ruins of Alexander's empire was centered at Pergamum, in western Asia Minor, not far from the site of ancient Troy. There, on a fortified hill, rose a new Greek city, the "Athens of Asia," wealthy and splendidly adorned, its gymnasium probably the largest in the Greek world. Within the city stood an altar dedicated to Zeus; its enormous proportions were typical of the Hellenistic tendency toward excess. Its frieze, large and swift flowing, depicted a battle of gods and Giants, symbolizing the image the Hellenistic age liked to present of itself—a time in which civilization triumphed over barbarism. Pergamum's bountiful rulers brought poets, scholars, and artists to their city and collected a large library. The liberality for which they were famous reached beyond their own realm to Athens, where they endowed schools and adorned the city with new buildings.

One of the reconstructed wings of the great altar of Zeus at Pergamum is shown at top. The altar's frieze extends almost 400 feet. Two of its mythological figures are shown here: at near right is Hecate, the goddess of magic; beyond her stands Nyx, a goddess of the night.

BOTH: STAATLICHE MUSEEN, BERLIN; F. L. KENETT

LOUVRE; GIRAUDON

THE HELLENISTIC SPIRIT

In the Hellenistic age Greek art flourished from Italy to India. Artists in great numbers left impoverished old city-states to settle and work in the powerful Greek kingdoms of the East. There, monarchs commissioned magnificent palaces and grandiose monuments to celebrate their rule; and ambitious Greek businessmen, who had made fortunes in the East and now wished to appear cultivated, spent their wealth ostentatiously on sculptures and paintings to adorn their lavish homes. Thus sovereigns and newly rich private citizens replaced the democratic communities as art patrons. Soon a homogeneous style of art came to predominate over a vast area. At the beginning of the Hellenistic period much of the sculpture that was being made was still inspired by masterpieces of the classical age, particularly by the idealized works of Lysippus and Praxiteles; yet by the second century, artists everywhere freely depicted a great range of subjects in a realistic manner, devoting particular attention to the portrayal of emotion. It was this Hellenistic art—vivid and technically refined—that the Romans copied, and that ultimately influenced European art so strongly.

Works by Praxiteles probably inspired the sculptor of the statue of Aphrodite at left, known as the Venus de Milo. *The* Three Graces *(opposite), a copy of a Hellenistic work, was found at Cyrene, in Libya.*

MUSEUM, CYRENE; GEORGE HOLTON, PHOTO RESEARCHERS

361

ISTANBUL ARKEOLOJI MUZELERI; ROLOFF BENY

WALTER C. BAKER COLLECTION

THE GREEK DIASPORA

To remain Greek, although they lived in the heart of Syria or Persia, Hellenistic colonists established gymnasiums in all of their settlements and patterned their cities, in every way they could, after the cities of their homeland. In order to assimilate the culture of their Greek conquerors, the natives of the countries in which they lived often abandoned their own traditions. Jewish youths neglected their religious obligations in order to compete in the gymnasium; their elders, to feel equal with the Greeks or impress their children with native Hebrew traditions, identified Moses with the mythological Musaeus, who had taught the arts of civilization to Orpheus. The Old Testament was translated into Greek, which had become the common language of the entire East. Throughout the East the upper classes transacted affairs in Greek, adopted Greek names, and identified the gods Baal and Ammon-Re with Zeus. They strove to associate themselves in every way with the civilization that was conquering the world. This unification of the East—the civilization into which Christianity was born—was to prepare society for the adoption of the revolutionary concept of one god.

A youth from Asia Minor, opposite, wears a cloak, donned after exercise in the gymnasium. The veiled dancer at right is probably from the great Hellenistic city of Alexandria.

363

HASSIA

BOTH: HARISSIADIS

ENDURING ATHENS

During the years when Hellenic culture spread in the wake of Alexander's conquests, Athens continued to be the intellectual capital of the Greek world. Alexandria became a center of scientific knowledge, and with its great library and museum, or "home of the Muses," a formidable rival to Athens; distant Susa in Persia and Antioch in Syria became renowned for the study of philosophy and rhetoric, respectively. Yet Athens remained supreme. From the late third century, when the Macedonians were expelled, until the time that the Romans conquered Greece, almost a century and a half later, the city enjoyed self-government, not because it was able to defend itself, but because it was so highly respected that other powers were reluctant to violate it. The Academy of Plato and his followers, Aristotle's Lyceum, the schools of rhetoric and of the Sophists attracted students from all over the Hellenistic world to listen to lectures and to attend the seminars for which the city was famous.

The temple of Olympian Zeus at Athens (opposite) was, according to the Roman historian Livy, "the only one in the world which has been conceived on a plan proportionate to the majesty of the god." The colossal structure was first begun in the sixth century; work was resumed in Hellenistic times, but the building was not completed until centuries after. Another of the great later-day monuments of Athens was the Theatre of Dionysus. Both the finely carved seat at right and figure of Silenus above come from the theatre.

BOTH: HARISSIADIS

365

THE ISLAND SHRINE

Perhaps as early as the second millennium B.C. the Aegean island of Delos had become a cult center. By the fifth century many sanctuaries, most of them dedicated to Apollo, had risen there. Delos became so important a shrine that it grew wealthy from the votive offerings of pilgrims. A league controlled by Athens protected and managed it, but in the power struggle following Alexander's death the islanders gained independence. They welcomed Egyptians and Persians, Romans and Greeks who, bearing gifts, came to worship the Greek gods during the Hellenistic age, and they welcomed foreign cults as eagerly. Soon it was no longer worship alone that brought visitors. Wharves and warehouses were built, and by the second century Delos, which had long been an entrepôt, had become a primary commercial center. It had the greatest slave market in the Greek world; money had become more important than religion to the old shrine. However, Delos was not destined to thrive much longer—in the first century B.C. trade routes shifted toward Rome, the island was laid waste by pirates, and eventually it was abandoned.

The religious and commercial center of Delos is one of the best preserved ancient sites; a view of it is shown above. At left is the courtyard of a luxurious Delian home, one of many built there by wealthy traders in the Hellenistic age. Often the walls and floors of such houses were decorated with brilliant mosaics, one of which is shown opposite; it depicts the god Dionysus riding on a leopard.

HANNIBAL

HARISSIADIS

366

10

THE

LASTING

LIGHT

The teachings of Plato are not alien to those of Christ.

—Justin Martyr

We are all Greeks.

—Percy Bysshe Shelley

In the year one of the Christian era, once-great Athens was only a run-down provincial seat in the wake of Roman advance, politically silent ever since Sulla's seizure of it in 86 B.C. Its academies were stultified. The great library which Aristotle had gathered and which the minor philosopher Apellicon had preserved, along with scrolls of Aristotle's own writings, had been carried off to Rome. So had innumerable treasures of art. The warehouses of the Piraeus, which once received goods from all the eastern Mediterranean and beyond, had become a transshipment center for old bronze and marble works to adorn the villas of wealthy Romans. The march of empire had virtually passed the city by. As Romans reached out, like Alexander before them, to grasp Asia Minor, Egypt, and the vast eastern interior beyond, apathetic Athens was little more than a well-looted mausoleum.

Yet the final decay of Athens as well as of its Hellenic sister states did not mean the extinction of Greek influence. On the contrary: even while most of them lay stunned and prostrate, a remarkable emanation from them continued—one might say, like that of some departed hero of an ancient tale who exerted extraordinary powers from the grave. In their prime of life the Greeks had possessed the quality of making their presence and ways felt vividly wherever they went, from the philosophers of Ionia, who puzzled over the nature of the universe, to the traders and settlers who took the culture of the vine and the olive to southern France and primitive Spain. In their later years the Greeks brought their influence to bear in large part upon those who had subjugated them, and through them, upon other cultures far and wide.

Before all-conquering Alexander struck deep into Asia, no artist of India had presumed to represent the image of the sublime Buddha. But Alexander's men carried images of Greek gods with them, and some centuries after their arrival the first sculptured figures of Buddha appeared in Gandhara, a region at the eastern foot of the Hindu Kush range—a type of figure, moreover, that appears to be modeled on the lineaments of Apollo and wears flowing Greek raiment (though with a third "eye" of Eastern insight implanted in the brow). Thus, Greek influence at its periphery gave shape to the image of the teacher of the East and thereby left a deep impress upon Buddhist religion.

Meanwhile, under Alexander's successor kings in the Near East a fusion took place in art. Ancient, hieratic Egypt had made the power of its monumental art strongly felt throughout archaic Greece; now the expressive forms of Greek art in its late flowering mingled with traditional Eastern ones; this in turn was to serve in forming the art of Byzantium. Traces of Greek influence are also to be found in the arts of the Egyptian Copts and the remote Ethiopians (see illustration, page 373). It was great Alexandria itself, however, with its intermingling of Greek and Roman, of Egyptian and Jew, that became the leading transmission center of Greek impulses. There the vast library assembled in the centuries after the death of the city's founder provided what one might term the first international meeting ground for scholars. (Before the despoliations it underwent at the hands of the emperors Aurelian and Diocletian in the third century A.D. and of Theodosius I in the fourth, it may have contained a half million rolls of parchment or papyrus.) For more than half a millennium, virtually every scientist of renown either studied or taught there, as did innumerable annotators and interpreters of ancient literary texts.

In the interplay of West and East, no movement was more profound than that which brought together the world of Greek philosophy—especially Plato's—and the body of Hebraic devotional tradition. The outcome was the Christian revolution. Though Christianity sprang from provincial Judea and claimed continuity from Judaism, surely it would not have grown into the sovereign faith it was soon to become throughout the Mediterranean world had it not included a powerful admixture of Greek ideas. The Jewish philosopher Philo of Alexandria, born some two decades before Christ, and a close student of the Pythagoreans, Platonists, and Stoics, was to be a major transmitter of Plato, and the mysticism derived from his thought, to the early Church. Saint John and Saint Paul were particularly influenced by Platonic thinking; and later, Saint Augustine was to remark that "only a few words and phrases" need be altered to bring Platonism into full accord with Christianity. Jesus himself taught in Aramaic, but it has been remarked by so distinguished an authority as the late Dean Inge that "the early Church spoke in Greek and thought in Greek."

Before this confluence, though, another had occurred that demonstrated surviving Greek influence in different fashion. This was the spell that moribund Hellas cast upon its master, all-conquering Rome. From the outset of their contacts with Greece, the Romans, uncertain as to their own origins, had felt a deep impulse to relate themselves and their background to this people across the sea, so senior to them in history, culture, and accomplishment. The Greeks in their time had pursued a hunt for high lineage too, producing their tales of godly ancestors and primordial heroes. Among the ambitious, status-seeking Romans the urge to establish a worthy genealogy was particularly strong.

Tradition had it that Rome had been founded by the brothers Romulus and Remus, reared by a simple herdsman but themselves

LOUVRE; PIERRE BOULOT, COURTESY *Life*

In the seventeenth century, Poussin painted classical subjects with classical grace. Here a detail symbolic of Greek influence on the ages shows Apollo and the Muse of lyric poetry.

The establishment of a Hellenistic kingdom in northern India after Alexander's conquest had a profound effect on Indian art. The figure of a bodhisattva, shown above, was strongly influenced by the example of classical Greek sculpture.

ROYAL ONTARIO MUSEUM

descended from a king. Late in the third century B.C. a tale arose linking Roman origins to Troy through the person of Aeneas of the Trojan royal house, who was represented as having become the ancestor, after his city's fall, of Rome's founder-brothers. Such a legend showed, for one thing, the Romans' increasing absorption with Greece and its literature. Very many educated Romans in the second century read Greek (and as Rome achieved supremacy in the eastern Mediterranean, knowledge of Greek became increasingly important as a means of communication between the masters and their Hellenized subjects). The playwrights Terence and Plautus adapted and imitated Menander and other writers of Greek New Comedy. Above all, the Romans read Homer. This we know from the innumerable uses to which Homer was put in Rome for purposes of citation and show of learning. No one read him more closely than a man who was born in northern Italy, near what is Mantua, and named Publius Vergilius Maro, the arch-poet of the Romans known to history as Vergil. Highly schooled, a friend of the poet Horace and the patron Maecenas, he set out in his later years to compose a vast epic poem that would ennoble the Roman presence. In the *Aeneid* he created the Roman *Odyssey* —and more.

To his patriotic and imaginative mind, the old story centering on Romulus and Remus was meager. The thought of an ancient connection with the Trojans, equal in valor to their Greek attackers, was prouder; and he found a way of making the Trojan-Roman lineage seem to outshine even that of the Greeks. A clue appeared in a passage in the *Iliad* about a child of Zeus named Dardanus, who had fathered the line of kings of Troy. Where had Dardanus come from? Vergil has it that he came from Italy, and had led his people to Troy, but with the thought of later returning to their homeland. Upon this idea Vergil, taking the side of what he termed "Priam's guiltless race," against Agamemnon's Greeks, constructs an elaborate tale. Aeneas, who is a son of Anchises (a descendant of Dardanus) and Venus (the Greek Aphrodite), is the one Trojan leader to survive the holocaust and is divinely appointed to return his folk to their Italian patrimony, where a great fate awaits them. After many voyagings and his affair with the Carthaginian queen Dido, Aeneas does find his way to Italy, there to become the progenitor of the Roman race.

There are vivid parallels between Vergil's epic and Homer's. Aeneas, like Odysseus, has fabulous adventures, including a descent into the underworld; Romans and Rutulians fight very much as Homer's Achaeans and Trojans did in the *Iliad*; gods intervene; and the long speeches of heroes and the tumultuous similes beloved by Homer are adopted almost as a canonical device. Yet while paying literary respect to Homer and thus to the Greeks, Vergil's tone and message depart from that of his great predecessor. Homer celebrated individual valor and *arete*; Vergil, although honoring *pietas*, or traditional Roman civic virtue, produces what is essentially a political poem, prophesying the power of the Roman state. The Romans, Jupiter promises at the very outset of the *Aeneid*, will enjoy a dominion without limits; they will be *rerum dominos*—"rulers of the world":

> . . . *An age shall come, as the years glide by,*
> *When the children of Troy shall enslave the children of*
>   *Agamemnon,*
> *Of Diomed and Achilles, and rule in conquered Argos.*
> *From the fair seed of Troy there shall be born a Caesar—*
> *Julius, his name derived from the great Iulus—whose empire*
> *Shall reach to the ocean's limits, whose fame shall end in*
>   *the stars.*

Vergil's work is only one example of the ambivalent attitude of Romans toward Greeks. The ever-loquacious historian Livy is intent on proving to his readers in instance after instance that the Romans are the world's elect. Yet the popular biographer Plutarch —a Greek writing for a Roman audience—makes a veritable cult of the Greeks in his *Lives*, where he pairs off Greek and Roman statesmen (Demosthenes with Cicero, Pericles with Fabius) in such a way as to make the point that leading Greeks had qualities every Roman should respect.

The homage Romans paid to Greece was shown not only by their thefts of works of art but by their continuing urge to copy Greek styles. Thus the Roman Forum was built in the Corinthian and Ionic architectural orders; while in the first centuries after Christ the remote Hellenized city of Aphrodisias in Caria in Asia Minor became by reason of its excellent marble and skilled craftsmen a veritable factory for the making of reproductions of classical Greek sculpture for export via Ephesus or Miletus on a thousand-mile trip to Rome's port of Ostia. The Romans conquered; but as their most stylish poet, Horace, himself remarked, "Captive Greece made captive her rude conqueror."

Vergil, for all his pride in Rome, did sense the glimmer of some era of finer feelings ahead; thus he dreamed in his celebrated fourth *Eclogue* of a time when "Our iron breed shall come to an end, and a golden race rise throughout the world." But in general the Romans—those ambitious climbers or *novi homines* of the ancient world—with their shrewd, materialistic approach, were not ready

A statue of Augustus, first of the Roman emperors, shows him with the physique of a Greek athlete; but the Hellenic ideal has been modified by the sculptor in order to convey the overwhelming power of the imperial presence.
VATICAN MUSEUM; ANDERSON

In later centuries the Persians, whose empire Alexander the Great had destroyed, looked on him as the greatest of rulers, and commemorated his feats in numerous works of art. This fifteenth-century Persian manuscript shows Alexander aboard a ship.

COURTESY OF THE FOGG ART MUSEUM

for such intimations. They looked upon the Greeks as a race of engaging artists and philosophers, patronized them, used them, but in their own stirrings of thought moved little beyond them. They adopted and adapted from Greek city-states many civil statutes, and, more importantly, from Greek society as a whole the idea of law as an accumulated body of ancestral precept, divine in origin, that should be binding upon all; upon this they built their own great structure of law. But they never seemed to penetrate to the core of Greek thought at its most advanced.

Early in their history they identified the Olympian gods with their own pantheon, at a time when many intelligent Greeks were looking elsewhere for truth. They were taken up with the powers of Mars and the charms of Venus when Greek thinkers were increasingly absorbed with the idea of *logos*, meaning the presence of an immanent reason governing the entire world, visible and invisible. Plato himself, in making his sharp distinction between the physical or sensory world and the ideal world, had taught that *nous*, or abstract mind, dominated the latter, while it was not concerned with the former. But with the Stoics, who came after him, the idea of *logos* as an everyday ethical principle came to the fore; and in Philo, the Hellenized Jew of Alexandria, *logos* is the divine designer who seeks to realize in the physical world the ideas long in his mind. Here Hebraic ideas of an all-knowing Creator intermix with Stoic and Platonic metaphysics; and soon the combination came to Rome. With it came ideas of abstinence, purification, mystical revelation, redemption—all derived from the mystery religions so prevalent in the Hellenistic world.

While these ideas remained distant or incomprehensible to many Romans, Plutarch in a flash of insight saw the approaching marriage of beliefs when he wrote, "There are not different gods in different nations, barbarians and Greeks, southerners and northerners. Just as the sun and moon and sky and earth and sea are common to all though named differently by different people, so the one Reason ordering this world, the one Providence governing it . . . have different honors and titles among different peoples according to their customs." Newer thoughts were to come, as when Saint John, at the outset of his Gospel, wrote, "In the beginning was the Word [in the Greek text, ὁ λόγος —*logos*], and the Word was with God, and the Word was God." And it was Paul, son of a Roman citizen in Tarsus, of Jewish descent and raised in the strict Hebraic faith in an area where Hellenic and Eastern influences particularly met, who set forth in his Epistles such transcendental phrases, Platonic in character, as "Now we see through a glass, darkly" and "The things which are seen are temporal; but the things which are not seen are eternal." Paul, converted to Christianity in about A.D. 35 after his early years of persecuting it, preached such doctrine to the early Christian believers in Antioch, to the Galatians, to the Corinthians, to the Athenians in their own Agora, and carried the burden and passion of his message of Christ the King to Rome as well—where he was imprisoned in A.D. 60, later to die a martyr's death. Wherever he went, Paul bore not only the witness of Jesus but also the heritage of Plato.

While Christianity invaded Rome's wavering mind with its Platonic mysticism and Hebraic rigor, restive Teutons, Goths, and tribesmen of eastern origin soon turned against Rome itself with sheer force. They sensed the weakness of an overextended civil structure ridden with rivalry and strife. By the third century A.D. the centralized machinery of heterogeneous Rome had become so creaky that the emperor Diocletian divided his vast state into two parts, East and West, and the center of power moved east. In the fourth century Constantine, a man of Balkan birth and the first emperor to give official sanction to Christianity, abandoned Rome, in his effort to bring the pieces of his empire together, and established his own seat at Byzantium. There, in what had hitherto been hardly more than a small port town, he built himself the glittering capital he called Constantinople, rifling art treasures from East and West to do so.

The eastern half of the Roman Empire came increasingly under the influence of Greek culture. Though Latin remained the official tongue of Constantinople through its age of splendor under Justinian in the sixth century, it was superseded by Greek in the seventh. And there Hellenic, Roman, and Eastern canons of art were combined to form that rigid and hieratic style known—to some with disdain, to others with admiration—as Byzantine.

Yet Greek influence did not remain confined to encrusted Byzantium, once Rome had been sacked by Alaric and other barbarian invaders. Though by now the Hellenic stream had been far diverted from its origins, it went on flowing into many lands, even through darkest times and often by roundabout ways. Aristotle, whose works had long been known in Rome, was first translated in part into Latin by the Roman scholar Boethius in the fifth century and was to exert a commanding influence on Christian schoolmen in centuries to come. Greek was carried as far west as Ireland and was studied there until the eighth century. At that time in Byzantium a controversy over the representation and worship of images was stultifying art. Yet Greco-Byzantine models had already spread to Europe—witness the mosaics at Ravenna that were to help set a style for the early Middle Ages.

Tales of Alexander's exploits entered folklore in an area extending from Iceland to Malaya. Here a miniature painting from Ethiopia shows the king and his nobles flying to heaven on great birds.
OTTO JAGER COLLECTION

The astrolabe above, one of the oldest in existence, was made by Moorish craftsmen early in the eleventh century. The instrument, used to determine the position of the stars and planets, was developed from ancient Greek prototypes.

ROYAL SCOTTISH MUSEUM

A thirteenth-century Arabic commentary on Euclid includes a diagram of the Pythagorean theorem. It was through Arabs, who conquered much of the Hellenized world, that Greece's mathematical knowledge reached the West.

BRITISH MUSEUM

Meanwhile another stream of ancient Greek emanation passed to Europe through a quite different channel—the Arabs. Striking out from their ancient deserts to overrun Egypt, and inspired under the banners of Mohammed to sweep across all North Africa and into Spain as well, they preserved far more than they destroyed, and passed their finds on to the West. Thus the thirteen books of Euclid's *Elements* became one of their prized possessions, first recorded Arabic in the eighth century (a later manuscript is illustrated on this page). Similarly the vast studies of the second-century A.D. Alexandrian astronomer, mathematician, and geographer Ptolemy (unrelated to the line of Macedonian monarchs of the same name in Egypt) were translated and disseminated by Arab scholars. This extraordinary man, creator of a brilliant mathematical theory of planetary motion about the earth, represented the culmination of classical science, and it was in large part through Arab transmission and commentary that his work exerted such a profound influence upon Europe. Finally, in the seventeenth century, the astronomer Copernicus was able to prove his geocentric theory wrong. Even then, however, Copernicus left the mathematical basis of Ptolemy's thinking all but intact. And Euclid, saved during the Dark Ages by Moslems, was to remain the god of Western geometry until far into the nineteenth century.

But primary to the medieval world was the transmission of Aristotle, much of whose work was also passed through either Arab or Byzantine hands. What the early Boethius had translated into Latin were only fragments. The great bulk of Aristotle's writings entered Europe by means of Arab scholars who put the original into their own tongue and glossed it, at such advanced seats of their learning as Córdoba and Toledo. From Spain, chiefly in the twelfth century, knowledge of Aristotle spread northward—either across the Pyrenees or via Palermo, the half-Arab, half-Western capital of Sicily. At the same time his texts were also coming from Constantinople through Eastern Church scholars who had translated from Greek to Latin. Aristotle became the subject of intense study and controversy at European universities, which were fast becoming major collecting points of ancient learning and centers of new instruction. Some of his work was banned at Paris in 1210 as inconsistent with Christian doctrine. But the mighty power of his logic and knowledge led theologians—Thomas Aquinas in particular—to see in his work a great encyclopedia of ancient learning and to seek to reconcile his systematic wisdom with Christian revelation. As Plato's mysticism inspired the Church Fathers, Aristotle's rigor shaped Saint Thomas' *Summa Theologica*—the vast metaphysical treatise that directed the thought of those in the Middle Ages who could read Latin manuscripts.

Many, of course, could not read at all—certainly not Latin. After convulsions caused by the invasions of Visigoth and Ostrogoth, Hun and Vandal, Europe slowly became literate again and found itself with many vernacular tongues, and with numerous classical tales transmitted into them. Thus a French troubadour fable based on distant legends of the Trojan War, *Le Roman de Troie*, by Benoît de Sainte-Maure, became popular. In the thirteenth century another French tale of chivalry and romance, permeated with classical allusions, *Le Roman de la Rose*, came into being at the hands of Guillaume de Lorris and Jean de Meun; it grew to be probably the most widely read story in the late Middle Ages. This long-drawn-out yarn, in effect an *ars amatoria*, or commentary on elegant seduction, shows that its authors were familiar with Vergil, with Greek legends as retold by Ovid, and very likely with Byzantine influences that had transmitted a certain polish to Western courts. England's first major poet, Geoffrey Chaucer, at the outset of his career was to try his hand at translating part of *Le Roman de la Rose*; and so we find him retelling his version of the very ancient story of the beautiful youth Narcissus, who was desired by all the girls but who would not give himself to them:

> *Narcisus was a bachelere,*
> *That Love had caught in his daungere,*
> *And in his net gan him so streyne,*
> *And dide him so to wepe and pleyne,*
> *That nede him muste his lyf forgo,*
> *For a fair lady, hight Echo,*
> *Him loved over any creature . . .*

Chaucer himself, like Shakespeare after him, very likely had "small Latin and less Greek." Dante Alighieri, whose greatest work preceded the beginning of Chaucer's by half a century, is also thought to have had almost no knowledge of Greek. Yet he had so acquainted himself with classical lore as to find in it the inspiration for his *Divine Comedy*—that incomparable achievement which both revived the epic form and sought a reconciliation between Christian and ancient ideals. In the *Inferno*, the most admired part of the work, Dante makes an imaginary visit to an underworld of memorable spirits—very much as Homer's Odysseus and Vergil's Aeneas had made their great descent. Dante chooses Vergil as his guide to this realm because he sees in him a prophet of Christianity, warm in his humaneness and prized for his premonition of a better world to come. At the same time, references to Aristotle and Greek history and myth abound in the *Comedy*—evidence that literary and philosophical knowledge of

The Greek motif of the good shepherd, seen in the early bronze on page 33 and the Acropolis figure on page 212, was adapted by Christian artists for the representation of Christ. The example above comes from Corinth and dates from very early in the Byzantine period. Images of Christ were also frequently modeled after statues of the handsome, youthful god Apollo.

BYZANTINE MUSEUM, ATHENS; HASSIA

the Greeks was much alive in Western minds again. And, though cast in the vernacular, his nobility of speech harks far back:

Per me si va nelle città dolente;
per me si va nell' eterno dolore;
per me si va tra la perduta gente.

I am the way into the city of woe.
I am the way to a forsaken people,
I am the way into eternal sorrow.

Soon after Dante's time, when direct acquaintance with Greek and Roman models still remained rare, a veritable hunger to rediscover them arose. The Italian poet Petrarch recommended that new authors copy ancient ones and tried (though without much success) to master Greek. His young friend Boccaccio in 1360 arranged to have a Byzantine scholar, Leontius Pilatus, appointed professor of Greek at Florence, and together with him made the first complete translation of Homer into Latin prose. Subsequent generations saw an immense increase in the work of rediscovery, translation, and adaptation, stimulated in part by the westward emigration of Byzantine scholars as the threatening Turks drew near, and then by the invention of printing. Herodotus and Thucydides were put into Latin in the mid fifteenth century; the scholar Ficino, employed by the Medici family, began his full rendering of Plato into Latin in 1462, completing it twenty years later; by 1475 the Vatican Library had on its shelves nine copies of the *Iliad* and four of the *Odyssey*, and translations of these works into modern languages were made during the following century.

Erasmus of Rotterdam, the leader in northern Europe of what was taking shape as a classical revival, proposed that every student should make the effort of reading the whole body of ancient literature, taking notes as he went. But well before this—in 1423, in fact—the Italian scholar Vittorino da Feltre had opened in Mantua a school dedicated in great part to such pursuit, seeking to combine in his pupils a harmonious blend of thorough classical knowledge and a devotion to Christian virtues. For Vittorino, the medieval tradition of training youths primarily in jousting, hunting, and prayer was not enough: he sought to build strong bodies, but in consort with searching minds, very much as Plato himself had done. So the pupil at Vittorino's school, while being taught to wrestle, throw javelins, and climb mountains, was also made to begin his study of Latin and Greek at the age of six. As a result of such thinking as Vittorino's, Renaissance men emerged, vigorous, well schooled, bold in action and yet conscious of the past.

The Renaissance, though, did far more than exhume antiquity.

It is presumed that Albrecht Dürer's drawing of Apollo, so typical of the Renaissance's revived interest in portraying the nude, was copied from a model or sketch of the Apollo Belvedere, *a statue which Dürer himself had never seen.*

BRITISH MUSEUM

It returned to it (first to Rome, and then to the Greece that lay behind it) in search of ideals of thought and behavior that would impart fresh values in a day when the spiritual power of the Church, grown both rigid and decadent, had lost its hold on many minds. Classical subject matter, in art or tale, had long been used in innumerable borrowings, some far removed from the meaning of the originals. It remained for Renaissance man not only to dig out the treasures of antiquity directly, but to relish their beauties for their own sake and to apply to himself the ideals of human grace, valor, and independence that he felt they embodied.

No movement in the Renaissance better illustrates this than the school of Neoplatonic thinking that flowered particularly at the court of the Florentine Medici, the most princely patrons of art and letters since the days of Roman emperors and aristocrats. Neoplatonism, owing much of its impetus to such scholar-translators and philosophers as Ficino and Pico della Mirandola, combined the ideals of bodily perfection with those of the purity and freedom of the soul. The Neoplatonists developed the language of men like Vittorino, who had tried to achieve a unity of the classical and Christian spirits. The perfect body in itself was, as the Greeks had felt, the image or mirror of a lofty spirit. Yet life was or should be (and here we come to Platonism and Christianity mixed) an advance from service of the material body to emancipation of the mind. Art, dedicated to beauty, the Neoplatonists believed, could serve to advance man toward the spiritual realm by bridging the divide between what was physically present in everyday man and what was divine in him.

This ideal was complicated in practice by the increasing lure of the pagan world, the more it came to light. Ghiberti, Brunelleschi, Donatello, all delighted in rummaging about ancient ruins for relics they could use as models. Greco-Roman mythological figures were found in great numbers, to be adapted as noble allegories; the educated gentry of Florence and all the other Italian cities loved to identify themselves with classical forebears, in paint, marble, or poetry. In his *Primavera* (shown at right) Botticelli adapted a classical theme to Neoplatonic sensibility with ineffable delicacy and restraint. Michelangelo, though also strongly influenced by Neoplatonism, was one of the first to admire the violent, late Hellenistic Laocoön group (see page 392) after its discovery in 1506; and he celebrated in his statuary the noble form at its most virile, and in his sonnets the beauties of naked young men. The direct study, or rather restudy, of the nude may have begun early in the fifteenth century, related both to classical finds and the particular Florentine interest in anatomy. The peak was reached

Many of Botticelli's paintings, such as La Primavera, *from which this detail depicting the three Graces comes, are based on classical art or on Greek philosophical themes. He even attempted to re-create one of Apelles' lost classical paintings.*
UFFIZI; SCALA

<hr />

377

NATIONAL PORTRAIT GALLERY, LONDON

LOUVRE; ARCHIVES
PHOTOGRAPHIQUES

STADELSCHES KUNSTINSTITUT, FRANKFURT; BRUCKMANN-GIRAUDON

Three men who represent the renewed interest in Greece that marked the eighteenth and early nineteenth centuries are Lord Byron (top), who promoted the cause of Greek independence and died fighting for it; the composer Gluck (center), whose operas strove to re-create Greek tragedy, in which the music played a great but not exclusive role; and the poet Goethe (bottom), who turned away from romanticism to a reverence for Greek ideals of beauty.

by Michelangelo himself, the greatest of whose brooding, anatomically detailed, undraped figures recall not so much the Laocoön group as the sculptures on the Parthenon pediment.

Well before this, Greek plays were being acted in translation in Italy, to commence a gradual revival of the theatre arts. As Gilbert Highet remarks in *The Classical Tradition,* the very basis of Western drama derives from the Greeks and Romans: the recognition of the play as potentially a form of high art, its use of complex plot, its division into acts, and the physical structure of the theatre. Attempts to write afresh in dramatic form, leaning on classics for substance yet using the language of the day, may have begun with a pastoral play, half-spoken and half-sung, on the ancient Orpheus theme written by the young scholar Politian for the court of Mantua in 1471. Opera, introduced as a new art form just at the end of the sixteenth century by such experimenters as Peri and Caccini, was an effort to incorporate music into spoken drama as the Greeks had once done—though precisely what the role of music had been in Greek drama, no one was certain, save that it had been pervasive. Renaissance plays and masques had contained what we would call "incidental" music or interludes of songs (and of course Shakespeare's plays include a multitude of lyrics); the new thought was to combine words and music throughout. The first attempts, with declaimed solo speeches, or recitatives, accompanied by instruments, seem clumsy; but very soon, in his *Orfeo* of 1607 and his *Combattimento di Tancredi e Clorinda* of 1624, the masterly Claudio Monteverdi achieved a union of word and tone of amazingly heightened emotional power. From here the line passes through the courtly, baroque operas of France (again, frequently on classical subjects) and Handel's vigorous oratoriolike ones (chiefly on biblical themes) to its first culmination in the works of Gluck, a major revolutionary in the art and a remarkable embodiment of later eighteenth-century neoclassicism. He abandons the declamatory style; his actor-singers (in his *Orfeo ed Euridice,* reduced to three) sing long arias of sustained and pensive beauty; choruses of Furies and Sacred Spirits hover in the background or come forth with turbulent or statuesque sound.

Shakespeare, though six of his plays and longer poems are based on Greek subjects, was quite clearly far more influenced by the Romans—particularly the dramatist Seneca, the poet Ovid, the historian Livy, and the biographer Plutarch. As everyone knows, even his plays dealing with nonclassical subjects abound in ancient allusions and images, but these appear to have come to him through Roman transmission. As for the Greek tragedians' canon of unity of time, place, and action, it is rarely reflected in his far-moving and multitudinous scenes. Messengers, as in Greek drama, do bring reports of what has occurred away from the central scene, and there are tellings of what happened anterior to the action, but generally Shakespeare likes to pack the entire complex story on the stage itself—battles, duels, marches, countermarches, in many a month and place.

It is with John Milton that we come to a man far more directly influenced by the Greeks—by Homer, father of the epic, whom he tried to emulate in a vast poem that would outdo Dante's and Vergil's ("While it pursues / Things unattempted yet in prose or rhyme"), and also by Athenian tragedians. His *Samson Agonistes*, stark, extremely concentrated, is highly reminiscent of Sophocles or Euripides. *Paradise Lost* and *Paradise Regained*, on the other hand, may seem endless to the modern reader, but it is a Homeric kind of endlessness, absorbed with noble speeches, spirits, marvels, and rolling similes, such as this, following Mammon's speech in revolt against the Almighty:

> He scarce had finished, when such murmur filled
> The assembly as when hollow rocks retain
> The sound of blustering winds, which all night long
> Had roused the sea, now with hoarse cadence lull
> Seafaring men o'erwatched, whose barke by chance
> Or pinnace anchors in a craggy bay . . .

Yet Milton could also write in a gentler, elegiac mood, coupling the pastoral style made fashionable in the Renaissance with a great mass of mythology, as when in his *Lycidas*, of less than 200 lines, he calls upon nymphs, dryads, muses, and "Sisters of the Sacred well" to help him commemorate his lost young friend Edward King: "Look homeward, angel, now, and melt with ruth. . . ." Here he is close in spirit to Poussin, that other master of classical evocation, whose vast landscapes with their calm figures breathe a sense of melancholy over something loved and lost.

In the courtly French theatre of the day, classical subjects were revived with stately magnificence but also often with somber power—nowhere more stirring than in Racine's great *Phèdre* of 1667, retelling the tale of Theseus' bride Phaedra. Tragically she falls in love with Theseus' stepson; with dark fate approaching she prepares to kill herself, facing death in a noble speech whose Alexandrine cadences represent the height of classical French: *"Jusqu'au dernier soupir de malheurs poursuivie, / Je rends dans les tourments une pénible vie."*

Against such nobility, the eruption at Versailles of ceiling paintings by Le Brun of gods and muses allegorically celebrating the glories of the French Jupiter, Louis XIV, was gilded vulgarity. It

Like many of his contemporaries the nineteenth-century American sculptor Horatio Greenough felt that his countrymen would "learn of the Greeks to be Americans." One of his statues shows George Washington clad in a toga and seated in a pose reminiscent of the Olympian Zeus of Phidias.

SMITHSONIAN INSTITUTION

was not until the latter half of the eighteenth century that another, stronger classical revival occurred. Again, as during the Renaissance, minds first turned to thoughts of Rome, stimulated particularly by the remarkable excavations at Pompeii. Yet an obscure German scholar, Joachim Winckelmann, was instrumental in attracting fresh attention to Greek art when he became infatuated with the study of it and in 1755 wrote his eloquent *Thoughts on the Imitation of Greek Works*. This essay, coming at a time when many men were surfeited with baroque extravagance and rococo frivolity, emphasized the "noble simplicity and serene greatness" of Greek art and likened it to the highest Greek literature. Soon another German, the dramatist Gotthold Ephraim Lessing, wrote *Laokoon*, a treatise that was to have enormous influence; in this essay he took that famous sculpture group as a model of dignity and restraint and proposed that new art emulate it.

No one today (the cycle of taste having revolved again) would call the Laocoön group "restrained." But the high seriousness of Lessing's subject and the eloquence of his argument drew many an artist directly back to Greece. "I want to work in a pure Greek style," wrote the painter Jacques-Louis David, turning against his own rococo background to become in a few years, with his lofty themes and severe line, the leader of French neoclassicism, favored both by the revolutionaries and the court of Napoleon. Meanwhile, diverse political overtones enlarged the revival. Revolution and the impulse toward republicanism made many men look back to Athens as a state near to their ideal, and the Hellenes' own war for independence from the Turks in the 1820's reinforced this attachment to them as the symbol and embodiment of man's dauntless mind and free spirit.

When in his "Ode on a Grecian Urn" John Keats exclaimed "O Attic shape! Fair attitude!" what he may well have been gazing at was a Wedgwood adaptation of a Greco-Roman vase, not Attic at all. That hardly matters; he was voicing a belief, shared by other romantic poets, in the liberating power of Greek beauty. Their romanticism also led them back to Plato, with his vision of a world of true Being of which ours is only the reflection. Plato's spirit pervades Wordsworth's "Ode on Immortality"—the poet being haunted with the sense of having had childhood glimpses of that perfect world, now lost to his sight. Goethe too was under Platonic spell when in *Faust* he wrote of our life being but a "colored refraction" (*"Am farbigen Abglanz / haben wir das Leben"*)—a close parallel to Shelley's mystical lines: *"Life, like a dome of many-colored glass, / Stains the white radiance of Eternity."*

Romanticism pursued both the "natural" and the ideal; its

A design for the stage setting of Eugene O'Neill's play Mourning Becomes Electra *shows its American heroine, who was modeled upon Aeschylus' Electra, a girl obsessed with her father's fate. She stands before her New England mansion, a house built in the Greek Revival style, like so many others of the region. The play, which was written in 1931, is but one of the many modern dramas based on Greek themes. In this, the twentieth century has maintained a tradition that has survived since the time of the Romans, whose drama was usually based on Greek themes. For the Greeks not only originated the theatre but provided it with an inexhaustible source of material.*

MUSEUM OF THE CITY OF NEW YORK

enemy was artifice; perhaps that explains why it found its spiritual home both in the wild moors of England and in the ruins of Athens. How to reconcile the two? Goethe in his later years, concerned with the contrast between the "storm and stress" of Western man and the classical ideal of perfection, tried to resolve it symbolically in the second part of *Faust* by having his turbulent hero mate with the most beautiful woman of antiquity, Helen of Troy. This was romantic imagination at its extreme. Yet, in a longer view, it was only another instance of the effort Western man has been making for centuries, turning to the Greeks not only for an image of the ideal but also for deeper light upon man's own nature and the powers around him.

Thus Western man has been drawn repeatedly to the Oedipus legend, a favorite subject to Renaissance humanists who discussed it, to Corneille, Dryden, and Voltaire who built plays on it, and to Sigmund Freud, who found in its tale of parricide and incest a clue to profound unconscious drives—the son's unacknowledged urge to replace the father and possess the mother. Igor Stravinsky and André Gide have made their own terse, brutal settings of the tale for our time, preferring it to such idyllic themes as that of Orpheus, beloved by Gluck.

Nineteenth-century Americans, romantically attracted, gave new cities in their countryside such names as Troy, Athens, Ithaca, and erected gleaming Greek Revival mansions. The twentieth-century dramatist Eugene O'Neill, drawing on Greek substance rather than outward form, interpreted a New England ancestral story in terms reminiscent of the tragic house of Agamemnon. The French Jean Giraudoux wrote *Amphitryon 38*—its title meaning that it was the thirty-eighth attempt over the centuries to retell the ancient Greek tale of Alcmene's husband, cuckolded by Zeus. T. S. Eliot's polished verse play *The Cocktail Party* harks back in theme directly to Euripides' *Alcestis*. One of the most revolutionary of contemporary artists, Pablo Picasso, has gone back repeatedly to the Greeks for both subject and style.

We are always going back to them—each in our own way, every generation in its way—because we sense that their gifts were incomparable. Democracy goes back to them. The cultivation of the body, of sports, of Western good taste and manners goes back to them. The idea of free scientific inquiry and philosophic speculation derives from them. Our pursuit of shapeliness and grace in the arts—insofar as we pursue it—was theirs also. Above all, when we speak of the ideal of all-around excellence in man, we are thinking as Greeks did, though we do not use their word for it. We are thinking of *arete*.

COLLECTION OF ROLAND PENROSE. COURTESY MUSEUM OF MODERN ART

REFLECTION
AND REVIVAL

During the Dark Ages that followed the fall of Rome, monks preserved some knowledge of antiquity in the West by copying Latin manuscripts; but when they came across a phrase or passage in Greek, they often failed to write it down, for knowledge of the language had disappeared. Instead they indicated that they had skipped over a section written in Greek, and thus incomprehensible to them. Much of the Hellenic legacy was forgotten, and the little that was remembered was often greatly distorted. Yet Greece nevertheless continued to exert a profound influence on men, even when the recipients of that influence were unaware of it. The tales of Greece—in the original and then in translation—were related over and over again by almost every generation that followed the return of the warriors from Troy; and even today men find them compelling. Along with its myths, Greece left other legacies to the arts. Century after century following the Renaissance, artists imitated Greek painting, sculpture, and architecture, and copied the matter and the forms of Greek poetry. (At left, a mythological drawing by Picasso, *The End of a Monster*, shows a minotaur-like creature dying before a beautiful nymph.) But the most lasting legacy of Greece was to the mind of Western man, for the Greeks endowed it with the tradition of inquiry and intellectual clarity that was to distinguish European civilization.

MUSEO NAZIONALE, NAPLES; ALINARI

Roman houses were often adorned with scenes from Greek history and mythology. Above, a mural from Pompeii depicts the sacrifice of Iphigenia; below, a mosaic shows the scientist Archimedes, who had helped defend the Greek city of Syracuse against the Romans, being killed by an enemy soldier. At right, an illustration from the oldest surviving copy of the Iliad, a lavish Greek edition made in Roman times, shows Hector with his family.

STADELSCHES KUNSTINSTITUT, FRANKFURT

SCANSANI-BIBLIOTECA AMBROSIANA DI MILANO

ROMAN INHERITANCE

More than any other, the Roman civilization was enriched by the legacy of Greece. Romans spoke Greek as well as Latin, worshiped gods similar to those of Greece, and adorned their temples and houses with art looted from Greek cities or made in imitation of Greek works. When they wrote poetry, it followed Hellenic forms; when they built temples, the facades were derivative too. Youths completed their education by travel in Greece, which remained a center of learning and art.

HOUVET

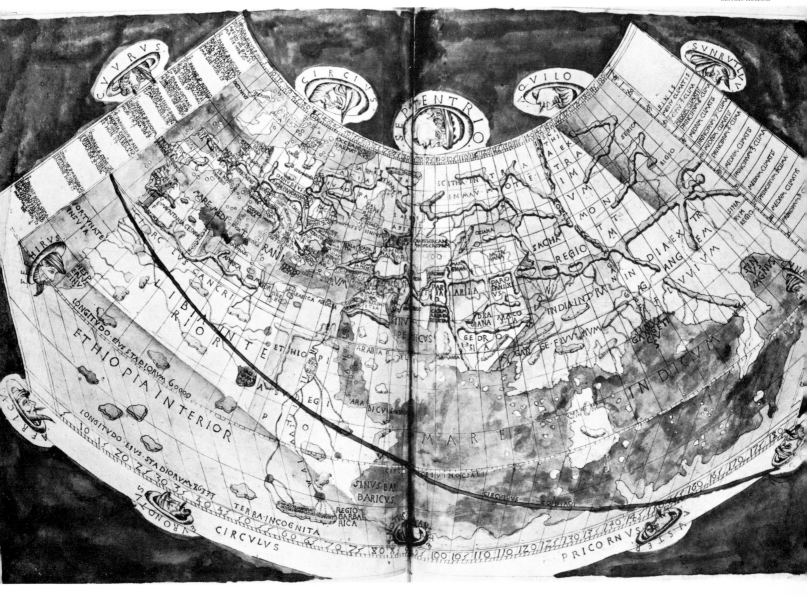
BRITISH MUSEUM

ARISTOTLE AND THE MIDDLE AGES

Stimulated in part by the discovery of long-lost writings of the ancient Greeks, a great period of philosophic inquiry commenced in twelfth-century Europe. Universities began to arise; scholars —notably Thomas Aquinas—attempted to organize all knowledge into a cohesive encyclopedic whole that would at the same time harmonize with Christianity; this structure was based on Aristotle's system of logic. Sections of Aristotle and some other classical texts were outlawed by the Church as incompatible with Christian teaching; but those classical works that survived were studied nevertheless and provided the basis for medieval man's sketchy knowledge of the physical world.

Aristotle is shown with scribes' tools (opposite) in a relief from Chartres Cathedral; his writings, more than any others, influenced the thought of the Middle Ages. Above, is a fifteenth-century copy of a world map by the second-century A.D. Greek, Ptolemy; medieval geography relied heavily on his descriptions of the world.

BIBLIOTHÈQUE NATIONALE

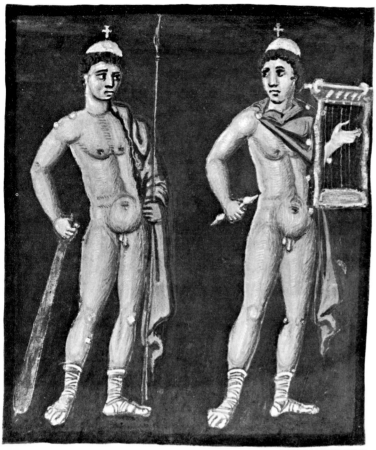

UNIVERSITY LIBRARY, LEYDEN

BIBLIOTHÈQUE NATIONALE; GIRAUDON

MEMORY OF MYTHS

"Greece had once the leadership in chivalry and learning; then chivalry passed to Rome together with the sum of learning, which now has come to France." So wrote the twelfth-century French poet, Chrétien de Troyes. Yet despite this tribute to Greece, medieval man had but a dim idea of what his own civilization had derived from the Greeks. In his mind, all of the figures of antiquity mingled: biblical patriarchs, Greek gods and mythological heroes, historical figures, and philosophers were undifferentiated, all of them worthies of a past that was distant and difficult to understand. The pagan gods, for example, were considered deified mortals, Apollo and Mercury being benevolent magicians so skillful that they had been made gods. Aside from Aristotle's philosophy, the one Greek legacy that the Middle Ages assimilated thoroughly was mythology, particularly the tale of Troy, which became a popular romance, favorable to the Trojan side.

The heavenly twins, Castor and Pollux, are seen above in an illustration from a Carolingian treatise. Both figures show the lingering influence of classical art, unlike the much later female nude at right, which nevertheless represents a classical theme—Ariadne abandoned on Naxos. Opposite, a medieval illumination depicting the entrance of the Trojan horse into Troy shows the city as a Gothic walled fortress and both its enemies and its defenders as medieval knights.

THE CLASSICAL REBIRTH

When Constantinople fell to the Turks in 1453, hundreds of Greek scholars, fleeing the infidel, sought refuge in Italy where they were welcomed as teachers of their ancient tongue. With their arrival, knowledge of Greek spread throughout Europe. In Venice, Aldus Manutius opened a Greek printing press; in Florence, crowds flocked to listen to lectures by Greek scholars, one of whom was reputed to be Plato's reincarnation. Philosophers, trying to re-create Plato's Academy, came together to study the philosopher's works, and each year on the anniversaries of his birth and death burned a candle before his portrait. Everywhere, interest revived in the Greek and Roman gods, and people named their children after classical heroes instead of saints. Roman antiquity received most of the attention during the Renaissance, but the Greeks were equally admired. The revival of knowledge of their language brought Homer, Plato, and the other Greek classics to the attention of Europe, which had seen them for centuries only in bad translation or naïve summaries, if it had seen them at all. It also inaugurated a critical study of the New Testament in its original tongue and, thus, indirectly led to the Reformation of the sixteenth century.

In the Vatican study of Pope Julius II, Raphael depicted the philosophers of The School of Athens; *Plato and Aristotle are at the center. Plato points upward as if to affirm his theory that only the ideal is real. Aristotle gestures to show that the concrete world is more important.*

RAPHAEL STANZE, VATICAN

VATICAN MUSEUM

USES OF A LEGACY

In 1506, when the Laocoön group was unearthed in a Roman vineyard, Michelangelo rushed to see the statue that had been described in antiquity as a "work of art to be preferred above all else in painting and sculpture." The statue was to have a profound effect on European art, for in it Michelangelo saw for the first time a classical precedent for the expressiveness and force he desired in his own work; and he and his successors utilized that precedent. In the centuries that followed the Renaissance, Greek art—and the Hellenistic and Roman works derived from it—were imitated again and again. Opera was born to re-create classical tragedy, with its musical accompaniment; poets wrote odes and lyrics filled with Greek motifs; painters and sculptors strove to attain the perfection of Greek art.

NATIONAL GALLERY OF ART, WASHINGTON, D.C., SAMUEL H. KRESS COLLECTION

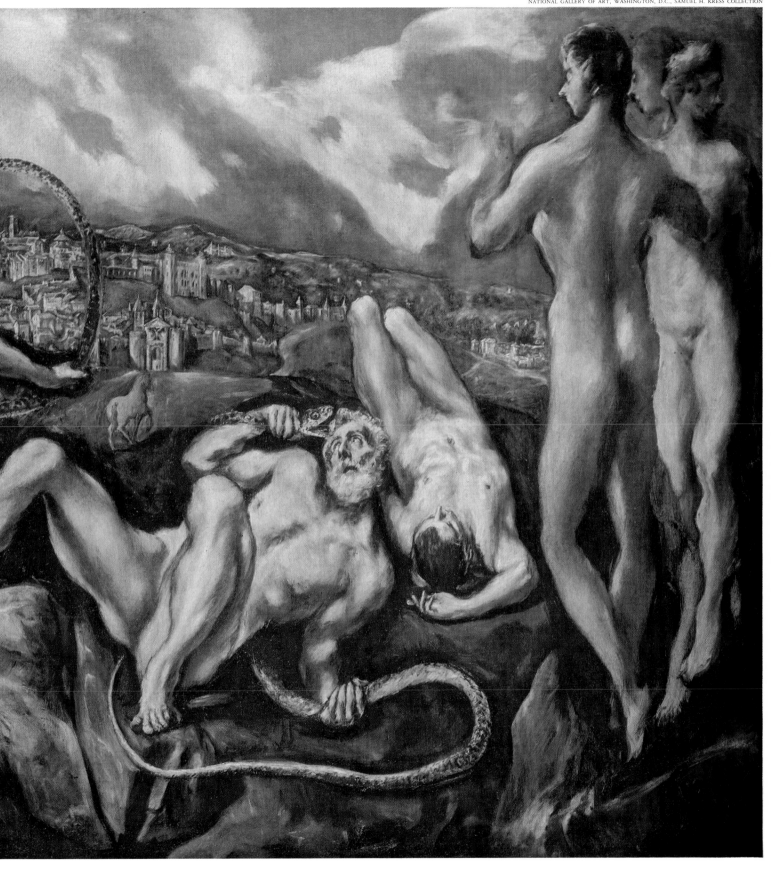

The famous and often copied Hellenistic statue of Laocoön and his sons, who were strangled by serpents after warning against the Trojan horse, is shown opposite. Above, is El Greco's seventeenth-century version of the episode, with the Spanish town of Toledo, its church steeples omitted, representing the pagan citadel of Troy.

A Wedgwood urn, below, modeled freely on a classical prototype, shows Apollo with his lyre and Melpomene, Muse of tragedy; it is one of many made in the eighteenth century to provide the public with examples of antique art. At right, the British antiquarian James Stuart is shown in Athens, drawing the Erechtheum. Stuart and a collaborator, Nicholas Revett, went to Athens at mid-century, recorded the city's sights, and published them to acquaint their contemporaries with Greek art.

NEW YORK PUBLIC LIBRARY

JOSIAH WEDGWOOD AND SONS LTD.

WORSHIPERS OF ANTIQUITY

When Isaac Newton discovered the laws of motion, he provided a scientific explanation for the structure of the universe; as a result of his work, eighteenth-century man saw not just a theological but a scientific order around him, much as the Greeks had done. Harmony and reason controlled the environment; and men—again like the Greeks—sought to reflect these qualities in their own lives. To achieve these in art, dramatists, sculptors, and poets followed antique models closely, sometimes so closely that originality was sacrificed. With its devotion to antiquity, the age encouraged the growth of archaeology. Travelers went to Greece in search of what they considered mankind's noblest works; and they brought back original statues and sketches of ruined temples that had lain forgotten for centuries. In America and France, where revolutions had been inspired, in part, by the example of ancient republics, their discoveries were especially welcome. In the new republics and elsewhere, buildings were constructed in the Greek style, furniture followed antique models, and women wore flowing gowns that imitated Grecian robes.

NEW YORK PUBLIC LIBRARY

Despite their use of Greek motifs, designers often failed to evoke the spirit of Greece. Above, a room in the Tuileries Palace, which was decorated by Napoleon's architects Percier and Fontaine, displays caryatids like those of the Erechtheum in a setting of imperial pomp.

In Philadelphia, a city whose very name is Greek, waterworks by the Schuylkill River were constructed in the classical style early in the nineteenth century; later an art museum was built above them and painted in the way the Greeks themselves had painted their temples. The Greek War of Independence helped inspire Americans to revive Greek architectural forms. Houses and churches, civic buildings and schools, were built like

classical temples in a style that could easily be copied by skilled carpenters. New American cities in the wilderness were given classical names—Ithaca, Syracuse, Athens, and Sparta; and in Michigan the town of Ypsilanti was named after the heroic brothers who were struggling against the Turks to restore to Greece the freedom it had once enjoyed, and of which the Americans considered themselves to be the New World heirs.

FRITZ GORO, COURTESY *Life*

PRADO, ANDERSON

NEW YORK PUBLIC LIBRARY, RARE BOOKS DIVISION

THE GREEKS IN MODERN EYES

Like other eras, our age has admired the Greeks for possessing just those qualities that it values most in itself. Modern men have esteemed the vigor and freedom of Greek life and stressed the irrationality of the Greeks more than their search for harmony. Again and again man's view of himself has been stated in terms borrowed from Greece. Sigmund Freud claimed that each man, in a sense, relived Oedipus' experience; other thinkers have used Prometheus' endless strivings or Sisyphus' endless torments as a symbol of human life. Many artists have freely adapted Greek styles; and some have followed Greek themes closely, like the novelist James Joyce, whose *Ulysses* is carefully plotted so that each episode echoes an incident in the *Odyssey*.

Artists, like writers, have demonstrated in modern times a preoccupation with Greek myths. Opposite is Goya's painting of Kronos devouring one of his children. Hans Erni's drawing of Oedipus and Jocasta is reproduced at right; above, is Matisse's illustration of the blinding of Polyphemus from an edition of Joyce's Ulysses.

NEW YORK PUBLIC LIBRARY,
SPENCER COLLECTION

A life-sized bronze by the contemporary English sculptor Michael Ayrton represents the mythical craftsman Daedalus, who was successful in his attempt to fly. For centuries Daedalus has served, like ancient Greece itself, as a symbol of man's unwearying aspiration toward a nobler life.
ARTIST'S COLLECTION

Recently the poet Robert Graves remarked sardonically that "translation is a polite lie, but nevertheless a lie." Still, translate we must, even at the risk of loss or distortion of the qualities of the original; and often poets have been the best conveyers from one tongue into another—none more controversial than Graves himself.

Dispute has long been embedded in the very subject of translation, and has become greater with the growth and change of modern languages and with our increasing distance from classical ones. Which serves the reader better when he approaches a work that is remote from him in speech and association: a literal rendering, or an imaginative effort at evoking its spirit? To ask the question is in a sense to beg it. For what is meant by "literal" or "faithful" as against "free"? Every translator is a creature of his own time and writes in terms of its limits and conventions. Every trot is tedious; interpretive readings may soon seem contrived; all translations age.

The problem of letter versus spirit is particularly acute when we come to translation from ancient Greek —a language distant from ours because of its highly inflected structure. When editing his recent anthology, *The Portable Greek Reader,* the poet W. H. Auden remarked that "the better a translation is as English poetry, the less like Greek poetry it is." On the other hand the poet-translator Paul Roche, in introducing his own version of Aeschylus' *Oresteia,* writes that "one language best translates another when it remains most true to itself. . . . English says most about Greek when it is most like English."

But this again raises the question, Whose English says most about Greek today? This has been of import in the making of this book, since it includes so many extended passages from Greek classics. In the last century and for some time thereafter, the fashion was to transmit Homer and the tragedians into a language echoing Shakespeare's, with romantic and neo-medieval overtones. The English poet laureate Robert Bridges, rendering the bold, swift speech of the *Iliad,* loaded it with quaint artifice:

And Priam all fearlessly from off his chariot alighted,
Ordering Idaeus to remain i' the entry to keep watch
Over the beasts; th'old king meanwhile strode doughtily
*   onward . . .*

Gilbert Murray sought to lend harsh Euripides a lilt like Swinburne's. Another translator of the romanticizing school, R. C. Jebb (preserved in Random House's *The Complete Greek Drama*) sometimes makes Sophocles sound like Malory's *Le Morte d'Arthur,* as when he has Oedipus say in response to the messenger who has come to try to rid him of his fears of guilt, "Indeed thou shouldst have guerdon due from me." "Guerdon"? What Oedipus actually is saying, as a recent translation by David Grene has it, is "You would not find me thankless if you did."

In most although by no means all instances, the decision reached in this book has been to turn to translators of our own time. This reflects no prima-facie prejudice against those who went before. Passages from philosophers in particular have been given in the versions of such masters from past eras as Benjamin Jowett (though contemporary classicists are also included— Kathleen Freeman, Hugh Tredennick, and A. E. Wardman, author of a readable version of Aristotle's abstruse *Politics*). It is in the realm of Homer, lyric poets, and dramatists, that our concentration on new readings has been the greatest, for we are experiencing a remarkable revival of translation of Greek masters by American and British poet-scholars not beholden to tradition. Because of the excellence of so much of their work, it has been amply represented here.

Just what caused the revival, in a time of supposedly diminishing interest in the classics, no one can clearly say. It may have been an implied protest against this diminution, abetted by translations worn and dated. It may also be that the free, experimental spirit alive in poetry today has encouraged a fresh shot at the classics —and damn the conventions. Graves' version of the *Iliad* is frankly insurgent. Richmond Lattimore, professor of Greek at Bryn Mawr and also a poet of high standing, has approached the *Iliad* as well as Greek lyrics and drama (he is represented here in all three sides of his work) with a desire to recover old rhythms yet to convey the sense in strong, uncloistered speech. Robert Fitzgerald, Boylston professor of poetry at Harvard, has put the *Odyssey* into lines (see pages 133–35) that seek to be as melodious and swift flowing as Homer's own. William Arrowsmith of the University of Texas combines vigorous rendering of tragedy (see *Hecuba,* pages 246–49) with boisterous fun in adapting Aristophanes. His co-worker on the new complete series of Greek comedy, Douglass Parker of the University of California, casts *Lysistrata* in a bold mixture of slapstick and rhetoric, wisecrack and doggerel (pages 254–56), which both men hold to be far more faithful to the gusto of the original than a literal transcript.

What unites all these men seems to be a devotion to their subject and an urge to make it most viable today. In this they are in lineage with one of their great predecessors, John Dryden, who felt that every "true" translation is in itself an act of sympathy. At the same time, they share a sense of modesty as to what a translator can accomplish. As Robert Fitzgerald wrote upon completing his recent version of the *Odyssey,* this poem, "considered strictly as an aesthetic object, is to be appreciated only in Greek. It can no more be translated into English than rhododendron can be translated into dogwood. You must learn Greek if you want to experience Homer." It is winning to hear one of the best translators of our times argue that his own work should be regarded only as a commentary on the original, not as a substitute for it.

ACKNOWLEDGMENTS

The editors wish to acknowledge the following individuals and institutions for their generous assistance and for their co-operation in making available pictorial material in their collections. We are especially grateful to T. Leslie Shear, Jr. of the Department of Greek of Bryn Mawr College for his valuable advice.

Acropolis Museum, Athens
  Nicholas Platon, Director
American School of Classical Studies, Athens
  Henry S. Robinson, Director
  Mrs. Poly Demoulini
Ashmolean Museum, Oxford, Department of Antiquities
Michael Ayrton
Walter C. Baker
Mrs. Ravelle Brickman
British Museum, London
  D. M. Bailey
  Dr. J. P. C. Kent
Corpus Christi College, Cambridge University, Lewis Collection
  A. G. Woodhead, Curator
Dr. Derek J. de Solla Price, Yale University
Dr. Sterling Dow, Harvard University
Editions d'Art Albert Skira, Geneva
  Peter Pfister
Alexander Eliot
André Emmerich Gallery, New York
Miss Alison Frantz
Sanford C. Frumker
Gabinetto Fotografico Nazionale, Rome
German Archaeological Institute, Athens
  Gerhard Neumann
Miss Fiorella Ginanneschi
Glyptothek und Museum Antiker Kleinkunst, Munich
  Dr. K. Vierneisel
Dr. Gilbert Highet, Columbia University
Hirmer Verlag, Munich
  Mrs. Bodil S. Fonbeck
Dr. Jotham Johnson, New York University
Kunsthistorisches Museum, Vienna
  Dr. Erwin M. Auer
Life Magazine, New York
  Miss Valerie Vondermuhll
The Metropolitan Museum of Art, New York
  Dietrich von Bothmer
  Miss Emma N. Papert
Musée Archéologique, Châtillon-sur-Seine
Museo Archeologico, Florence
Museo Nazionale, Naples
Museo Vaticani, Rome, Archivio Fotografico
Museum of Fine Arts, Boston
  Cornelius C. Vermeule III
  Miss Elizabeth P. Riegel
National Archaeological Museum, Athens
  Christos Karouzos, Director
National Gallery of Art, Washington, D.C.
  Mrs. Betty S. Gajdusek
New York Public Library
  Karl Kup
  Miss Elizabeth Roth
  Wilson G. Duprey
  Mrs. Maud D. Cole
NY Carlsberg Glyptothek, Copenhagen
Roland Penrose
Miss Judith Perlzweig
Spiros G. Ponty
Thaddeus L. Smith
Soprintendenza alle Antichità della Campania, Naples
Soprintendenza alle Antichità d'Etruria, Florence
Miss Bianca Spantigati
Staatliche Museen, Berlin
  Dr. N. Kunisch

Dr. U. Gehrig
Städelsches Kunstinstitut, Frankfurt
State Hermitage Museum, Leningrad
  M. I. Artamonov, Director
Miss Lucy Talcott
University Library, Leyden
  M. Obbema
Martin von Wagner-Museum, Würzburg
PHOTOGRAPHY: Athens, Dimitrios Harissiadis; Berlin, Walter Steinkopf; London, Derek Bayes, R. B. Fleming and Co., Ltd.; Munich, C. H. Moessner; Naples, F. Clements; Paris, Madame Simone Guiley-Lagache, M. M. Chuzeville; Vienna, Photo Meyer.

Maps and drawings by Cal Sacks. Map (redrawn) on pages 114–15 reproduced from *Ulysses Found,* © 1963 by Ernle Bradford, by permission of Harcourt, Brace & World, Inc.

Grateful acknowledgment is made for permission to quote from the following works (the page on which the quotation appears is indicated in boldface type):

INTRODUCTION: **8** from *Greek Poetry for Everyman,* translated by F. L. Lucas; by permission of The Macmillan Company, N.Y., and J. M. Dent & Sons Ltd., London.

CHAPTER 1: **26, 27** excerpts from *The Odyssey,* translated by Robert Fitzgerald. Copyright © 1961 by Robert Fitzgerald. Reprinted by permission of Doubleday & Company, Inc., N.Y., and William Heinemann Ltd., London. **28** Hesiod, translated by T. F. Higham, in *The Oxford Book of Greek Verse in Translation;* by permission of The Clarendon Press.

CHAPTER 2: **48, 56** from *Mythology,* by Edith Hamilton. Copyright 1940, 1942 by Edith Hamilton. Reprinted by permission of Little, Brown and Company, Boston. **53** excerpt from *The Odyssey,* translated by Robert Fitzgerald. Copyright © 1961 by Robert Fitzgerald. Reprinted by permission of Doubleday & Company, Inc., N.Y., and William Heinemann Ltd., London. **54** from *The Persian Wars,* by Herodotus, edited by Francis R. B. Godolphin, translated by George Rawlinson. Copyright 1942 by Random House, Inc., N.Y. Reprinted by permission. **55** from Euripides' "Bacchae," translated by William Arrowsmith, in *The Complete Greek Tragedies,* David Grene and Richmond Lattimore, editors; The University of Chicago Press. © 1958. **57** from Sophocles' "Antigone," translated by Elizabeth Wycoff, *The Complete Greek Tragedies,* The University of Chicago Press. © 1954.

CHAPTER 3: **78** from *The Anger of Achilles,* by Robert Graves. Reprinted by permission of Willis Kingsley Wing and Cassell & Co. Ltd. Copyright © 1959, by International Authors, N.Y. **79, 92, 93** from *The Iliad of Homer,* translated by Richmond Lattimore; by permission of The University of Chicago Press. Copyright 1951 by The University of Chicago. **79** excerpt from *The Odyssey,* translated by Robert Fitzgerald. **80, 90** from *The Persian Wars,* by

Herodotus, edited by Francis R. B. Godolphin, translated by George Rawlinson. 93 from *The Iliad*, translated by A. T. Murray, the Loeb Classical Library; by permission of Harvard University Press, Cambridge (Mass.).

CHAPTER 4: 114 from *Ulysses Found*, by Ernle Bradford; by permission of Harcourt, Brace & World, Inc., N.Y. 118 from *The Ancient Greeks*, by M. I. Finley; by permission of The Viking Press, Inc., N.Y. 119 from *The Greeks*, by H. D. F. Kitto; Penguin Books, Baltimore. © H. D. F. Kitto, 1951. 124 from *The Persian Wars*, edited by Francis R. B. Godolphin, translated by George Rawlinson. Copyright 1942 by Random House, Inc., N.Y. Reprinted by permission. 125 Alcaeus, translated by C. M. Bowra, in *The Oxford Book of Greek Verse in Translation;* by permission of The Clarendon Press, Oxford.

POETS AND TELLERS OF TALES: 129, 138 Hesiod, translated by Jack Lindsay, in *The Oxford Book of Greek Verse in Translation;* by permission of The Clarendon Press, Oxford. 130–33, 137 reprinted from *The Iliad of Homer*, translated by Richmond Lattimore; by permission of The University of Chicago Press. Copyright 1951 by The University of Chicago. 133–35 excerpt from *The Odyssey*, translated by Robert Fitzgerald. Copyright © 1961 by Robert Fitzgerald. Reprinted by permission of Doubleday & Company, Inc., N.Y., and William Heinemann Ltd., London. 137 from *The Anger of Achilles*, by Robert Graves. Reprinted by permission of Willis Kingsley Wing and Cassell & Co., Ltd. Copyright © 1959, by International Authors, N.Y. 138–42 from *Greek Poetry for Everyman*, translated by F. L. Lucas; by permission of The Macmillan Company, N.Y., and J. M. Dent & Sons Ltd., London. 139 Pindar, translated by H. T. Wade-Gery and C. M. Bowra, in *The Oxford Book of Greek Verse in Translation;* by permission of The Clarendon Press, Oxford. 140–44 reprinted from *Greek Lyrics* (2nd edition) translated by Richmond Lattimore; by permission of The University of Chicago Press. Copyright 1949, 1955, and 1960 by Richmond Lattimore. 141 Theocritus, translated by Sir William Marris, in *The Oxford Book of Greek Verse in Translation;* by permission of The Clarendon Press, Oxford. 142 from *Pindar: The Pythian Odes*, translated by H. T. Wade-Gery and C. M. Bowra; The Nonesuch Press Ltd. 143 Archilochus, after J. H. Merivale, as adapted by G. B. Grundy, in *Ancient Gems in Modern Settings;* Basil Blackwell, Publisher, Oxford.

CHAPTER 5: 163, 173, 178–80 from *The Persian Wars*, by Herodotus, edited by Francis R. B. Godolphin, translated by George Rawlinson. Copyright 1942 by Random House, Inc., N.Y. Reprinted by permission. 164–65, 170–71 from Thucydides' *History of the Peloponnesian War*, translated by Richmond Crawley, revised by R. Feetham, Everyman's Library; by permission of E. P. Dutton & Co., Inc., N.Y., and J. M. Dent & Sons Ltd., London. 169,

170 from "Athens and Sparta," by A. H. M. Jones, in *The Greeks*, edited by Hugh Lloyd-Jones; by permission of C. A. Watts & Co. Ltd., London. 169–70 from Plutarch's "Lycurgus," in *Paideia*, by Werner Jaeger; by permission of Oxford University Press, Inc., N.Y. 172 from *Terpsichore and other Poems*, translated by H. T. Wade-Gery; Golden Cockerell Press. 173 from *The Greeks and Their Gods*, by W. K. C. Gutherie; by permission of Methuen & Co., Ltd. Publishers, London. 173 from *Hellenistic Culture*, by Moses Hadas; by permission of Columbia University Press, N.Y. 181 from the *Oresteia;* by permission of the translator, Professor George Thomson, University of Birmingham, England.

CHAPTER 6: 198 from *Greek Poetry for Everyman*, translated by F. L. Lucas. 201 from *Early Greek Philosophy* (4th edition), by John Burnet. 206, 207 from the *Oresteia*, translated by George Thomson.

DRAMATISTS AT THEIR HEIGHT: 242–44 reprinted from Aeschylus' "Agamemnon," translated by Richmond Lattimore, in *The Complete Greek Tragedies*, edited by David Grene and Richmond Lattimore; by permission of The University of Chicago Press. © 1953 by The University of Chicago. 244–46 reprinted from Aeschylus' "Libation Bearers," translated by Richmond Lattimore, in *The Complete Greek Tragedies*, edited by David Grene and Richmond Lattimore; by permission of The University of Chicago Press. © 1953 by The University of Chicago. 246–49 reprinted from Euripides' "Hecuba," translated by William Arrowsmith, in *The Complete Greek Tragedies*, edited by David Grene and Richmond Lattimore; by permission of The University of Chicago Press. © 1956 by The University of Chicago. 250–54 reprinted from Sophocles' "Oedipus the King," translated by David Grene, in *The Complete Greek Tragedies*, edited by David Grene and Richmond Lattimore; by permission of The University of Chicago Press. © 1942 by The University of Chicago. 254–56 from *Lysistrata*, translated by Douglass Parker; by permission of The University of Michigan Press, Ann Arbor. Copyright © by William Arrowsmith 1964.

CHAPTER 7: 258 from *Greek Poetry for Everyman*, translated by F. L. Lucas. 259 from Thucydides' *History of the Peloponnesian War*, translated by Richard Crawley, revised by R. Feetham, Everyman's Library; by permission of E. P. Dutton & Co., Inc., N.Y., and J. M. Dent & Sons Ltd., London. 260, 268 from *Everyday Things in Ancient Greece*, by Marjorie and C. H. B. Quennell; by permission of B. T. Batsford Ltd., London, and G. P. Putnam's Sons, N.Y. 263, 266, 269 from *Women in Antiquity*, by Charles Seltman; by permission of St. Martin's Press, Inc., N.Y., and Thames & Hudson Ltd., London. 264, 271 from *The Life of Greece*, by Will Durant; Simon and Schuster, N.Y. Copyright, 1936, by Will Durant. 274 from Plato's *Symposium*, translated by Michael Joyce, Every-

man's Library; E. P. Dutton & Co., Inc., N.Y., and J. M. Dent & Sons Ltd., London.

CHAPTER 8: 292, 301, 307, 308–9 from Thucydides' *History of the Peloponnesian War*, translated by Richard Crawley, revised by R. Feetham, Everyman's Library; by permission of E. P. Dutton & Co., Inc., N.Y., and J. M. Dent & Sons Ltd., London. 297 from Euripides' *Medea*, translated by Rex Warner. 300 from *A History of Greece* (3rd edition), by J. B. Bury; by permission of Macmillan & Co. Ltd., London. 301 from *The Life of Greece*, by Will Durant. 302–3 from Aristophanes' *The Clouds*, translated by William Arrowsmith; by permission of The University of Michigan Press, Ann Arbor. Copyright © by William Arrowsmith 1962. 304 from Sophocles' "Oedipus the King," translated by David Grene, in *The Complete Greek Tragedies*. © 1942 by The University of Chicago. 305 from Sophocles' *Oedipus at Colonus*, translated by Robert Fitzgerald; Harcourt, Brace & World, Inc. 306 from Euripides' "Trojan Women," translated by Richmond Lattimore, in *The Complete Greek Tragedies*. © 1958 by The University of Chicago.

PRIME MOVERS OF THOUGHT: 321 from Plato's *Apology*, translated by Hugh Tredennick, Penguin Books Ltd., Harmondsworth, England. 322–23 from *Ancilla to the Pre-Socratic Philosophers*, by Kathleen Freeman, 1957; by arrangement with Harvard University Press, Cambridge (Mass.), and Basil Blackwell, Publisher, Oxford. 324–26, 331 from Plato's "Lysis" and "Laws," in *Socratic Discourses;* Everyman's Library edition. Reprinted by permission of E. P. Dutton & Co., Inc., N.Y., and J. M. Dent & Sons Ltd., London. 326–29 from Plato's *Phaedo*, translated by Hugh Tredennick; Penguin Books Ltd., Harmondsworth, England. 329–30 from Plato's *Timaeus*, translated by Benjamin Jowett; by permission of The Clarendon Press, Oxford. 330 from *The Works of Aristotle*, translated by W. D. Ross; by permission of The Clarendon Press, Oxford. 331–32 from *The Philosophy of Aristotle*, edited by Renford Bambrough. Copyright © 1963 by Renford Bambrough; by arrangement with The New American Library, Inc., N.Y. 333 from *Epicurius: The Extant Remains*, translated by Cyril Bailey; by permission of The Clarendon Press, Oxford. 334–35 from *The Persian Wars*, by Herodotus, edited by Francis R. B. Godolphin, translated by George Rawlinson. Copyright 1942 by Random House, Inc., N.Y. Reprinted by permission. 335–36 from Thucydides' *Peloponnesian War*, translated by Benjamin Jowett.

CHAPTER 9: 342 from *The Persian Expedition*, by Xenophon, translated by Rex Warner; Penguin Books Ltd., Harmondsworth, England. 348 from Arrian's *Anabasis*, translated by E. Iliff Robson, The Loeb Classical Library; Harvard University Press, Cambridge (Mass.)

CHAPTER 10: 371 from *The Aeneid of Vergil*, translated by C. Day Lewis. 376 from Dante's *Inferno*, translated by John Ciardi.

A

NOTE: *Page numbers in boldface type indicate that the subject is illustrated.*

INDEX

of Women, 266, 276
See also ATHENS, SPARTA, Education in

EGYPT, 15, 117–19, 125, 177, 179, 203, 259, 337
Architecture, 208, 215
Art, 207, 368
in Hellenistic age, 347, 350–53 *passim*
Religion, 9, 48, 80, 204
Sculpture, 126, 185, 202, 209, 210

EKKLESIA. See ASSEMBLY OF ATHENS

ELECTRA (daughter of Agamemnon), 108, 109, 381

ELECTRA (daughter of Atlas), 60

ELEUSINIAN MYSTERIES, 56–57

ELEUSIS, 56, 69
Bay of, 179

ELGIN, LORD, 6, 213

ELIOT, T. S.
The Cocktail Party, 381

EMPEDOCLES, 295, 323 (*quoted*)

EOS, 91

EPAMINONDAS, 344

EPHEBE, by Critios, 204, **205,** 210–11

EPHESUS, 53, 117, 120, 177

EPHORS, 173, 174
See also SPARTA, Government in

EPHORUS, 339

EPICURUS, 265, 321
Principal Doctrines, 333 (*excerpt*)

EPIDAMNUS (DURAZZO), 294

EPIDAURUS, 162, 215, 233
Theatre at, 7, 236 (*diagram*), 237, **238–39,** 339

EPONYMOUS HEROES, ALTAR OF THE, 165

ERASISTRATUS, 352

ERASMUS, DESIDERIUS, 376

ERATOSTHENES, 337

EREBUS, 49

ERECHTHEUM, 6, 7, 217, 221, 225, **226–27,** 394

ERETRIA, 176, 178

ERNI, HANS
Oedipus and Jocasta, 399

EROS (god), 49, 54, 55, 57, 85

EROS (love), 257
Socrates on, 273–74

EROTES, **288–89**

ERYMANTHUS, MOUNT, 78

ESQUILINE VENUS, 193

ETHIOPIA, 179
Art of, 369, 373

ETRUSCANS, 119, 145, 282

EUBOEA, 26, 117, 176

EUBULUS, 266

EUCLID, 352
Proof of Pythagorean theorem, 337, 374

EUMAEUS, 88, 115, 135

EUMENIDES, by Aeschylus, 181 (*excerpt*)

EUNOMIA, 169, 174, 257

EUPATRIDS, 164, 166, 169

EUPHRATES RIVER, 29

EURIPIDES, 59, 80, 83, 266, 270, 279 (*quoted*), 297, 301, 303–6 *passim*
Alcestis, 80, 297, 381
Andromache, 263 (*excerpt*)
Bacchae, 55 (*excerpt*), 338
Hecuba, 241, 246–49 (*excerpt*)
Heracles, 80
Iphigenia in Aulis, 338
Medea, 85, 217, 297, **298–99**
The Trojan Women, 305, 306 (*excerpt*)

EUROPA, 60, 81, 113

EURYCLEIA, 88, 115, 135

EURYDICE, 86, 107

EURYMACHUS, 133, 134

EURYMEDON RIVER, 258

EURYSTHEUS, 78, **96,** 97

EVANS, SIR ARTHUR, 7

EXPOSURE OF INFANTS, 175, 276

F

FARMING. *See* AGRICULTURE

FATE (*MOIRA*), 59, 101, 257

FATES, 52, 60, 297

FERTILITY RITES AND SYMBOLS, 37, 84, 260, 265, 272
Fertility deities, 38, 39, 52, 53, 57, 60, 63, 69, 75, 81, 302

FICINO, MARSILIO, 376

FINLEY, M. I., 8 (*quoted*)

FITZGERALD, ROBERT
Translation of the *Odyssey,* by Homer, 133–35

FLORENCE. *See* RENAISSANCE

FOSTER, JOHN, 6

FREEMAN, KATHLEEN
Translation of pre-Socratic writings, 322–23

FREUD, SIGMUND, 381, 399

FURIES, 49, 52, 109, 181, 207, 244, **304**

FURNITURE, 8, 261, **262**

G

GAEA, 49, 53, 60

GAMES. *See* ISTHMIAN, OLYMPIC, PAN-ATHENAIC, PYTHIAN GAMES

GANDHARA, 368

GANYMEDES, 64, **65**

GAUGAMELA, BATTLE OF, 347, 350

GAZA, 350

GELON, 123

GEOMETRY. *See* MATHEMATICS

GEROUSIA. See COUNCIL OF ELDERS

GERYON, 78

GIANTS, 49, 60
Battle of gods and, 50, **74–75,** 79

GIDE, ANDRE, 381

GILGAMESH, 81

GIRAUDOUX, JEAN
Amphitryon 38, 381

GLUCK, C. W., 9, 378

GODS, 48–59 *passim,* 62–77 *passim*
Assimilation with other deities, 52, 117, 353
Genealogy, 60–61 (*chart*), 89
Man and, 9, 33, 48, 50–52, 57, 59, 81, 86–87, 122, 241
See also separate listings for individual gods

GOETHE, J. W. VON, 378
Faust, 380–81

GOLDEN FLEECE, 52, 84–85, 106, 107

GOMME, A. W., 175

GORDIAN KNOT, 347

GORGIAS, 275

GORGONS, 82, 206, **207**

GOYA, FRANCISCO
Kronos, 398

GRACES, 52, 60, 360, **361**

GRANICUS RIVER, 347

GRAVES, ROBERT, 86
Translation of the *Iliad,* by Homer, 78, 137

GRAVESTONES
Attic, 196, 197, 271, **272**
Spartan, 170

GRECO, EL
Laocoön, 392–93

GREEK LANGUAGE, 8, 34–35, 45, 129, 145, 257
in Post-classical times, 369, 370, 373, 376, 383, 391

GREEK REVIVAL. *See* ARCHITECTURE

GREEK WAR FOR INDEPENDENCE, 380, 396–97

GREENOUGH, HORATIO
George Washington, 379

N

O